CHINA'S NEW PLACE IN A WORLD IN CRISIS

ECONOMIC, GEOPOLITICAL AND
ENVIRONMENTAL DIMENSIONS

Other titles in the China Update Book Series include:

2002   China: WTO Entry and World Recession

2003   China: New Engine of World Growth

2004   China: Is Rapid Growth Sustainable?

2005   The China Boom and its Discontents

2006   China: The Turning Point in China's Economic Development

2007   Linking Markets for Growth

2008   China's Dilemma: Economic Growth, the Environment and
        Climate Change

All books in The China Update Book Series are edited by Ross Garnaut and Ligang Song, except China's Dilemma, edited by Ligang Song and Wing Thye Woo.

Print copies of the books can be obtained from ANU E Press.
Electronic copies can be downloaded free from http://epress.anu.edu.au

CHINA'S NEW PLACE IN A WORLD IN CRISIS

ECONOMIC, GEOPOLITICAL AND ENVIRONMENTAL DIMENSIONS

Ross Garnaut, Ligang Song and Wing Thye Woo (eds)

ANU
THE AUSTRALIAN NATIONAL UNIVERSITY

E PRESS

B | Brookings Institution Press

社会科学文献出版社
SOCIAL SCIENCES ACADEMIC PRESS(CHINA)

ANU

E PRESS

Published by ANU E Press
The Australian National University
Canberra ACT 0200, Australia
Email: anuepress@anu.edu.au
This title is also available online at: http://epress.anu.edu.au/china_new_place_citation.html

CHINA BOOK
INTERNATIONAL

Co-published with SOCIAL SCIENCES ACADEMIC PRESS (CHINA) under the China Book International scheme. This scheme supports co-publication of works with international publishers.

National Library of Australia
Cataloguing-in-Publication entry

Title:	China's new place in a world in crisis : economic geopolitical and environmental dimensions / editors Ross Garnaut, Ligang Song, Wing Thye Woo.
ISBN:	9781921536960 (pbk.)
	9781921536977 (pdf)
Notes:	Includes index.
	Bibliography.
Subjects:	Economic development--Environmental aspects--China
	Energy consumption--China.
	Industrialization--China.
	China--Economic conditions.
	China--Economic policy.
	China--Environmental conditions.
	China--Commercial policy.
Other Authors/Contributors:	
	Garnaut, Ross.
	Song, Ligang.
	Woo, Wing Thye.
Dewey Number: 338.951	

Cover design and layout by Teresa Prowse, www.madebyfruitcup.com

Cover image: "black and white of Shang" iStock photo # 2552759.
www.istockphoto.com/stock-photo-2552759-black-and-white-of-shang.php

Contents

Part I China's New Place in World Economy and Politics

Part II Macroeconomic Adjustments Amid Global Recession

Tables

Figures

Abbreviations

AusAID	Australian Agency for International Development
ABARE	Australian Bureau of Agricultural and Resource Economics
ABM	Asian Bond Market
ABS	Australian Bureau of Statistics
ACCC	Australian Competition and Consumer Commission
ACFTU	All-China Federation of Trade Unions
ACU	Asian currency unit
ADB	Asian Development Bank
AEU	Asian Economic Union
AFF	Asian Financial Fund
AFP	Agence France-Presse
AIG	American International Group
AMF	Asian Monetary Fund
APEC	Asia-Pacific Economic Cooperation
ASEAN	Association of South-East Asian Nations
BIS	Bank for International Settlements
BAU	business as usual
BHPS	British Household Panel Survey
BoP	balance of payments
CAS	Chinese Academy of Sciences
CCS	carbon capture and storage
CDM	Clean Development Mechanism
CDP	currency depreciation pressure index
CDS	credit default swaps
CIA	Central Intelligence Agency
CN	cluster number
CPI	consumer price index
CRB	Commodity Research Bureau
DRC	Development Research Centre
EABER	East Asia Bureau of Economic Research

EC	European Commission
ECU	European currency unit
EIA	Energy Information Administration
ETS	emissions trading scheme
EU	European Union
FAI	fixed-asset investment
FD	first-difference
FDI	foreign direct investment
FIEs	foreign-invested enterprises
FIRB	Foreign Investment Review Board
FTA	free trade area
GATT	General Agreement on Tariffs and Trade
GDP	gross domestic product
GHG	greenhouse gas
GTAP	Global Trade Analysis Project
HILDA	Household Income and Labour Dynamics in Australia
IE	Ireland
IEA	International Energy Agency
IETS	international emissions trading scheme
IIP	international investment position
IMF	International Monetary Fund
IPCC	Intergovernmental Panel on Climate Change
IPOs	initial public offerings
IRP	interest rate parity
IVA	industrial output
LU	Luxembourg
M&A	mergers and acquisitions
NDRC	National Development and Reform Commission
MFA	Multi-Fibre Arrangement
MNEs	multinational enterprises
MOFCOM	Ministry of Commerce
MV	market variability
NAFTA	North American Free Trade Agreement
NBER	National Bureau of Economic Research
NBS	National Bureau of Statistics

NCB	National Census Bureau
NEA	national emissions account
NFA	net foreign asset
NIEs	newly industrialising economies
NSEs	non-state enterprises
ODA	official development assistance
OECD	Organisation for Economic Cooperation and Development
PBOC	People's Bank of China
PMA	Petroleum Marketers Association
PMI	purchasing managers' index
PPI	producer price index
ppm	parts per million
PPP	purchasing power parity
RCA	revealed comparative advantage
REER	real effective exchange rate
RMB	renminbi
ROA	return on assets
ROE	return on equity
RUMiCI	Rural–Urban Migration in China and Indonesia
SAFE	State Administration of Foreign Exchange
SDRs	special drawing rights
SMEs	small and medium-sized enterprises
SOEs	state-owned enterprises
SSPC	Survey of Population Changes
SWFs	sovereign wealth funds
TFP	total factor productivity
TVEs	town and village enterprises
UN	United Nations
UNCTAD	United Nations Conference on Trade and Development
UNEP	United Nations Environment Program
UNFCCC	United Nations Framework Convention on Climate Change
USBS	United States Bureau of Statistics
USD	US dollar
USFHA	United States Federal Highway Administration
USGS	United States Geological Survey

VAT	value-added tax
WA	Western Australia
WGQ	Wigner-Gabor-Qian
WTO	World Trade Organization

Contributors

Prema-chandra Athukorala
Arndt Corden Division of Economics, Research School of Pacific and Asian Studies, The Australian National University, Canberra.

Cai Fang
Division of Labour and Human Capital, Institute of Population and Labour Economics, Chinese Academy of Social Sciences, Beijing.

Chunlai Chen
Crawford School of Economics and Government, The Australian National University, Canberra.

W. Max Corden
Department of Economics, University of Melbourne, Melbourne.

Peter Drysdale
East Asian Bureau of Economic Research, Canberra; Crawford School of Economics and Government, The Australian National University, Canberra.

Fan Gang
National Economy Research Institute, China Reform Foundation, Beijing.

Christopher Findlay
School of Economics, University of Adelaide, Adelaide.

Kyoji Fukao
The Institute of Economic Research, Hitotsubashi University, Tokyo.

Ross Garnaut
Vice-Chancellor's Fellow and Professorial Fellow in Economics, University of Melbourne, and Distinguished Professor of Economics, The Australian National University, Canberra.

Stephen Howes
Crawford School of Economics and Government, The Australian National University, Canberra.

Yiping Huang
China Center for Economic Research, Peking University, Beijing; China Economy and Business Program, Crawford School of Economics and Government, The Australian National University, Canberra.

Anna Janus
Tsinghua Brookings Institution, Tsinghua University, Beijing.

Sherry Tao Kong
Research School of Social Sciences, The Australian National University, Canberra.

Guonan Ma
Bank for International Settlements, Hong Kong.

Will Martin
The World Bank, Washington, DC.

Huw McKay
Westpac Bank, Sydney.

Xin Meng
Research School of Social Sciences, The Australian National University, Canberra.

Ken Peng
Citigroup, China.

Chen Ping
China Center for Economic Research, Peking University, Beijing; Center for New Political Economy, Fudan University, Shanghai.

Minggao Shen
Caijing Magazine, Beijing.

Ligang Song
China Economy and Business Program, Crawford School of Economics and Government, The Australian National University, Canberra.

Dewen Wang
Division of Labour and Human Capital, Institute of Population and Labour Economics, Chinese Academy of Social Sciences, Beijing.

Xiaolu Wang
National Economy Research Institute, China Reform Foundation, Beijing.

Hugh White
Strategic and Defence Studies Centre, The Australian National University, Canberra; Lowy Institute for International Policy, Sydney.

Wing Thye Woo
Brookings Institution, Washington, DC; University of California (Davis); Central University of Finance and Economics, Beijing.

Xiao Geng
Tsinghua Brookings Institution, Tsinghua University, Beijing.

Jinjun Xue
Center for International Economic Policy Study, School of Economics, Nagoya University, Nagoya.

Xiuke Yang
Tsinghua Brookings Institution, Tsinghua University, Beijing.

Tangjun Yuan
The Institute of Economic Research, Hitotsubashi University, Tokyo.

Qu Yue
Division of Labour and Human Capital, Institute of Population and Labour Economics, Chinese Academy of Social Sciences, Beijing.

Dandan Zhang
Research School of Social Sciences, The Australian National University, Canberra.

Yongsheng Zhang
Development Research Centre, People's Republic of China.

Haiwen Zhou
Bank for International Settlements, Hong Kong.

Acknowledgments

The China Economy and Business Program gratefully acknowledges the financial support for the China Update 2009 from The Australian Agency for International Development (AusAID), and the assistance provided by Rio Tinto through the Rio Tinto – ANU China Partnership.

China's place in a world in crisis

Ross Garnaut

The world and China's place in it have been transformed over the past year. The pressures for change have come from the most severe global financial crisis ever, and from what so far is the largest decline in output in a comparably short period in the history of the world economy.

China and its economic prospects have also changed, but not so much as China's place in a changing world. After a challenging year, China is confirmed on a course of continuing strong growth. There are still questions about longer-term sustainability, but there is now considerable cause for confidence that there will be positive answers. The global financial crisis has accelerated China's emergence as a great power, in advance of China or its global partners thinking and working through the consequences for managing the implications for the governance of world affairs.

These are the themes of this year's *China Update*.

The global China boom was at its height when the *China Update*'s annual assessment was released a year ago (Song and Woo 2008). World resources and food prices were at record levels. Developing-country growth for 2007 was the strongest ever; even though things fell apart from September, growth for the year was more than 13 per cent for China, more than 9 per cent for India, more than 6 per cent for Africa and more than 8 per cent for all developing countries.

In 2009, economic growth is somewhat subdued but still strong in China and the large, successful developing countries. The economic outlook is now deeply problematic in the industrialised and poor developing countries.

The financial crisis of 2008 can now be traced back to weaknesses in the US financial system that began to be revealed from 2006. The crisis came in September 2008 with the collapse of several Wall Street investment banks. There was an immediate breakdown of the system of international financial intermediation, which had been smoothly transferring China's unprecedented surpluses to cover the unprecedented current payments deficits of the United States and Australia in particular (Garnaut forthcoming).

The financial crisis precipitated a global recession. In China, the recessionary pressures from the international economy reinforced the effects of an earlier tightening of monetary policy. This tightening had been designed to bring to an end level of inflation that had been worrying the authorities for more than a year. The restrictive monetary policy had pricked the bubble in the Shanghai and Shenzhen stock exchanges and caused a pause in the real estate boom in a number of major cities. The sudden drying up of orders from importers of Chinese goods in the industrialised countries caused retrenchment in the export factories and the abandonment of expansion plans in export-oriented enterprises. Tens of millions of urban workers returned to the farms, villages and townships of rural China.

Suddenly some of the long-term questions about the sustainability of China's early twenty-first-century growth strategy demanded immediate answers. Could China replace export-oriented growth with similarly strong growth focused on opportunities in the domestic market? Could China expand expenditure enough and quickly enough if developments in the international economy prevented the accommodation of China's huge and growing external surpluses?

Other long-term issues of the sustainability of China's early twenty-first-century growth strategy remained to be answered. Was it possible for the world to manage the huge expansion of supply and delivery capacity for natural resources to fuel, feed and fabricate the demands of Chinese economic growth, at costs and prices that would be consistent with continuing growth in living standards in the whole world? Would China and the world find ways of breaking the nexus between economic output and emissions of the greenhouse gases that were rapidly increasing the risks of dangerous climate change?

Between last year's and this year's updates came the thirtieth anniversary of the commencement of reform—the anniversary of the time when Deng Xiaoping took control of the Central Committee of the Chinese Communist Party in December 1978 and moved decisively to implement policies of market-oriented reform and opening to the outside world. Each of the decennial anniversaries had coincided with crises for reform—the three substantial crises of the reform period. In late 1988, high inflation and disagreements within the leadership on how to handle it were setting the scene for the tragic developments of June 1989 and the only substantial challenge to reform. In late 1998, China had embarked on but did not yet know the fate of its risky policy response to the East Asian financial crisis: the maintenance of a fixed exchange rate against the US dollar and huge Keynesian fiscal expansion at a time when exports had stagnated and foreign exchange reserves were in rapid decline. Now, China has embarked on another huge fiscal and monetary expansion, this time in response to a global rather than a regional financial crisis and recession (Garnaut 2009).

Soon after the breaking of the global crisis, China embarked on an even larger expansion than in the late 1990s. It was the largest fiscal expansion of any country in response to the crisis of 2008. There was an even larger monetary expansion. The strongly restrictive instructions to the state banks were reversed in the final months of 2008 and replaced with instructions to expand lending.

There was much less risk in the expansionist strategy this time than during the East Asian financial crisis. China's extraordinarily large foreign exchange reserves meant that a flank that had been vulnerable in the late 1990s was now thoroughly covered. And the success of Keynesian policies through the East Asian financial crisis increased confidence in expansionary policies in the global recession.

It was clear by January that the immense and timely fiscal and monetary expansion was having a large effect. Chinese growth through 2009, from the December quarter of 2008 to the December quarter of 2009, is now likely to be comparable with annual growth in the years leading into the crisis. Chinese exports remain weak and the impetus to growth is coming from expansion of domestic demand. This is stabilising net exports, and as 2009 proceeds will make the external accounts a negative factor on Chinese growth. China will be a helpful stabilising factor in the global economy. Already the strong recovery of Chinese import demand has taken global energy and minerals prices off their late-2008 lows, to points halfway between the averages in real terms of the late twentieth century and the heights of the boom.

China's strong growth in the early twenty-first century before the global crisis was raising four large questions about its sustainability.

First, there were questions about the extent to which it depended on growth of exports and a rising surplus in foreign trade. The strong growth in exports and huge and increasing trade surpluses were placing large structural pressures on its trading partners. At a time of weakness in the global trading system, this was threatening protectionist reactions. The payments surpluses were the other side of the coin of payments deficits in and transfers of capital to a few deficit countries—first of all the United States. This was convenient to the United States and other deficit countries, which were able to avoid hard choices of their own involving reduction of expenditure through the cutting of public expenditure, including on defence, the increasing of taxation and the raising of interest rates. Some analysts saw it as postponing and therefore exacerbating major adjustments that had to happen sometime and would be the more painful and costly for delay.

Second, there were questions about the extent to which growth on an unprecedented scale was placing pressure on local, national, regional and global environmental amenity. Increasingly, developments in China were seen as being of central importance to the emerging risks of dangerous climate change. Here the external costs of Chinese growth were carried by the global community and any solution to the global problem would need to involve all substantial economies including China (Garnaut 2008).

Third, the established patterns of growth in the early twenty-first century were associated with wide and increasing dispersion in the distribution of incomes. Inequality had fallen in the early years of reform with its concentration on agricultural and other rural development. By the early twenty-first century, the high earnings and ease of financing of projects in state-owned enterprises for capital-intensive projects were the first of several sources of bias concentrating incomes growth in the hands of relatively well off people in the cities, and especially in the wealthy coastal cities. The feeling among many ordinary people that they were not receiving an equitable share of the rich fruits of rapid economic growth was the source of social tension manifested, for example, in many protests against decisions of officials.

Fourth, there were questions about the effects of rapidly rising expenditure in China on global markets for food, minerals and energy resources. Chinese demand was a major influence on unprecedentedly high food, metals and energy prices in the time leading up to global recession. Would continued strong growth in China as it became a larger economy raise the prices of these commodities so high that they might not be compatible with continued growth in incomes and living standards on a global scale? The satisfactory resolution of the food and resource supply issues would require smoothly functioning goods, capital, transport and enterprise markets.

Could these sources of risk to continued strong economic growth be corrected without risking growth itself?

These four questions about the sustainability of growth were closely interrelated. The trade surplus was the other side of the coin to prodigious and rapidly growing savings rates—far higher than China's extraordinarily high investment rates. Inequality of earnings contributed to exceptionally high savings rates, since those who were well off saved a higher proportion of their incomes than the poor. The high profits and high incomes in the state-owned enterprises were two important elements in the growing inequality of incomes. The retention of a high proportion of these firms' earnings for investment in heavy industry and infrastructure perpetuated and exacerbated the inequality of incomes and contributed to disproportionate pressure on the environment and demand for minerals and energy resources.

There had been much discussion before the global crisis of changes in strategy that would reduce pressures arising in each of these four areas. President, Hu Jintao, and Premier, Wen Jiabao, in successive statements had emphasised the importance of expanding expenditure and promoting development in rural areas and shifting the balance in resource allocation towards such human services as health and education. Improved environmental amenity was to be an important focus of increased expenditure and there was increasing official focus on China's role as a victim and source of and contributor to solutions to the global warming problem.

The adjustments would be associated with less intensive use of resources.

Only small progress had been made in giving effect to these official statements of good intentions before the international crisis. The appreciation of the Chinese against US currencies by about 20 per cent in three years or so from July 2005 would, when accompanied by expansion of public expenditure in rural areas, contribute to easing external balance, reduction in inequality and pressure on the environment and natural resources.

There was a sense in which these four sets of questions about sustainability of established patterns of rapid growth in China could be partially self-correcting. By the mid-1990s and more strongly from the early twenty-first century, labour was becoming scarce enough in many parts of China for real wages to rise rapidly. This contributed to rising consumption and potentially to reduced competitiveness of exports and import-competing production of labour-intensive goods and lower shares of investment in heavy industry with their impacts on resources and the environment.

These were possibilities that had not been realised before the crisis. Productivity, output and incomes rose even more rapidly than real wages and consumption. Rates of return on investment continued to be high and to rise. It would take even higher rates of growth in output and incomes and even higher rates of growth in real wages for these market processes to make inroads into China's surplus savings and income inequalities. Faster growth in itself, even with the structural change associated with rapid increases in real wages, would increase pressure on resources and the environment in the absence of other corrective measures.

Now the crisis makes large and immediate structural change a condition of continued rapid economic growth. The rest of the world is rapidly reducing its deficit of savings relative to investment. This is part of the cautious response of households and businesses, and is in any case forced by the collapse of the banks that once transferred funds smoothly from the surplus to the deficit countries.

China cannot continue to grow with rapid increases in its net exports, payments surplus and foreign exchange reserves.

It can, however, continue to grow rapidly. This requires the rapid expansion of domestic demand. There are limits to the rate of increase in private consumption, so much of the expansion, especially in the early stages, must take the form of public expenditure—investment and consumption—and of private investment. The investment share of output and expenditure is likely to have to rise for a while from current levels. If spent well—and there are still abundant opportunities for productive and highly profitable investment in China—this would require even higher rates of growth of output than in the Chinese experience before the crisis. Higher growth, in turn, would bring forward pressures for real wages to rise and for consequential structural change.

This is the world that China has entered in the aftermath of the global crisis. It is a world of development that will be associated with major reductions in China's trade and payments surpluses. Over time, it is likely to be associated with moderation of income inequalities—although not necessarily in the near term.

Early correction of growing inequalities, as well as reduction of the pressure on resources and the environment from rapid economic growth, would require the successful implementation of complementary policies. Reduction in income equalities would require much of the expansion of public expenditure to be focused on the supply of education, health services and transport and communications infrastructure on lower income and especially rural communities. For China to reconcile continued rapid economic growth with playing its proportionate part in a global effort to mitigate human-induced global warming would require deliberate measures to tax or to regulate emissions, and to accelerate commercialisation of new, low-emissions technologies. Success in breaking the nexus between economic growth and greenhouse gas emissions would moderate growth in demand for non-renewable resources.

The early Chinese stimulus packages contained elements of increased expenditure directed to income distribution and environmental issues. This component has tended to expand in successive packages.

The sustained rapid growth of China and other large developing countries in the early twenty-first century has been changing the international economic and strategic balance. The tectonic plates of global economic weight and therefore eventually strategic influence have been shifting towards a quadripolar world in which four great powers will need to work cooperatively to achieve major international objectives: the United States, the European Union, China and India. Effective international action on most issues will require cooperation between the four, and leadership from China and the United States.

This is a world so changed that it will take time to develop the ideas and the institutions through which international cooperation can be effective.

The global crisis has not changed the directions of movement of the tectonic plates. It has accelerated the movement, by substantially slowing the growth of the major industrialised countries while affecting much less the major developing countries. This reduces further the time within which new approaches to and institutions for management of the new international order must be developed. Less time means greater chance of damaging mistakes.

These are the issues covered by the contributions to this book. How have China's growth prospects been affected by the global crisis? How will the crisis and China's response to it affect the prospects for progress on the great internal issues in China's development? How will the crisis and the international community's response to it affect the rapidly emerging new international order, in which China and other major developing countries have much larger roles?

The next three chapters discuss some ways in which the crisis has affected ideas in China and elsewhere about international institutions that are necessary to make the new world work.

Woo (Chapter 2) notes that the crisis completes the discrediting of the advice from the Washington-based global financial institutions on the policy response to the East Asian financial crisis a decade ago. This validates the search for alternative regional institutions for financial cooperation. Woo favours a plurality of institutions providing international public goods, including one or more with East Asian regional roots. His practical suggestion is modest: support for an Asian finance facility, in which the United States would be invited to participate, as a defence against financial contagion. The strong reserves position of East Asian economies places them in a good position for effective cooperation in this area.

Several chapters discuss the haunting question: did developments in China contribute to the global financial crisis? Chen (Chapter 3) takes pre-emptive action by identifying flawed economic and financial analysis of financial markets at the centre of the problem. He notes that some US analysts have seen strong causal roles either for low Chinese savings, high external payments surpluses and a low exchange rate, or for the complementary imbalances between China and the United States. He sees the antidote to future crises mainly in financial reform in industrialised countries and expresses concern that currently proposed remedies for the global recession will be too weak for the task.

Corden (Chapter 6) considers the matter carefully and concludes that the Chinese surpluses might have made some small contribution to the crisis. Flaws in developed financial markets were more important.

Ma and Zhou (Chapter 4), Corden (Chapter 6) and Wang and Fan (Chapter 8) all discuss the puzzling and important reality that lies behind the Chinese payments surpluses: the exceptionally high Chinese savings rates. Corden presents the data simply and shows that China's exceptional trade and current account surpluses are recent phenomena—mostly since 2005. He notes that Chinese household savings are high (15 per cent of GDP despite an unusually low household income share), but these are of modest dimension compared with enterprise savings (28 per cent of GDP). Ma notes as well the high contribution of government surpluses (reductions of debt), which have risen strongly since 2002. Wang and Fan explore the links between high and increasing inequality in the distribution of income and the savings rate.

Ma and Zhou carefully analyse the factors contributing to rising savings shares in recent years and possible future tendencies. The age structure of the Chinese population has been highly and increasingly favourable for high savings in recent years. They conclude that it is unlikely that the external accounts will turn around into deficits, but the surpluses will not continue to grow and will probably decline. Xiao, Yang and Janus (Chapter 9) analyse the determinants of profitability of state-owned enterprises and so illuminate one of the sources of high and increasing inequality and also high savings rates in China. They explain proposals to reduce the privileged positions and improve the performance of firms operating in the sector.

Several chapters note that whether or not the dependence of growth in recent years on increasing exports and net exports was favourable for China, it will not be possible after the global crisis. The industrialised countries will not be prepared or able to fund the deficits that would need to be the counterparts of Chinese surpluses.

Is an alternative pattern of development built around expanding domestic demand feasible? The general view is that it is necessary, feasible and, if implemented well, desirable on other grounds as well.

Wang and Fan remind us of the long history of analysis of deficiencies in demand, from Marx through to Keynes in theory and Roosevelt in practice. They describe a simple model to illustrate how increased investment alone will not fill the gap on a long-term basis. They note, following Keynes, the essential role of government expenditure in filling the demand gap from time to time. They might have added that increased investment can and must take a major part of the load for a while.

Even if China were successful in shifting the balance between savings and investment by increasing the consumption share of expenditure, it would still have such large external assets that their disposition would be of major importance for China and the rest of the world. Ma and Zhou note that China has moved quickly from being a substantial net debtor in 1999 (net foreign liabilities of 9 per cent of GDP) to being a large net creditor (33 per cent of GDP in 2007). As Corden observes, this was an outcome of other objectives and policies and policy constraints, and not the result of deliberate policy.

Ma and Zhou note the highly unbalanced and unusual composition of China's external assets and liabilities. Its assets are concentrated in fixed-interest securities, especially in the United States. Its liabilities are concentrated in direct foreign investment in China. They contrast the low returns on this asset portfolio with outcomes for Hong Kong, which holds a much higher proportion of its external assets in higher yielding securities including equities. It is inevitable and unexceptionable for China to seek to rebalance its foreign financial assets in the period ahead.

It is natural and unexceptionable in principle for China to hold a much higher proportion of its foreign assets in equities. Drysdale and Findlay (Chapter 16) show that this is easier said than done by reference to the nationalist reaction in Australia to increased Chinese interest in direct investment in the resources sector. Australian policy has found itself in a conceptual tangle. The substantive Australian national interest can be secured through long-established policy on foreign direct investment. Chen makes the interesting suggestion that China would face less resistance to direct investment abroad, and might make better investments, if it diversified the holding of its assets through endowment of a range of public institutions.

Chen (Chapter 15) reminds us that direct foreign investment into and out of China is keeping this dimension of globalisation alive when the financial crisis has closed down most direct foreign investment into industrialised countries. Direct foreign investment into China fell somewhat in the last quarter of 2008 as the financial crisis struck its heaviest blow, but picked up much of the lost ground in the first quarter of 2009. The moderate decline in investment into China has been mainly in real estate. There was a large decline in direct foreign investment in the world as a whole and into and out of industrialised countries in 2008, but Chinese investment abroad doubled. This was an important support for continued growth in developing countries in particular. In Australia, it allowed production to continue at some resources projects, and development to proceed at others, when this would not otherwise have been possible after the crisis.

Huang, Peng and Shen (Chapter 7) assess the economic outlook after the crisis and the expansionary policy and conclude that China is back on a path of reasonably strong growth. In an analogue of the discussion of direct foreign investment, they note that after falling initially, Chinese imports are steadying and are contributing a stabilising element to global trade. Chinese import demand has lifted prices for minerals and energy commodities from the trough into which they retreated in the immediate aftermath of the crisis.

Martin (Chapter 14) reminds us of one area in which the global trading system moved forward in 2009: with the European Union and the United States finally applying Uruguay Round liberalisation of textile and clothing trade to China, the world is operating without systemic quantitative restrictions on trade in these products for the first time in half a century. Chinese shares of the previously restricted markets have increased sharply, but this has been partially matched by a decline in Chinese shares of other markets, which had been open from earlier times.

Three chapters take us deep into analysis of the Chinese labour market. Athukorala, Fukao and Yuan (Chapter 10) apply the theories of development in labour-surplus economies to the experience of China. The rising profit shares of value added are consistent with the theory and with Hong Kong's experience at an earlier stage of its development. The demographic structure of China has supported exceptionally rapid growth of the labour force, well in excess of growth in the population, over the later reform period. Nevertheless, Chinese real wages have been growing rapidly since the mid-1990s, and especially since 2002. Real wage growth has been strongest in the coastal areas and in state-owned enterprises, but has been considerable in all geographic regions and classes of ownership. Labour productivity growth has been so strong that the labour shares of enterprise value added and unit labour costs have continued to fall despite rapid increases in real wages.

Cai, Wang and Qu (Chapter 11) introduce new dimensions into labour market analysis by referring to regional differences in patterns of internal migration and capital flows. Labour-intensive production for export in coastal areas was running into competitiveness issues before the global financial crisis with the rapid growth in real wages. The crisis provides an opportunity for productive structural change. Productivity growth has generally run ahead of rapidly rising real wages, but requires continuing change in the structure of production. China is not a single, homogeneous economy in relation to all the factors affecting comparative advantage in production. International trade analysis needs to take account of changing comparative advantage among regions of China as well as among national economies.

Kong, Meng and Zhang (Chapter 12) focus on the impact of the financial crisis. They note that it is one factor applying pressure to employment through 2009, alongside new labour laws that increase the cost of employing labour and the restrictive monetary policy before the crisis. They note the huge numbers of people who returned to their home areas from urban jobs as the crisis hit late in 2008. They present official data on the number of people who had not recovered employment some time after the Spring Festival in 2009. The data from their own Australian National University—Beijing Normal University survey suggested a higher proportion of people who had not returned to employment—in the range of 13–19 per cent of the total urban labour force from rural areas before the crisis.

McKay and Song (Chapter 13) place Chinese economic development in the reform period on a larger canvas. They compare resource use, urbanisation and industrialisation with industrialised countries at corresponding stages of development, focusing especially on the United States, Japan and South Korea. China is unexceptionable in an East Asian context. However, the high intensity of energy use has implications for emissions of greenhouse gases that were not known to be important for the countries that experienced industrialisation earlier in history.

This sets the stage for three papers on environmental management in Chinese development, with a special focus on the global warming issue.

Zhang and his colleagues in the Development Research Centre (Chapter 17) make an analytically outstanding contribution to the Chinese and international discussion of mitigation responses to global warming. They are uniquely placed to be influential, so that their contribution is of special importance. Their chapter argues that China and other developing countries should be prepared to accept binding caps on emissions, so long as the caps are set fairly, by carefully defined and appropriate criteria. They recognise the problem of carbon leakage, with emissions-intensive industries moving to countries with weaker policies, and see this as a reason for seeking caps in all countries. Like carbon leakage, the problems commonly identified in relation to carbon embedded in industrial products are best managed through all countries accepting a cap. Once entitlements have been defined, trade in entitlements will reduce the costs of reducing emissions. Once entitlements are defined for each country, all countries have powerful national interests in reducing emissions. The authors endorse the per capita basis for allocating entitlements, but argue for applying that in a very different way to Garnaut (2008): they see per capita entitlements as covering historical as well as future emissions, whereas the Garnaut Review looked forward to convergence on equal per capita entitlements at some time in the future. Zhang and colleagues accept that there was an alternative approach to dealing with the historical legacy proposed in the Garnaut Review, built around the industrialised countries taking special financial responsibility for research, development and commercialisation of low-emissions technologies, and for adaptation to unavoidable climate change in developing countries. If there is to be an effective international agreement on greenhouse gas mitigation that adds up to a global solution, we must have before us for discussion concrete proposals that can add up to a solution. No single proposal—neither that of the Garnaut Review nor that of Zhang and colleagues—will immediately receive the support of all relevant parties. By putting concrete proposals for discussion, however, we can come to understand what is important to various parties to the discussion and work towards a productive outcome.

Howes (Chapter 18) takes a look at China's own domestic commitments to reductions of emissions below business as usual and comments that these would meet foreign expectations of China in an early phase of global mitigation. This provides an opportunity for China to play a major role in the search for a global agreement by committing itself firmly in international fora to outcomes that are already covered by domestic policy. Howes notes the welcome increase in Chinese willingness to consider international commitments to contain the growth in emissions within the right context—embodied, for example, in the Zhang contribution to this book, and in two other major recent Chinese papers.

Xue (Chapter 19) discusses the general tendency for environmental concerns to rise in importance with economic development. This is elevating environmental issues in the Chinese policy agenda—rather earlier and more strongly than one would expect at China's income level. In the special case of global warming, this is a necessary condition for China's effective participation in a global mitigation effort. We could add that the sufficient condition is the presence of an international agreement to which China is a party.

White (Chapter 5) explores the implications of continued rapid economic growth in China and of the likelihood that China's relative economic performance will be enhanced rather than diminished by the global crisis. Strategic weight is closely related to economic size, although there has been some stickiness in the bringing to account of Chinese strong economic growth of the past three decades. This stickiness is likely to be a temporary phenomenon, followed by a catching up. The trigger for the catching up might be the realisation that the time when the economic size of China exceeds that of the United States is not far in the future. A politically stable Asia Pacific region will require China and the United States to accept that its exercise of power will need to be qualified by recognition of the interests and perspectives of the other. This will not be easy for either, and especially for the United States after its long period of strategic superiority in Asia.

References

Garnaut, R., 2008, *The Garnaut Climate Change Review*, Cambridge University Press, Melbourne.

Garnaut, R., 2009, 'Thirty Years of Chinese Reform and Economic Growth' in J. Lin, Y. Yao and H. Wu (eds), *Reform and Development in China: What can China Offer the Developing World*, Routledge Publishing.

Garnaut, R. and Llewellyn-Smith, D. forthcoming 2009, *The Great Crash of 2008*, Melbourne University Press.

Song, L. and Woo, W. T. (eds), 2008, *China's Dilemma: Economic Growth, the Environment and Climate Change*, Asia Pacific Press, Canberra, The Brookings Institution Press, Washington, DC, and Social Sciences Academic Press, Beijing.

China and international financial reform 2

Wing Thye Woo[1]

Unhappiness with the international economic architecture all round

The founding principle of economics is that the division of labour increases output. The growth experience of China in the past three decades confirms the validity of this basic insight by Adam Smith on the productivity effects of task specialisation. Thanks to China's rapidly increasing labour-intensive manufactured exports to the rest of the world, China has industrialised at a record pace and hence has also reduced rural poverty at a record pace through the reduction of surplus agricultural labour. China is now the world's largest exporter of textiles, shoes and toys, and also the world's largest recipient of foreign direct investment (FDI). China has clearly been a big beneficiary of the post-World War II global economic system that has promoted economic globalisation.

Economic globalisation has been driven by two processes: the deregulation of international trade; and the opening of national capital markets to achieve an integrated global financial system. The pillar of the international economic architecture that had fundamental responsibility for encouraging trade deregulation was first the General Agreement on Tariffs and Trade (GATT) and is now the World Trade Organisation (WTO). The pillar that has encouraged the lifting of obstacles to cross-country capital movements is the International Monetary Fund (IMF), beginning in the 1980s.[2] The increase in economic globalisation has made the currency of the United States, the US dollar, the keystone of the international economic architecture because the US dollar is the currency most commonly used to denominate cross-country transactions in goods, services and financial assets.[3]

China is of course not the only country that has performed well under this postwar international economic architecture. Economic globalisation

15

also accelerated the development of other Asian countries such as Malaysia, South Korea, Taiwan and Thailand. India, too, attained a higher rate of economic growth after it started steady opening of its economy to international trade and investment from 1991 onwards. In fact, quite a number of advanced economies, most notably in Europe, have deepened their economic integration beyond the standard WTO and IMF norms in liberalisation of the trade account and the capital account. If there were not general recognition in Western Europe that WTO-plus and IMF-plus levels of economic integration would produce large economic benefits, the EU project would not have been realised in just 50 years after so many centuries of strife between distinct nation-states. The establishment of the North American Free Trade Agreement (NAFTA) in 1994 was an endorsement by the North American economies of Western Europe's judgment about the material benefits of WTO-plus and IMF-plus economic integration.

There is now, however, increasingly widespread dissatisfaction with the trade and financial components of the international economic architecture that have created so much prosperity in so many countries. The growing unhappiness with the financial components has quite disparate origins. First, the present frailties of the US economy and its damaged financial system have spurred renewed concern about the stability of an international financial system that operates largely on a US dollar standard. Zhou Xiaochuan (2009), Governor of the People's Bank of China, has recently revived the suggestion by Robert Triffin that the amount of special drawing rights (SDRs) issued by the IMF be greatly increased so that they can displace the US dollar as the medium of exchange in international transactions.

Another way to displace the US dollar from its central role in international transactions (and hence as a reserve currency) is for East Asia to provide an alternative medium of exchange (and hence an alternative store of value) by creating a common Asian currency. After all, the combined China–Japan–South Korean gross domestic product (GDP) will exceed US GDP in 2025, with China's GDP alone exceeding US GDP by 2040. In the opinion of Haruhiko Kuroda, President of the Asian Development Bank (ADB), a common East Asian currency is a realistic objective:

> The more we think about a single currency the greater the political factor seems to dominate. Especially in Asia, where political systems vary so much from country to country and political rivalries between countries are still so intense, we tend to be pessimistic about

a single currency even in the long run...[H]owever, if we look at the younger generations who are free from old nationalistic sentiment, we can be more optimistic. ('The case for Asian monetary union', *Wall Street Journal*, 1 June 2004)

The second area of unhappiness with the financial component of the international economic architecture is the growing rejection of the 'Washington Consensus' that has undergirded the policy advice of the IMF. The East Asian financial crisis exposed the inadequacy of the Washington Consensus, which downplayed the existence of speculative bubbles and the importance of investments in science to sustain high growth.[4] The resulting one-size-fits-all approach of the IMF's rescue packages has seriously eroded the trust in the technical competence of the IMF, and this trust has been the basis for the unusual monopoly status that the IMF enjoys as the world's sole monetary body. This is unlike the World Bank, which faces potential scrutiny from the regional development banks such as the ADB, the Inter-American Development Bank, the European Bank for Reconstruction and Development and the African Development Bank.

Dissatisfaction with the WTO-led trade system has also been growing in recent years. The turn against free trade is well illustrated by the surveys in 2003 and 2007 of the public's attitude towards trade, conducted in 30 countries by the Pew Research Center (2003, 2007). The decline in support for free trade is most pronounced in the United States. The proportion of US residents who had a positive view of trade in 2007 was only 59 per cent—the lowest satisfaction level in the sample. This was also a dramatic drop from the 78 per cent reported in the 2003 survey.

This rise in discontent with trade is a global phenomenon. Of the 38 countries in the sample, 27 reported a drop in support for free trade, two countries were unchanged in their views and nine countries increased their support. The most alarming sign of a threat to the WTO system is that six of the G7 countries (the United States, France, Germany, Italy, the United Kingdom and Canada) view trade in a more negative light than before. None of the nine countries that had become more ardent supporters of trade is a major trading power at present.

A large part of the unhappiness with the WTO-led trade system has come to rest on the persistent trade account surpluses of China, which reached 11.3 per cent of GDP in 2007. At a US congressional hearing in March 2007, Morris Goldstein (2007) opined that the renminbi was overvalued by 40 per cent against the US dollar and accused China of exchange rate manipulation—a charge echoed by Fred Bergsten (2007). On 12 June 2007, Peter Mandelson, the trade commissioner for the European Union, described China's trade policy as 'illogical', 'indefensible' and 'unacceptable' and accused China of doing nothing to rein in rampant counterfeiting ('Surplus fuels EU–China war of words', *Financial Times*, 13 June 2007). On 14 June 2007, a bill was introduced in the US Senate 'to punish China if it did not change its policy of intervening in currency markets to keep the exchange value of the currency, the yuan, low' ('4 in Senate seek penalty for China', *New York Times*, 14 June 2007). In the 2007–08 period, the US trade representative launched a record number of WTO suits against China's trade practices.[5]

This chapter will confine itself to the narrow task of analysing the desirability from China's viewpoint of supporting new forms of international monetary-financial cooperation in order to reform the international monetary system in the direction of reducing the global role of the US dollar and to improve the global ability to fight financial market disorders.

Starting on the road to a common Asian currency?

In retrospect, the East Asian financial crisis of 1997–98 gave a huge boost to the impetus towards Asian economic integration. The yearning for greater economic integration in post-crisis Asia was due as much to the consequences of the typhoon that appeared in the Gulf of Siam on 2 July 1997 as it was to the causes of the financial typhoon and the responses of the international financial institutions, the United States and Western Europe.

East Asians drew two lessons from the East Asian financial crisis. The first lesson is that the Washington Consensus doctrine is blind to the ability of the financial markets to price financial assets incorrectly on a large scale. A better picture of the working of financial markets is that of Paul Volcker (1999), who said:

> International financial crises, I might even say domestic financial crises, are built into the human genome. When we map the whole thing, we will find something there called greed and something called fear and something called hubris. That is all you need to produce international financial crises in the future.

Because the IMF (under the influence of the Washington Consensus) regarded the collapse of output in Asia as the inevitable consequence of an unsustainable economic system that was created by government policies catering to crony capitalism, the initial IMF rescue packages stressed severe monetary-fiscal tightening and a drastic overhaul of the economic system and incentive structure (for example, immediate increases in the capital adequacy ratio and abrupt large-scale closures of financial institutions) to restructure the economy in order to restart growth. This initial misjudgment explains why the IMF kept under-predicting until the end of 1998 the strength of the growth that occurred.

The second important lesson drawn by East Asians is that the only form of reliable help during an economic emergency is self-help. The IMF could not be counted on to always be correct in its diagnosis on its first reading of the situation. Moreover, the United States could not be expected to be always ready to help out countries in desperate straits. In the three-decade-long rule of Indonesian President General Suharto, he had been bailed out several times by the United States and its allies (notably, Australia, Japan, the Netherlands and the international financial institutions), and it was thus quite natural for him to expect some external aid when things started going awry in the last quarter of 1997. Suharto was mistaken. He did not realise that with the end of the Cold War in 1992, he was dispensable to US security and ideological interests just like his fellow general, Joseph Mobuto of Congo-Zaire.

The only countries that were willing to commit immediate large-scale financial assistance to the crashing East Asian economies were neighbouring Japan and Australia. Japan proposed the Asian Monetary Fund (AMF). Japan did not succeed, however, in establishing the AMF. There were three key reasons for the failure of the initiative. First, some important industrialised countries believed in the crony capitalism explanation of the crisis, and concluded that an AMF would merely mean throwing more money to the undeserving, corrupt elite of these countries. Second, some other industrialised countries wanted to protect the monopoly position of the IMF so that they could continue to command a disproportionate influence on world affairs. Third, China was not prepared to be rushed by events into supporting a new regional institution without careful consideration of all the implications.

These two lessons propelled the East Asian countries after their recovery to go on a reserves-accumulation spree to insulate themselves from future speculative attacks—that is, to be independent of the supervision of the IMF. These lessons also led the Asian countries—the 10 Association of South-East Asian Nations (ASEAN) countries, China, Japan and South Korea, collectively called ASEAN+3—to start the process of currency and financial cooperation when they met in Chiangmai, Thailand, in 2000. The resulting 'Chiangmai Initiative' had two major components.

The first component was that countries agreed to come to one another's aid if similar speculative attacks were to reoccur. This pooling of reserves to defend the existing values of their exchange rates was enabled by each country entering into a web of bilateral swap arrangements. The second component was the establishment of an Asian Bond Market (ABM) to keep funds within the region. The assumption was that if there was a panic-led capital flight from one Asian country, the existence of the ABM would channel these funds to the other Asian countries. The ABM was a defensive mechanism (just like the antiballistic missile) and it worked by reducing the probability of a collective capital flight from Asia.

At the May 2006 meeting of the ADB in Hyderabad, India, the bank led the calls for the introduction of an Asian currency unit (ACU) to coordinate exchange rate movements within the region. This proposal was similar to the first major step towards currency unification in Europe when the European currency unit (ECU)—more popularly known as the European currency snake—was introduced in 1976 to coordinate a joint float against the US dollar. Would Asia, in three years after Hyderabad, as Europe did in 1979, form the Asian equivalent of the European monetary system? And would it then grow into an Asian monetary union in another 20 years?

Given the many parallels[6] between the rapid developments in Asia in the past decade with the movement in Europe from the Treaty of Rome in 1957, which established the European Economic Community, to the Maastricht Treaty in 1993, which formalised the European Union, the sense of history repeating itself is naturally a strong one. Is there an Asian Economic Union (AEU) in the offing? Will it come soon, just like a late industrialiser taking off at explosive speed compared with the first industrialiser?

We know enough from painful experience, however, to be wary of linear thinking; otherwise, there would never be any turning points in history. We do well to remember Karl Marx' words: 'History repeats itself, first as tragedy, second as farce.'[7]

The economic basis for exchange rate coordination and a common currency

The basic question is whether the final realised form of the Asian Economic Union (AEU) will be closer to the European Union or to NAFTA. The European Union and NAFTA are similar in that they permit the free movement of goods and capital within their respective groupings. They also, however, differ in many significant aspects. Unlike the European Union, NAFTA allows only limited labour mobility across countries (notably, there are restrictions on labour movements from Mexico to the United States and Canada), it has no plans to coordinate exchange rate policies and it does not envisage an eventual political union.

Even so, recent events do not suggest that the European Union and NAFTA will continue to evolve steadily towards their stated final forms. When the citizens of France and the Netherlands, in 2005, and of Ireland, in 2008, were allowed to express their choice at the voting booth about the desirability of moving on to the next stage of integration, they rejected the motion. It is commonly believed that if the United Kingdom and Italy had conducted referendums on the issue, their citizens would have also rejected continued European integration. During the US primary elections for nomination as the candidate of the Democratic Party, Hillary Clinton and Barack Obama expressed the possibility of renegotiating the terms of NAFTA.

Amid these contrary developments within the European Union and NAFTA in the past few years, more prominent Asian voices have, however, emerged in support of building an AEU. For example, in 2005, Haruhiko Kuroda, the President of the ADB, called for Asia to move 'towards a borderless Asia'; and, in 2008, he reported that despite Asian economic integration being a challenging task, 'Asia is poised to take these steps' (Kuroda 2005, 2008).

So far, no prominent proponent of an AEU has advocated a future political union as a final objective. While political objectives such as the avoidance of armed conflict among traditional competitors might suffice to drive the economic integration agenda, it would be more rational to also explicitly acknowledge the economic costs of these political decisions. To put the issue more fundamentally, is there a case for exchange rate coordination (and, maybe, monetary integration) within an AEU in the absence of political unification?

In our opinion, we cannot compare the relative merits of an EU-type AEU and an NAFTA-type AEU without stating what the world will look like in the future. Luckily for us, the conventional views of the state of the world in 2025 and 2050 are conveniently contained in a Goldman-Sachs study (O'Neill et al. 2005). Projections have been made for the inflation-adjusted GDP in the major countries in the European Union, NAFTA and the AEU for 2025 and 2050 (Table 2.1).

Table 2.1   The world economy in 2005, 2025 and 2050 according to GDP

Case 1 NAFTA GDP: United States dominates now and in the future

	United States	Canada	Mexico
2005	12.5	1.2	0.7
2025	19.6	1.8	2.4
2050	37.7	3.0	7.8

Case 2 EU GDP: Fairly equal in size

	France	Germany	United Kingdom
2005	2.3	3.1	2.3
2025	3.2	3.9	3.3
2050	4.9	5.4	5.1

Case 3 Asia GDP: Japan dominates now; China dominates in the future

	China	South Korea	Japan
2005	1.9	0.8	5.3
2025	11.7	2.6	6.7
2050	48.6	3.7	8.0

Note: GDP is measured in US$ trillion in 2005 prices.

Source: O'Neill, J., Wilson, D., Purushothaman, R. and Stupnytska, A. 2005, *How solid are the BRICs?*, Global Economics Paper, no. 134 (15 December 2005), Goldman Sachs.

Case 1 in Table 2.1 focuses on the three NAFTA countries: the United States, Canada and Mexico. If we select for the normalisation of GDP in each year, the current GDP of the country that had the smallest GDP in 2005, the GDP ratio of the United States–Canada–Mexico in each year would be: 17.9:1.7:1.0 in 2005; 8.2:0.8:1.0 in 2025; and 4.8:0.4:1.0 in 2050.

While the United States will become increasingly large vis-a-vis Canada and decreasingly large vis-a-vis Mexico, the fact is that the United States is the overwhelmingly dominant country in NAFTA at present and will continue to be so in the future. In 2050, the United States will be 12 times larger than Canada and almost five times larger than Mexico. Given this great disparity in economic size, it will always be true that independent economic shocks in Canada and Mexico will have very limited impact on the US economy, while a sneeze by the United States could send powerful tremors to the other two NAFTA members. In such an unequal situation, the survival of individual currencies is natural because the giant US economy sees no advantage in allowing its monetary policy to be influenced by the concerns of the smaller economies, and Canada and Mexico could use the exchange rate as an additional instrument to help offset shocks (especially trade shocks) originating from the US economy.

Case 2 in Table 2.1 reports the GDP of the three largest economies in the European Union: Germany, the United Kingdom and France. Again, using the smallest country in 2005 (France in this case) to normalise GDP, we see that the GDP ratio of Germany–the United Kingdom–France will be: 1.3:1.0:1.0 in 2005; 1.2:1.0:1.0 in 2025; and 1.1:1.0:1.0 in 2050.

The GDP ratios reveal clearly that the biggest EU economies are of the same magnitude now and will continue to be so in the future. This means that independent shocks in each country will have sizeable spill-over effects on the others. This high level of economic interdependence among EU members means that the welfare of each member will be increased if national economic policies are coordinated in a manner that reduces negative spill-over effects. One instrument for achieving this welfare-enhancing cooperative solution is a common currency.

Furthermore, in the political dimension, the natural compromise solution for a group of equally powerful countries is a common currency rather than the adoption of any particular national currency. The fact that Europe is anxious to undertake political union in order to minimise the possibility of another war between Germany, the United Kingdom and France means that a common currency is a necessary by-product. In 1950, when the French Foreign Minister, Robert Schuman, pushed for the creation of the European Coal and Steel Community—the forefather of the European Union—he explicitly admitted that this was a way to prevent further war between France and Germany. With the steel and coal industries under the control of a supranational organisation, war would have been 'not only unthinkable but materially impossible' (<http://en.wikipedia.org/wiki/European_Coal_and_Steel_Community>).

Case 3 in Table 2.1 projects that the distribution of GDP of the three major East Asian economies—Japan, China and South Korea—will display drastic changes over time. The GDP ratio of Japan–China–South Korea will be: 6.6:2.4:1.0 in 2005; 2.6:4.5:1.0 in 2025; and 2.2:13.1:1.0 in 2050.

Unlike the European Union, an AEU will not be a club of equals at any point in time; and, unlike NAFTA, there is no stable dominant economic giant across time. Japan is the economic giant in 2005, but China will be the economic giant in 2050. If there is a compelling economic argument to form a yen bloc today, the same economic reasoning would dictate that this yen bloc transform itself into a yuan bloc by about 2035.

Because Chinese policymakers must be well aware of the changing balance in economic power within East Asia in the next three decades, it is hard to see why China today would want to support the establishment of a regional economic architecture that would establish a yen bloc. Similarly, even if China were to agree to the formation of a yen bloc now, it is hard to see why it would not seek to change the fundamental nature of the regional financial architecture after 2035. It is, in short, politically unrealistic to expect a common currency for East Asia in the foreseeable future.

Moreover, it is also economically undesirable for East Asia to adopt a common currency because there has not been serious consideration of complete integration of national labour markets in the official and academic discussions of an AEU. If economy A is entering into inflation while economy B is entering into recession, A will want to raise the interest rate while B will want to lower the interest rate. The uncomfortable reality is that whatever the compromise interest rate policy might be, it will be optimal only if labour from B can move freely and without cost to A.[8] Without unhindered labour mobility across A and B as the adjustment mechanism to a common monetary policy, the benefits of a common currency could be greatly reduced, if not overwhelmed.

Our opinion is that the NAFTA-like disparity in economic power in an AEU at present and in the future and the absence of policy-induced integration of national labour markets mean that the only stable configuration is the survival of individual East Asian currencies with limited coordination among them in normal times. It therefore appears to us that the many present efforts to promote closer exchange rate cooperation will not succeed in the long run.

China should support the creation of an Asian financial facility as a means of reforming the international financial architecture

In our opinion, the present deep global financial crisis has given Asia an opportunity to establish a feasible form of Asian financial cooperation as part of its efforts to help reform the international financial architecture. At the G20 summit meetings in Washington, DC, on 15 November 2008 and in London on 2 April 2009, French President, Nicolas Sarkozy, and UK Prime Minister, Gordon Brown, called on the G20 to establish an IMF greatly enhanced in both financial lending power and regulatory supervisory power. We agree that an improved IMF is highly desirable, but a greatly enhanced Asian swap facility—the Asian Financial Fund (AFF)—would be a superior first line of defence against financial contagion in Asia, because Asia collectively now has enough reserves to fend off unwarranted speculative attacks on a subset of its members. It must be emphasised that the core mission of the AFF is to combat financial contagion and not to finance balance-of-payments adjustment caused by economic mismanagement. This present emphasis by the AFF on the former is what distinguishes it from the IMF, which has both functions as its core mission.

An AFF is necessary because it is simply impossible (and certainly inefficient) to increase the size of the IMF enough to enable it to have in-depth expertise on most of the countries to be able to respond optimally in a timely manner to each national crisis. Furthermore, the IMF's policies are decided by executive directors who usually take their orders from their national ministries of finance and central banks, and it would be credulous to think that a significant proportion of these national economic agencies have up-to-date understanding of most of the emerging economies. Even if the improved technical competence of the IMF is not doomed to disappoint the emerging economies, they will be disappointed by the long time required for an improved IMF to appear. The negotiations on meaningful IMF reforms will inevitably be cantankerous and hence protracted.

The Sarkozy–Brown proposal for a new Bretton Woods should be recognised as part of the continuing effort by Old Europe to maintain its disproportionate representation in global governance bodies such as the UN Security Council, the IMF and the World Bank.[9] The proposal to make the unreformed IMF the super financial policeman of the world is foolish because the concentration of so much power in its hands would magnify the impact of any incorrect operational procedure and allow the mistake to remain unchecked for a longer time. If need be, the assignment of global financial regulation to an expanded Bank for International Settlements (BIS) would be a better alternative. The IMF should forgo its dream of jurisdictional expansion and become instead a more specialised agency that undertakes macroeconomic surveillance for the world and balance-of-payments assistance for the emerging economies.

Right now, East Asia has a thin network of swap lines to defend its currencies. It would be desirable to hasten the evolution of the existing swap facility into the AFF by two actions. First, the existing swap facility specifies that a cumulative drawing that exceeds 20 per cent of a country's quota requires the country to accept IMF supervision. This 'flight-to-the-IMF' clause should be removed because painful memories of 1997–98 make it politically suicidal for any East Asian leader to do so.

Second, the Asian swap facility must now establish a surveillance mechanism to pre-qualify its members for emergency loans (Wang and Woo 2004). Without a credible procedure to pre-qualify members, the removal of the 'flight-to-the-IMF' clause will guarantee that the present system of (bilateral and multilateral) swap arrangements will not be sustainable and will not increase to meaningful sums. This is because the members want the pooled funds to be used only to defend an exchange rate against speculative attacks not justified by fundamentals. The members will not support using the pooled reserves to defend an exchange rate that has been rendered overvalued by inflationary domestic policies. Without pre-qualification of potential borrowers, no member will be willing to risk committing a large part of its reserves to the swap facility.

During the height of the East Asian financial crisis, the United States, Western Europe and China opposed the establishment of an Asian Monetary Fund to help handle the crisis. Why should they now support the setting up of the AFF, which will have some of the same features as the rejected AMF? There are six reasons for a change of mind.

The first reason is that the 2008 global financial crisis has removed all doubt that financial panic and not crony capitalism was the cause of the East Asian financial crisis, and that the IMF's programs made matters worse.

The second reason is that the United States and Western Europe cannot really stop such a move anyway because: 1) East Asian economies now have the requisite amount of foreign exchange reserves to undertake self-insurance against speculative attacks on a subset of their members; and 2) China has now changed its mind about the desirability of a regional financial institution.

The third reason is that there is now realisation by the United States that, when dealing with Asia, it should rely less on the hard power of a formal dominant role in global leadership and more on the soft power of US example—such as helping Asia do what is best for Asia (which is an excellent start for the United States' re-engagement with Asia). The United States' support for the AFF is a much-needed change towards an inclusive US approach that is diversified in modality to handle each specific multilateral issue. Such a change in modality by the United States would be a realistic response to the shift towards Asia as the centre of gravity for the world economy.

The fourth reason is that with the end of the Cold War, the international agenda of the United States is no longer so similar to that of the Western European countries. This is why when President Sarkozy pressed former US President George W. Bush in October 2008 to convene a G7 summit to deal with the global financial crisis, Bush chose to convene a G20 summit instead. The international economic agendas of the United States and some of the major developing countries now share many more common elements that are at odds with the position of the European Union—for example, on agricultural subsidies.

The fifth reason is that the United States and the rest of the interested world will be members of the AFF just as they are now influential members of the ADB. The creation of the AFF would not mean the disappearance of their policy engagement with Asia. Furthermore, just as we have the system of the World Bank and several regional development banks (such as the Inter-American Development Bank and the African Development Bank), it is also natural and desirable to have regional financial institutions in addition to the IMF. The IMF by no means becomes obsolete with the establishment of the regional financial institutions. The IMF can play a very helpful role in speeding up the institutional maturity of these regional financial institutions and in keeping up the competition of ideas.

The sixth reason is that the AFF could expand over time to be an Asia-Pacific Economic Cooperation (APEC)-level institution and be a good partner to the IMF because 'two heads are better than one' in analysing unexpected, quickly evolving crises and preventing their contagion. In short, the better way to improve the supply of global public goods is not to simply increase the size of the existing providers but to increase the number of providers while seeking to improve the performance of existing ones.

Of course, over time, depending on the progress in reforming the operations and the governance of the IMF, and the new needs created by greater Asian economic integration, the Asian community might empower the AFF to also extend adjustment loans with conditionality to countries that needed balance-of-payments assistance because of past economic mismanagement. It is important to note that pooling national foreign exchange reserve funds and using them to enhance regional welfare is independent of whether the AFF will promote exchange rate coordination or not. One activity does not imply the other.

Summing up

Our formulation of an Asian Financial Fund is operationally the establishment of a large Asian swap facility that has its own surveillance mechanism to pre-qualify members for emergency loans. The primary mission of the AFF is to calm panic in the foreign exchange markets and not to defend currencies that have been rendered overvalued by domestic inflationary policies. The AFF's goal is to attenuate the cost of bad luck and not the cost of bad policies.

Given the large size of East Asian foreign reserves, the AFF should take on the additional task of designing a pooling scheme where part of the East Asian reserves could be safely used to finance sound infrastructure projects in the poorest Asian countries. This outcome would be superior to the present practice of putting almost all of the East Asian foreign reserves into the assets of G7 economies.

It is important that the AFF does not suffer from the institutional inertia that is characteristic of the current global organisations such as the United Nations, the World Bank and the IMF. The leadership structure of the AFF should be designed to avoid simply locking in the balance of economic power that exists at the time of its founding—unlike the unchanging composition of the permanent members of the UN Security Council, the head of the World Bank always being a US appointee and the head of the IMF always being a European. If the AFF can adopt a self-updating type of leadership structure, its first contribution to the world (as well as to the East Asian region) will be the provision of an example to inspire positive developments in the reform of the leadership structure in global organisations.

References

Bergsten, C. F. 2007, The dollar and the renminbi, Statement before the Hearing on US Economic Relations with China: Strategies and options on exchange rates and market access, 23 May 2007, Subcommittee on Security and International Trade and Finance, Committee on Banking, Housing and Urban Affairs, US Senate, Washington, DC.

Goldstein, M. 2007, Assessing progress on China's exchange rate policies, Testimony before the Hearing on Risks and Reform: The role of currency in the US–China relationship, 28 March 2007, Committee on Finance, US Senate, Washington, DC.

Kuroda, H. 2005, Towards a borderless Asia: a perspective on Asian economic integration, Speech, 10 December 2005, Asian Development Bank, Manila, <http://www.adb.org/Documents/Speeches/2005/ms2005088.asp>

—— 2008, The challenges of economic integration, Speech, 12 September 2008, Asian Development Bank, Manila, <http://www.adb.org/Documents/Speeches/2008/ms2008070.asp>

Marx, K. 1852, *The Eighteenth Brumaire of Louis Bonaparte*, Marxists web site <http://www.marxists.org/archive/marx/works/1852/18th-brumaire/>

Mundell, R. A. 1961, 'A theory of optimum currency areas', *American Economic Review*, vol. 51, pp. 657–65.

O'Neill, J., Wilson, D., Purushothaman, R. and Stupnytska, A. 2005, *How solid are the BRICs?*, Global Economics Paper, no. 134 (15 December 2005), Goldman Sachs.

Pew Research Center 2003, 'Views of a changing world', *Pew Global Attitudes Survey*, Pew Research Center, Washington, DC, <http://pewglobal.org/reports/pdf/185.pdf>

—— 2007, 'World publics welcome global trade—but not immigration', *Pew Global Attitudes Survey*, Pew Research Center, Washington, DC, <http://pewglobal.org/reports/pdf/258.pdf>

Volcker, P. 1999, 'A perspective on financial crises', in J. Sneddon Little and G. Olivei (eds), *Rethinking the International Monetary System*, Federal Reserve Bank of Boston, Conference Series, no. 43, June 1999.

Wang, Y. and Woo, W. T. 2004, 'A timely information exchange mechanism, an effective surveillance system, and an improved financial architecture for East Asia', in Asian Development Bank, *Monetary and Financial Integration in East Asia: The way forward. Volume 2*, Palgrave Macmillan, pp. 425–58.

Woo, W. T. 2004, 'Serious inadequacies of the Washington Consensus: misunderstanding the poor by the brightest', in J. Joost Teunissen and A. Akkerman (eds), *Diversity in Development: Reconsidering the Washington Consensus*, December 2004, Forum on Debt and Development, The Hague, Netherlands.

Zhou, X. 2009, *Reform the International Monetary System*, People's Bank of China, Beijing.

Endnotes

1. This chapter is part of the first phase of my project on China's New International Economic Responsibilities.

2. In the aftermath of the 1997–98 capital account crises in East Asia, however, the IMF has been more muted and circumspect in its advocacy of capital account opening. Another international organisation that champions capital account liberalisation is the Organisation for Economic Cooperation and Development (OECD), which makes an open capital account a prerequisite for membership.

3. The euro and the yen are also major currencies but they are seldom used in transactions that do not involve agents in the Euro Zone countries and Japan.

4. See Woo (2004) for a review and critique of the Washington Consensus doctrine.

5. In the February–April 2007 period, the United States filed a WTO suit against Chinese subsidies to exports, Chinese import restrictions on copyright-intensive imports and China's weak protection of copyrights. On 19 December 2008, the United States filed a WTO suit against China's programs to establish global brands for its products because they were seen as export subsidies.

6. The Chiangmai Initiative turned out to be only the first part of a more comprehensive program of regional economic integration. In November 2001, China and ASEAN agreed to start negotiations for an ASEAN+1 free trade area (FTA) that would be achieved in 2010. By November 2002, China and ASEAN had made enough progress to sign the framework agreement for the ASEAN+1 FTA. This fast pace of economic embrace between ASEAN and China had the synergistic effect of accelerating what had been a leisurely paced process of incremental economic integration within ASEAN, and of energising Japan into active FTA negotiations with ASEAN. The ambition of Asian economic integration, or at least its rhetoric, has continued to broaden. The annual ASEAN+3 conference in 2005 was

supplemented by the East Asian Summit (effectively an ASEAN+6 conference) to include Australia, India and New Zealand; and the host of the 2005 conference, Prime Minister Abdullah Badawi of Malaysia, expounded on his vision of an Asian community.

7. This is the common paraphrase of the opening sentences in Marx (1852).

8. This is the fundamental insight of Mundell (1961).

9. The veracity of this statement is striking in that the G20 summit in November 2008 turned out to be a G22 summit because some of the European members pressed successfully for the inclusion of the Netherlands and Spain.

From an efficient to a viable international financial market 3

Chen Ping

Introduction

This ongoing grand crisis originated in the United States, then transmogrified into an international crisis. It represents a natural experiment. The positive side of this crisis is its fundamental lesson. It is not a theoretical debate confined to ivory towers, but a historical event that has destroyed social confidence in the mainstream equilibrium theory of the so-called efficient market. This has accelerated the rise of the non-linear evolutionary theory of the viable market. Four observations reveal where the equilibrium theory of asset pricing and business cycles went wrong: 1) exchange rate resonance driven by US business cycles; 2) the meso-foundation of macro-fluctuations; 3) the endogenous nature of persistent cycles in financial macro-indexes; and 4) the trend of collapse and higher moment risk in the derivative market. The new perspective of non-linear population dynamics in continuous time provides a better alternative to existing rational-actor/linear models of finance, not only for understanding the cause of the present situation, but to inform efforts related to redesign and reform. The systematic failure in the mortgage security market, unprecedented concentration in the international financial market, and unfettered speculation in the commodity and currency markets have all contributed to the current disaster. A new international financial order can be achieved if a robust and workable international antitrust law can be enacted and a Tobin tax on foreign exchange transactions can be established through global efforts. An overhaul of financial theory is needed to develop a viable market for sustainable economies.

33

Empirical observations and policy implications: econometric illusion in the efficient market and an alternative strategy for a viable market

Our empirical analysis of business cycles draws on tools developed by the new science of complexity and non-linear dynamics, which were applied to US economic time series (Chen 1988, 1996a, 1996b, 2002, 2006, 2007). The policy recommendations were reached based on alternative scenarios tested under the rubric of non-linear evolutionary dynamics in finance and economics (Chen 2005, 2008). The debate begins by examining exchange rate co-movements and the nature of business cycles, before proceeding to examine the misleading role of linear models in asset pricing.

Exchange rate resonance among major currencies and a Tobin tax to discourage short-term speculation

What was the source of the US financial crisis? US Federal Reserve Chairman, Ben Bernanke, has attributed it to over-consumption in the United States and over-saving in China, while Treasury Secretary, Tim Geithner, has blamed China's exchange rate policy. Is there any empirical evidence in the conventional arena predicting the unstable nature of the international financial market? Econometric tests based on regression analysis cannot reach a conclusion since their results depend on untenable assumptions about underlying dynamic structures. In contrast, our observations are based on non-parametric analysis of the currency depreciation pressure index (CDP), which is constructed in terms of covered interest rate parity (IRP). We can consider CDP as a disequilibrium measurement of the degree of deviation from IRP (Jia and Chen 2009). We plot major currency trajectories over time (Figure 3.1), including the euro, the Japanese yen, British pound sterling and the Chinese renminbi. Equilibrium theory asserts that an efficient market should be characterised by the absence of arbitrage opportunity. If equilibrium theory is valid in the international financial market, we should see horizontal lines in time, not wave-like resonance. Its relation with monetary instruments is shown in Figure 3.2.

Figure 3.1 Currency depreciation pressure indexes for the euro, yen, pound sterling and renminbi, January 1999 – February 1999

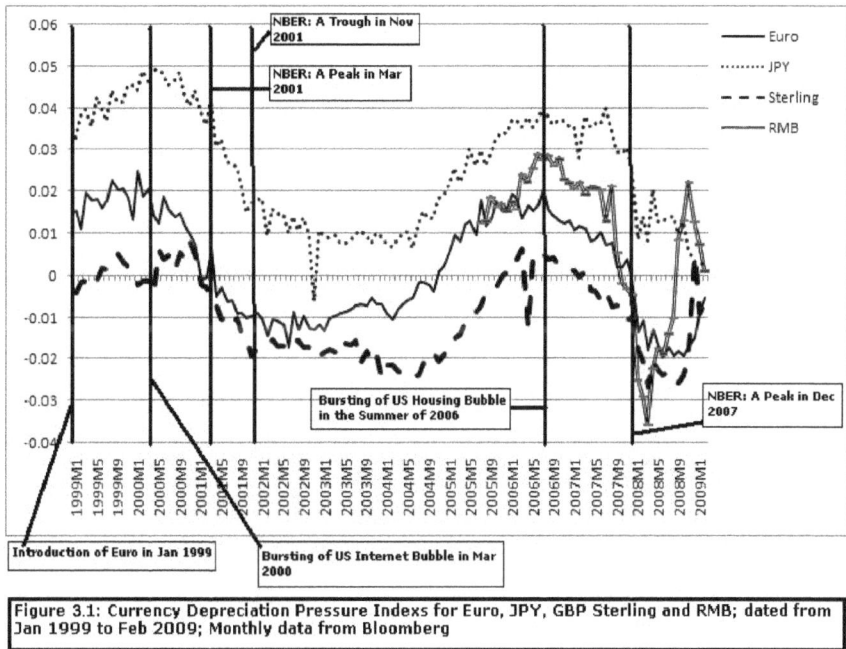

Figure 3.1: Currency Depreciation Pressure Indexs for Euro, JPY, GBP Sterling and RMB; dated from Jan 1999 to Feb 2009; Monthly data from Bloomberg

Source: Monthly data from Bloomberg.com.

The wave-like resonance patterns among the major-economy exchange rates in Figure 3.1 have a close correlation with the US business cycles as defined by the National Bureau of Economic Research (NBER). The vertical axis is the CDP measure of depreciation pressure.

Figure 3.2   Time trajectories of various US interest rates

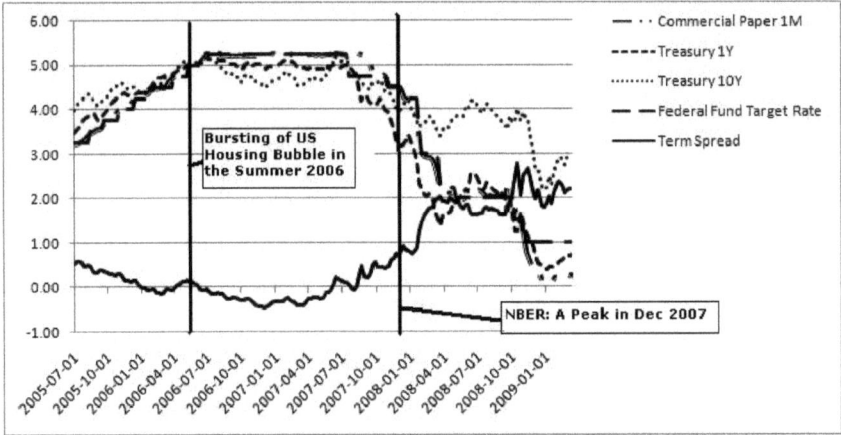

Figure 3 depicts various of US Interest Rates, including 1-month Commercial paper rate, 1-year Treasury Bill rate, 10-year Treasury Bill rate, Federal Fund Target Rate as well as term spread. We use weekly data, downloaded from Federal Reserve at St. Luis!

Source: Weekly data from Federal Reserve Bank at St Louis.

From Figure 3.2, we can see clearly that only long-term interest rates signal the boom and bust in business cycles.

Based on the above observations, we see no evidence of an equilibrium-efficient market encapsulated in risk-free arbitrage in the currency market. Detailed studies show little correlation between exchange rate resonance and other fundamental variables in the US economy, such as trade and budget deficits. On the contrary, there is strong evidence of US power in the international market, since the exchange rate resonance is clearly driven by US business cycles. This implies that the US economy is the dominant market for international capital flow—which it is. No other currencies have countervailing power against the tide of the US economy. This implication is important for designing the new international financial order. Even if the US economy declines significantly, there is no candidate to replace the US dollar as the world's reserve currency in the near future.

Endogenous nature of US persistent business cycles and a new perspective on risk management

If the exchange rates of major countries are driven by US business cycles, the next question must be about the nature of business cycles. Are they generated by external shocks (Frisch 1933; Lucas 1972) or by internal instability (Schumpeter 1939; Chen 1988, 1996a)? This issue is essential, since all textbook investment strategies related to diversification and hedging are based on a simple assumption that an efficient market is characterised by a random walk or Brownian motion, without countenancing the possibility of non-linear deterministic patterns such as persistent cycles and chaos (Friedman 1953; Fama 1970, 1991; Black and Scholes 1973). The application of a new technique of time-frequency analysis based on WGQ (Wigner-Gabor-Qian) transformation in time-frequency space has led to the development of a powerful tool for non-stationary time-series analysis, which can replace these conventional models (Chen 1996a, 2005, 2008). Solid evidence of endogenous persistent cycles is shown in Figure 3.3, while the equilibrium illusion of white noise is simply created by the first-difference (FD) filter (Figure 3.4), which is a high-frequency noise amplifier by nature (Chen 2008).

Figure 3.3   Endogenous nature of S&P 500 index movements

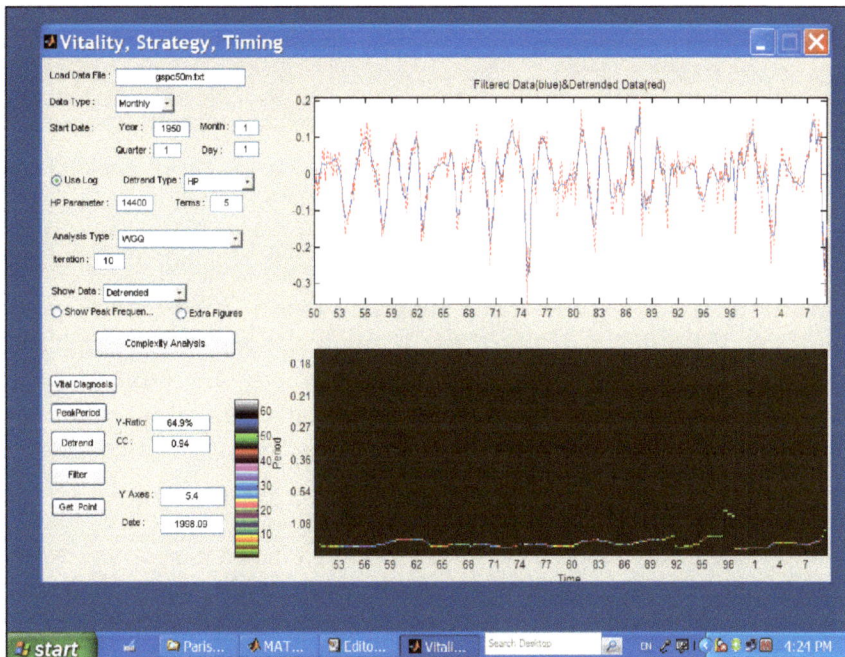

Source: (Chen 1996b, 2005).

As shown in Figure 3.3, deterministic cycles can explain 64.9 per cent of variance from HP-detrended cycles filtered by WGQ transformation in time-frequency space. The cross-correlation with original cycles is 0.94. We found these persistant cycles can be explained by colour chaos. Colour means that its intrinsic period is about four to five years. Colour chaos is deterministic chaos in continous-time. Its correlation dimension is 2.5 (Chen 2005). Colour chaos can be considered as the non-linear model of Schumpeter's biological clock, a better alternative model of random walk or white noise in equilibrium theory of business cycles.

Figure 3.4. The frequency response function for the FD filter

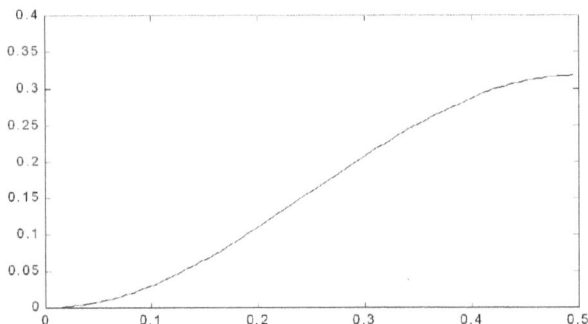

Here, $X(t) = FD[S(t)] = S(t + 1) - S(t)$; the horizontal axis is the frequency range from zero to 0.5. Clearly, this is a whitening device, which suppresses low-frequency signals in business-cycle range but amplifies high-frequency noise for creating an equilibrium illusion of an 'efficient market' dominated by white noise.

What can be learnt from these observations? First, white noise plays only a non-dominant role in the financial market. For example, the white noise component represents only about 30 per cent of the variance of the HP-filtered cycles. Second, the equilibrium theory of efficient markets provides a distorted image of reality. We find that the intrinsic frequency of stock market indexes is remarkably stable about the business-cycle frequency, while the price level varies erratically. Therefore, *price does not contain all the information about market movements*. Market trends, cyclical periods and correlation phases are more essential information than the price level for business decision making and macro-management. Third, the equilibrium theory of asset pricing offers a misleading recipe for risk management. A diversification strategy works only if market movements have no systematic trends and persistent cycles and all players make independent rational decisions without correlated actions. If business cycles play a leading role in market movements, cash-flow management should be the key factor in risk management—a fact that is often missing from traditional asset-pricing theory. Investors do not just make a simple choice between stocks and bonds. Cash can become king when uncertainty is pervasive. That is why securitisation is not capable of preventing crises such as the sub-prime debacle. On the contrary, complex tools of derivative trading amplify market resonance under the guidance of equilibrium finance theory.

The meso-foundation of macro-fluctuations and competition policy in the global economy

Lucas (1972) made a strong claim that business cycles could be explained by an equilibrium (rational expectations) mechanism of workers' choices between work and leisure. His micro-foundations theory has, however, been rejected by empirical observations based on the principle of large numbers (Chen 2002). It was Schrödinger (1948), the founder of quantum mechanics and quantum biology, who found a salient relationship between the number of micro-elements and the variability of aggregate fluctuations.

Equation 3.1

$$\text{Market variability (MV)} = \frac{STD(S_N)}{Mean(S_N)} \approx \frac{1}{\sqrt{N}}$$

The implication of Equation 3.1 is very clear. The more micro-elements involved, the less will be the aggregate fluctuation. This is the principle of large numbers. This relation holds not only for static aggregation, but for some dynamic systems such as the population dynamics of the birth–death process (Chen 2002). Empirically speaking, since we can measure market variability (MV) from aggregate indexes, we can also infer the effective cluster number (CN), N, at the micro-level. Therefore, we have a powerful tool to identify the source of aggregate fluctuations—if there is an explanation for micro-foundations (the structural level of households and firms) or an explanation for meso-foundations (the structural level of financial intermediates and industrial organisation in the form of clusters). The empirical results are shown in Table 3.1.

Table 3.1 Market variability and effective number for various aggregate indexes

Item	MV (%)	CN
Real personal consumption	0.15	800,000
Real GDP	0.2	500,000
Real private investment	1.2	10,000
Dow Jones Industrial (1928–2009)	1.4	9,000
S&P 500 Index (1947–2009)	1.6	5,000
NASDAQ (1971–2009)	2.0	3,000
Japan–US exchange rate (1971–2009)	6.1	300
US–euro exchange rate (1999–2009)	4.9	400
Texas crude oil price (1978–2008)	5.3	400

Notes: For non-stationary time series, market variability is measured via the HP filter; the average is estimated from a moving time window in the range of the average length of business cycles, here proxied at five years (Chen 2002).

Sources: US aggregate indexes and exchange rates are sourced from the Federal Reserve Bank of St Louis; stock indexes data are from < yahoo.finance >; the oil price index is from the US Energy Information Administration.

The number of households, corporations and public companies and their implied orders of market variation (MV) in 1980 are given in Table 3.2.

Table 3.2 Numbers of households and firms in the United States, 1980

Micro-agents	Households	Corporations[a]	Public companies
N	80,700,000	2,900,000	20,000
MV (%)	0.01	0.1	0.7

[a] Here, we count only those corporations with more than $100,000 in assets.

Source: The data are from the US Bureau of Census.

From Tables 3.1 and 3.2, we can see that household fluctuations contribute only about 5 per cent of fluctuations in real gross domestic product (GDP) and less than 1 per cent in real investment; and small firms can contribute 50 per cent of fluctuations in real GDP or 8 per cent in real investment, while public companies can generate about 60 per cent of aggregate fluctuations in real investment. Clearly, there are very weak 'micro-foundations' but strong evidence of a 'meso-foundation' in macroeconomic fluctuations. The doctrine of 'too big to fail' might be true at the micro-level in the cases of external shocks, but it is not true at the macro-level in terms of the meso–macro relationship. This fallacy of composition still fools equilibrium economists in their representative model of macro behaviour.

More surprisingly, the order of market variability in the oil and currency markets is much higher than real investment and the stock market, which indicates the ugly fact of financial concentration generated by giant financial corporations. This is the real root of this grand crisis!

Dan Gilligan, President of the Petroleum Marketers Association (PMA), has revealed that financial giants such as Morgan Stanley, Goldman Sachs, Barclays and JP Morgan were manipulating the oil price (Gilligan 2009). They put hundreds of billions of dollars in the oil futures market, in addition to money invested by large institutional fund managers such as the California Pension Fund, the Harvard University Endowment, and other institutional investors. They started their speculation in 2000, when the US Congress deregulated the futures market, granting exemptions for complicated derivative investments called oil swaps, as well as electronic trading on private exchanges. Volatility in the price of oil increased dramatically. Later in the decade, within one year, the oil price rose from $67 a barrel to $147 a barrel, then collapsed back down to $45. On one occasion, the oil price jumped $25 in one day! Surprisingly, changes in oil demand and supply in this period were less than 5 per cent, while changes in the price of oil were larger than 100 per cent! From the middle of June to the end of November 2008, when a US congressional investigation started, about $70 billion of speculative capital left the futures market. At that time, demand for oil dropped 5 per cent, but the price of oil dropped more than 75 per cent to $100 a barrel. Gilligan estimated that about 60–70 per cent of oil contracts in the futures market were controlled by speculative capital at the peak. In the past five years, hedge funds and global banks have poured capital into the oil market. Their 'investment' rose from $13 billion to $300 billion. Something must be done to stabilise commodity futures markets.

Rethinking the theoretical foundation of trend collapse, higher moment risk and the financial crisis in the derivatives market

In the 2008 financial crisis, credit default swaps (CDS) played an important role when the fall of Lehman Brothers generated a tremendous loss for AIG. We suspect that the oversimplified model of CDS options based on orthodox pricing theory played a significant role in ignoring underlying market instability.

An important discovery related to the principle of large numbers is the viable dynamics for sustainable markets. For stochastic dynamics with a growth trend, there exist stochastic models with the distinct feature of market variability (Chen 2002, 2005; Li 2002). Their results are quite enlightening. Random walks are damping, Brownian motion is explosive, but the birth–death process tends to a constant in the form of the principle of large numbers. The random walk and Brownian motion are representative agent models by nature. Only the birth–death process is a population model, which is capable of describing social interaction and collective action in behavioural finance.

It is possible to modify the option-pricing model based on the population model of the birth–death process in stock-price movements (Zeng and Chen 2008). For the representative agent model of geometric Brownian motion, the probability of stock-price movement can be described by a binomial tree (Cox et al. 1979). Credit default swap valuation is also based on a similar model (Duffie 1999). For our model in the birth–death process, stock-price changes can be understood by a trinomial tree: in addition to the probability of prices moving up and down, there is a chance of a stable price. This complexity might exhibit the so-called volatility smile (changing market volatility driven by irrational herd behaviour in the financial market) observed in option prices. A more general model of evolution in probability distribution can be derived in terms of a master equation (Tang and Chen 2009). Based on empirical observation, transition probability can be described by a non-linear function; its solution can be approximated by expansion in terms of higher moments. If we consider only the first and second moment (that is, mean and variance in portfolio theory), the solution will converge to that of the Black–Scholes model, in which an arbitrage-free portfolio can be constructed. If, however, we add the third and fourth moments, the model solution might produce complex patterns, such as a trend collapse and market crisis (Figures 3.5a and 3.5b). In other words, *financial crisis can be understood as higher moment risk.*

Figure 3.5a Observed market crisis*

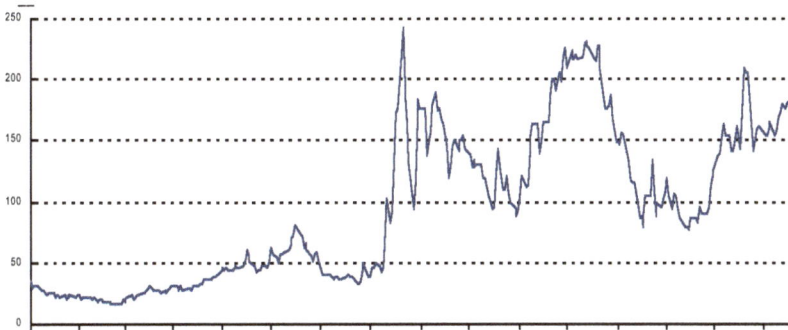

* The observed TED (three-month interest rate spread between euro dollar LIBOR rate and US Treasury bill rate) series (January 2007 – April 2008).

Source: <http://www.tedspread.com>

Figure 3.5b Model simulation*

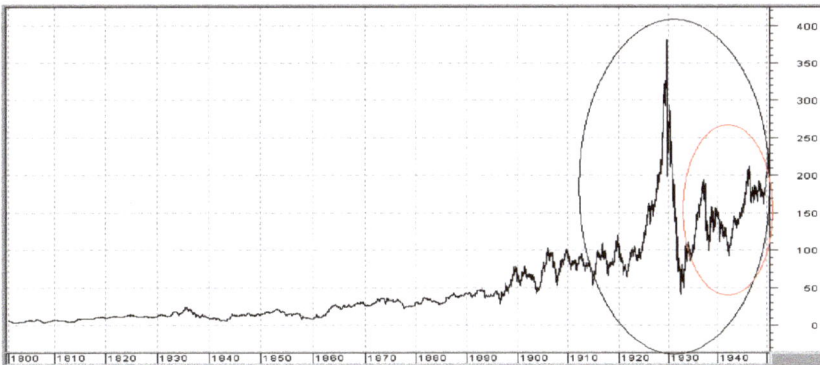

* The Dow-Jones Industrial Average Index (DJIA) during the Great Depression.

Source: Metastock.

Now, we have a better understanding of why the derivative market might collapse on a large scale. When the option-trading mechanism is simple enough, Black could adjust the model parameters such as market volatility so that the theoretical solution could close on the empirical price. In a complicated over-the-counter derivative market without regulation, however, such as the credit default swap market, trading based on an oversimplified binomial-tree model would mislead the market without empirical calibration. This grand crisis has provided a striking example of how a linear model for a complex market can create such tremendous turmoil. Only new thinking in asset-pricing theory can prevent a similar crisis in the future.

Economic complexity of transaction costs and the selective mechanism of industrial organisation

The US Administration has long realised the critical role of prudent financial regulation. Mainstream economists, however, still argue that the market can be self-regulating, following the Coase theory of transaction costs. Coase (1937) claimed that the foundation of the firm was the incentive to reduce transaction costs. Coase (1960) believed that social conflicts could be solved via bilateral exchange without interference from a third intermediary such as government or legal action. Coase (1988) assumed that the US financial market was an ideal model of the Coasian world of zero transaction costs. He seemingly ignored the fact that regulating the financial market greatly increased transaction costs. Coase (1979) raised the issue when he openly placed doubts on anti-bribery legislation for the media industry. He simply ignored the social costs that emerged when bribery and market manipulation generated system instability, which could potentially cost much more than regulation. The real aim of the Coase theory was to reject antitrust policy when he met the Chicago School (Kitch 1983). This study revives the old debate about antitrust policy from the new perspective of market instability and economic complexity. Coase is wrong simply because he ignored the issue of economic complexity (Chen 2007). Firm's driving force is value creation, not transaction costs reduction. Innovation creates both instability and complexity that are sources of increasing transaction costs in division of labour. Bilateral exchange cannot solve conflicting interests in pollution and market manipulation. Government regulation and people's participation are essential in maintaining an orderly market and resolving social conflicts. Whether regulation is proper or not, it cannot be judged by transaction costs in the short term, but by social effects in the long term. Coase theory is another type of perpetual motion machine without heat (that is, transaction costs) dissipation, which is against the second law of thermodynamics. The simple fact of global warming is clear evidence of increasing energy consumption. China could avoid a financial crisis mainly because its policy is selectively open to constructive FDI, not speculative hot money.

The danger of the Friedman theory of exogenous money and the tripolar world of the Great Depression

So far, the weak effect of expansionary monetary policy reminds us of the danger of the exogenous theory of business cycles, discussed previously. The current monetary policy adopted by mainstream economists is strongly influenced by Friedman's theory of exogenous money and his misleading explanation of the Great Depression (Friedman and Schwartz 1963). Friedman assumed monetary movement was exogenous, so central bankers' monetary policy had no historical and structural constraints. The discovery of monetary chaos challenged the monetarist theory of exogenous money but supported the Austrian theory of endogenous money (Chen 1988, 2005). Few economists, however, realised the danger of monetarist policy in dealing with an economic crisis such as the failure of the Washington Consensus, with crises in Latin America and East Asia and the transitional crisis in Eastern Europe and the former Soviet Union (Chen 2006, 2008).

Friedman claimed that expansionary monetary policy alone could have prevented the Great Depression, though there is no solid empirical evidence to support his theory. It would be very dangerous for Bernanke and other central bankers around the world to follow Friedman's theory in dealing with the current crisis.

On the contrary, we have solid evidence supporting the Austrian theory of endogenous money. In 1998, China had to confront severe deflation in the aftermath of the East Asian financial crisis. China managed to maintain sustained growth mainly through fiscal policy—manifest in large investments in infrastructure. So far, we already see that the effectiveness of monetary policy is highly constrained by historical policy and economic structure. When the business sector is heavily in debt, expansionary monetary policy can move only short-term interest rates and might be powerless to determine medium and long-term interest rates when investors feel uncertain about the economic outlook due to the danger of deep recession, possible inflation and currency depreciation. Since late 2008, major countries have rapidly adopted crisis policies such as monetary expansion, fiscal stimulus and enhancing regulation in the financial market, such as over executive pay and leverage restriction. From our observation, the US Administration has tried only to treat the symptoms rather than to cure the American disease, which is the huge power of the financial sector to crowd out the industrial sector. So far, we see no attempt by policymakers to break up monopolistic financial firms such as AIG and Citibank. Thinking strategically, we should prepare for the worst scenario and then work out the best solution.

Kindleberger (1986) has produced a highly relevant analysis that is helpful in understanding the current crisis. Friedman believed that the Great Depression was triggered by one simple event: the death of New York Federal Reserve Governor, Mr Strong, which left a vacuum in the Fed's monetary policy. Kindelberger pointed out that the global depression was caused by the collapse of globalisation based on British leadership. The three world powers after World War I—the United Kingdom, the United States and France—were kicking the ball among themselves and eventually provoked a collapse in the whole global system. We have a similar situation today, since the United States has lost its automatic world leadership via excessive military expansion and excessive consumption. The world order has changed since the 1980s; unless the United States, Europe and China coordinate their efforts, we could face a situation worse than the Great Depression in the 1930s.

What is the worst situation that might result from this grand crisis? Japan's stock market and real estate crisis of the 1990s lasted more than a decade. US President Roosevelt's 'New Deal', including Keynesian policy in fiscal stimulus and welfare policy, did not end the Great Depression, which lasted 11 years until it ended with World War II. There may be little chance of World War III among the major nuclear powers; however, the next wave of government default could destabilise small countries (such as happened in the recent Baltic crises), worsen existing wars in the Middle East and intensify regional and ethnic conflicts in South Asia and Africa. The possibility of a regional nuclear war in the Middle East and South or North-East Asia should not be fully discounted.

The best-case scenario is that current globalisation can be stabilised. This is possible only if trust in security matters and financial coordination can be consolidated among the major military and economic powers, including the United States, the European Union, China, Russia and Japan. The Cold War did not turn into a 'hot war' since the Yalta bipolar structure was stable during the Cold War era. Since the Soviet Union dissolved, the unipolar structure based on US dominance is significantly unstable in a world of disequilibrium with increasing disparity between rich and poor countries.

The American disease and the China puzzle

Before discussing China's role, we need to understand the world today from an evolutionary perspective. Bernanke once suggested that the US imbalance was rooted not in excessive consumption but in China's excess saving. I have a different view on this. The United States is much more powerful than China and the other Asian economies combined. Its financial power still dominates the international financial order—as we already know from the foregoing discussion.

The United States' trouble in the financial markets began with former President Ronald Reagan's contradictory economic policies in the 1980s. On the one hand, Reagan launched a tremendous military expansion; on the other hand, he provided substantial tax cuts and deregulated the financial sector. Growing public debt financed the budget deficit that resulted, which drove up interest rates and the dollar and ruined the competitiveness of the US manufacturing industry. As we know, the response to this was outsourcing—first to Japan and then to East Asia. The United States pushed Japan to appreciate the yen, but that did not solve its trade deficit. Instead, it threw the manufacturing industry out of Japan and to the 'Asian tigers' and mainland China. Ever since, the United States has been putting pressure on the Chinese Government to appreciate its currency, but without success.

The United States' fundamental problem is that the financial sector has replaced the industrial sector as the driver of its economy. You cannot cure that disease by playing currency or monetary games. Since the 1970s, no matter how the exchange rate has fluctuated, the United States has had a persistent trade deficit, while Germany and Japan have had a persistent trade surplus. This has nothing to do with exchange rates, but with US policy. The United States has advanced technology and abundant resources, but continues to waste immense resources on military spending and financial speculation. What is needed is a fundamental change in its policy framework.

As for China, of course it has suffered from US foreign policy, but it has also benefited. During the East Asian financial crisis, China followed the United States' recommendation that it should not devalue its currency. Before and during that crisis, mainstream American economists had one single policy recommendation for Latin America, Hong Kong and China: dollarisation, dollarisation and dollarisation! Remember that most Chinese reformers tried very hard to learn about the market economy from the US textbook. They all considered US Treasury Bonds a risk-free investment compared with risky stocks and corporate bonds. The Chinese Government therefore decided to target China's exchange rate with the dollar and buy US Treasury securities. This was thought to be the best way to preserve the value of Chinese savings—or at least a much better way than to invest them in China's own enterprises. Once China chose that road, however, US Treasuries turned out to be a trap. In such a situation, China had fewer options than Japan and European countries in the currency game, because of the asymmetrical policy adopted by the United States. When the dollar goes down, Japanese or Europeans can buy US assets, but Chinese cannot— blocked as they are by the United States' national security policy. At the same time, American and other foreign banks and firms are invited to be strategic partners with China's state-owned firms for improving China's competitiveness. Does the United States think that China is blind and will sell her security interests to US firms?

I would still claim that this asymmetrical trade policy has in fact done more good for China than for the United States in the changing world balance. US administrations have repeatedly used political pressure in exchange rate policy. It did not resolve the US deficit problem, but it did accelerate the economic integration of East Asia. How did that happen? If world trade were free and based on rules of symmetry, China would be buying much more US technology than it really does. Since the United States does not allow exports of high-tech products to China, China can import only second-hand technology. The United States does, however, export high technology to Japan and other East Asian countries, and this preferential trade policy has created an arbitrage opportunity for these countries. It is not by accident that, since the 1980s, China has had a persistent trade deficit with Japan, then with South Korea and with South-East Asian countries. In fact, these deficits are quite comparable with China's trade surplus with the United States. What does this mean? It means that the United States has given away a huge trade opportunity to China's neighbours.

What, however, are the real results of this policy? After the East Asian financial crisis, all these countries realised that China was a more reliable partner in international trade than previously thought, since China did not devalue its currency despite the crisis. They also realised that their economies benefited greatly from China's rapid growth. So, geopolitically speaking, these countries went from being insecure neighbours to Chinese partners. South Korea, the larger of the Association of South-East Asian

Nations (ASEAN) countries and Vietnam, in addition to Hong Kong and Taiwan, became increasingly integrated in the rapidly growing Chinese economy.

Today, East Asia is the third-largest economic zone in the world, with relatively stable exchange rates to the dollar, which also help to stabilise the US currency. If US policymakers realise that this can be the basis for closer economic cooperation, I would say that our future is bright. If, however, the United States considers this a challenge rather than an opportunity, it signals a troubling future.

This is the geopolitical heritage of the Reagan regime and the US imbalance. So far, the United States is still able to maintain its financial power in spite of increasing deficits. One critical factor in this is China's exchange rate policy. So far, both Chinese and Americans are happy about the past but worry about the future. Unlike her Asian partners, China does not get any credit from US policymakers. Perhaps the United States should think about how to win other people's trust rather than just other people's money.

We need to explain one of the 'China puzzles': why China has a much higher saving rate than industrialised countries—or why do poor countries end up subsidising the rich ones such as the United States? Some Western observers speculated that China's rapid growth was not based on technological progress and organisational innovation but on suppressing workers' wages and thus household consumption. They claim, therefore, that appreciation of the Chinese currency will not only solve the United States' problem of a persistent trade deficit, it will stimulate the consumption and welfare of the Chinese people. Is it that simple?

My observation is that China's high savings are the result of asymmetrical power in the credit market and marketing networks, since non-linear pricing is the main tool used by the multinational companies that dominate China's export market. More than half of China's exports are by foreign firms—and most export channels are controlled by multinational firms such as Wal-Mart. Chinese companies and the Chinese Government have no pricing power in the international market. For any Chinese product sold in the United States, Chinese companies receive 2–5 per cent of the sale value. As a result, China's domestic market is more open and more competitive than those of the United States, Japan or any other country in Asia and Europe. If we look, for instance, at China's car industry, we see that the market, unlike in the United States, is not dominated by the 'big three'; there are more than 100 companies competing with each other. Their profit margins are very thin compared with their giant foreign competitors. In order to survive, they have to upgrade their technology through self-financed investment. Small and medium firms have little access to the stock or bond markets. The distorted financial market leads to a very high saving rate in Chinese firms.

Since China launched its reforms some 30 years ago, its annual growth rate in residential income and consumption has been about 7 and 6 per cent, respectively. China's high-saving puzzle cannot be explained by households; it is has to do with the behaviour of firms. If we look at the composition of China's immense bank deposits, the deposits of individuals represent some 50 per cent, with more than 30 per cent coming from firms. If there is so-called excess saving, China's domestic interest rate should be even lower than those in the United States. In fact, China's interest rate in the domestic market is much higher than that paid on US Treasuries. In rural industries, the grey-market interest rate is more than 20 per cent. Clearly, strong market competition leads to strong competition in investment in technological upgrading among all industries and firms. The Chinese Government has very limited means to cool investment since public investment is much smaller than private investment; in addition, regional governments have strong incentives to promote manufacturing industries.

I would guess that if the US Government adopts new antitrust laws and breaks up monopolistic firms, as it did with AT&T, US industries will become more competitive and US households will behave more like Chinese households—investing in education and technology rather than in big houses and cars. In the end, you would see more balanced trade in the world market.

Bernanke points out China's high saving rate, rather than the low saving rate in the United States, as a possible source of financial instability. We might ask a more fundamental question about the driving force of growth: should it be consumption, investment, new technology or new industry?

US policymakers are talking loudly about economic stimulation to stimulate consumption. Economic indicators are often focused on the building of new houses and the sale of new cars, while there is soft talk about expanding the military industry. Can the United States recommend the same policy to developing countries without creating unequal competition in the global market?

Let's assume that one country spends most of its income on consumption, while another country spends more on innovation. Which country do you think will win the international competition? That's a very simple question—no matter what natural resources and property rights we take into account. You don't need a grand theory; commonsense will do to answer this simple question.

China's realistic role in a changing world order

There is much debate about China's role in a changing world order—from the 'China threat' to 'G2' status. As a personal observation, China's success is based on a decentralised experiment in searching for a Chinese model of global competition. There are several features of the Chinese system that are different from mainstream economics based on the Anglo-Saxon model—so-called laissez-faire economics.

First, China has been a unified country since 200 BC—formed not by market forces but by political organisation based on a small-scale, self-sufficient economy. China has only 10 per cent arable land and has experienced frequent wars and natural disasters. Historically, there has been persistent demand for effective governments rather than small governments. China developed resource-saving but labour-consuming technology while the West developed labour-saving but resource-consuming technology under different ecological conditions (Chen 1990, 1993). The Chinese model is therefore different from the Western model because there is a trade-off between stability and complexity (Chen 2005). This implies that developing countries should explore technologies appropriate to them and develop effective government to meet historical challenges. There is no universal recipe to fit a diversity of situations.

Second, China's shift of its development basis from inland to coastal areas was based on a strategic evaluation of the changing world order. The Korean War, the Vietnam War and the United States' policy of containment forced China to channel domestic savings into building up its defence industry and technological foundation. When US interest shifted to the Middle East, Deng Xiaoping's open-door policy seized the opportunity and developed the coastal economy, which became the engine of China's technological progress and export-led growth. China's competitiveness is not based on cheap labour, but on a cheap welfare system. Four-fifths of the population live on collectively owned land without paying expensive social security taxes. China's main strength lies in its human capital.

A large number of engineers and scientists were trained in Mao's era. China's effort in transforming defence industry into civilian industry has been more successful than the United States, East Europe and the former Soviet Union. That is why China's open-door policy did not create a dependent economy; simply because China's domestic industry could rapidly learn and compete with multinational companies. Cheap labour alone never leads to take-off in developing countries. In contrast, land and asset privatisation in Eastern Europe and the former Soviet Union led to a significant decline in agricultural and industrial output, a rapid increase in income inequality and a breakdown of the social welfare system. This process is visible again in the recent crisis in Baltic countries (Chen 2006).

Third, China is still a developing country with large regional disparities and tremendous population pressures under limited resources. Small and medium firms engage in the export market, mainly because market channels in the domestic market are far behind those in industrialised countries. It would be naive to demand that the Chinese currency ascend to reserve currency status, which could lead to premature liberalisation of the capital account. From international experience, Germany has more rigorous regulation of its financial market, so that German industry has firm support from the financial sector, while Japan wrongly accepted US advice in liberalising its financial market and lost a decade. China's policymakers should be careful in learning and experimenting in the international financial market.

We suggest that China could learn from other countries and play a constructive role in the global arena.

First, the European Union grew out of the European Coal and Steel Community in 1951, when France and Germany became partners instead of rivals. If China, Japan, South Korea and the ASEAN countries could build up a similar economic program—such as the joint development of offshore oil reserves—East Asia could integrate into an Asian union. Political wisdom with long-term vision is needed for Asian leaders in facing the current crisis. In Chinese, 'crisis' implies both danger and opportunity. The Japanese, South Korean and Chinese populations are ageing; therefore, there is diminishing chance of military conflict but increasing desire for economic cooperation. Even if US-led globalisation falls apart, East Asia could still maintain a stable and healthy economy. In doing so, other countries might join the East Asian community, including Australia, New Zealand, Russia, India and the Pacific United States, so that a better name in the future might be the 'Pacific Union', in parallel with the European Union and North America. The next phase of globalisation would then have a tripartite regional foundation that would be more promising than the existing US-led globalisation.

Second, the euro, yen and renminbi cannot yet displace the US dollar. The financial innovation of the 'euro dollar' market was created in 1957 by the Soviet Union and British banks in order to get around the controls of US financial power. Growing US deficits led to rapid expansion of the euro dollar market. In the current grand crisis, European banks have experienced heavy losses, caused by the US sub-prime crisis. This in turn has hurt South Korea, Brazil, Russia and other developing countries, as they have lost money on deposits in the euro dollar market. Chinese financial managers realised too late that the so-called 'risk-free' Treasury bonds were in fact risky assets, and they bought too many US Treasury bonds to 'preserve asset value'. China should cooperate with other Asian countries to develop an 'Asian dollar' market centred in Shanghai, since China could constructively utilise its excess foreign reserves. Currency and sovereign bond swaps can be integrated into the Asian dollar market, increasing its depth and sophistication over time. If the US Federal Reserve printed too much money, thereby destabilising the global economy, higher uncertainty would raise interest rates in both the euro and Asian dollar markets. Market forces would effectively discipline central bankers if their monetary policy was irresponsible or near-sighted. Goodwill alone is not a sufficient condition for a sound international order. International competition is a necessary condition for international stability.

Third, China's recent investment in foreign natural resources has caused a series of public relations problems since China's operation of state-owned enterprises (SOEs) is not compatible with Western laws. China should learn from the US model of land-grant universities and non-profit university endowment funds, rather than the Singaporean model of sovereign wealth funds. SOEs transformed into publicly listed, shareholder companies owned by university funds, pension funds, and so on, would greatly improve China's image abroad and its educational foundation at home. Currently, China's technological attainment depends heavily on foreign technology. China's higher education system is essentially a teaching rather than a research system. By dividing state assets among a dozen or so competitive 'land-grant' university endowment funds, China could build up a strong system of innovation by integrating research, education and production. Western media could easily understand the nature and objective of a Peking University Fund or Fudan University Fund along the lines, for example, of the Texas University Fund and Columbia University Fund as qualified investment institutions.

Basic considerations in reforming the international financial market

Based on the above discussion, there are some basic considerations for reforming the international financial market.

First, current economic and financial bureaucracies are heavily influenced by equilibrium economists and financial interests. It would be helpful to establish a non-governmental expert forum under the United Nations; their policy recommendations could be more constructive for discussions among world leaders.

Second, regulation and supervision should centre on an international competition or antitrust policy. The market shares of giant financial companies in the commodity market, currency market and some key financial sectors should be subject to an upper limit, such as 5 per cent. Trading volume should be monitored frequently and transactions above a certain threshold should be reported and regulated.

Third, a Tobin tax on currency exchanges is essential to protect small countries without large foreign reserves. Tobin tax receipts should be housed in a specific development fund for helping developing countries.

Fourth, each country has the sovereign right to match its exchange rate regime to its development stratagem. Its exchange rate can be used in special drawing rights (SDR, a reserve assets created by IMF) calculations with gradual adjustment every five years or so. An economic council under the United Nations, which is responsible for coordinating major countries in stabilising their exchange rates, could regulate the IMF. An orderly adjustment of exchange rates could be conducted every five years or so except in emergency situations.

Fifth, an overhaul of financial theory and financial regulation would speed up the academic debate about rethinking economic history and economic theory (Chen 2008). This conference on China's new place in a world in crisis is a small step in this direction.

References

Black, F. and Scholes, M. 1973, 'The pricing of options and corporate liabilities', *Journal of Political Economy*, vol. 81, pp. 637–54.

Bloomberg.com, data source for exchange rate and interest rate.

Chen, P. 1988, 'Empirical and theoretical evidence of monetary chaos', *System Dynamics Review*, vol. 4, pp. 81–108.

—— 1990, 'Needham's question and China's evolution—cases of non-equilibrium social transition', in G. Scott (ed.), *Time Rhythms and Chaos in the New Dialogue with Nature*, Iowa State University Press, University of South Dakota, Vermillion.

—— 1993, 'China's challenge to economic orthodoxy: Asian reform as an evolutionary, self-organizing process', *China Economic Review*, vol. 4, pp. 137–42.

—— 1996a, 'Trends, shocks, persistent cycles in evolving economy: business cycle measurement in time-frequency representation', in W. A. Barnett, A. P. Kirman and M. Salmon (eds), *Non-linear Dynamics and Economics*, Cambridge University Press, Cambridge, pp. 307–31.

—— 1996b, 'A random walk or color chaos on the stock market? Time-frequency analysis of S&P indexes', *Studies in Non-linear Dynamics & Econometrics*, vol. 1, no. 2, pp. 87–103.

—— 2002, 'Microfoundations of macroeconomic fluctuations and the laws of probability theory: the principle of large numbers vs. rational expectations arbitrage', *Journal of Economic Behavior & Organization*, vol. 49, pp. 327–44.

—— 2005, 'Evolutionary economic dynamics: persistent business cycles, disruptive technology, and the trade-off between stability and complexity', in K. Dopfer (ed.), *The Evolutionary Foundations of Economics*, Cambridge University Press, Cambridge, pp. 472–505.

—— 2006, 'Market instability and economic complexity: theoretical lessons from transition experiments', in Y. Yao and L. Yueh (eds), *Globalisation and Economic Growth in China*, World Scientific, Singapore, pp. 35–58.

—— 2007, 'Complexity of transaction costs and evolution of corporate governance', *Kyoto Economic Review*, vol. 76, no. 2, pp. 139–53.

—— 2008, 'Equilibrium illusion, economic complexity, and evolutionary foundation of economic analysis,' *Evolutionary and Institutional Economics Review*, vol. 5, no. 1, pp. 81–127.

Coase, R. H. 1937, 'The nature of the firm,' *Economica,* vol. 4 no. 16, pp. 386–405.

—— 1960, 'The problem of social cost', *Journal of Law and Economics,* vol. 3 no. 1, pp. 1–44.

—— 1979, 'Payola in radio and television broadcasting', *Journal of Law and Economics*, vol. 22, no. 2, pp. 269–328.

—— 1988, *The Firm, the Market, and the Law*, University of Chicago Press, Chicago.

Cox, J., Rubinstein, M. and Ross, S. 1979, 'Option pricing: a simplified approach', *Journal of Financial Economics*, vol. 7, no. 3, pp. 229–63.

Duffie, D. 1999, 'Credit swap valuation', *Financial Analysis Journal*, vol. 55, no. 1, pp. 73–87.

Energy Information Administration, Data source of oil prices, <http://www.eia.doe.gov>

Fama, E. F. 1970, 'Efficient capital markets: a review of theory and empirical work', *Journal of Finance*, vol. 25, pp. 384–433.

—— 1991, 'Efficient capital market II', *Journal of Finance*, vol. 46, no. 5, pp. 1575–617.

Friedman, M. 1953, 'The case for flexible exchange rates', in M. Friedman, *Essays in Positive Economics*, University of Chicago Press, Chicago.

Friedman, M. and Schwartz, A. J. 1963, *Monetary History of United States, 1867–1960*, Princeton University Press, Princeton, NJ.

Frisch, R. 1933, 'Propagation problems and impulse problems in dynamic economics', *Economic Essays in Honour of Gustav Cassel*, George Allen & Unwin, London.

Gilligan, D. 2009, 'Did speculation fuel oil price swings', 1 December, *60 Minutes*, 2009, CBS Television, <http://www.cwpma.org/Template. php?-p=HomeNewsPopup&-d=News&-r=52.0>

Jia, J. C. and Chen, P. 2009, *Exchange rate resonance—observations based on deviations from interest rate parity*, CCER Working Paper, June, Peking University, Beijing.

Kindleberger, C. P. 1986, *The World in Depression, 1929–1939*, Revised and enlarged edition, University of California Press, Berkeley.

Kitch, E. W. (ed.) 1983, 'The fire of truth: a remembrance of law and economics at Chicago, 1932–1970', *Journal of Law & Economics*, vol. 26, no. 1, pp. 163–234.

Li, H. J. 2002, Which type of stochastic processes could better address the issue of microfoundations of macro fluctuations? Thesis, Mathematics School, Peking University, Beijing.

Lucas, R. E., jr, 1972, 'Expectations and the neutrality of money', *Journal of Economic Theory*, vol. 4, pp. 103–24.

Schrödinger, E. 1948, *What is Life?* Cambridge University Press, Cambridge.

Schumpeter, J. A. 1939, *Business Cycles: A theoretical, historical, and statistical analysis of the capitalist process*, McGraw-Hill, New York.

Tang, Y. N. and Chen, P. 2009, *The trend collapses and the premium of turbulence: the premium of collective behavior and the dynamics of financial crisis*, CNPE Working Paper, March, Fudan University, Shanghai.

US Bureau of Census, Data source of household numbers and firm numbers.

Zeng, W. and Chen, P. 2008, 'Volatility smile, relative deviation, and trading strategy—a general diffusion model for stock price movements based on non-linear birth–death process', [in Chinese], *Economic Journal Quarterly*, vol. 7, no. 4, Peking University, Beijing, pp. 1415–36.

Acknowledgments

This chapter was presented in various forms at several international meetings on the current economic crisis. The author thanks participants for stimulating discussions at the IRE & EPS Conference on 'Looking for Solutions to the Crisis: The United States and the new international financial system', New School University, New York, 14 November 2008; the IDEAs Conference on 'Re-Regulating Global Finance in the Light of the Global Crisis', Tsinghua University, Beijing, 9–12 April 2009; the Shadow Gn Meeting, Luiss University, Rome, 14 May 2009; the IRE & EPS meeting on 'Financial and Banking Crisis: Looking for solutions', Paris, 15–16 June 2009.

China's increasing external wealth 4

Guonan Ma and Haiwen Zhou[1]

Introduction

While balance of payments (BoP) statistics reflect cross-border flows over time, the international investment position (IIP) data record an economy's international financial assets and liabilities or its international balance sheet at a given point in time. Similar to BoP statistics, external assets and liabilities are classified by instrument into positions of direct investment, portfolio investment and other investment. There is an additional category of foreign reserves on the asset side. In a matter of less than 10 years, China's net foreign asset (NFA) position—the difference between international assets and liabilities—has swung from being a net debtor of about 9 per cent of GDP in 1999 to a net creditor of more than 30 per cent of GDP in 2007.[2] China's NFA position in absolute terms now ranks as the second largest in the world, after Japan. Moreover, the sum of China's external assets and liabilities expanded by 90 times in the past two decades. Finally, while China has accumulated a huge stock of inward direct investment on the liability of its international balance sheet, it holds the world's largest official reserves on the asset side. As China's role in the global financial system grows, the stakes are high for China and the rest of the world.

This chapter examines the following questions related to China's international investment position: why has China become such a big creditor at an early stage of development? Will its NFA position be maintained during the next 20 years? Will China continue to integrate financially with the rest of the world, as gauged by the size of its external balance sheet? What are the main features of the composition of China's international assets and liabilities?

The chapter builds on numerous related research efforts. Lane and Milesi-Ferretti (1999, 2007, 2008) have covered much ground in the field of international investment positions. They developed an IIP data set for more than 100 countries, including China, when few people were officially compiling IIP data. Lane and Milesi-Ferretti have since explored many themes related to IIP. Nevertheless, systematic research on China's external balance sheets remains limited. Lane and Schmukler (2007) compare the net position, size and structure of the Chinese and Indian external balance sheets mostly on the basis of their data set constructed before the official publication of the Chinese IIP data. McCauley and Chan (2008) project China's external banking position in the coming years based on a cross-sectional study of the economies of the Organisation for Economic Cooperation and Development (OECD).

There have been very different perspectives on China's puzzlingly large NFA position when its capital–labour ratio is still quite low. According to the neoclassical growth model, higher returns to capital should attract capital inflows, so that a low-income, catch-up economy should be a net debtor borrowing foreign savings. Dollar and Kraay (2006) conjecture that domestic economic and financial distortions in China have led to a large current account surplus and net capital outflows. They calibrate a theoretical model to predict a net debtor position of 17 per cent of wealth for China in the mid-2000s and use non-structural regressions to predict China's NFA position to be negative 5–10 per cent of GDP in two decades. In contrast, McKibbin (2005) and Peng (2008) highlight the macroeconomic consequences of a demographic transition and project that in the coming decades, China will likely run a current account surplus and thus maintain a large positive NFA position.

The purpose of this chapter is to shed light on the empirical importance of some of these medium-term economic and demographic factors influencing China's net and gross external investment positions as well as their compositions. In particular, based on an analysis of the time-series data, we examine the roles of relative income growth, demographic shifts, government debt, domestic financial development and the real effective exchange rate in shaping China's NFA position. We also explore determinants of China's gross external investment position: the sum of foreign assets and liabilities in a cross-sectional regression. Finally, we offer an overview of the evolving structure of China's international balance sheet and explore its implications.

Three main findings are summarised. First, while a marked growth differential vis-a-vis the OECD attracts capital inflows, China's growing creditor position can be attributed largely to rapid demographic transition. If this result holds, China might not turn into a meaningful net debtor in the coming two decades. This conclusion stands in contrast with the predictions of Dollar and Kraay (2006) that suggest China should turn into a large debtor before long, but is broadly consistent with the predictions of McKibbin (2005) and Peng (2008). Second, the scale of China's international balance sheet has expanded substantially in the past two decades and will likely continue to do so in the coming decade, suggesting growing interactions between China and the global financial market. Third, China's external assets and liabilities have become more lop-sided over time, with assets mostly in fixed-income instruments and held by the official sector and liabilities mainly taking the form of inward private direct investment.

The chapter is organised as follows. The next section highlights the key trends in China's IIP. The third section explores the question of why China's positive NFA position is so large when its income level is still low, while section four presents empirical results regarding key determinants of China's growing NFA position. Section five examines the outlook for the gross size of China's international balance sheet, and section six discusses the key features of the composition of China's international assets and liabilities. The final section concludes.

China's international balance sheet: an overview

China started officially publishing its IIP data in 2004—too recently to provide figures for a meaningful analysis of the historical trends. We have adopted an approach similar to Lane and Milesi-Ferretti (1999) and construct a longer and more consistent IIP time series for 1985–2003 (Ma and Zhou forthcoming). Our approach differs from the previous methodology in at least two aspects. First, we take the first year of the official IIP data (2004) as the starting point to ensure that our estimated series can be integrated with the official statistics. Second, we estimate the breakdown of the inward direct investment position between equity and inter-company loans so that we can estimate the Chinese IIP on three alternative bases: historical cost, current cost and market value. Unless specified, this chapter uses the current-cost estimate.

Several features of China's external balance sheet can be identified from our new estimates (Table 4.1 and Figures 4.1–3). First, China's NFA position—the difference between external assets and liabilities—has surged since the mid-2000s (Table 4.1 and Figure 4.2). Before 2004, China was mostly a small debtor. In 1999, China's NFA position was in a trough of negative $100 billion, or about −9 per cent of GDP. The turning point was 2004, when China's creditor position started growing substantially. By 2007, China's NFA position in dollar terms was the second-largest globally, exceeding $1 trillion, or more than 30 per cent of GDP. In the next section, we will take a closer look at the puzzle of why China has become such a big lender when its income level is still less than one-tenth of the OECD average.

Figure 4.1   The size of China's gross foreign assets and liabilities (US$billion)

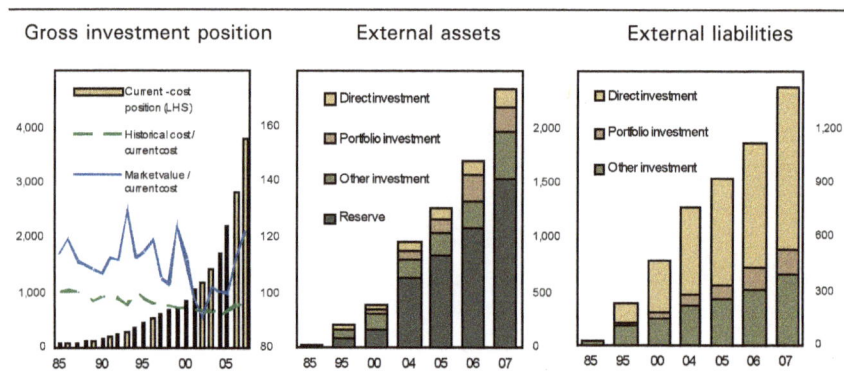

Gross investment position   External assets   External liabilities

Notes: Calculated at current costs. Gross investment position is the sum of foreign assets and liabilities.

Sources: State Administration of Foreign Exchange and authors' own estimates.

Figure 4.2   China's net foreign asset position and stock market index

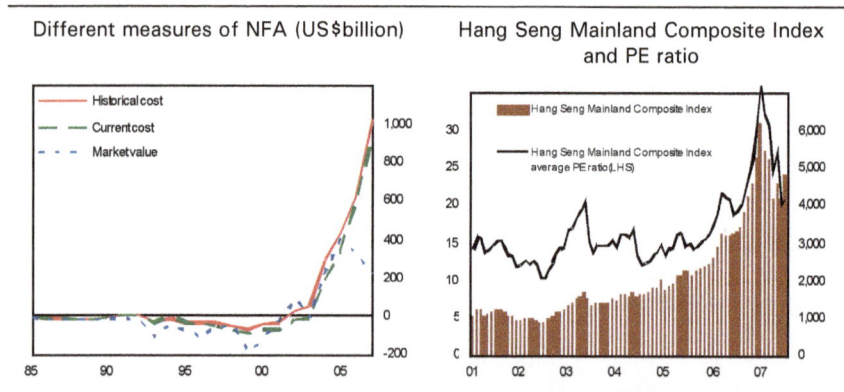

Different measures of NFA (US$billion)   Hang Seng Mainland Composite Index and PE ratio

Notes: NFA is the net foreign asset position, which equals foreign assets less foreign liabilities.

Sources: State Administration of Foreign Exchange and authors' own estimates.

Table 4.1 China's international investment position (US$billion)

	1985	1995	2000	2004	2005	2006	2007
Net foreign asset position	**-5.8**	**-38.5**	**-74.3**	**190.4**	**343.1**	**579.0**	**1027.4**
(Percentage of GDP)	*(1.9)*	*(5.3)*	*(6.2)*	*9.9*	*15.3*	*21.8*	*30.4*
Assets	**18.2**	**191.2**	**385.4**	**954.6**	**1260.0**	**1690.9**	**2428.0**
(Percentage of GDP)	*5.9*	*26.3*	*32.2*	*49.4*	*56.3*	*63.6*	*71.8*
Direct investment abroad	0.9	33.3	51.8	77.5	101.9	137.4	169.6
Portfolio investment	0.0	12.1	41.1	92.0	116.7	229.2	284.6
– Equity securities	0.0	0.0	0.0	0.0	0.0	1.5	19.6
– Debt securities	0.0	12.1	41.1	92.0	116.7	227.8	265.0
Other investment	14.7	72.3	126.9	166.6	215.7	251.5	426.5
Reserve assets	2.6	73.6	165.6	618.5	825.7	1072.8	1547.3
Liabilities	**24.0**	**229.8**	**459.7**	**764.2**	**916.9**	**1111.9**	**1400.6**
(Percentage of GDP)	*7.8*	*31.6*	*38.4*	*39.6*	*41.0*	*41.8*	*41.4*
Direct investment inward	3.2	109.2	289.6	496.1	588.4	691.6	891.8
Portfolio investment	1.0	14.6	30.1	56.6	76.6	120.7	146.6
– Equity securities	0.0	3.9	17.8	43.3	63.6	106.5	129.0
– Debt securities	1.0	10.7	12.3	13.3	13.0	14.2	17.6
Other investment	19.8	106.0	140.0	211.5	251.9	299.6	362.2
Memo: market value							
Direct investment abroad	*2.4*	*42.9*	*76.8*	*96.3*	*123.2*	*177.1*	*218.6*
Direct investment inward	*7.3*	*159.1*	*359.4*	*476.6*	*559.2*	*992.4*	*1659.5*

Notes: Calculated at current costs. The 2007 data on NIIP and GIIP have been updated but the updated detailed compositions were not available at the time of the publication. The net foreign asset position is foreign assets minus foreign liabilities.

Sources: State Administration of Foreign Exchange and authors' own estimates.

Figure 4.3 Composition of China's international investment position (US$billion and per cent)

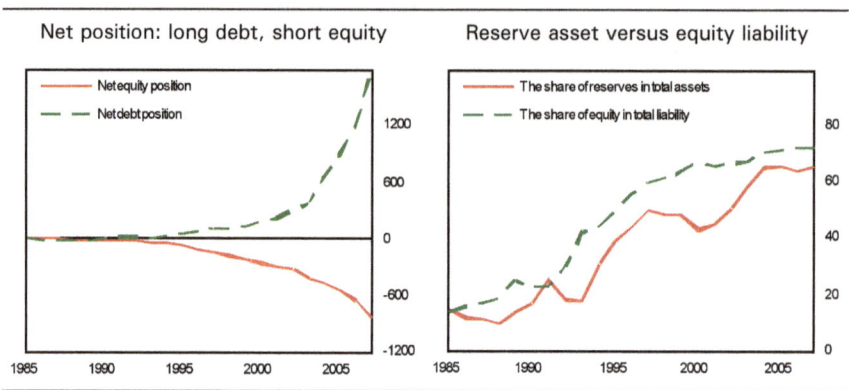

Net position: long debt, short equity   Reserve asset versus equity liability

Notes: Calculated at current costs; net equity position is asset minus liability of direct investment and equity portfolio investment; net debt position is asset minus liability of all the other categories.

Sources: State Administration of Foreign Exchange and authors' own estimates.

Second, the size of China's international balance sheet—the sum of foreign assets and liabilities—has expanded considerably in the past two decades. China's gross external investment position rose by more than 88 times during 1985–2007 (Figure 4.1) and exceeded $3.8 trillion by 2008, ranking third in Asia, after Japan and Hong Kong Semi-Autonomous Region (Table 4.2). Measured against GDP, however, China's gross position only slightly exceeds 110 per cent and remains well below the East Asian average of 250 per cent. Since the gross position of foreign assets and liabilities serves as an indicator of international financial integration, we will also examine whether China's financial integration and interactions with the rest of the world will continue expanding over time.

Finally, the structure of China's external balance sheet has become more asymmetric over time. China's 'long debt, short equity' asymmetry has become more pronounced, as the absolute sizes of its net negative equity position and positive net fixed-income instrument position have been growing (Figure 4.3). Moreover, 70 per cent of China's foreign liabilities today are concentrated in equity instruments (mostly direct investment), in contrast with the mid-1980s, when 80 per cent of its total foreign liabilities were owed by the public sector in the form of multilateral and bilateral borrowings. Finally, reserves increasingly dominate China's foreign assets, representing two-thirds of its total today, in comparison with 15 per cent 20 years ago. In other words, the monetary authority has become the largest holder of Chinese foreign assets (Figure 4.1).

Table 4.2   International investment positions: China and Asia, 2007
(US$billion and per cent)

	China	Hong Kong	Japan	Singapore	Korea
(1) Gross external assets	2,428.0	2,730.6	5,355.2	879.9	587.6
(2) Gross external liabilities	1,400.6	2,208.7	3,160.3	725.2	820.1
(3) Gross position = (1) + (2)	3,828.5	4,939.3	8,515.5	1,605.1	1,407.7
(4) Gross position as percentage of GDP	113.1	2,383.8	194.4	995.1	145.1
(5) NFA = (1) – (2)	1.027.4	521.9	2,194.9	154.7	–232.5
(6) NFA as percentage of GDP	30.4	251.9	50.1	95.9	–24.0

Notes: All are in 2007 data; China calculated at current costs; gross position is the sum of foreign assets and liabilities.

Sources: State Administration of Foreign Exchange; International Monetary Fund; various governments; authors' own estimates.

Why is China lending so early to the rest of the world?

China's net creditor position has been growing rapidly since 2004. Its NFA position exceeded $1 trillion or 30 per cent of GDP by 2007, when Chinese per capita GDP was only $2500—one-tenth of the OECD average. According to the neoclassical model, this is puzzling, given China's still low levels of income and capital–labour ratio as well as its exceptional growth momentum (Dollar and Kraay 2006). According to conventional wisdom, China should be importing large amounts of foreign savings rather than lending abroad. This seems to be a case of the 'Lucas paradox', 'allocation puzzle' or 'perverse capital flows'.[3]

China's growing NFA position in the latter half of the first decade of the 2000s appears to have been driven mostly by its concurrently surging current account surplus (Figure 4.4). The Chinese current account surplus rose from being essentially balanced in the early 2000s to some 10 per cent for 2007. Between 2004 and 2007, China's cumulative current account surplus reached $1.3 trillion—similar to the change in its NFA position during the same period. Underpinning such large rises in the current account surplus has been the high and rising domestic saving rate relative to its already high domestic investment rate. China's gross domestic saving rate rose from 38 per cent of GDP in 2000 to a record high of nearly

50 per cent in 2007, widening the saving–investment gap from 2 per cent of GDP to about 7 per cent. Factors shaping China's saving–investment gap and current account balance are therefore also likely to be a central part of the puzzle.

Figure 4.4   Current account balance, saving–investment gap and NFA position as a percentage of GDP

Gross domestic saving and investment rates

Current account balance and NFA position

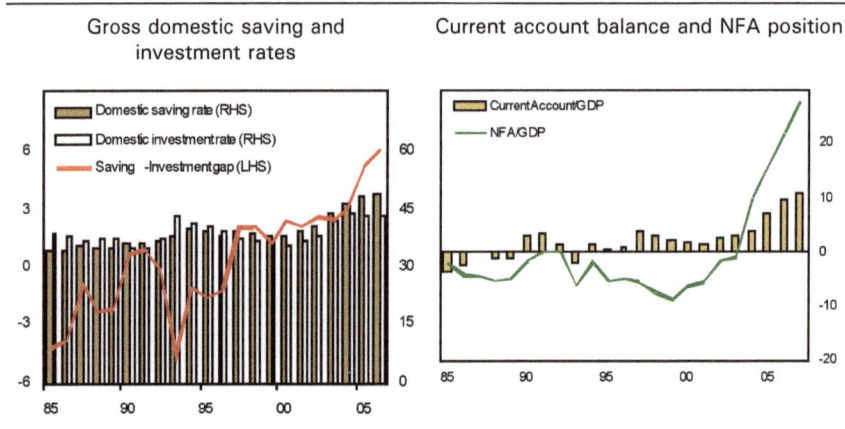

Note: NFA is net foreign asset, which equals foreign assets less foreign liabilities.

Sources: State Administration of Foreign Exchange; authors' own estimates; Ma, G. and Zhou, H. (forthcoming), *China's evolving external wealth and rising creditor position*, BIS Working Papers, Bank for International Settlements, Basel.

In the literature, three broad strands of explanation for China's unusually high gross domestic saving rate have been proposed.[4] The first strand interprets high household saving as being linked to precautionary motives and/or demographic trends. Diminished provision of social services, reduced job security and limited access to consumer credit during the economic transition of the 1990s are thought to be important reasons. Less attention has been given to the fact that the working-age population has risen relative to the total population. The second explanation is a high corporate saving rate, owing to strong corporate profits and a policy of no dividend payments. Finally, high government saving could in part help explain China's high saving rate because of buoyant revenues and low government consumption.

These explanations address their effects mostly on saving only and appear insufficient in explaining the large saving–investment surplus that has driven China's creditor position. To gauge the plausible empirical magnitudes of a range of the factors thought to directly shape China's

NFA position, this chapter follows Lane and Milesi-Ferretti (2001) and estimates a parsimonious reduced-form model. The five determinants of the NFA position considered in our analysis are relative income growth, demographics, government debt, domestic financial depth and the exchange rate. In particular, one main contribution of our chapter is to compare the roles of the demographic trends with relative growth in shaping China's NFA position.

The first factor is the growth differential. According to the standard neoclassical growth model, relatively high growth at home can be viewed as a low-income economy catching up and could indicate a higher marginal product of capital, which should attract foreign capital inflows and discourage overseas investment. In other words, higher returns on capital at home should facilitate foreign liability expansion and dampen acquisition of foreign assets. We therefore expect a negative relation between the growth differential and the NFA position. As China turned itself into a big net exporter of capital, it was among the fastest-growing economies in the world.

A second factor is demographic transition—a window whereby the labour force temporarily grows faster than the population dependent on it, resulting in a falling dependency rate. For many economies, this demographic window lasts for more than five decades (Lee and Mason 2006), but it has taken China only half that time to achieve; China's overall dependency ratio fell from 55 per cent in 1985 to 38 per cent in 2007 (Figure 4.5). According to the life-cycle hypothesis, a falling dependency burden helps lift the saving rate of households and thus funds additional investment, leading to higher per capita income growth (Williamson and Higgins 2001). A falling overall dependency rate also indicates additional labour supply, which, together with more liberalised rural–urban migration (Wang and Mason 2008), boosts firms' profits and corporate saving by restraining wage increases. Finally, a lower dependency ratio could also suggest less government consumption on health care and pensions and thus higher government saving.

Figure 4.5   China's demographic transition and NFA position (per cent)

Working-age share and overall
dependency rate

Young and elderly dependencies

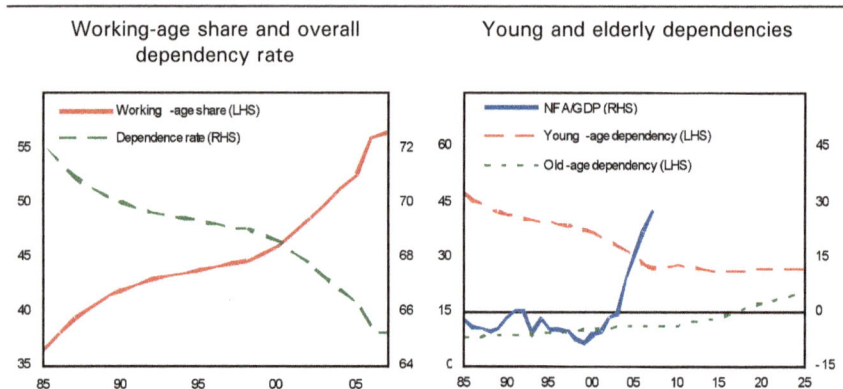

Notes: The working-age share is the ratio of the working-age population (aged between fifteen and sixty-five) to the total population. Young-age (old-age) dependency is the ratio of those aged below fifteen (above sixty-five) to the working-age population. The overall dependency rate is the sum of young and old-age dependencies.

Source: Ma, G. and Zhou, H. (forthcoming), *China's evolving external wealth and rising creditor position*, BIS Working Papers, Bank for International Settlements, Basel.

Although the saving story of lower dependency is well understood, the potential asymmetrical demographic effects of young and old-age dependencies on domestic investment and thus the domestic saving– investment gap are less well known. A lower youth dependency should boost savings but not necessarily investment, all else being equal (Higgins and Williamson 1997). This is because a lower youth dependency could reduce demand for investment in housing, schools and hospitals. Falling youth dependency therefore tends to boost the saving–investment surplus, thus impacting favourably on the current account balance.

In contrast, the effect of elderly dependency on the current account is ambiguous in theory, depending on the relative demographic effects on saving and investment. A rising elderly dependency rate can dampen investment more than saving, also leading to a current account surplus (Lueth 2008; Peng 2008), mainly because a diminishing labour supply and a rising capital–labour ratio tend to discourage domestic investment. Alternatively, it could worsen the current account balance if the saving effect outweighs the investment effect (Kim and Lee 2007; IMF 2008). One striking feature of China's demographic transition during 1985–2007 is that its youth dependency fell by half, while its elderly dependency edged up only slightly, resulting in a stable overall dependency ratio (Figure 4.5).[5] An interesting empirical question asks what is the possible net effect of this particular demographic transition on China's saving–investment gap and consequently its current account surpluses or increased net capital outflows.

The third factor considered in this chapter is the government debt stock. This factor is found to negatively affect an economy's NFA position, as a larger stock of government debt tends to reduce gross domestic saving and increase external borrowing (Lane and Milesi-Ferretti 2001). China's government debt level rose from 4 per cent of GDP in 1985 to a peak of 30 per cent in 2002, but has since trended lower (Figure 4.6). This appears to be consistent with the argument that high government saving could in part have supported China's high domestic saving rate in recent years (Li and Yin 2007), contributing to China's swing from being a debtor to a creditor during the early 2000s.

Figure 4.6   China's NFA position, government debt and real effective exchange rate (per cent and index)

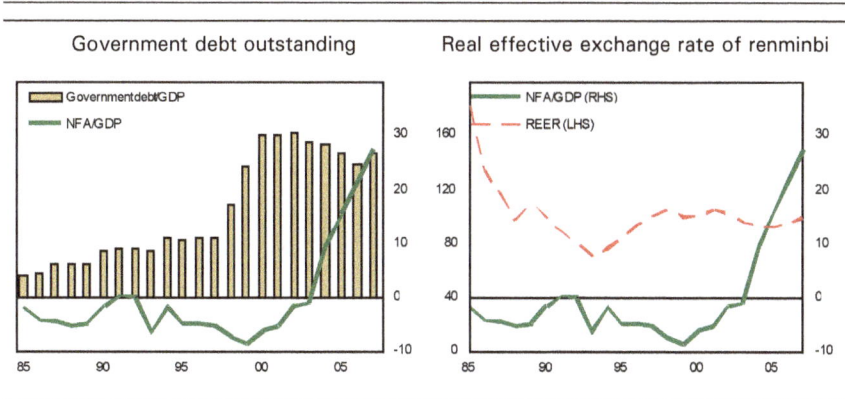

Government debt outstanding   Real effective exchange rate of renminbi

Note: REER is the real effective exchange rate (2000 = 100).

Source: Ma, G. and Zhou, H. (forthcoming), *China's evolving external wealth and rising creditor position*, BIS Working Papers, Bank for International Settlements, Basel.

The fourth variable is domestic financial development. Its effect on the saving–investment balance and thus the NFA position is generally ambiguous. One theory suggests that financial underdevelopment results in over-saving (failure of consumption smoothing) and excessive financing constraint on domestic investment spending, both of which contribute to a rise in the saving–investment gap (Mendoza et al. 2007; Chamon and Prasad 2008). This could spur overseas diversification (thus facilitating foreign asset accumulation) and discourage foreign investors (hence limiting foreign liability accumulation), boosting the NFA position of the home economy. Financial underdevelopment should therefore limit the ability of an economy to absorb foreign capital. Conversely, advances in the domestic financial sector in an economy should relate negatively to its net external position.

Finally, a more controversial determinant is the exchange rate, the effects of which on the NFA position could work through the trade and valuation channels. One theory is that an undervalued renminbi boosts corporate profits and savings on the one hand and depresses domestic investment by raising the prices of imported capital goods on the other (Eichengreen 2006; Goldstein and Lardy 2008). A stronger renminbi should therefore trim China's current account surplus and negatively affect its NFA position (Figure 4.6). This needs to be tested, however, as Chinn and Wei (2008) find limited empirical support for the role of the exchange rate in current account adjustment.

Specification and estimation

To test the empirical importance of these proposed determinants of the NFA position, we estimate the following regression equation on the 1985–2007 time-series data.

Equation 4.1

$$nfa_t = \alpha_0 + \beta_1 GROWTH_t + \beta_2 YOUNG_{t-1} + \beta_3 OLD_{t-1} + \beta_4 DEBT_t + \beta_5 FINANCE_t + \beta_6 REER_t + \varepsilon_t$$

in which nfa is the ratio of the NFA position over GDP; GROWTH is the log of the ratio of China's real GDP over that of the OECD; YOUNG (OLD) is the young (old) age dependency ratio; DEBT is the ratio of (domestic and external) government debts outstanding to GDP; FINANCE is an indicator of domestic financial development; REER is the real effective exchange rate of the renminbi; and ε is the error term. We construct two alternative measures of domestic financial depth (Ma and Zhou forthcoming). Finally, to address the concerns of non-stationarity in the time-series data, we also estimate the first-difference form of Equation 4.1.

Equation 4.2

$$\Delta nfa_t = \alpha_0 + \alpha_1 \Delta GROWTH_t + \alpha_2 \Delta YOUNG_{t-1} + \alpha_3 \Delta OLD_{t-1} + \alpha_4 \Delta DEBT_t + \alpha_5 \Delta FINANCE_t + \alpha_6 \Delta REER_t + \pi_t$$

Results for Equations 4.1 and 4.2 are presented in Tables 4.3 and 4.4. Most of the coefficients are consistent with our prior expectations. Our findings confirm both predictions that higher growth tends to attract more capital inflows into China, turning it into a net borrower. On the other hand, the falling young-age dependency tends to contribute to the current account surplus, turning China into a net lender. There is also some evidence suggesting that outstanding government debt negatively affects the NFA in China's case. Our findings, however, seem to suggest limited roles for financial depth and the real effective exchange rate. Since the first-difference equations appear to yield more stable coefficients and suggest a more plausible size of impact while avoiding the non-stationarity problem, our discussions of the medium-term outlook for the NFA position will be based on the estimates reported in Table 4.4.

Table 4.3 Determinants of China's net foreign asset position (in level)

	1	2	3	4	5	6
GROWTH	−0.73[c]	−0.79[c]	−0.67[c]	−0.64[c]	−0.72[c]	−0.68[c]
	(-4.38)	(−4.82)	(−5.69)	(−5.84)	(−4.47)	(−6.58)
YOUNG	−2.78[a]	−1.79	−3.43[c]	−3.28[c]	−3.17[c]	−3.50[c]
	(−1.98)	(−1.25)	(−4.67)	(−4.69)	(−2.90)	(−5.41)
OLD	36.67[b]	44.27[c]	30.09[c]	28.99[c]	35.25[b]	30.80[c]
	(2.55)	(3.01)	(4.02)	(4.15)	(2.57)	(4.64)
DEBT	−1.38[c]	−1.50[c]	−1.23[c]	−1.19[c]	−1.32	−1.23[c]
	(−3.66)	(−4.19)	(−4.95)	(−4.86)	(−3.82)	(−5.11)
FINANCE	0.02		0.01			
	(0.46)		(0.23)			
CAPITAL		0.06		0.03		
		(1.43)		(0.88)		
REER	−0.07	−0.16			−0.04	
	(−0.54)	(−1.18)			(−0.37)	
Constant	−139.72	−231.13	−67.65	−65.68	−112.97	−69.11
	(−0.92)	(−1.47)	(−0.94)	(−0.93)	(−0.82)	(−0.99)
Adjusted R^2	0.89	0.91	0.90	0.90	0.90	0.91
Durbin-Watson stat.	1.73	2.00	1.61	1.67	1.61	1.58

[a] denotes significance at the 10 per cent level

[b] denotes significance at the 5 per cent level

[c] denotes significance at the 1 per cent level

Notes: Equation 4.1; the sample period covers 1985–2007; t-statistics are in parentheses.

Source: Ma, G. and Zhou, H. (forthcoming), *China's evolving external wealth and rising creditor position*, BIS Working Papers, Bank for International Settlements, Basel.

Table 4.4   Determinants of China's net foreign asset position (in first difference)

	1	2	3	4	5	6
GROWTH	−0.20	−0.23	−0.26	−0.29	−0.29	−0.31
	(−0.57)	(−0.58)	(−0.88)	(−0.89)	(−0.82)	(−1.03)
YOUNG	−5.52[b]	−4.39[a]	−5.30[c]	−4.08[a]	−3.48[b]	−3.43[b]
	(−2.71)	(−1.75)	(−2.79)	(−1.85)	(−2.36)	(−2.47)
OLD	25.43	17.38	30.60	21.32	15.33	17.67
	(1.10)	(0.73)	(1.68)	(1.12)	(0.68)	(1.10)
DEBT	−0.24	−0.31	−0.33	−0.40	−0.40	−0.43
	(−0.52)	(−0.63)	(−0.88)	(−1.00)	(−0.86)	(−1.13)
FINANCE	−0.08		−0.07			
	(−1.40)		(−1.40)			
CAPITAL		−0.03		−0.02		
		(−0.46)		(−0.39)		
REER	0.05	0.04			0.02	
	(0.38)	(0.30)			(0.15)	
Constant	−4.53	−2.73	−4.63	−2.60	−1.39	−1.49
	(−1.18)	(−0.62)	(−1.25)	(−0.61)	(−0.43)	(−0.49)
Adjusted R^2	0.19	0.09	0.23	0.14	0.13	0.19
Durbin-Watson stat.	2.50	2.50	2.53	2.54	2.50	2.53

[a] denotes significance at the 10 per cent level

[b] denotes significance at the 5 per cent level

[c] denotes significance at the 1 per cent level

Notes: Equation 4.2; the sample period covers 1985–2007; t-statistics are in parentheses.

Source: Ma, G. and Zhou, H. (forthcoming), *China's evolving external wealth and rising creditor position*, BIS Working Papers, Bank for International Settlements, Basel.

The estimated coefficient of the growth differential suggests that for each 1 percentage point growth differential vis-a-vis the OECD, China's NFA/GDP ratio will decline by 0.25 percentage points per annum. This is consistent with the neoclassical growth model in which a faster-growing economy tends to attract more capital inflows. Since the China–OECD growth differential averaged more than 7 per cent per annum during 1985–2007, the relative growth factor would cumulatively push China into a net debtor position of 40 per cent of 2007 GDP, *ceteris paribus*.

The declining young-age dependency ratio appears to be a major determinant of China's NFA position, overwhelming the effect of the growth differential. Our estimate suggests that China's NFA position has improved by 4.5 percentage points of GDP, on average, for each 1 percentage point decline in its young-age dependency. In just two decades, China's young-age dependency ratio dropped by nearly 20 percentage points—enough to boost China's NFA position by 90 per cent of 2007 GDP cumulatively, all other things being equal. The estimated coefficient for the old-age dependency is positive, favouring the view that ageing might lead to increased capital outflows, given limited international mobility of labour and capital–labour substitutability (Lueth 2008). Nevertheless, we find the magnitude of the estimated coefficient implausibly large.

The coefficient for government debt also has the expected negative sign. Our estimates support the views of Kuijs (2006) and Li and Yin (2007) about the role of fiscal policy for China's high saving rate and exceed the absolute values obtained by Lane and Milesi-Ferretti (2001), suggesting that a rise of 1 percentage point in the debt/GDP ratio leads to a decline of 0.35 percentage points in the NFA/GDP ratio. China's debt/ GDP ratio rose from 4 per cent to 26 per cent between 1985 and 2007, cumulatively contributing to a debtor position of about 8 per cent of 2007 GDP. Nevertheless, since 2003, a lower government debt level might have contributed to the observed swing to a net lender position by an estimated 1.5 per cent of GDP.

The sign of the financial development coefficient varies and is statistically insignificant in all cases. Our evidence therefore fails to confirm the view that financial underdevelopment is a major factor behind China's large current account surplus and growing creditor position. One possibility is that both indicators might be less than ideal measures of the institutional quality of the domestic financial sector. Nevertheless, no matter how one measures this institutional quality, a more puzzling question is why the apparent financial underdevelopment has not retarded China's economic growth so far.

Finally, the estimated coefficient for the renminbi's real effective exchange rate changes sign from equation to equation and is statistically insignificant in all cases, suggesting limited empirical evidence for the exchange rate as a major determinant of China's NFA position in our specification. This is consistent with the findings by Chinn and Wei (2008) and Cheung et al. (2009) and raises questions about the view that an undervalued renminbi adds to corporate profits and thus lifts the saving rate and current account surplus in China (Eichengreen 2006). For instance, the suggested association of strong corporate profits with an undervalued currency can induce far more investment spending than additional corporate saving thus generated, potentially worsening the current account balance and NFA position.

These results provide us with useful benchmarks about the outlook for China's NFA position. Assuming that in the next two decades China grows at a pace 5 percentage points above that of the average OECD annually and that the ratio of government debt to GDP rises by 10 percentage points cumulatively, this would cause China's NFA position as a share of GDP to fall by 22.5 and 3.5 percentage points, respectively. In other words, these two factors combined could trim China's NFA position to below 5 per cent of GDP by 2025, *ceteris paribus*.

Much of the uncertainty in the outlook for China's NFA position comes from the demographic impacts. We obtain fairly robust estimates for the impact of the young-age dependency, but China's young-age dependency is projected to change little between 2007 and 2025 (UN 2006) and might therefore cease to be a major driver of China's NFA position going forward. Meanwhile, China's old-age dependency ratio is projected to double to 20 per cent. Our estimated coefficient for the old-age dependency is, however, implausibly large and positive, suggesting that it is risky for us to assess its quantitative impact. Since existing empirical findings for East Asia are divided over the effect of ageing trends on the saving–investment balance (Higgins and Williamson 1997; Bosworth et al. 2004; Kim and Lee 2007; IMF 2008; Lueth 2008), the projected rise in old-age dependency could boost or weaken China's NFA position. The net effect on the current account could also be tempered by a concomitant rise in the overall dependency rate. One possible scenario is that the combined effect of the young and old-age dependencies on China's NFA could be negligible in the coming two decades.

These results together—taken at face value—suggest that China could remain a net creditor over the next generation and at least is very unlikely to become a meaningful debtor in the next two decades. This projection is broadly in line with the findings by McKibbin (2005), Kuijs (2006), Eichengreen (2006) and Peng (2008), but contrasts with those of Dollar and Kraay (2006), who predict that, with further economic liberalisation, China will swing into a substantial debtor position of at least 5 per cent of GDP in 20 years.

Caution, however, is called for in interpreting these results, in part because the estimation method, data sample and quality have limitations. For instance, the IIP and BoP statistics themselves are obviously subject to measurement errors. Moreover, this is a partial model that could miss some of the general equilibrium effects. In the context of global imbalances, any outcome of China's current account and NFA position would depend not only on domestic developments but on the accommodation of the rest of the world. Finally, we have not controlled for some of the potentially important policy and institutional factors, such as a withdrawal of public service provisions and protection of property rights—in part because measuring such factors is challenging.

China's expanding international balance sheet

China's gross external investment position—the sum of its international assets and liabilities—also matters because it can serve as an indicator of its financial integration and interactions with the rest of the world (Lane and Milesi-Ferretti 2003, 2007). Moreover, adjustments in gross positions could entail large cross-border flows, potentially overwhelming the domestic financial system and thus posing challenges to policymakers. Finally, a bigger international balance sheet could affect monetary and financial stability, as the impact of a given shock could be magnified. This section explores the medium-term outlook for China's gross position in the coming decade.

China's gross position has expanded considerably in the past two decades but remains relatively small. Scaled by GDP, China's international balance sheet has increased steadily over time, from 14 per cent of GDP in 1985 to 113 per cent by 2007 (Figure 4.7). Nevertheless, this is still below the average 350 per cent reached by OECD countries and 250 per cent for Asian economies, implying that China's external assets and liabilities have room to expand substantially in the coming decade. When scaled by trade flows and domestic financial wealth, however, China's gross position has exhibited markedly different dynamics. The gross position relative to trade flows has not been monotonic—first peaking about 1998 but trending lower since. China's financial integration seems therefore to have trailed its trade integration since the East Asian financial crisis.[6] Alternatively, the gross position relative to domestic financial wealth displays even greater instability over time. Scaled by the sum of domestic credit, bonds outstanding and stock-market capitalisation, China's gross position peaked in 1996 but has since declined. According to this measure, China's international financial integration has stalled in recent years.

Figure 4.7 China's gross external investment position

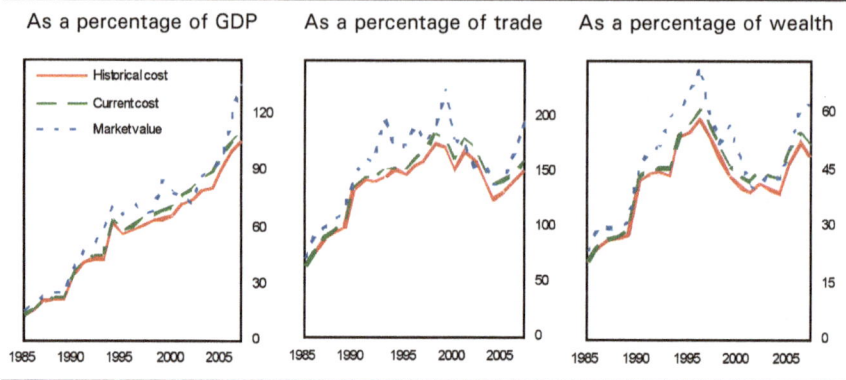

As a percentage of GDP   As a percentage of trade   As a percentage of wealth

Historical cost
Current cost
Market value

Notes: The gross position is the sum of foreign assets and liabilities; trade is gross goods and services trade flow; wealth is domestic financial wealth defined as the sum of domestic credit, domestic bonds outstanding and domestic stock-market capitalisation.

Source: Ma, G. and Zhou, H. (forthcoming), *China's evolving external wealth and rising creditor position*, BIS Working Papers, Bank for International Settlements, Basel.

What might be the medium-term outlook for China's cross-border asset trade with the rest of the world? This question can be answered in part by examining the likely size of China's international balance sheet in 10 years if it opens up its capital account and maintains its recent path of development. We conduct this forward-looking exercise by first relating the gross position to a set of determinants across the OECD members, which by selection have achieved high degrees of capital mobility. We then apply the estimated parameters from the cross-country estimation to the assumed paths for China's growth and trade in order to project the magnitude of its gross position in a more liberalised environment in 2015.

Equation 4.3 gives the cross-sectional regression specification.

Equation 4.3

$$\text{giip}_i = \theta_0 + \theta_1\,\text{SIZE}_i + \theta_2\,\text{OPEN}_i + \theta_3\,\text{INCOME}_i + \theta_4\,\text{FINANCE}_i + \theta_5\,\text{EURO}_i + \theta_6\,\text{CENTRE}_i + \lambda_i$$

in which the dependent variable giip is the ratio of the gross position to GDP. The independent variables are standard ones examined by Lane and Milesi-Ferretti (2008) and McCauley and Chan (2008). 1) *SIZE* is country size as measured by GDP. Large economies tend to hold less external assets and liabilities relative to their size, because of greater room for domestic diversification. We therefore expect a negative coefficient for *SIZE*. 2)

OPEN is trade openness measured by the sum of exports and imports of goods and services as a ratio of GDP. Since trade and financial openness are considered to complement each other, we expect a positive correlation. 3) INCOME is per capita GDP, which is expected to be positively related to the gross position, as higher levels of income enhance risk tolerance and facilitate international diversification. 4) FINANCE is domestic financial development proxied by the two indicators discussed in section four. Its relation with the gross position is ambiguous in theory but is often thought of as being complementary. 5) We also introduce two dummies: EURO for the euro area and CENTRE for financial centre. This is a cross-sectional regression on the OECD sample. To help smooth the trend and limit the influence of possible outliers, unusual movements and measurement errors, all of the above variables are the 2001–05 averages.[7]

Table 4.5 shows that the estimated coefficients for trade openness, economic development and the two dummies are all positive and statistically significant. Also, the dummies for the euro zone and financial centre exert great influence on the gross position. The estimates for the coefficient of country size have the anticipated negative sign but are only marginally significant. Finally, the estimated coefficients for the two indicators of domestic financial development have the expected positive signs but are statistically insignificant.

We take the estimated parameters of Column 3 in Table 4.5 as a basis for our projections. To ensure that our projections are reasonable, we first conduct an informal model consistency simulation on the real Chinese data for the years 2004–07. We find that on the basis of the estimated coefficients from the cross-sectional regression, the real Chinese data fall nicely between our two fitted values based on the full sample and that without Luxembourg and Ireland. We shall take these two fitted values of the gross position as the upper and lower bounds of the band for our projection (Table 4.6).

Table 4.5 Determinants of the gross external investment positions of the OECD economies

	(1)		(2)		(3)		(4)	
	Full sample	Without LU & IE	Full sample	Without LU & IE	Full sample	Without LU & IE	Full sample	Without LU & IE
GDP	-0.07 (-1.50)	-0.05 (-1.29)	-0.07 (-1.49)	-0.05 (-1.30)	-0.07 (-1.65)	-0.05 (-1.38)		
Trade	0.64[a] (3.78)	0.43[a] (2.82)	0.63[a] (3.71)	0.43[a] (2.79)	0.63[a] (3.85)	0.43[a] (2.86)	0.79[a] (6.08)	0.54[a] (6.43)
Euro dummy	0.62[a] (4.52)	0.51[a] (3.98)	0.63[a] (4.47)	0.51[a] (3.99)	0.62[a] (4.55)	0.51[a] (4.06)	0.57[a] (4.78)	0.47[a] (4.27)
Financial centre dummy	1.43[a] (5.06)	1.18[a] (8.21)	1.44[a] (5.13)	1.19[a] (8.32)	1.47[a] (5.02)	1.19[a] (8.63)	1.43[a] (4.90)	1.14[a] (10.31)
Nominal GDP per capita	0.61[a] (5.51)	0.55[a] (6.67)	0.62[a] (5.71)	0.55[a] (6.81)	0.63[a] (6.00)	0.56[a] (6.70)	0.62[a] (5.81)	0.55[a] (6.34)
Finance	0.06 (0.73)	0.03 (0.70)						
Capital market			0.04 (0.52)	0.01 (0.13)				
Constant	-3.02 (-1.60)	-1.49 (0.88)	-2.91 (-1.53)	-1.39 (0.82)	-2.74 (-1.55)	-1.36 (-0.85)	-4.20[a] (-3.07)	-2.42[b] (-2.19)
Adjusted R²	0.90	0.89	0.90	0.86	0.90	0.86	0.90	0.86

[a] denotes significance at the 1 per cent level
[b] denotes significance at the 5 per cent level

Notes: Equation 4.3; the full sample has 30 observations; LU and IE stand for Luxembourg and Ireland, respectively; the euro dummy takes the value of 1 for Euro members and zero otherwise; for Luxembourg, Switzerland and the United Kingdom, the dummy takes the value of 1, and zero otherwise; t-statistics are in parentheses.

Source: Ma, G. and Zhou, H. (forthcoming), *China's evolving external wealth and rising creditor position*, BIS Working Papers, Bank for International Settlements, Basel.

Table 4.6   China's projected gross external investment position
(US$billion and per cent)

	2004	2006	2007	2010	2015
Fitted value of gross position from full sample	1,730.4	2,989.7	4,312.7	6,109.5	14,894.1
Fitted value of gross position without LU & IE	1,151.4	1,916.2	2,690.0	3,838.92	9,114.62
Real gross position	1,718.8	2,802.9	3,765.4	-	-
Fitted value of gross position/ GDP from full sample (%)	89.6	113.0	133.0	142.8	192.2
Fitted value of gross position/ GDP without LU & IE (%)	59.6	72.4	82.9	89.7	117.6
Real gross position/GDP (%)	89.0	105.4	111.3	-	-

Notes: Calculated at current costs; LU and IE stand for Luxembourg and Ireland, respectively.
Sources: State Administration of Foreign Exchange and authors' own estimates.

To obtain the projected values of China's gross external international position for 2015 on the basis of the OECD experience, we assume that for the next 10 years, the annual growth rates of China's nominal GDP per capita and trade flows (both in dollar terms) average 12 per cent, respectively, compared with their historical averages of 13 per cent and 21 per cent for the past 10 years. On these assumptions, China's gross position could triple in absolute terms by 2015, as indicated by the midpoint of the two fitted values. China's gross position would rise to about 150 per cent of GDP. This forward-looking result stems from a cross-sectional regression of the OECD experience and the assumed paths of China's trade and growth, and thus is conditioned on China's domestic development as well as the accommodation of the global financial system. In particular, the current global financial crisis generally could curtail cross-border asset trade and thus slow the expansion of China's international balance sheet. The bottom line, however, is that with a more liberal capital regime, China's external balance sheet could expand, indicating China's growing role in and increased exposure to global finance in the years ahead.

The evolving structure of China's foreign assets and liabilities

The gross and net international investment positions of an economy's external balance sheet often interact with its composition to jointly shape their dynamics. This section first highlights some of the medium-term features of China's external capital structure and discusses factors shaping these trends and their implications for risk–return balance and risk–return trade-off for China. China's external capital structure exhibits three prominent features.

First, sector wise, official reserves increasingly dominate China's foreign assets, representing two-thirds of its total today, in comparison with 15 per cent 20 years ago (Figure 4.3). If the new China Investment Corporation is included, the external assets held by the Chinese official sector are estimated to top $1700 billion in 2007—far exceeding China's NFA position of $1 trillion. This points to a significant net foreign liability position of some $700 billion for the Chinese non-official sector.

Second, in terms of instruments, while 70 per cent of China's foreign liabilities were concentrated in equity (mostly direct investment) in 2007, some three-quarters of its foreign assets were estimated to be in the fixed-income instruments. As a result, the absolute sizes of its net negative equity position and positive net debt instrument position have grown over time (Figure 4.3). This 'long debt, short equity' asymmetry is more pronounced than in most emerging economies (Lane and Schmukler 2007).[8]

Third, regarding currency composition, while China's foreign assets are denominated almost entirely in foreign currencies, 70 per cent of its foreign liabilities are denominated in the domestic currency—mainly because of its large inward direct investment position. Other things being equal, a 10 per cent appreciation of the renminbi is estimated to translate into a valuation loss of almost 3 per cent of 2008 GDP, given that China's gross liability position is 43 per cent of GDP.

Many factors could affect the composition of China's external balance sheet. We highlight only three in this chapter. The first is the particular sequence of China's capital account opening. The previous policy of favouring capital inflows and discriminating against outflows, for instance, could help explain the fact that compared with China's external assets, its external liabilities are more diversified among local/foreign as well as private/public players. Also, the commanding role of inward direct investment in China's external liabilities could be attributed in part to the longstanding policy of promoting this form of inflow and restricting portfolio inflows.[9]

A second factor is changing exchange rate expectations. The Chinese renminbi has been heavily managed but market expectations swung quite sizeably over time. Typically, in time of depreciation in expectations, there is understatement of China's foreign assets due to capital flight, and in time of appreciation in expectations, there is understatement of China's foreign liabilities due to hot money inflows. Before 2002, the perceived renminbi weakness during the East Asian financial crisis encouraged Chinese households and firms to hang on to their dollar deposits and avoid dollar loans, with the government struggling to protect the official reserves (Figure 4.8). This pattern reversed considerably during 2002–07, as the Chinese private sector attempted to shift the exchange rate risk onto the public sector by selling dollars to the central bank, which resulted in a large build-up of China's official reserve assets (Goldstein and Lardy 2008).

The third factor is domestic financial development. The underdevelopment of China's domestic capital market could also have constrained foreign investors from participating in local securities markets and forced domestic firms to turn increasingly to foreign direct investment. Moreover, the small size of China's domestic capital markets relative to cross-border capital flows in turn might also give rise to apprehension on the part of the regulatory authorities, resulting in a tiny portfolio liability position in China's external balance sheet. On the other hand, China's banking sector still dominates its domestic financial system and thus helps explain why the position of other investment (mostly bank-related instruments) is more than twice the size of the portfolio investment position on both sides of the Chinese international balance sheet.

China's external capital structure raises a number of issues related to the risk–return trade-off. First, the official sector as a prominent asset holder and China's highly skewed 'long debt, short equity' position could indicate a deliberate past policy choice to place a big premium on stability, since it offers policymakers some comfort in times of distress. Reserve assets tend to be placed in liquid but low-yield fixed-income products, while equity investment on the liability side is often riskier and thus more costly. This imbalance in China's international balance sheet also suggests that China might have fared relatively better than most in the current global financial crisis and thus is well positioned to rebalance its external portfolio on a longer-term basis in the future. Large overseas direct investment from China into the rest of the world is therefore expected only in the foreseeable future.

Second, low returns on China's net foreign assets mean that it has so far accumulated its net foreign assets principally through its trade surplus over time. One can compare an economy's NIIP with its cumulative net exports of goods and services, with the gap serving as an indicator of the cumulative total returns on its net external position. As Figure 4.9 shows, China's cumulative trade balance of goods and services exceeds its net foreign asset position, whereas Hong Kong's cumulative net exports of goods and services account for less than one-third of its NFA position (Yong and Chen 2005). In other words, Hong Kong attains its big net foreign asset position mostly by high net returns (income and valuation changes) from cross-border asset trade, whereas China achieves this principally by accumulating trade surpluses over time.

Conclusions

This chapter has investigated the medium-term trends of and outlook for China's net and gross international investment positions as well as the composition of its external balance sheet. We find that the marked decline in young-age dependency could have been a major determinant of China's position as an emerging big net creditor. Faster growth and higher government debt only partially offset this demographic effect. Moreover, the roles of the exchange rate and financial depth in shaping China's NFA position appear mixed. Our findings suggest that the probability of China swinging into a meaningful debtor position in the coming two decades is low. As the gross size of its international balance sheet could triple within the next 10 years, China is likely to be a bigger player in the global financial system while also becoming more exposed to external shocks. Finally, the composition of China's external assets and liabilities is highly skewed, reflecting past developments in policy, institutions and markets and suggesting substantial potential for portfolio rebalancing going forward.

A number of implications can be drawn from these findings. First, with a very different pattern of demographic shifts expected in the coming two decades, China's NFA position is expected to adjust gradually, facilitated by continued strong economic growth and a more flexible renminbi. This should assist an orderly global rebalancing without creating excess stress on the rest of the world. Second, as China's NFA position is unlikely to reverse sharply into that of a net debtor, the pressure from large and sudden reversals in cross-border flows arising from big position adjustments under a more open capital account should be manageable, other things being equal. This should be positive for China's goal of greater renminbi convertibility. Third, a bigger international balance sheet indicates growing interactions between China and the global financial system and highlights the need for China to enhance risk management and financial market development, and for the rest of the world to learn to cope with a rising China. Finally, China's lopsided external balance sheet could offer room for marked portfolio rebalancing in the coming decades—increased overseas equity investment on the asset side and greater portfolio investment inflows on the liability side.

References

Bosworth, B., Bryant, R. and Burtless, G. 2004, *The impact of ageing on financial markets and the economy: a survey*, Brookings Institution Working Paper, Brookings Institution, Washington, DC.

Chamon, M. and Prasad, E. 2008, *Why are saving rates of urban households in China rising?*, IMF Working Paper, no. WP/08/145, International Monetary Fund, Washington, DC.

Cheung, Y., Chinn, M. and Fujii, E. 2009, *China's current account and exchange rate*, NBER Working Paper, no. 14673, National Bureau of Economic Research, Cambridge, Mass.

Chinn, D. and Prasad, E. 2003, 'Medium-term determinants of current accounts in industrial and developing countries: an empirical exploration', *Journal of International Economics*, vol. 59, pp. 47–76.

Chinn, M. and Wei, S. 2008, A faith-based initiative: do we really know that a flexible exchange rate regime facilitates current account adjustment?, Manuscript, January.

Debelle, G. and Faruqee, H. 1996, *What determines the current account? A cross-sectional and panel approach*, IMF Working Paper, no. 96/58, International Monetary Fund, Washington, DC.

Dollar, D. and Kraay, A. 2006, 'Neither a borrower nor a lender: does China's zero net foreign asset position make economic sense?', *Journal of Monetary Economics*, no. 53, pp. 943–71.

Eichengreen, B. 2006, 'Global imbalance, demography and China', in M. Balling, E. Gnan and F. Lierman (eds), *Money, Finance and Demography: The consequences of ageing*, a volume for the 26th SUERF Colloquium, Lisbon.

Goldstein, M. and Lardy, N. 2008, *Debating China's Exchange Rate Policy*, Peterson Institute for International Economics, Washington, DC.

Gourinchas, P. and Jeanne, O. 2007, *Capital flows to developing countries: the allocation puzzle*, NBER Working Papers, no. 13602, November, National Bureau of Economic Research, Cambridge, Mass.

Higgins, M. and Williamson, J. 1997, 'Ageing structure dynamics in Asia and dependence on foreign capital', *Population and Development Review*, vol. 23, no. 2, June, pp. 261–93.

Horioka, Y. and Wan, J. 2008, 'Why does China save so much?', in B. Eichengreen, C. Wyplosz and Y. Park (eds), *China, Asia, and the New World Economy*, Oxford University Press, Oxford, pp. 371–91.

International Monetary Fund (IMF) 2008, *Regional Economic Outlook: Asia and Pacific*, November, International Monetary Fund, Washington, DC.

Kim, S. and Lee, J. 2007, 'Demographic changes, saving, and current account in East Asia', *Asian Economic Papers*, vol. 6, no. 2, pp. 22–53.

Kraay, A. 2000, 'Household savings in China', *The World Bank Economic Review*, vol. 14, no. 3, pp. 545–70.

Kuijs, L. 2005, *Investment and savings in China*, World Bank Policy Research Working Paper, no. 3633, The World Bank, Washington, DC.

—— 2006, *How will China's saving–investment balance evolve?*, World Bank Policy Research Working Paper, no. 3958, The World Bank, Washington, DC.

Lane, P. and Milesi-Ferretti, G. 1999, *The external wealth of nations: measures of foreign assets and liabilities for industrial and developing countries*, IMF Working Paper, no. WP/99/115, International Monetary Fund, Washington, DC.

—— 2001, 'Long-term capital movements', *NBER Macroeconomic Annual*, National Bureau of Economic Research, Cambridge, Mass., pp. 71–135.

—— 2003, *International financial integration*, IMF Staff Papers, vol. 50, Special Issue, International Monetary Fund, Washington, DC.

—— 2007, 'The external wealth of nations mark II: revised and extended estimates of foreign assets and liabilities, 1970–2004', *Journal of International Economics*, vol. 73, pp. 223–50.

—— 2008, *The driver of financial globalisation*, Institute for International Integration Discussion Paper, no. 238, January, Department of Economics, College of Liberal Arts and Sciences, University of Connecticut.

Lane, P. and Schmukler, S. 2007, 'International financial integration of China and India', in A. Winter and S. Yusuf (eds), *Dancing with the Giants: China, India and the global economy*, The World Bank, Washington, DC, pp. 101–32.

Lee, R. and Mason, A. 2006, 'What is the demographic dividend', *Finance and Development*, vol. 43, no. 3, September, International Monetary Fund, Washington, DC.

Li, Y. and Yin, J. 2007, 'A study on China's high saving rate', *Economic Research*, no. 6, pp. 14–26.

Loayza, N., Schimdt-Hebbel, K. and Serven, L. 2000, 'Saving in developing countries: an overview', *The World Bank Economic Review*, vol. 14, no. 3, pp. 393–414.

Lueth, E. 2008, *Capital flows and demographics—an Asian perspective*, IMF Working Paper, no. WP/08/8, International Monetary Fund, Washington, DC.

Lucas, R. 1990, 'Why doesn't capital flow from rich to poor countries?', *American Economic Review*, vol. 80, pp. 92–6.

Ma, G. and Zhou, H. (forthcoming), *China's evolving external wealth and rising creditor position*, BIS Working Papers, Bank for International Settlements, Basel.

McCauley, N. R. and Chan, E. 2008, 'Hong Kong and Shanghai: yesterday, today and tomorrow', in Takatoshi Ito and Andrew K. Rose (eds), *Financial Sector Development in the Pacific Rim*, East Asia Seminar on Economics, vol. 18, National Bureau of Economic Research, Cambridge, Mass.

McKibbin, W. 2005, *The global macroeconomic consequences of a demographic transition*, Lowy Institute Working Papers, no. 7.05, November, Lowy Institute, Sydney.

Mendoza, E., Quadrini, V. and Rio-Rull, J. 2007, *Financial integration, financial deepness and global imbalance*, NBER Working Paper, no. 12909, National Bureau of Economic Research, Cambridge, Mass.

Modigliani, F. and Cao, S. 2004, 'The Chinese saving puzzle and the life-cycle hypothesis', *Journal of Economic Literature*, vol. XLII, March, pp. 145–70.

Peng, X. 2008, 'Demographic shift, population ageing and economic growth in China: a computable general equilibrium analysis', *Pacific Economic Review*, vol. 13, no. 5, pp. 680–97.

Prasad, E., Rajan, R. and Subramanian, A. 2006–07, 'Patterns of international capital flows and their implications for economic development', *The New Economic Geography: Effects and policy implications*, Federal Reserve Bank of Kansas City and Brookings Institution, Kansas City and Washington, DC.

United Nations (UN) 2006, *World Population Prospects: The 2006 revision*, United Nations, New York.

Wang, F. and Mason, A. 2008, 'Demographic factors in China's transition', in L. Brandt and T. Rawski (eds), *China's Great Economic Transformation*, Cambridge University Press, Cambridge.

Williamson, G. and Higgins, M. 2001, 'The accumulation and demography connection in East Asia', in A. Mason (ed.), *Population Change and Economic Development in East Asia—Challenges met and opportunities seized*, Stanford University Press, Palo Alto, Calif.

Zhou, X. 2009, Some observations and analysis of the saving rate problem, Speech at Bank Negara Malaysia High Level Conference, Kuala Lumpur, Malaysia, 10 February 2009.

Endnotes

1. Guonan Ma is a senior economist at the Bank for International Settlements (BIS) and Zhou Haiwen is a staff member of the State Administration of Foreign Exchange of China (SAFE). The views expressed in this chapter are those of the authors and do not necessarily reflect those of their affiliated organisations. We are grateful for the comments and suggestions by Claudio Borio, Stephen Cecchetti, Yin-Wong Cheung, Andrew Filardo, Marion Kohler, Li Jiange, Robert McCauley, Anella Munro, Frank Packer, Thomas Rawski, Eli Remolona and Wang Xin, although any errors remain ours. We also thank Eric Chan and Marek Raczko for their excellent research support.

2. There are three basic measures of the international investment position: historical cost, current cost and market value. The Chinese official IIP statistics are based principally on the historical-cost approach. On the basis of the official statistics, China's net foreign asset position exceeded 30 per cent of GDP in 2007. Following the US Bureau of Economic Analysis (Nguyen 2008), we adopt the current cost value as our featured or benchmark IIP measurement in this chapter, unless otherwise specified.

3. Lucas (1990) argues that the levels of capital flows from rich and capital-abundant economies to poor and capital-scarce economies are too low, relative to what the neoclassical growth models predict. Gourinchas and Jeanne (2007) and Prasad et al. (2006–07) go one step further: the former show developing economies with faster growth attract less capital (the 'allocation puzzle'), while the latter demonstrate a positive correlation between the current account balance and growth among emerging markets.

4. See Loayza et al. (2000) for an overview of the determinants of domestic saving in developing economies. Most of the literature also focuses on the Chinese saving rate instead of the saving–investment gap. For an overview of China's household, corporate and government saving patterns, see Zhou (2009). For further discussion, see Kraay (2000); Modigliani and Cao (2004); Fehr et al. (2005); McKibbin (2005); Kuijs (2005, 2006); Dollar and Kraay (2006); Eichengreen (2006); Li and Yin (2007); Chamon and Prasad (2008); and Horioka and Wan (2008). Also, empirical studies on medium-term factors behind the current account, see Debelle and Faruqee (1996) and Chinn and Prasad (2003).

5. The significant decline in the young-age dependency started in the early 1980s and was attributable in part to the baby boom during the 1950s and 1960s and the sudden fall in the birth rate due to the one-child policy vigorously implemented from the late 1970s.

6. This is perhaps due to a combination of large-scale withdrawals of international capital from Asia during the East Asian financial crisis, a policy response of fortified capital controls to support the official pledge of no renminbi devaluation and accelerated trade flows after China's entry to the World Trade Organisation.

7. To further mitigate possible heteroskedasticity in our cross-sectional regressions, we: 1) take logs of all the variables except the two dummies; 2) introduce White heteroskedasticity-consistent co-variances; and 3) regress the samples with and without Luxembourg and Ireland (the two main outliers).

8. Moreover, compared with other instruments, the position of portfolio investment has been tiny on both the asset and the liability sides of China's external balance sheet.

9. In recent years, China has moved towards a more balanced management of capital inflows, with an increased emphasis on portfolio investment. China's external positions could therefore rebalance across instruments in the coming years.

The geo-strategic implications of China's growth

5

Hugh White

Geo-strategy returns

In the 20 years since the Berlin Wall fell, the common working assumption among policymakers and analysts of international affairs alike has been that the end of the Cold War marked not just the end of a particular geo-strategic episode, but the end of an era in which geo-strategy as traditionally conceived—focusing on strategic competition between states and especially between major powers—played a significant role in shaping the international system.

Many compelling arguments supported this idea. In an era without the sharp ideological divisions of the twentieth century, it was argued, there would be little to disagree about or compete over. In an era of globalisation, the disruption to trade and other forms of communication caused by competition and conflict would be too costly to contemplate. In an era of unipolarity, the United States' overwhelming military preponderance would deter any government from challenging the US-led global order, which it was clearly committed to perpetuate. And, after 9/11, non-state actors such as terrorists, and the weak and rogue states that allowed them to flourish, seemed much more dangerous and claimed most of the political and intellectual attention previously devoted to geo-strategic concerns. It became commonplace to assert that in the new century serious challenges to the global order arose not from traditional strategic competition but from the toxic combination of terrorists, weak and rogue states and weapons of mass destruction.

This set of ideas has by no means faded away. It remains central, for example, to the views of US Secretary of Defence, Robert Gates (2009), about America's future defence needs. In the past year or two, however, it has been challenged by authors who have started to pay attention to the way in which shifts in the relative power of states could produce pressures for change in the global order of a quite different kind, and potentially of much greater magnitude and significance, than those posed by non-state actors and weak and rogue states.[1] They argue that economic growth in many countries around the world—though very much a product of the US-led globalised order of recent decades—could nonetheless undermine that order because it will produce changes in relative power among states, which the order will struggle to accommodate.

This argument is supported by some simple but powerful insights. First, in a globalised world, states still seem to act very much as states always have, and though their actions do not necessarily conform to the dire predictions of the hardline realists,[2] nor do they invariably reflect an unwaveringly rational commitment to enlightened mutual self-interest. Pride and fear still shape state's actions, primarily because they shape citizens' expectations of their states and their leaders. In a globalised world, states still act as states always have because most citizens still seem to relate to their states very much as they always have: in a deeply emotional and tribal way. Nationalism in it various forms remains as strong as ever, not just among the peoples of emerging nations but among those of established powers.

Second, the nature and scale of the terrorist threat, though still serious, is now seen as less apocalyptic than it was in the first shock after 9/11. This opens political and intellectual space to explore these other challenges to international order and it undermines hopes that any emerging geo-strategic competition might be subsumed in the common cause of fighting jihadist terrorism (Bell 2008). Third, it has become clearer that in a globalised world, interdependence cuts two ways, constraining the United States as well as potential challengers to the international order. It transpires that the United States cannot act with as much freedom as some expected to impose its will on an unruly world, because it too will suffer so badly from any resulting disruption. Fourth, the past decade has brought a more sober and realistic understanding of the limits to US military power. It is now clear that the United States cannot use force as easily and cheaply as many had assumed to uphold its vision of global order.

For all these reasons, geo-strategy is back. We are again exploring how the international order—the set of understandings and expectations that shapes relationships between states—is formed by the perceptions and realties of power, and especially how changes in relative power affect the workings of the international order. Moreover, after a period during the Cold War in which geo-strategic calculations were based more on military than on economic factors, we are rediscovering the centrality of economic power as the key driver of geo-strategic relationships. There is a simple reason for this: we are living through a period of remarkable economic transformation. The number of people engaged in the modern global economy has doubled in the past two decades and could double again in the next few decades. This has produced by far the largest increase in economic activity of any comparable period in history, as huge populations around the world have moved from low-productivity to high-productivity forms of work.[3] This in turn is driving shifts in relative economic weight of a scale and speed that we have not seen for many decades, if ever. Policymakers and analysts are starting to realise that if the trends of recent decades persist, the United States will not retain the unchallengeable economic primacy it enjoyed throughout the past century. In this century, there are likely to be many very strong states that the United States will have to deal with.

Much of the analyses of these trends, including those cited earlier, explore the general implications of the rising power of the whole class of emerging economies for the international order.[4] This is useful as far as it goes, but exploring the geo-strategic consequences of the emerging economies as a group runs the risk of understating the significance of the most important of them. China's growing economic weight is far more significant than that of any other emerging power in its implications for future international order—because it is by far the largest of the emerging economies and because its growing power so profoundly affects the regional order in North-East Asia, which is by far the most important focus of geo-strategic competition on Earth.

It is easy to underestimate the geo-strategic implications for the international order of China's growing economic weight because so little seems to have happened so far. China's economy has grown strongly and steadily for more than 30 years and its relative economic strength has grown remarkably, yet its place in the international order has not so far changed nearly as radically. It is tempting to conclude that China's economic growth has little geo-strategic impact. This assumes, however, that geo-strategic change follows steadily and smoothly as economic weight shifts. That is not necessarily so. The geo-strategic consequences of economic change can be 'sticky': the status quo can persist for years as economic weight shifts and then fall swiftly when the pressure becomes too great to bear. East Asia's stable strategic order has persisted through several decades of fast Chinese growth, but that does not necessarily mean no changes are in store. It could mean that change, when it comes, is swifter and more disruptive for having been delayed.

China grows

The tipping point might not be far away. For several decades, it has been relatively easy to overlook the strategic implications of China's growing economic weight, but in the past couple of years attention has started to focus on an unmistakable and fast-approaching geo-strategic milepost: the point at which China overtakes the United States to become the largest economy in the world. Statistically, it has been clear for a long time that if the trends of recent decades are sustained, China's output will overtake the United States' some time in the next few decades, but only in the past year or two has this become an imminent and inescapable probability. Only in the past year or two have strategic policymakers and analysts started to take notice.

The Australian Government's Defence White Paper released in May 2009 predicted that on some measures China's economy could overtake the United States' to become the largest in the world by about 2020 (Commonwealth of Australia 2009:34, para. 4.23). By 'some measures', the White Paper presumably meant purchasing power parity (PPP), because the date at which China's gross domestic product (GDP) in market exchange rate terms overtakes the United States' is at present much more remote, and PPP is clearly the more relevant measure of economic weight for geo-strategy.[5] The date of 2020 is at the closer end of the range of credible crossover dates. The middle of the range of estimates is probably closer to 2030, but from a geo-strategic point of view, a decade here or there is not very important. What matters is the recognition that the United States will probably loose the advantage in sheer economic scale that it has enjoyed ever since it rose to global power well within the time frames of today's strategic and defence policymakers. This probability is no longer a statistical curiosity but an active factor in shaping policy.

Of course, this prediction could prove false. China's economic growth might falter for one or more of a wide range of reasons—social, economic, political, environmental or indeed strategic. After three decades of rapid growth, however, sustained by continual adaptation and reform within China, there is no compelling reason to assume that China cannot sustain growth in the next three decades at rates sufficient to overtake the United States in output. And although it is too early to be sure, it seems probable that the global financial crisis will, if anything, accelerate the power shift from the United States to China. If or when it happens, China's ascent to the leading position in the global economy will mark the end of 130 years of US economic primacy.

Why does that matter to geo-strategy? The connection between economic and strategic power is complex in detail, but historical evidence suggests that it is simple in essence: in the modern era, economic scale is the necessary and sufficient precondition for strategic weight. In the nineteenth century, the United Kingdom's global maritime primacy lasted as long as its economic primacy—and not much longer. The United States took its place as the world's strongest strategic player soon after it displaced the United Kingdom as the world's biggest economy, in the 1880s. It is possible that the foundations of US strategic power lie elsewhere than in its economic strength, but one must at least note that it has never exercised any significant strategic power beyond its own immediate region except when it has commanded the world's largest economy.

Some would argue that this is too simple. The Central Intelligence Agency (CIA) in its November 2008 report, *Global Trends: 2025 report*, used a compound measure of national power incorporating GDP, defence spending, population and technology. It is not clear how valid this compound measure is over longer time frames, because in the long run, all other things being equal, defence spending and technological strength will tend to follow economic weight. In the short term, however—the next two or three decades anyway—it would certainly be wrong to assume that as China overtakes the United States in economic output it will necessarily assume its position as the global superpower. The United States will continue to enjoy a significant advantage over China in many other aspects of power—including the soft power of culture and the hard power of armed force—because while these kinds of power are no doubt based ultimately on economic power, their development can lag economic growth by decades. China is establishing the long-term sources of these different kinds of power through immense investment in education. It will be some decades, however, before it can challenge the United States—for example, in its capacity to project substantial military force to any corner of the globe. It will be a long time, if ever, before China could emulate the United States' position in recent decades as the world's leading power.

Primacy fades

China does not, however, have to replace the United States as the global hyper-power in order to overturn the US-led global order of recent decades. China's growing power can reshape the global order by challenging the United States' position in the new century's economic and strategic centre of gravity: Asia. China's growing economic weight will erode US strategic primacy in the Western Pacific—indeed, it is already doing so. This process has political, diplomatic, economic and military aspects. Others have written about the ways in which China has increased its diplomatic and economic influence in Asia in the past decade (Osbourne 2007). Here, I want to just touch on the specific military aspects of the power transition now under way in Asia. Economic strength is the foundation of strategic power, but military capability is its most direct and tangible expression, and economic growth shapes geo-strategic affairs most directly by supporting expanded military capabilities. The extent to which growing Chinese military capabilities reflect the geo-strategic significance of China's growing economic weight is often underestimated because US defence spending remains so much larger, and its aggregate capabilities remain so far superior. That, however, misses the point in two ways. First, China does not need to compete with the United States globally in order to erode US primacy in Asia. Second, China does not need to be able to emulate the United States in military capability, but simply limit US options. In both these respects, the military-strategic competition between the United States and China is asymmetrical, in ways that benefit China.

In military terms, American strategic primacy in Asia has been based on its capacity to exert what naval strategists call 'sea control' over the Western Pacific. Sea control is the ability to use the sea, especially to project force. The United States' military position in Asia has depended primarily on its capacity to project force by deploying aircraft carriers and amphibious forces anywhere in the Western Pacific with relatively low risk. Now, however, US sea control is slipping away as China develops the capacity to deny important areas of the Western Pacific—especially those closest to China—to the US Navy's surface fleet.

This process has been going on for some time. China's military priorities started to shift from continental to maritime capabilities after the collapse of the Soviet Union alleviated what had been its most pressing strategic risk. China started to acquire highly capable air and naval systems from its former Soviet adversaries in the early 1990s, and this process has accelerated since 1996. In that year, the United States deployed carriers to the waters around Taiwan in a show of support for Taipei after China used missile tests to intimidate Taiwanese voters in that year's presidential election. Historians might judge that this was the last time in which the United States could exercise the assured sea control that once characterised and in important ways constituted its strategic primacy in Asia. Since then, Chinese submarine forces have improved markedly, to the point where they now pose a significant threat to US carriers and other surface ships, and China has also reportedly developed more exotic sea-denial capabilities, including ballistic missiles capable of hitting aircraft carriers at long range. The costs and risks to the United States of deploying carriers or amphibious forces to the waters around Taiwan or elsewhere in China's extended maritime approaches—including around Korea and Japan—have already increased sharply. This limits US options and raises the threshold for intervention to the point that naval power projection might no longer be a viable military option for the United States in any future confrontation with China unless absolutely vital US interests are at stake. Moreover, the trends clearly suggest that this problem will intensify. Ten years from now, the costs and risks will be even higher, further raising the threshold of US military intervention in any strategic crisis in East Asia.

Of course, during the Cold War, the United States faced formidable Soviet sea-denial forces in the Western Pacific, but in those days it was clear that US strategic interests vis-a-vis the Soviet Union were so vital that the United States would accept huge strategic costs and risks to defend them. Since the Cold War, US interests in Asia are less compelling. Since 1989, successive US administrations have persuasively affirmed continued US interests and engagement in Asia, but all interests have their limits, and it is clear that nothing in Asia matters to the United States today as much as containing the Soviet Union did—unless it is to prevent the appearance of another strategic 'peer competitor'.

That leads us to the question of how the United States responds to China's challenge. First, however, we need to explore how serious that challenge is. The arguments presented so far suggest that the economic foundations and military dimensions of US primacy in Asia have already been significantly eroded as China's economy has grown, and will continue to do so in coming years. Some will argue, however, that the true foundations of US primacy are not to be found in its armed forces or its economic output, but in its ideas, values and institutions. This is a hard argument to evaluate. Clearly, many of what Americans regard as American values are highly attractive to many others around the world, including in Asia. The universality of these values, however, which US leaders so often assert,[6] tends to undermine their belief that they are distinctively American and that global support for them constitutes any substantial adjunct to US power. In the end, the argument that American values support US power probably presupposes that a significant proportion of the world's population believes that only in a global order dominated by the United States can those values flourish. There could be some truth in the basic proposition, but there is little evidence that many people in places such as China see things this way. They certainly seek many of the values that the United States champions, but they do not necessarily believe that only US global leadership can deliver them.

Of course, anyone who foreshadows the eclipse of US primacy in Asia must be uncomfortably aware that such predictions have been made and proved wrong many times before. Previous predictions, however, have been made at times of transient US uncertainty and have underestimated the country's remarkable power of reinvention and innovation. This time, it is different, because what threatens US primacy in Asia is not the grave but inevitably transient strategic and economic problems that beset the new president, but something much deeper. US primacy in Asia is not challenged by US weakness but by China's strength. This is new. Never before has US primacy been challenged at its most fundamental source— by its eclipse as the world's most productive economy.

The source of that challenge runs very deep. In a sense, it began a century ago, as the Chinese toppled the moribund empire and started trying to build a modern state that could regain China's traditional place in the world. That proved to be a long and tragic struggle, but today's China is the result. By adopting so many (though not all) of the economic, political, institutional and technological ideas that have made the rich world's workers so productive in the past two centuries, China is now within sight of regaining its position as the world's biggest economy, which its huge population secured for it until the Industrial Revolution boosted the United Kingdom's productivity so spectacularly. As China emulates the productivity of a modern advanced economy, its sheer scale ensures that it will end up producing more. In geo-strategy, destiny is not so much demographics alone, but the combination of demographics and labour productivity

For Americans, this prompts the uncomfortable speculation that US power has not resulted from any special quality of their country. Instead, it is a product of the simple circumstance that the United States has remained for more than a century the most populous country to have consistently maintained the productivity-promoting practices, policies and institutions that first appeared with the Industrial Revolution. It also enjoyed the advantage of being spared the worst ravages of war. Now, after 30 years of peace and stability during which market economics have been supported by relatively stable government at home and peace abroad, China is doing what the United States did, but on an even bigger scale.

Asia transforms

What does all this mean for Asia? China's economic growth has profound geo-strategic implications because it challenges the United States' economic primacy, which has been the foundation of US strategic primacy, which has in turn been the foundation of the international order that has kept East Asia so peaceful for nearly four decades. Since the early 1970s, Asia has enjoyed the most prosperous and cooperative period in its long history, and in retrospect, it seems clear that the main cause has been the emergence of a set of stable and uncompetitive strategic relationships between Asia's most powerful states: the United States, China and Japan. Former US President Richard Nixon's visit to China initiated this period, because it marked the point at which US strategic primacy in Asia ceased to be opposed actively by China. Instead, a stable triangular power balance evolved in which China and Japan both accepted US primacy in return for the assurance it gave them in relation to one another and to the Soviet Union. As a result, US failure in Vietnam was followed by decades of uncontested primacy, which created the necessary conditions for so much else: the success of the Association of South-East Asian Nations (ASEAN); Indochina's recovery; the economic growth of Japan, South Korea, Taiwan and China; Asia's regional integration; and Australia's enmeshment in Asia.[7]

As the economic foundation of the United States' primacy erodes, the Asian order that has been built on it will change. There is no reason to expect that China will continue to accept US primacy as the basis of the regional order in Asia while its own power approaches and exceeds the United States', and it therefore no longer need rely on the United States for assurance against Russia and Japan. Of course, China will want Asia to remain peaceful and harmonious, but it will not see US primacy as necessary for that. It will see increased Chinese power and influence in Asia as perfectly compatible with the perpetuation of a stable and cooperative regional order. Whether that proves to be correct or not will depend on how China chooses to use its growing power, and on how others respond.

It is hard to get a clear picture of Chinese ideas about its future role in Asia. China's own history offers little guidance, because it has never before exercised great power in an Asia of modern nation-states. In one view, Beijing might be content to establish a modest sphere of influence over its immediate periphery, but its immediate periphery includes Japan, so even this apparently modest goal would require it to establish clear primacy over the other major Asian power. It seems inevitable therefore that China will aim for a wider leadership role in Asia; but of what kind? There is no evidence that Beijing seeks the kind of 'hard' militarised hegemony that we associate with the communist strategic policies of Joseph Stalin and Leonid Brezhnev. Certainly, Chinese military developments do not support such fears. It is much more likely that China will seek a kind of 'soft' hegemony, comparable with the leadership that the United States exercises in the Western hemisphere under the Monroe Doctrine. As keen students of history, the Chinese would understand that the Monroe Doctrine has delivered the United States substantial economic, political and strategic benefits at relatively low cost for a very long time. It is hard to see why they should want anything more—but it is also not clear why, as its power grows, China would aim for anything less.

Much will therefore depend on how the United States responds to China's rise. 'Monroe-style' primacy cannot be shared, so for China to achieve this ambition, the United States would need—perhaps very gradually—to concede its strategic position in Asia to China and withdraw. That seems on the face of it rather unlikely—as Secretary of State, Hillary Clinton (2009), said recently, 'The United States is not ceding the Pacific to anyone'—but it cannot be completely discounted. Two other outcomes are, however, more probable: either the United States elects to share power with China or it tries to maintain primacy by contesting China's challenge. Whichever option the United States takes, Asia's international order emerges very different from the one that has served the region so well for the past almost four decades. Moreover, any of them would be likely to carry significantly greater risks of strategic competition and even conflict between Asia's major powers than we have seen since the Vietnam War. US withdrawal would substantially increase the intensity of strategic competition between China and Japan. A US decision to contest China's challenge would inevitably increase strategic competition between them and probably lead to a polarisation of the region into US and Chinese camps. Even a decision by the United States to share power with China would entail a risky and complex negotiation involving not only these two powers but Japan and eventually India to establish what would in effect be a concert of Asia's major powers.[8]

Unfortunately, the most risky of these outcomes is also the most probable. To share power with China under some kind of concert arrangement would require the United States to treat China as an equal in every respect of international power: acknowledging unreservedly the legitimacy of its political system, its international interests even when they clash with the United States' and—within the limits set by the UN Charter—the legitimacy of China using its armed forces to protect those interests. It does not seem at all likely that the United States will in fact be willing to concede this much to China, and it is unlikely to do so unless and until it is brought face-to-face with the costs and risks of any alternative way of responding to China's growing power. There is an element of denial in US approaches to the strategic implications of China's rise: a reluctance to accept and address the direct implications of well-established trends. The result is an unexamined assumption that for the United States, retaining primacy in Asia is the only possible strategic objective. US debates have not yet, however, faced the question of how far they are willing to go and how much they are willing to spend to preserve primacy against a country that can match the United States in economic output.

China also has hard choices to make if it is to help build a power-sharing 'concert of Asia'. It will have to forgo aspirations to lead Asia itself and accept that the United States will remain a major player—and a major constraint on China's freedom of action. Even harder, perhaps, would be the need for China to accept Japan as an equal participant in Asia's strategic affairs. Japan is too strong to be left out of the top tier of any new Asian order and it is hard to see how it could remain a strategic client of the United States within a concert of Asia. The cooperative US–China relationship that would be required for a concert of Asia to work would be too close for Japan to be comfortable about relying on the United States for protection from China's power. The stronger Beijing becomes, and the more important to Washington it grows, the less sure Tokyo can be that Washington will always put Japanese interests ahead of Beijing's. Unless Tokyo can establish an independent strategic position, with all that that entails, it can therefore be expected to exercise a strong and probably effective veto over US–China strategic accommodation.

Overcoming all these obstacles would take remarkable diplomacy and statecraft from all three major powers. That makes it unlikely that we will see a new concert of Asia that will accommodate China's growing economic and strategic weight. More probably, we will see a steady increase in strategic competition between the United States and China. It is important to recognise that this is not necessarily China's fault. China's growth is certainly driving geo-strategic change in Asia, but how that change unfolds and what it means for Asia depend as much on how other countries respond as on how China seeks to use this power.

Hard choices

It is tempting to see the challenges to Asia's geo-strategic order posed by China's growing economic weight as a problem for the next generation of policymakers, or indeed to deny that it is a problem at all. The first response seems to be exemplified by Australia's new Defence White Paper, which while acknowledging, as we have seen, the speed and significance of China's economic rise, nonetheless defers any serious policy response to the 2020s and beyond. The second response typifies that of most in the US policy community, who either assume that China's economic growth will stall before it can overtake the United States or that US primacy can somehow be sustained—by soft or hard power or by both—long after the economic power that underpins it has been overtaken.

The reasons for these evasions are plain. Acknowledging the geo-strategic implications of Asia's economic transformation impels policymakers and analysts towards momentous and profoundly difficult choices. For Americans, the choice is between order and primacy. For decades, there has been no such choice, because US primacy has been the essential condition of Asia's stability. In future, however, the United States might be able to sustain primacy only at the expense of order. An effort to maintain US primacy would involve the construction of a coalition of US allies to contest the Chinese challenge to the United States' position, of which the trilateral alignment of the United States, Japan and Australia— and the quadrilateral alignment involving India as well—can be seen as the first rough drafts. Such moves risk drawing Asia towards a divided future dominated by strategic competition between armed camps. The costs of such a future in terms of lost opportunities for trade, investment and integration of all kinds are potentially immense, and the risks of all-out conflict are significant too. It is easy to mount arguments as to why

Americans would prefer not to share power in Asia with China; it is harder to explain why the costs and risks of doing so outweigh the costs and risks of entering sustained strategic competition with a country of China's immense strategic potential. History might be a poor guide here: China is not the Soviet Union. The United States cannot be sure that it would win such a competition, or that victory in such a competition, if it could be attained, would be worth the cost.

The United States' allies in Asia likewise face tough choices once they confront the geo-strategic implications of China's rise. For Australia, the choices are especially momentous, because the eclipse of US primacy would mark not just the end of the post-Vietnam order that has kept Asia so peaceful and Australia so secure in recent decades. It would mark the end of the Anglo-Saxon maritime domination of Asia, which has been seen by Australians as the necessary and sufficient condition for their security since a colony was founded at Sydney Cove in 1788. Australians need to decide whether they should follow their traditions and instincts by urging the United States to contest the Chinese challenge to this deepest foundation of Australian security, or whether they owe the forces of history and encourage the United States to accept a different, lesser but still critical role in Asia as a balancer of China in a concert of equals. And if, regardless of what they say, the United States decides to contest China's challenge, Australians would need to decide whether they should support the United States in doing so or slide towards an uneasy and insecure neutrality. Either way, Australia faces much greater strategic risks than it has been used to since the 1960s.

References

Bell, C. 2008, *The End of the Vasco da Gama Era*, The Lowy Institute, Sydney.

Castles, I. 2008, 'PPP is not "basically a con"', *East Asia Forum*, 3 December 2008, <www.eastasiaforum.org/2008/12/03/ppp-is-not-basically-a-con/>

Central Intelligence Agency (CIA) 2008, *Global Trends: 2025 report*, November, Central Intelligence Agency, Washington, DC, <http://www.dni.gov/nic/PDF_2025/2025_Global_Trends_Final_Report.pdf>

Clinton, H. 2009, Remarks at the global press conference, Foreign Press Centre, Washington, DC, 19 May.

Commonwealth of Australia 2009, *Defending Australia in the Asia-Pacific Century: Force 2030*, Department of Defence, Canberra.

Friedman, G. 2008, *The Next One Hundred Years*, Doubleday, New York.

Gates, R. M. 2009, 'A balanced strategy: reprogramming the Pentagon for a new age', *Foreign Affairs*, vol. 88, no. 1 (January–February), pp. 28–40.

Kagan, R. 2008, *The Return of History and the End of Dreams*, Knopf, New York.

Mearsheimer, J. 2001, *The Tragedy of Great Power Politics*, Norton, New York.

Obama, B. 2009, Remarks by the President on a new beginning, Cairo University, Cairo, Egypt, 4 June 2009, <http://www.whitehouse.gov/the_press_office/Remarks-by-the-President-at-Cairo-University-6-04-09/>

Osbourne, M. 2007, *The Paramount Power*, The Lowy Institute, Sydney, <http://www.lowyinstitute.org/Publication.asp?pid=370>

White, H. 2008a, 'Australia in Asia: exploring the conditions for security in the Asian century', in D. I. Shambaugh and M. B. Yahuda (eds), *International Relations of Asia*, Rowan and Littlefield, Lanham, Ml., pp. 215–33.

—— 2008b, 'Why war in Asia remains thinkable', *Survival*, issue 6 (December), pp. 85–104, <http://www.informaworld.com/smpp/b=all~content=t713659919~tab=issueslist~branches=50-v5050>

Yueh, L. 2009, *Law and Economics of Globalisation*, Elgar, United Kindom.

Zakaria, F. 2008, *The Post American World*, Norton, New York.

Endnotes

1. Four notable examples are Zakaria (2008); Kagan (2008); Bell (2008); CIA (2008).
2. See, for example, Mearsheimer (2001).
3. This argument is explored in Yueh (2009).
4. See also Friedman (2008).
5. See an interesting essay by Castles (2008).
6. For the latest example, see Obama (2009).
7. For a fuller account of this view of Asia's recent strategic history, see White (2008b).
8. For further exploration of these issues, see White (2008a).

China's exchange rate policy, its current account surplus and the global imbalances[1]

6

W. Max Corden[*]

This chapter is stimulated by current views prevalent in the United States about Chinese exchange rate policy. The Chinese currency, the renminbi (RMB), was fixed to the US dollar from 1997 to 2005. In July 2005, a new regime was instituted, and from then on there was some appreciation of the RMB–dollar rate. It appreciated cumulatively about 9 per cent by the end of 2007. In general, US critics have not considered this appreciation as being sufficient. The common argument was that, if the RMB were allowed to float, it would appreciate substantially more and this would reduce China's high current account surplus as well as the US deficit. In this view, the Chinese exchange rate regime and policy within the regime have been (more or less) the causes of the current account imbalance. It is implied that the Chinese exchange rate intervention caused the Chinese current account surplus and at least played a role in causing the overall US current account deficit.[2]

Table 6.1 shows the Chinese current account surplus as a percentage of gross domestic product (GDP) from 2000 to 2008. Of course, these figures give the overall Chinese surplus and not just the bilateral surplus with the United States.

Table 6.1   China: surplus on current account (per cent of GDP)

2000	1.7	2005	7.2
2001	1.3	2006	9.5
2002	2.4	2007	11.0
2003	2.8	2008	10.0
2004	3.6		

Source: International Monetary Fund (IMF) 2009, *World Economic Outlook*, April 2009, International Monetary Fund, Washington, DC.

Until 2005, China was criticised for fixing the value of the RMB to the US dollar. After that it was criticised for not allowing the RMB to appreciate enough. The real objection, however, was clearly to the large current account surplus, rather than to a fixed exchange rate per se. After all, fixing an exchange rate to the dollar was common under the Bretton Woods system, and even after the general breakdown of this system some countries (notably in Latin America) fixed their exchange rates to the dollar without any complaints from the United States. Furthermore, there are no International Monetary Fund (IMF) rules that prohibit this. Similarly, there can be no good objection to some intervention in the foreign exchange market. Many countries have exchange rate regimes that involve some management or 'manipulation'.

Section one of this chapter discusses the relationship between exchange rate intervention and the current account outcome in the Chinese case. Section two discusses the possible reasons or justifications for Chinese policies and developments that have led to this outcome. Finally, section three deals with the implications for other countries, particularly the United States, of China's current account surplus and of China's growth. This discussion includes some reflections on how Chinese surpluses have been related to the current world credit crisis. Is China to blame?

This chapter is written in memory of James Meade, whose student I was in the 1950s. Inevitably, I have absorbed his taxonomic approach and therefore will expound various alternative views or positions.

The role of the exchange rate and other factors in determining China's surplus

Many kinds of exchange rate regimes are compatible with a current account surplus

It could be argued that exchange rate regimes are not really connected with global current account imbalances. Global current account imbalances have been associated with all kinds of exchange rate regimes. Spain has a large deficit while the Netherlands has a surplus; yet both have a fixed exchange rate to the euro—that is, they are both part of the euro zone. Of course, the euro itself floats relative to the principal non-euro currencies. In the 1980s, the US current account deficit and the Japanese surplus were the main international imbalances and Japan certainly had to suffer continuous criticism from the United States. Now, again, Japan is one of the major surplus countries and, as usual, the United States is the major deficit country. Both the United States and Japan, however, have floating rate regimes—and in the case of Japan there is only occasional intervention. A floating rate regime between them is therefore obviously no inhibition to a current account imbalance.

Suppose a country has a floating exchange rate regime with no intervention in the foreign exchange market at all. Nevertheless, its government wishes to induce a current account surplus, with the accompanying depreciation of the exchange rate. This is certainly possible if there is international capital mobility. The government can loosen monetary policy and so induce capital outflow through the lower domestic interest rate. Alternatively, it can contract fiscal policy, leading to a reduced budget deficit and thus, again, a lower domestic interest rate and thus depreciation, capital outflow and a current account surplus. In both cases exchange rate intervention is not needed to bring about a current account surplus. This argument does not, however, apply to China because capital outflows are strictly controlled, as is the interest rate.

Why did China's current account surplus increase?

How then does the system work in China? What determines the current account balance? In particular, why did the current account surplus increase so sharply from 2005 (Table 6.1)? The diagrammatic exposition in the next section is my attempt at a stylised story. There are two essential points. The first is that the current account balance has not been planned by the central authorities but rather has been an unplanned by-product of a variety of developments and policies. Exchange rate policy, as reflected in intervention in the market, has just been one part of the story. Hence, the remarkable increase in the surplus from 2005 (as shown in Table 6.1) was not necessarily intended by central policymakers. The second point is that exchange rate policy can and does affect the surplus: if it were desired to reduce the surplus, a policy that brought about significant real appreciation could achieve it. In practice, however, exchange rate policy has been targeted on another objective, which I shall discuss.

Where did the sudden rise in the surplus from 2005 come from? First, let me summarise the point of view of Anderson (2008). In this view, which tells only one part of the story, 'the main shock was a dramatic fall in import growth' (Anderson: 62). The turn around 'came almost completely from net trade in heavy industrial products (aluminium, machine tools, cement, key chemical products, and especially steel and steel products)'. This was the result of an earlier domestic investment boom in that category of products, which, in turn, was stimulated by an earlier rise in domestic demand for such products. At the same time, between 2002 and 2006, national savings increased by more than 10 per cent of GDP. This, in turn, came from the corporate sector, and especially the heavy industrial sector. Anderson gives more details, but his main point is that the increased current account surplus resulted from a combination of a rise in the excess of savings over investment and a decline in the growth rate of imports, both originating in a particular sector of the economy.

Figure 6.1 China's merchandise trade, 2000–07 (US$ billion)

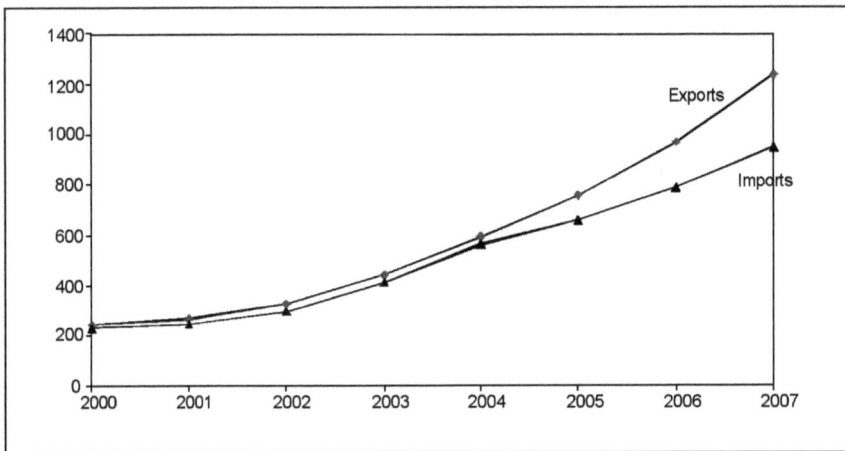

Source: Based on data compiled from UN Comtrade database.

There have, however, also been other factors.[3] The overall picture is that there has been an acceleration of the rate of growth of exports and a decline in the rate of growth of imports (Figure 6.1). The average annual rate of growth of exports increased from 23.8 per cent (2000–04) to 26.3 per cent (2005–07), while the average annual rate of import growth declined from 26.3 per cent (2000–04) to 19.8 per cent (2005–07). There have been steady productivity improvements in the labour-intensive exports sector. Furthermore, as is pointed out in Athukorala (2009), in 2001, China joined the World Trade Organisation (WTO) and this significantly improved the attractiveness of China's domestic investment climate for export-oriented production. Consequently, the process of relocation to China (from Japan, Taiwan and South Korea especially) of final assembly activities of information and communication technology products accelerated. This showed up in the export statistics with a time lag.

How it all fits together: a diagram

Allowing for considerable oversimplifications, the Swan diagram (from Swan 1963) is helpful, especially in illustrating the sharp increase in China's current account surplus. It is a diagrammatic summary of one of the main messages that originated in James Meade's classic *The Balance of Payments* (1951).

In Figure 6.2, the vertical axis shows an index of China's competitiveness. An upward movement can be brought about by a real depreciation or by an improvement in productivity in export and import-competing industries. As I have noted, there have been steady productivity improvements in labour-intensive exports. In addition, on the import-competing side, one can regard the expansion of heavy industrial product industries, as highlighted in the Anderson story, as also being a productivity improvement. As noted above, WTO accession contributed significantly to improve investor confidence in the Chinese economy and this might also be regarded as a productivity improvement in the export sector.

Figure 6.2   The Swan diagram for China

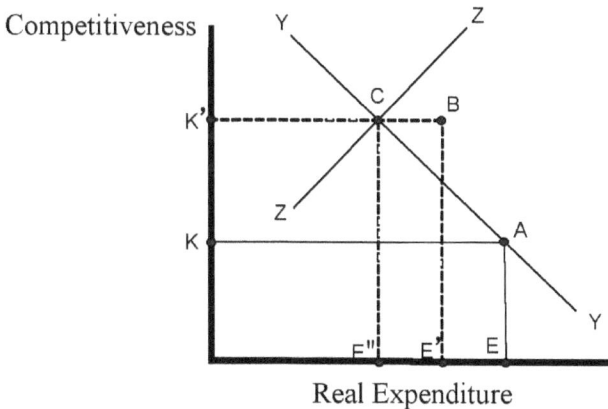

We start with competitiveness at K. It is determined primarily by the real exchange rate. It increases to K' from 2005 to 2007 owing to the productivity improvements just discussed, slightly offset by real appreciation owing to the change in the exchange rate regime in 2005. The horizontal axis shows total expenditure, on consumption and on investment. We start at E. A decline in consumption (rise in savings) brings expenditure to the left, to E'. This would also result from a decline in investment. The line or curve YY is the 'internal balance' line. Internal balance can be defined as the target level of spending on home-produced goods designed to avoid excessive inflation while maximising domestic output. The line shows various combinations of competitiveness and expenditure that would attain such internal balance.

In the diagram, we start in internal balance at point A. The improvement in competitiveness combined with the increase in saving (decline in expenditure) would bring the system to point B. This is, however, a situation of excess demand or potential inflation, so monetary policy in the form of controls on bank lending induces a reduction in expenditure, whether on lending for consumption or for investment, bringing expenditure down to E'' and the new equilibrium to C. If the current account had been in balance at A (hence savings were equal to investment and expenditure equalled income), it would be in surplus at C.

A movement upwards along the YY curve improves the current account (greater surplus or reduced deficit).[4]

Thus, in China's case, monetary policy has been targeted on the internal balance objective. This has been broadly achieved. In principle, competitiveness could then be targeted on the current account objective. Competitiveness depends, however, on much more than the nominal exchange rate, especially when it is a bilateral nominal rate. Since inflation in China and its trading partners has not been high, perhaps there has not been a great difference between the (trade-weighted) nominal and the real exchange rate. There is, however, uncertainty about productivity changes in the tradeable sectors and these cannot really be controlled. Thus policy could not easily regulate the movement from K to K'. Furthermore, the position of the internal balance line is also uncertain and this line can move about in response to productivity changes in the non-tradeable sectors as well as structural changes and demand patterns in the economy.

It follows that the current account outcome is to some extent endogenous. Nevertheless, if the Chinese authorities were really determined to reduce or even eliminate the surplus they could presumably do so by sufficient nominal appreciation of the exchange rate. In order to maintain internal balance this would have to be associated with an easing of monetary policy leading to an increase in real expenditure. Just as variations and flexibility in monetary policy can roughly achieve and maintain internal balance, so a flexible exchange rate policy might be able to achieve and maintain an external balance objective. At the same time, it needs to be remembered from the discussion above that the steep increase in the surplus from 2005 was not the result of deliberate shifts in exchange rate policy and was, indeed, not easily predictable. The main point, to be discussed below, is that exchange rate policy has not been targeted on external balance—that is, on a current account objective. There have been other objectives.

The motivations for China's policies

The Chinese current account surpluses, and especially the big increases in them since 2005, are by-products of various developments, such as productivity improvements, but also of a variety of policies, including, of course—perhaps crucially—exchange rate policy. I shall now review these policies and their implications

The first policy is to maintain what I (following Meade) have called 'internal balance', but is generally described as avoiding, or limiting, inflation, while adequately stimulating the economy through monetary policy. The monetary effects of exchange rate intervention must then be sterilised. This policy has been broadly successful and the objective can hardly be disputed.[5]

The second policy is to intervene in the foreign exchange market so as to prevent excessive appreciation relative to the US dollar and, to an extent, stabilise the exchange rate. It is this policy that has been under continuous criticism in the US Congress and by some US economists. The policy is defended by Fan Gang, a Professor at the Chinese Academy of the Social Sciences, who gives a useful Chinese point of view that I paraphrase here (Fan 2008).

The primary purpose of Chinese exchange rate policy is to maintain employment in export industries and, presumably, also related employment in urban areas. Furthermore, large variations in the exchange rate would lead to speculation and China's immature and fragile financial system would not be able to bear those risks. In addition, the Chinese are opposed to large policy changes; they prefer to move policies in small steps. In any case, it is not clear what the long-run equilibrium exchange rate should be or what rate would finally satisfy the US Congress.

To summarise, there have been two parts to Chinese exchange rate policy. The first part is 'exchange rate protection'—namely, a policy designed to maintain profitability and employment in the export sector by means of undervaluation of the exchange rate.[6] The second part is to maintain a stable exchange rate, avoiding a floating rate and sharp changes in a fixed but adjustable rate. US critics of Chinese exchange rate policy have frequently advocated either that the RMB should float or that there should be a steep once-for-all appreciation. Hence, there have been two reasons for rejecting this advice.

Third, for some years after the East Asian financial crisis of 1997–98, China, as well as other East Asian countries, built up foreign exchange reserves deliberately as a form of self-insurance. It was provision against a balance-of-payments crisis so as to avoid the need to call for rescue from the IMF. At least since 2006, however, China's reserves have been well above the level that seemed to be required.

The fourth set of policies explains why national savings by households and private and public corporations have been remarkably high.[7] Relative to GDP, aggregate savings are estimated to have been about 50 per cent of GDP in 2006. There are several relevant policies here. Household savings have been fairly high (about 15 per cent of GDP in 2006) owing to reduced social welfare arrangements, lack of pensions and the inadequacy of financial intermediation (Woo 2008). Enterprise savings have been exceptionally high (28 per cent of GDP in 2006) and have steadily increased owing to low wages and an absence of payments of taxes or dividends to the government.[8] The labour share of industrial value added in China during 2002–05 was less than 30 per cent (compared with an industrial-country average of more than 65 per cent). Notwithstanding reported increases in average urban wages, unskilled workers' wages have not increased much because of continuous massive labour inflows from the rural economy to urban centres. The outcome has thus been a persistent increase in company profits and thus savings.

The net result of the current account surplus and intervention in the foreign exchange market has been that by 2008 the central bank held nearly US$2000 billion of reserves—a substantial part held in the form of US Treasuries. While some build-up of reserves made sense as a precaution against a balance-of-payments crisis, this amount of reserves can hardly be justified other than as a by-product of other policies that I have just described—policies that were either seen as desirable for other reasons or could not easily be changed.[9]

It could thus be argued that the policies that led to such large current account surpluses and the build-up of massive foreign financial assets have not been in the Chinese interest. It surely cannot be in the long-term Chinese interest to accumulate vast amounts of dollar-denominated foreign assets (notably US Treasuries) earning a low return and very likely to lose real value relative to the prices of non-dollar goods owing to continued dollar depreciation. By 2007, the Chinese authorities seemed to be well aware of this and planned to diversify their international investments. Also, probably China's national savings have been too high for a reason I have just mentioned above—namely, that state-owned enterprises have used their profits for investment (or deposited them with banks) rather than paying more as dividends to the government. These extra government revenues could have been used to provide various much-needed government services to a population that, in part at least, is still quite poor.

On the other hand, it might have been rational to park temporarily a significant proportion of Chinese savings abroad until the public administration system had improved, to allow more funds to be distributed to provincial governments for various social and infrastructure improvements. In addition, the capital market and banking system might also have needed improvements before some of the internationally accumulated funds could be efficiently invested domestically. Temporarily, some of China's savings have thus been parked abroad, awaiting improvements in public sector management and in the capital market. I emphasise the word 'temporarily'. I have called this the 'parking theory' (Corden 2007).

On balance, this has probably not been a conscious motive explaining the massive accumulation of reserves. The explanations given earlier are sufficient. The 'parking theory' can be used not to explain the motivation of real policies but rather to assess the net result of these policies. Has the net result been favourable for China? My suggestion is that it might indeed have been favourable, but only in the short run. With the accumulated reserves steadily growing, the net result—the degree of 'parking'—went too far, at least by 2007.

International implications of China's surplus and growth

How some countries' surpluses led to other countries' deficits

For the world as a whole, total current account surpluses must add up to other countries' deficits. These surpluses and deficits make up the 'global imbalances' that have been of so much concern. The main concern has been that deficit countries—notably, the country with the biggest deficit, the United States—cannot run such deficits indefinitely.

The world general equilibrium effects of the Chinese surplus cannot be analysed on their own. They must be aggregated with the effects of all the other surpluses (the main surplus countries having been China, Japan, Germany, the various oil exporters and East Asian developing countries other than mainland China). In 2007, the Chinese surplus was 21.4 per cent of the total surplus of all the surplus countries. These were the 'savings glut' countries—namely, the countries where savings exceeded investment, even though in some cases the surpluses resulted from declines in investment rather than increases in savings.[10]

Treating these surpluses as *exogenous*—determined by a variety of factors influencing total savings and investment in each country—they led to a fall in the world real interest rate. One should also take into account here the moderating effect on the fall of the world real interest rate of the exogenous increase in the US fiscal deficit (explained by political factors). This fall in the real rate of interest led in many countries, especially in the United States, to a credit boom and thus to increases in borrowing for investment and for consumption. These increases in spending generated deficits in many countries and possibly also reduced some surpluses. This was the *endogenous* effect of the decline in real interest rates that created the current account deficits to match the surpluses of the 'savings-glut' countries.[11]

It follows that through the world general equilibrium process involving a sharp decline in the world real interest rate, the surplus of China was a part-cause of the deficit of the United States. The exogenous increase in the politically determined US fiscal deficit (or shift from surplus to deficit), however, as well as the exogenously determined surpluses of savings-glut countries other than China, also contributed to explaining the US deficit.

It is worth noting that if US savings had not declined as much as they did, the US deficit might indeed have been avoided, or moderated. The worldwide fall in interest rates and the credit boom would, however, have been greater. Therefore, other countries would have had to borrow more and thus go into greater deficits. Alternatively, in the absence of such extra borrowing, recessions would have developed in many countries, essentially because an excess of world savings was not absorbed sufficiently by extra private investment or government borrowing. Equilibrium would then be restored in a Keynesian process through falling incomes.

Sectoral effects of the surpluses of the 'savings-glut' countries

What were the effects of the surpluses of China and the other savings-glut countries on various sections or interest groups in the deficit countries? For brevity, I will refer specifically to the United States, as it has been the principal deficit country. Also, China has had the largest surplus since 2006, so it will represent all surplus countries. It is important to bear in mind that I am not concerned here with bilateral balances. Essentially the effects in the United States (and other deficit countries) come under two headings—namely, trade effects and capital market effects.

Beginning with the trade effects of China's surplus, China exports mainly labour-intensive goods and their prices have fallen relative to the general price level in the United States. Hence, US producers of such goods have been adversely affected. The adverse effect on US import-competing producers, reflected in relatively lower wages and perhaps increased unemployment, has been the main effect that has carried political weight. It explains hostility to China ('China-bashing') in Congress and the US pressure for appreciation of the RMB. The other side of this coin is that consumers of such goods in the United States have benefited. As I will note below, US exporters to China have benefited from China's high growth (though not from its real productivity-adjusted depreciation). These exporters have probably been the main interest group that has acted as a counterweight to the 'China-bashers'.

The extraordinary growth of China, rather than just its current account surplus, has increased demand for many commodities and thus benefited producers of oil and of commodities such as iron ore, copper and coal, which are exported by many countries, notably the oil exporters, but also countries such as Australia, Brazil and Chile. Exporters of various other products, especially capital goods and 'high-tech' products, often coming from the United States or Germany, have also benefited. Chinese growth has, however, also harmed other countries, especially importers of oil.

The capital market effects in the United States of the Chinese surplus are usually not so clearly perceived. Lower interest rates benefit all borrowers, and especially the US government, which is a major borrower. Hence, future US taxpayers benefit. On the other hand, Americans who are savers lose.

What about the value of the dollar relative to other industrial-country currencies, especially the euro and the yen? Since a large part of surplus countries' accumulation of foreign reserves (notably of China) has gone into dollar-denominated securities or investments of various kinds, especially US Treasuries, the surpluses have kept the dollar up, in spite of the growing US deficit. This also, of course, has had sectoral positive and negative effects.

Looking at the total effects of all these worldwide relative price changes, positive and negative, one cannot really say clearly whether the net effects of the surpluses of China and other 'savings-glut' countries have been beneficial or not for the rest of the world. One must certainly remind politicians and the public that cheaper imports from China have benefits for consumers and that lower interest rates and readier availability of credit certainly have benefits for government treasuries and private sector borrowers. Indeed, a major beneficiary has been the US Treasury and hence US taxpayers in the future.

It might be sufficient to make the point that when China, at the margin, exports goods to other countries in exchange for importing bonds and other financial instruments—especially from the United States—it is engaging in *inter-temporal* trade. There are likely to be gains from this kind of trade as from the usual trade in goods and services (Corden 2007).

The causes of the current crisis: is China to blame?

It has been argued that the current world credit crisis has its origin in the excessive credit expansion in the United States and elsewhere, and in turn this has had its underlying origin in the high savings of the 'savings-glut' countries, which include China. This credit expansion led to excessive leverage, the housing booms and, in general, to irresponsible lending by financial intermediaries and to unwise or excessive borrowing by households, private equity and (to a lesser extent) non-financial firms. While in the developing-country debt crises of the 1980s and 1990s the blame was generally put on the borrowers, this time some would put the blame on the original lenders—that is, the net savers, especially China.

High savings need not—and should not—lead to crises. It is not unreasonable that in some countries savings exceed investment, for whatever reasons, and in others investment exceeds saving. There is an international capital market and its role is to intermediate between lenders and borrowers, just as such a market intermediates within countries. As expounded above, the mechanism of adjustment is the world real interest rate. Such an international market makes international inter-temporal trade possible, just as markets make possible ordinary trade in goods and services.

What, then, has gone wrong to create the disastrous world credit crisis, leading to worldwide recession?

Before the crisis, when world savings increased, there seemed to be a lack of demand for funds from private corporations, or even governments, that wished to borrow and invest in order to increase physical or human capital, and where a reasonable return could be expected. In the United States, in the case of the private non-financial corporations, this reluctance to borrow is explained by the rebound from the 'dot com' bubble. In Latin American and East Asian countries other than China, it is explained by the rebound from earlier debt crises. Perhaps the financial intermediaries did not try hard enough to find such customers who were willing to borrow for investment with good prospects. Alternatively, one could simply regard these special explanations as pointing to an unfortunate coincidence. Just when world savings increased sharply, sound investment opportunities had declined.

The result was that much lending took place for more risky purposes, especially residential housing, and for consumption. This was the result of the so-called 'search for yield'. In the United States, in effect consumption rather than investment was mainly financed. Also, the gap in demand for funds was partially filled by the US fiscal deficit, which resulted from tax cuts and the need to finance the Iraq war. It might be recalled that John Maynard Keynes focused on the lack of perceived investment opportunities ('animal spirits') as a major cause of lack of aggregate demand. In this case, world aggregate demand was maintained for some years, principally by increased US private consumption as well as, earlier, the US fiscal deficit, but perhaps at the cost of a later crisis.

Thus, there are several steps in the story. First there was the 'savings glut' coming principally from Japan, China, the oil exporters and Germany. Then there was the lack of sufficient demand for funds for fruitful investment for a variety of special reasons. Thus, the high savings were not matched adequately by sound investment worldwide. Finally, there was the response in the world capital market, leading to 'search for yield', excessive leverage, unwise lending, and so on. Hence China played a role in initiating this sad story, although—as I have noted earlier—in 2007, the Chinese surplus was only 21.4 per cent of the total surplus of all the surplus countries.

There has, however, been another factor explaining the crisis. This is simply that the large financial intermediation industry, including commercial banks and prominently including investment banks has failed to do its job properly. The 'fatal flaw' has been the invention and use of new financial instruments that have been poorly understood and have created a serious information problem. Instead of the declining phase of a US housing bubble having an adverse financial impact that was confined to a limited number of US states, the manner of financing through securitisation of mortgages and their purchase worldwide created a worldwide financial crisis.

Conclusion

Finally, what has been the impact of China's growth, as distinct from its surplus, on the world economy? China's entry into the world economy has certainly been a major shock. And that is not just because it has generated exceptionally large current account surpluses since 2005. Even more important, it has created over a much longer period the shock of its massive growth acceleration.

Its government has chosen to be exceptionally outward looking in its approach. The Chinese emphasis has been on export expansion rather than just import substitution. This approach has been consistently urged on developing countries by advisors from industrialised countries, and in this Chinese case has been notably fruitful. Surely, the world has to adapt to China's growth and its dramatic transformation, welcoming the reduction of Chinese poverty and enjoying the improved terms of trade that incidentally China has effectively bestowed on many of its trading partners. From Australia and many other countries, it is buying more commodities; from the United States, it is buying more government bonds (of which the US Treasury has been a massive supplier) and many other goods and services, and to many countries, notably the United States; and in Europe, it is selling more labour-intensive goods. All these effects have improved its trading partners' terms of trade. Of course, there are also losers. These include producers of labour-intensive goods in industrialised and developing countries. The Chinese shock is, however, one that should be lived with, adapted to and not resisted.

References

Anderson, J. 2008, 'China's industrial investment boom and the renminbi', in M. Goldstein and N. R. Lardy (eds), *Debating China's Exchange Rate Policy*, Peterson Institute for International Economics, Washington, DC.

Athukorala, P. 2009, 'The rise of China and East Asian export performance: is the crowding out fear warranted?', *The World Economy*, vol. 32, pp. 234–66.

Athukorala, P. and Yamashita, N. 2009, 'Global production sharing and Sino–US trade relations', *China and World Economy*, vol.17, pp. 39–56.

Bernanke, B. S. 2005, *The Global Savings Glut and the US Current Account Deficit*, Federal Reserve Board, Washington, DC.

Corden, W. M. 1994 *Economic Policy, Exchange Rates, and the International System*, Oxford University Press and Chicago University Press, Oxford and Chicago.

—— 2007, 'Those current account imbalances: a sceptical view', *The World Economy*, vol. 30, pp. 363–82.

Fan, G. 2008, 'Renminbi revaluation and US dollar depreciation', in M. Goldstein and N. R. Lardy (eds), *Debating China's Exchange Rate Policy*, Peterson Institute for International Economics, Washington, DC.

Goldstein, M. and Lardy, N. R. 2005, 'China's revaluation shows size really matters', *Financial Times*, 22 July.

Goldstein, M. and Lardy, N. R. (eds) 2008, *Debating China's Exchange Rate Policy*, Peterson Institute for International Economics, Washington, DC.

Meade, J. E. 1951, *The Balance of Payments*, Oxford University Press, London.

Riedel, J., Jing, J. and Jian, G. 2007, *How China Grows: Investment, finance, and reform*, Princeton University Press, Princeton.

Siebert, H. 2007, 'China: coming to grips with new global player', *The World Economy*, vol. 30, pp. 893–922.

Swan, T. W. 1963, 'Longer-run problems of the balance of payments', in H. W. Arndt and W. M. Corden (eds), *The Australian Economy: A volume of readings*, Cheshire, Melbourne.

Wolf, M. 2008, *Fixing Global Finance*, Johns Hopkins University Press, Baltimore.

Woo, W. T. 2008, 'Understanding the sources of friction in U.S.–China trade relations: the exchange rate debate diverts attention away from optimum adjustment', *Asian Economic Papers*, vol. 7, pp.65–99.

Yu, Y. 2007, 'Global Imbalances and China', *The Australian Economic Review*, vol. 40, pp. 3–23.

Endnotes

* © The Royal Economic Society 2009. This paper appears in the *Economic Journal* (vol. 119, issue 541) and is printed here with permission of the Royal Economic Society.

1. At the James Meade Centenary Meeting at the Bank of England on 12 July 2007, I presented a paper entitled 'Exchange rate policies and the global imbalances'. The present chapter, essentially completed in March 2009, is a substantially revised and expanded version of this 2007 paper. For excellent and comprehensive overviews of Chinese issues, I have found particularly useful Riedel et al. (2007), Siebert (2007), Yu (2007) and Woo (2008). I am indebted to Jim Riedel for an understanding of Chinese macroeconomic processes and to Prema-chandra Athukorala and David Vines for valuable comments on a draft of this chapter.

2. The best reference on US attitudes, and many aspects of the RMB issue, is Goldstein and Lardy (2008). The critical view of Chinese policy can be found particularly in the contribution in that volume by Michael Mussa, while a thorough review of US Congressional attitudes is in the contributions of Gary Clyde Hufbauer and Claire Brunel, and of Stephen S. Roach. For an earlier view that more RMB appreciation was desirable, see Goldstein and Lardy (2005).

3. A concise overview of China's 'unbalanced' growth experience can be found in the contribution by Bert Hofman and Louis Kuijs in Goldstein and Lardy (2008).

4. In Figure 2, I have also drawn the curve ZZ, which shows all the combinations of competitiveness and expenditure that would yield the same current account outcome as at C. If that were the 'external balance target' and competitiveness could be manipulated to achieve external balance, it would have meaning, in the same way as YY has meaning,

because monetary policy is managed to attain internal balance. With the curve ZZ added, I have drawn the complete Swan diagram.

5. In a fast-growing economy, the demand for money has also been growing, and hence it has not been necessary to sterilise the monetary effects of exchange rate intervention completely, and indeed inflation has also not been zero. The inflation rate has been volatile. For a neat summary of money supply, inflation and sterilisation, see Siebert (2007: 903). On monetary policy, see also Eswar Prasad in Goldstein and Lardy (2008).

6. For extensive discussion of 'exchange rate protection', see Corden (1994). It is closely related to 'export-led growth'.

7. Note the following complication. When total expenditure (consumption plus investment) is determined by the internal balance policy for any given competitiveness level (as is clear from Figure 2), the excess of savings over investment (equals excess of income over expenditure) is also given, and hence the current account surplus is given. Thus, the ratio of savings to GDP and the ratio of investment to GDP cannot both be independently determined. In fact, both are influenced by the credit controls imposed on the banks, required for implementing the internal balance policy.

8. The figures come from Goldstein and Lardy (2008: 112).

9. This is how it looked in 2007. Now, in March 2009, when there has been a drastic fall in exports because of the world credit crisis and US recession, one cannot completely rule out the possibility that the reserves will be useful after all.

10. The term 'savings glut' originated in Bernanke (2005). Note also that there has been a massive shift of production bases from Japan, South Korea and Taiwan (and earlier from Hong Kong) to China within global production networks. China's contribution to aggregate global surpluses has therefore been partly counterbalanced by declines in surpluses of these other surplus countries in the Asian region. See Athukorala and Yamashita (2009).

11. On the world general equilibrium process leading to the 'global current account imbalances', see Corden (2007) and Wolf (2008: c 4). The latter explains clearly how the United States has been the 'borrower and spender of last resort'.

Macroeconomic performance amid global crisis 7

Yiping Huang, Ken Peng and Minggao Shen

The turnaround of macroeconomic conditions

The Chinese economy took another drastic turn at the beginning of 2009. According to a survey by the China Center for Economic Research, the average forecast of gross domestic product (GDP) growth for the second quarter of 2009 by 20 international and domestic institutions went up to 7 per cent from the real performance of 6.1 per cent during the first quarter. This confirms broad confidence in the belief that the Chinese economy has probably already bottomed out.

This improvement in sentiment is attributable mainly to better-than-expected economic data in early 2009—especially stabilisation of industrial production and a rebound in fixed-asset investment. In particular, the purchasing managers' index (PMI) of the manufacturing sector rose from 36 in November 2008 to about 53 in April and May 2009. This implied that managers' expectations shifted from sharp contraction to steady expansion.

The quick turnaround probably surprised most capital market investors and financial industry analysts. We, however, have been of the view that China should be able to maintain relatively strong growth in 2009 and 2010, relying on the government's strong capability for mobilising resources. Excessive pessimism among some investors and analysts earlier was, in our view, caused by two key factors: misinterpretation of economic trends and underestimation of the government's capability.

First, economic data weakened sharply during the fourth quarter of 2008. The growth of industrial production decelerated from above 15 per cent early that year to about 3–5 per cent at the end of 2008. In particular, the growth in power generation shifted from above 10 per cent to −9 per cent. Demand for key commodities, such as steel, copper and aluminium, also collapsed. These changes led to widespread worries that the Chinese economy was falling off a cliff.

In the meantime, however, data on underlying demand in the economy were stronger. Growth in retail sales—a key indicator of consumer spending—continued to grow strongly. Net exports also continued to surge, as imports declined much faster than exports. The real growth of fixed-asset investment moderated—from 20–25 per cent in the year to the start of 2008, to 10–15 per cent at the end of the year—caused mainly by a collapse in real estate investment.

The inconsistency between rapidly weakening production-based data and relatively resilient expenditure data could be explained by inventory adjustment. De-stocking is a common phenomenon during economic downturns. In the years preceding the recent downturn, inventories accumulated drastically because of a long period of economic boom and commodity price inflation. These trends, however, reversed from mid-2008 as the global economy fell into recession while commodity markets tanked. This led to a massive reduction of inventories.

This implied, however, that the weakening of production activities was exaggerated compared with moderation in underlying economic demand. Meanwhile, it also suggested that once the de-stocking process ended, industrial production could stabilise, unless the slowdown in economic demand accelerated. In particular, the potential pick-up of underlying demand could lead to re-stocking and faster acceleration of production than underlying demand.

Second, many investors and analysts were sceptical about the government's ability to support growth. One representative view was that, after 30 years of economic reform, China was already a 'typical capitalist economy'. With limited policy influence, a typical capitalist economy would likely be subject to violent economic cycles.

This view reflected, however, a significant underestimation of the government's ability to influence economic activities in China. True—the economy has become more market oriented in past decades, but the government managed to deliver steady economic growth during the East Asian financial crisis. Compared with 10 years ago, the government's ability to mobilise resources has actually strengthened, not weakened.

Ten years ago, government revenue accounted for 11 per cent of GDP. Today, its share is already 21 per cent. Ten years ago, the average ratio of non-performing loans of the Chinese banks was close to 40 per cent. Today, not only is this ratio about only 7 per cent, the banks are all well capitalised and quite liquid. Ten years ago, state-owned enterprises (SOEs) as a whole made net losses. Today, they are generally profitable. Clearly, the government's ability to influence economic activities goes well beyond direct budget spending.

The evolution of these two factors contributed to the turnaround of China's macroeconomic conditions in early 2008. A recent increase in GDP forecasts reflected improvement in the general sentiment, especially in international capital markets. Chinese economists as a whole were never as pessimistic as their counterparts overseas.

There is now a consensus that the growth in the Chinese economy has already passed its lowest point. Some believe that China will lead the world out of recession this time around; however, important issues remain. Is China's growth recovery sustainable? Will the government-supported cyclical rebound enhance or hinder structural transition of the Chinese economy? What other policy options are available to improve the sustainability of strong growth? These are some of the key questions we address in this chapter.

An update of macroeconomic performance

Only a year ago, the Chinese authorities were still busy fighting inflation. In February 2008, the increase in the consumer price index (CPI) reached a cyclical high of 8.7 per cent, led by above-20 per cent inflation in the price of food. The People's Bank of China (PBOC) adopted various measures to tighten monetary policy, including raising policy rates, increasing reserve requirements and appreciating the currency.

From mid-2008, however, macroeconomic conditions turned down. GDP growth decelerated from 9 per cent in the year to the first quarter of 2008 to 6.7 per cent in the year to the fourth quarter. The slowdown of the economy was partly attributable to the tightening policies implemented earlier; but it was caused mainly by weakening of the global economy following the US sub-prime crisis.

This development abruptly ended the first phase of the debate about decoupling the Chinese and US economies. The decoupling thesis was, at the minimum, unrealistic given China's open-door policy and integration with the world economy during the past 30 years. The current US financial crisis affected the Chinese economy mainly through the following three channels: weakening of exports, reversal of capital flows and loss of investor confidence.

Responding to the changing macroeconomic conditions, the PBOC quickly started to loosen monetary policies, with the first rate cut in September 2008. Currency appreciation also came to an abrupt halt during the second half of the year. Most importantly, the PBOC's credit policy shifted from strict control of loan growth in early 2008 to effective encouragement of loan extension in early 2009.

Export growth collapsed from 20–30 per cent on a year-to-year basis a year ago to about −20 per cent in recent months (Figure 7.1). Recently, there have been signs of stabilising consumer confidence and financial conditions in the United States. Despite the initial improvement, however, both indicators remain at extremely low levels and it will be some time before they can translate into a recovery of China's exports. Port traffic in May still showed no meaningful improvement from April—and still weakening shipping rates echoed this disappointing trend.

China's exports are therefore not likely to recover significantly any time soon. This is determined fundamentally by the dim outlook for the major industrial economies, which account for more than 60 per cent of China's export market. Even the more optimistic views suggest stabilisation of the US economy about the turn of the year, with recovery of the European and Japanese economies lagging that of the United States.

Meanwhile, the steady recovery of Chinese investment paints a more upbeat picture for imports into China, especially imports of investment goods. The recent rally in global dry-bulk freight rates shows a greater increase for rates bound for China and Hong Kong than elsewhere in May compared with April. For example, routes such as Singapore–China and South Korea–China have shown a near-50 per cent rebound since the low in mid-April, while those to Japan and the United States have risen 10–15 per cent from their more recent lows.

Commodity prices picked up significantly in May (Figure 7.2). Crude oil prices rose to around $70 a barrel, compared with the recent low of $32 a barrel. Assuming stable import volumes, petroleum and related products could add more than $1 billion a month to China's import bill. Other commodity prices have also seen varying degrees of rebound—evident in the Commodity Research Bureau (CRB) industrial price index.

Figure 7.1   Chinese export growth and US financial conditions index
(per cent year-on-year, index)

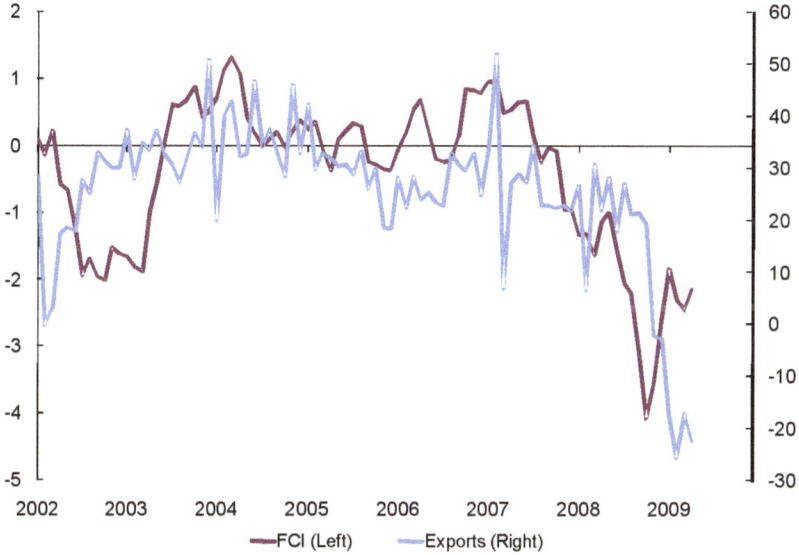

Source: Citi Investment Research and Analysis.

Figure 7.2   CRB industrial commodity prices and crude oil price
(index, $/barrel)

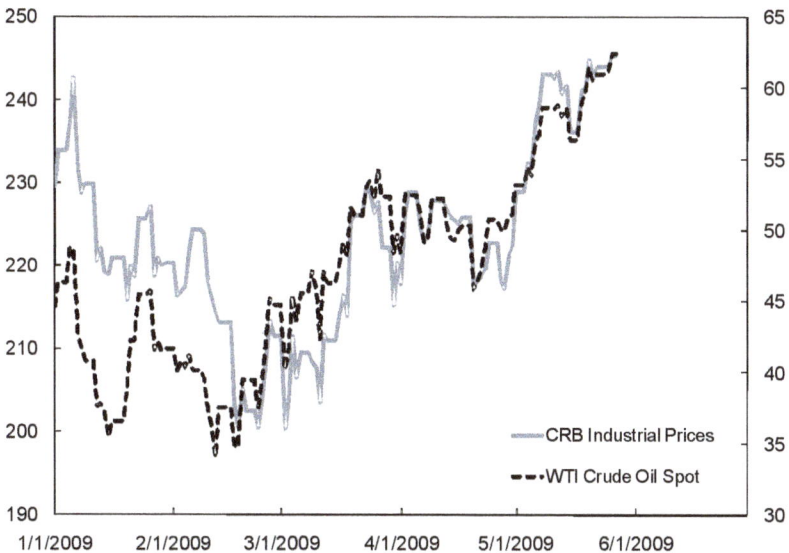

Source: Citi Investment Research and Analysis.

The faster recovery of imports than of exports suggests that the trade surplus and the current account surplus could shrink further. This would present a greater drag on GDP growth in the coming quarters. During the first quarter, the nominal trade surplus was greater than a year ago; but, removing price changes that penalised imports much more than exports, the surplus was really $7 billion short. This produced a 0.2 percentage point drag on GDP growth in that quarter.

An extended weakness in exports and the surplus would be an additional burden on fiscal expansion to protect growth, which could worsen structural imbalances. Given this backdrop, foreign exchange policy is likely to remain unchanged until exports return to growth and the surplus stabilises.

Recent calls for internationalisation of the Chinese yuan will occur only at a gradual pace, with little meaningful impact on transaction volume or currency value in the coming year; the authorities made this clear recently through both word and deed. The State Council said it would keep the yuan stable, boost credit finance and tackle slowing external demand— the biggest challenge to the economy. This explains why Chinese yuan fixing has bucked the falling US dollar recently and weakened against the dollar.

With exports in the gutter, it is difficult for production to provide an extra lift to growth in the near term (Figure 7.3). The recent return of the PMI to above 50 is consistent with modest production growth going forward. The below-40 reading in November 2008—similar to the levels in the United States and Europe during the same period—was obviously an overshooting.

The government's stimulus policies, meanwhile, could brighten the outlook for production. So far, however, firms are still not expanding, even though the worst of the de-stocking has passed. Stimulus projects are still in their early stages, which could be helping digest inventories but is yielding little boost to new production.

Figure 7.3 Industrial production and purchasing managers' index
(per cent year-on-year)

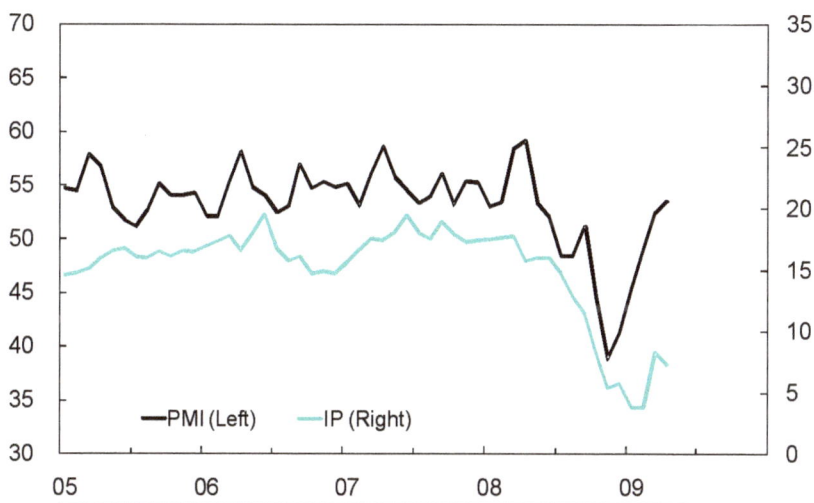

Sources: National Bureau of Statistics and Citi Investment Research and Analysis.

Going forward, investment growth could be slower than what was achieved during the first months of the year. The value of land and used facilities and equipment is included in fixed-asset investment (FAI). These values take a significant share of the total investment (as much as one-third for some projects) and are generally accounted for in lump sums at the beginning of the project. In January–April, the number of new projects totalled more than 86 000, worth RMB3.7 trillion—up 45 per cent and 91 per cent year-on-year, respectively. These projects will take several years to complete, but the land involved is already accounted for and naturally frontloads growth. As a result, FAI growth should start to decelerate soon.

The beginning of construction will probably draw mostly on the inventory of suppliers. This has probably widened the gap between industrial production and FAI growth. Going forward, however, greater investment demand will need to come from current production.

Many observers are puzzled by the gap between tepid levels of power generation and improving economic growth prospects. Indeed, the first four months of 2009 saw FAI increase 30.5 per cent while industrial production grew 5.5 per cent—all accompanying a 3.8 per cent drop in power output.

The power gap can be attributed to several factors, including greater declines in heavy-industry output such as metals, export weakness and the aforementioned land component of investment. Ultimately, however, the gap will narrow, not only via slower investment growth but by a pick-up in electricity production.

Steel output fell 5 per cent year-on-year in April, while non-ferrous metals output declined by 8.6 per cent (Figure 7.4). This highlights the sharp declines in heavy-industry output. Heavy industry accounts for 70 per cent of total industrial production—up from 60 per cent in 1998. It has outgrown light industry by 3 percentage points on average in the past 10 years. From July 2008 through to April this year, heavy-industry growth plummeted by 12 points, while light-industry growth fell by 6 percentage points (Figure 7.5). This steep fall in heavy-industry production contributed to the sharp decline in power consumption.

While export business is likely to remain weak for some time, investment should start to have an impact. Especially encouraging is the stabilisation of residential investment (Figure 7.6).

Figure 7.4   Growth of metal production
(per cent year-on-year)

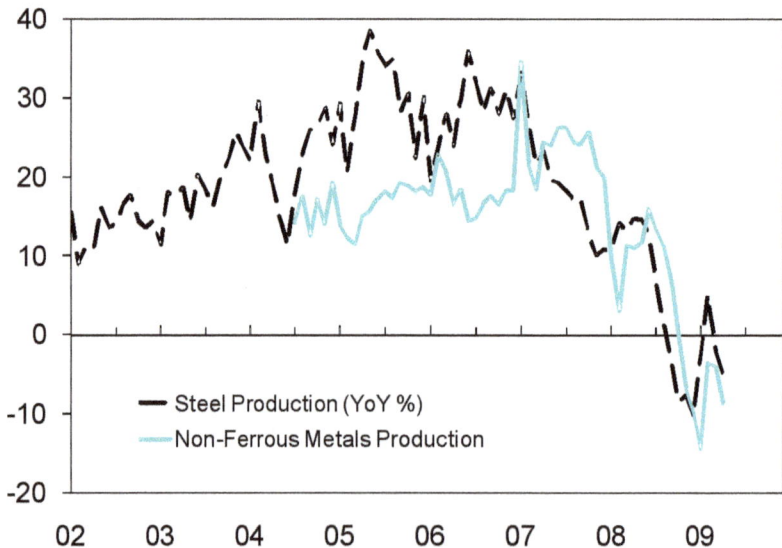

Source: China Steel and Non-Ferrous Metal Industry Association.

Figure 7.5   Growth of industrial production: heavy versus light industry
(per cent year-on-year)

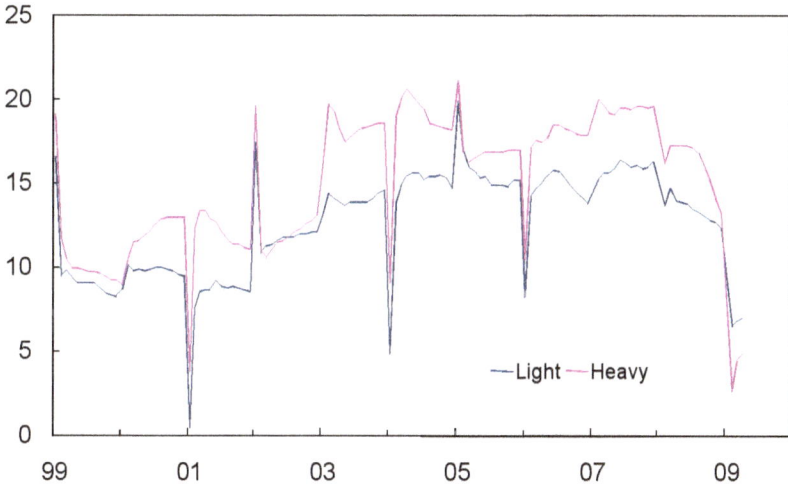

Source: National Bureau of Statistics.

Figure 7.6   Growth of fixed-asset investment: state-owned enterprises, residential and other

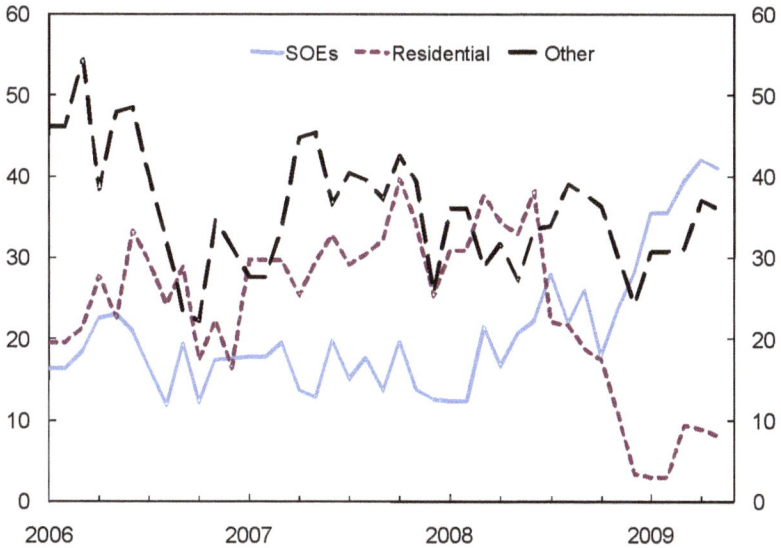

Source: CEIC Data Company.

Figure 7.7 Growth of power generation and industrial production
(per cent year-on-year)

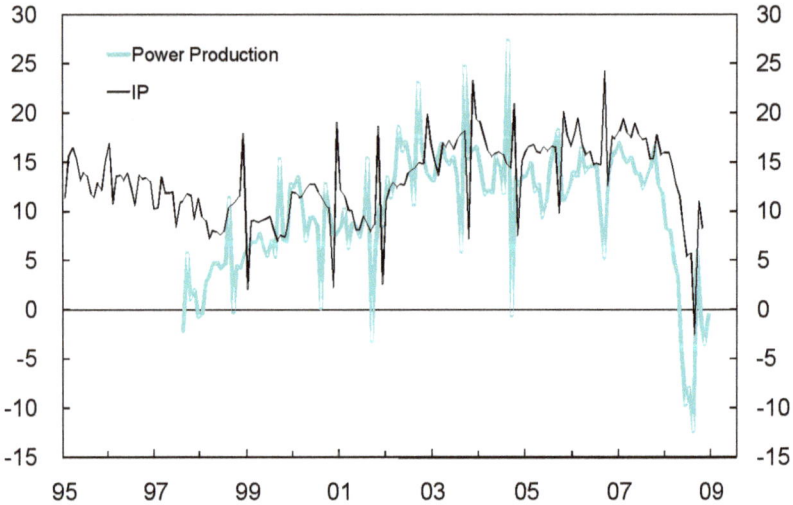

Sources: National Bureau of Statistics and National Power Distribution Center.

The recent sales boom in the property sector—likely to be short-lived—has not alleviated developers' financial pressures or greatly reduced the likelihood of major bankruptcy events. Recent successful land auctions suggest private investment in housing could also resume later this year. In addition, the government's low-cost housing projects have already begun and should add to demand for metals and other heavy industrial products in the second half of the year. All these are factors that should help narrow the power gap (Figure 7.7).

Given the general outlook for the economy, the current risks of deflation and inflation are probably becoming more balanced. The base effect will keep the year-on-year CPI headline negative for several more months, but the monthly changes have already returned to more normal seasonal patterns (Figure 7.8). Especially for the non-food CPI, the April reading of 0.1 per cent month-on-month was the first monthly increase since October 2008. Sharp deflationary pressures are probably behind us, along with severe de-stocking and housing price declines.

Figure 7.8   Headline CPI, 2007, 2008 and 2009
(per cent month-on-month)

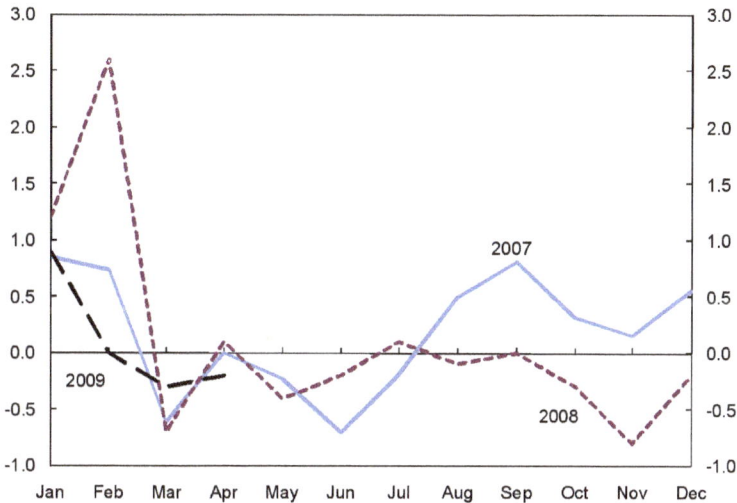

Source: Citi Investment Research and Analysis.

Inflationary pressures also are not significant. Some observers are probably paying too much attention to the inflation/reflation risk in the United States and China. Recent money growth could be expected eventually to lead to inflation. The current negative output gap is, however, a more powerful cap on price levels than the quantity of money, as continued de-leveraging (and the lack of re-leveraging) has sharply reduced the velocity of money circulation. More importantly, after widespread criticism, the PBOC and the US Federal Reserve might be anxious to re-establish their credibility once signs of inflation emerge. The greater risk now therefore might still be for policymakers to act too quickly, which could hurt the momentum for recovery.

Normalising inflation should bring higher bond yields. Without excessive pricing pressures in either direction, the negative base effect for the CPI will ease significantly by August. This could bring the year-on-year CPI rate to 2 per cent. Under this scenario, bond yields will probably rise (Figure 7.9). The flush liquidity conditions now could delay this rebound in yields, but not for long.

Figure 7.9   CPI and bond yields (per cent year-on-year)

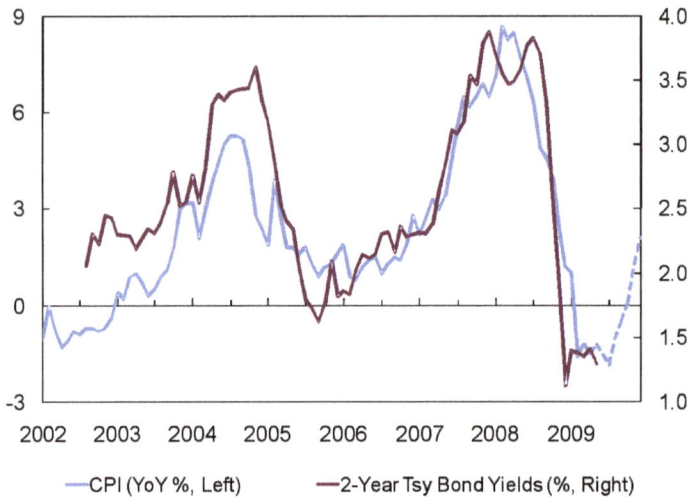

—CPI (YoY %, Left)   —2-Year Tsy Bond Yields (%, Right)

Source: People's Bank of China.

The turning point for the producer price index (PPI) could also be near. Commodity prices rebounded smartly in May, with the CRB industrial prices index up 7 per cent and crude prices up 15 per cent. The PMI for input prices turned the corner last December and rose above 50 in April, which has probably continued in May. Because PPI inflation peaked in July–August 2008 at about 10 per cent year-on-year, the base effect would keep PPI negative until the fourth quarter.

Against this backdrop, monetary policy has room to stay loose. Officials have sworn to keep monetary policy loose, maintaining that an asset bubble now is more tolerable than not having sufficient liquidity. Credit expansion could stay at a fast pace as well, probably with about RMB300 billion in new loans each month. The current rate of RMB500–600 billion, however, is still too aggressive, producing credit growth in excess of 30 per cent year-on-year.

The first wave of commercial bills issued after the crash is approaching expiration, which could create some refinancing needs (Figure 7.10). This will not be a big problem, but could create bigger new loans, while outstanding amounts rise more slowly. Those looking to earn a safe interest spread might find this more difficult, as some banks have reduced their deposit rates voluntarily due to excess liquidity.

Figure 7.10 New loans (RMB billion)

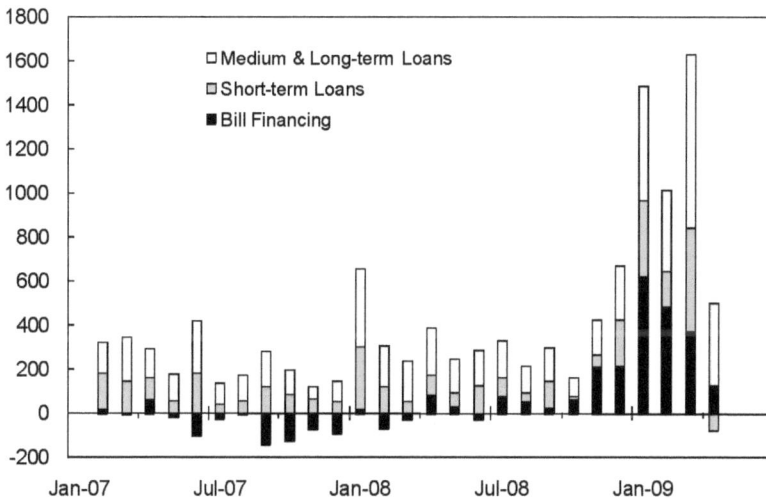

Source: People's Bank of China.

Policymakers will probably protect the recovery with ample liquidity and the ever-ready next round of stimulus, but there will probably be little action in the near term. Recent statements from officials have been mixed, recognising the progress made so far and raising concerns about loan quality and an excessive rebound in property prices. Some local governments have resumed policies to limit property speculation. The credit expansion will probably continue to slow, but will remain at a historically rapid pace.

Sustainability of rapid growth

The rebound in economic activity gives rise to the hope that not only will China come out of recession first, it will lead the world along the path of recovery. A critical question remains, however, about the sustainability of China's rapid growth. The recovery in growth is mainly the result of government policy—but has the government made the best policy choices?

The most direct consequence of the financial crisis is the collapse of China's exports. This probably provided a golden opportunity for China to rebalance its growth pattern, especially by reducing its dependency on external markets. The Chinese Government made its best effort to offset the loss of this source of growth by boosting domestic investment.

This government-sponsored growth recovery, however, creates a set of new issues. As investment surged sharply, domestic demand became even more unbalanced. The rush to plan and implement investment projects also raises questions about efficiency and investment returns. More importantly, the stimulus policies strengthened the state sector significantly while weakening the relative position of private enterprises.

Some policymakers argue that investment inefficiency should be tolerated, as the stimulus policies are temporary crisis-fighting measures. The government will, however, have to deal with the aftermath of the financial crisis and the stimulus packages. Some observers are perhaps hoping that the export market will return once the global economy recovers.

The truth, however, is that despite the expected recovery of the US economy in the coming years, American households might increase their saving ratios. This means that growth in US consumption and Chinese exports is likely to be weaker in the future than before the crisis. Chinese growth will therefore have to rely increasingly on domestic demand going forward.

Unfortunately, there is a significant risk with the current momentum of domestic demand. The extraordinary credit expansion seen in the first quarter of 2009 has already slowed significantly in recent months and is likely to moderate further. The dramatic growth in state investment crowded out private sector activities. The majority of new loans, for instance, went to the state sector. Abundant liquidity has already started to push up asset prices around the country, especially in the property sector. While improvement in property market sentiment should be welcomed, as it could help to stabilise investment and other economic activities, the premature creation of a property bubble could be costly later.

According to policymakers, the purpose of the government's stimulus policy is to support growth. The purpose of maintaining strong growth is to create enough jobs; and the purpose of job creation is to maintain social stability. Boosting state investment is, however, probably not an efficient way of ensuring social stability. China is probably able to support strong growth in the near term, but state investment-led growth might not create enough jobs to offset job losses in the export sector. If that is the case, social stability could still be at risk despite strong growth.

The more efficient way of achieving social stability in a time of crisis is to provide direct welfare and income support to households. According to surveys by PBOC officials, the costs of keeping factories in production are often four times the cost of providing direct support to households.

More importantly, sustainability of rapid growth in the long run depends on a more rapid rise in consumption. To boost consumption, the government will need to improve the social welfare system as well as changing income distribution among the government, enterprises and households.

Therefore, for short-term and long-term growth and stability purposes, it should be much more effective for the government to spend resources on boosting consumption rather than on stimulating state investment. If the government doesn't do it now, it will have to do it after 2010. Unfortunately, conditions will be much less favourable by then as the non-performing loans of the banking sector will be much bigger, fiscal conditions will be much weaker and debt burdens much higher.

Economic crisis, Keynesianism and structural imbalance in China 8

Xiaolu Wang and Fan Gang

Economic crisis and demand insufficiency: theories and practices

About 140 years ago, Karl Marx raised a famous explanation for economic crisis in *On Capital* (1867). He regarded the economic crises occurring periodically in the capitalist world as the result of the incompatibility between rapidly expanding production capacity and the mode of income distribution inherently associated with the capitalist system. Such incompatibility restricts the consumption capability of the majority of the people, and thus leads to overproduction. Cyclical economic crises that destroy the surplus production capacity are regarded as the only way to resume general equilibrium between aggregate supply and demand. This way of dealing with economic crises will, however, always brew the next one. Marx believed that this was an inherent and unsolvable conflict inside the capitalist economic system, and the highly developed production power could be finally released only if this system was replaced by one with public ownership and public distribution of income.

Although his conclusion was proved incorrect by the experience of the capitalist society unfolding later on, his judgment about demand insufficiency was validated more than half a century after *On Capital* was published. Altogether, there were seven economic crises in the Western world from the 1870s until the Great Depression in the 1930s, occurring on average once in every eight to 10 years. The most severe was the Great Depression that started in 1929, when the size of the US economy shrank by 30 per cent between 1929 and 1933 and the unemployment rate increased from 3 to 25 per cent. It took 10 years—until 1939—for the United States to restore its 1929 gross national product (GNP) (US Bureau of the Census 1975:126, 226).

During this period of crisis, John M. Keynes published *The General Theory of Employment, Interest and Money* (1936), which stated the theory of insufficiency of effective demand. He argued that the marginal propensity to consumption was below unity and was usually affected by many objective and subjective factors. When total production was increasing, there needed to be expanding investment to fill the gap. There is, however, no automatic mechanism to keep investment equal to saving. Insufficiency of effective demand, overproduction and unemployment therefore occur from time to time. He further pointed out that in richer countries, the marginal propensity to consume was lower, so that this problem tended to occur more often.

The principle outlined by Keynes seems simple and reasonable. Unlike Marx, Keynes did not treat insufficiency of effective demand as an unsolvable flaw in the capitalist system. Instead, he suggested that the demand gap be filled by either increasing government expenditure or decreasing the interest rate to stimulate private investment. He pointed out that government expenditure could lift effective demand by more than the initial increase in expenditure via the multiplier effect. The higher the marginal propensity to consume, the greater is the multiplier—making, the expansionary fiscal policy more effective.

US President Franklin Roosevelt's 'New Deal' after 1933 coincided with Keynesian theory. The Roosevelt Administration expanded investment in the construction of infrastructure—such as roads, airports, schools and hospitals—held work-relief projects and established an unemployment benefit system. The decline of the US economy was soon moderated from −14.7 per cent in 1932 to −1.8 per cent in 1933, and then returned to a positive growth rate, of 9.1 per cent, in 1934. After several years' recovery, by 1939, the economy had grown out of the crisis.

Roosevelt went beyond Keynes. The most distinctive measures were the establishment of the social security system in 1935 and the passing of the *Fair Labor Standards Act* in 1938. In addition, the Roosevelt Administration introduced progressive income taxes and death duties, which meant fairer income distribution between rich and poor. To some extent, these institutional innovations turned the United States from a traditional inchoate capitalist society to a welfare state on the basis of a free market. These institutional changes reduced income inequality, moderated social conflicts and lifted up total consumption.

Keynes did not fully agree with those (such as Karl Marx) who treated demand insufficiency as a result of insufficient consumption. Keynes (1936) argued that increases in other investment and consumption could help to drive up effective demand although an increase in capital stock was far more valuable for a society. Once investment increased, consumption would automatically increase even without changing the propensity to consume. He also accepted, however, that the best solution might be to increase both investment and the propensity to consume at the same time. He argued that over-investment meant that any further investment would make losses, which could happen only in a situation in which all the capital goods were in abundant supply and there was full employment.

One important issue Keynes did not explore further, however, is that demand insufficiency situation itself—that is, a tendency for total investment to be less than total saving—can be a result of market saturation caused by overcapacity. In this case, further investment—led, say, by lowering the interest rate—will lift aggregate demand only in the short run, before these investment projects are completed. After that, additional production capacity is created—thus, the demand–supply imbalance will appear again and could become more severe.

This is really an issue of saving–investment imbalance. Let's consider a simple two-sector model. Sector A produces consumer goods for the society and sector B produces capital goods for sector A and for itself for the renewal and possible expansion of capital stock. Each year the society consumes 80 per cent of its products in value and saves 20 per cent for investment. The total products of the society therefore consist of 80 per cent of consumer goods and 20 per cent of capital goods in value. Assuming the two sectors are equally productive and equally capital and labour intensive, and the economy is initially in equilibrium, sector A should share 80 per cent of the total capital stock and employment and B should share the remaining 20 per cent of the total capital stock and employment.

Now if the society increases the saving rate from 20 per cent to 50 per cent, consumption demand will decrease and there will be more financial resources available for investment. Meanwhile, the reduction in consumption demand will lead to an overcapacity in sector A, causing reallocation of capital and labour from A to B so that production comprises 50 per cent consumer goods and 50 per cent capital goods.

If, however, the structural adjustment is completed in this way, sector B will at some future time have severe overcapacity, because the demand of sector A for capital goods will fall proportionally to its reduction in production—namely, a drop of 37.5 per cent (1–50 per cent/80 per cent)[1]—and this will cause further demand reduction in sector B. A more likely situation is that the resource reallocation can be only partially completed—thus, there will be insufficiency of demand in both sectors. As a result, there will be a reduction in total investment. This is because, with decreasing demand in both sectors, further investment would make losses.

In this situation, a loose monetary policy to stimulate investment can help to create short-term demand for capital goods in both sectors. However, increases in production capacity, once completed, will soon become overcapacity. The economy is unable to get out of the crisis, unless the propensity to consume resumes its initial level or the economy can export its capital goods to other countries without keeping a trade balance.

Now we add a public sector into the model and assume that the stimulatory investment is made only by the government and it invests only in a non-production public sector such as infrastructure. This will create a better situation and the economy will be lifted out of the recession. Without readjusting the saving and consumption rates, however, crisis will return when fiscal expansion stops. This is because, without expansionary government investment, the demand for capital goods will be less than the initial level. This will force the government to continue an expansionary fiscal policy with continued budgetary deficits, and will finally lead the economy into stagflation. This implies that production is restricted by the low propensity to consume, which is below its optimal level.

The policy implication is that when there is insufficient consumption, the typical Keynesian-style investment expansion or loose monetary policy is not enough, and institutional change and policy adjustment to stimulate consumption—such as establishing or improving social security and welfare systems—are necessary.

Before and after World War II, all industrialised countries completed the necessary institutional changes. While the basic market mechanisms remained, they changed the initial result of income distribution by establishing social security, social services and transfer payment systems. These entitled everyone to be educated, to be fairly paid and to be protected by medical care and pension systems. This reduced income inequality and largely changed the phenomenon of consumption insufficiency common in the old capitalist world. This moderated the traditional mechanism causing economic cycles.

How to weigh the advantages and disadvantages between social welfare policies and a free market, or between equality and efficiency, remains a hot topic of debate to this day—for which a common solution has not been found. From a historical perspective, however, most informed people agree that the institutional innovation in a certain level of social security and income redistribution in industrialised countries brought these countries new life in the twentieth century.

Over-consumption in the United States and over-saving in China: two types of imbalance

In terms of building and developing the social welfare system, the United States did not go as far as European countries. It retained large income inequality. The most recently available Gini coefficient for the United States is 0.408 (World Bank 2008), which indicates it has the largest income inequality in the industrialised world.

There were two basic elements enabling the United States to avoid severe crisis between the Great Depression of the 1930s and the current financial crisis.

First, the United States was heavily involved in World War II in the 1940s, the Korean War in the 1950s, the Vietnam War in the 1960s, the Gulf and Kosovo wars in the 1990s and the Afghanistan and Iraq wars in the 2000s, and conducted an arms race and arms exports during (and after) the Cold War. Arms demand digested the United States' expanding production capacity and largely moderated its demand insufficiency problem.

Second, for a long time, excessive borrowing has sustained an expansion of consumption in the United States. In 2007, personal consumption accounted for 70 per cent of gross domestic product (GDP)—twice as high as that in China—and total consumption accounted for 86 per cent of GDP. The net saving rate in the United States was −1.7 per cent and the outstanding debt of US households accumulated to US$13.8 trillion, equivalent to total US GDP, in 2007. Adding government, financial and non-financial business debt, total outstanding debt amounted to US$47.9 trillion—equal to 3.5 times US GDP in 2007 (CEIC 2009; Roach 2008). Table 8.1 presents data showing the levels of outstanding US debt and its structure. Sub-prime loans were securitised and sold to other countries via 'financial innovation', which formed the basis of worldwide financial bubbles and finally caused the global financial crisis.

Table 8.1   Outstanding debt in the United States (US$trillion)

Year	Government	Household	Non-financial business	Financial sector	Sum	GDP	Debt/GDP (%)
1950	0.2	0.1	0.1			0.3	
1970	0.5	0.5	0.5	0.1	1.6	1.0	149
1990	3.5	3.6	3.8	2.6	13.5	5.8	232
2007	7.3	13.8	10.6	16.2	47.9	13.8	347

Sources: CEIC n.d., *CEIC Database*, CEIC Data Company Limited, <www.ceicdata.com>; United States Bureau of the Census 1975, *Historical Statistics of the United States: Colonial times to 1970*, United States Bureau of the Census, Washington, DC, Part 2, pp. 973, 989.

In general, the United States transformed itself from over-production to an over-consumption by large levels of military spending and excessive borrowing. Neither of these were sustainable. The fact that the unbalanced structure of the United States could be maintained for so long was partially related to another type of structural imbalance in China.

In contrast with the US economy, China retained a very high saving rate and correspondingly low consumption. China's massive exports filled the US gap between consumption and production. China's large foreign exchange reserves financed US consumption and investment based on borrowing. Conversely, without the over-consumption in the United States, China's rapidly expanding production capacity would have been obstructed earlier by the insufficiency of domestic demand.

In the past 50 years, there has been a continued decrease in China's consumption rate and a continued increase in the saving rate The rate of final consumption in GDP dropped rapidly between 2000 and 2007, from 62 per cent to 49 per cent. The household consumption rate dropped from 46 per cent to 35 per cent during the same period. The recent consumption rate is the lowest in the world, and is far lower than that in most countries. Although investment has grown rapidly, it has lagged behind the growth in savings. Due to the insufficiency of domestic demand, firms have relied more and more on the international market for sales and the economy for growth. This has formed a complementary economic relationship between China and the United States. The opposite trend of changing saving and consumption rates in China and the United States is shown in Figures 8.1a and 8.1b.

Figure 8.1a Final consumption rate and gross saving rate in China, 1952–2008 (per cent)

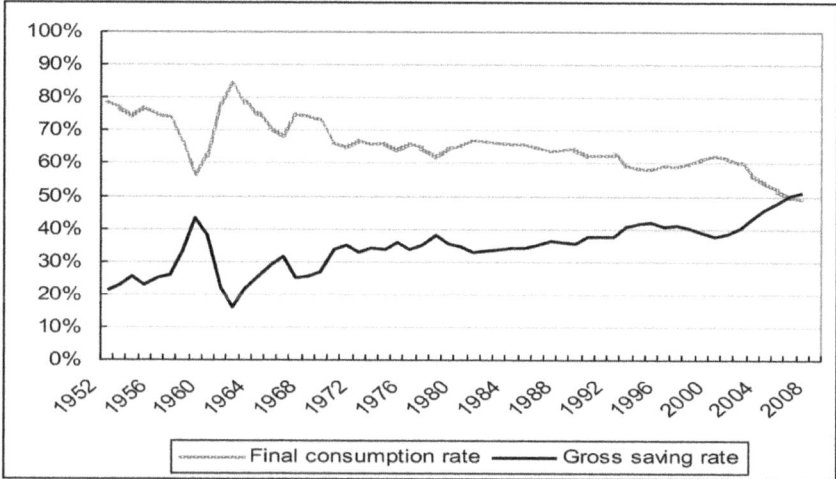

Figure 8.1b Final consumption rate and gross saving rate in the United States, 1952–2008 (per cent)

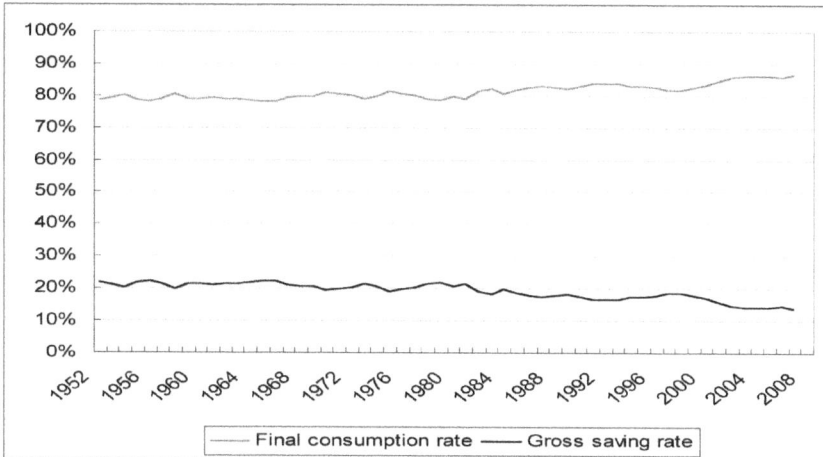

Note: Final consumption rate and gross saving rate are the ratios of final consumption and gross savings to GDP.

Sources: National Bureau of Statistics (NBS) various years, *China Statistical Yearbook*, China Statistics Press, Beijing; CEIC n.d., *CEIC Database*, CEIC Data Company Limited, <www.ceicdata.com>

In 2007, China's exports to the United States accounted for 19 per cent of its total exports. China's bilateral trade surplus with the United States (US$163 billion) accounted for 62 per cent of China's trade surplus and 5 per cent of China's GDP. According to the US statistics, the US–China trade deficit is even larger (US$256 billion), because it includes trade via Hong Kong; it accounted for 36 per cent of the total trade deficit in the United States. This indicates a close relationship between China and the United States with regard to domestic imbalances. Net exports (as a percentage of GDP for each country) for China and the United States have changed radically in the past two decades (Figure 8.2). They have exhibited a kind of symmetrical pattern in the past decade, which indicates the increasing bilateral dependency between the two countries.

Figure 8.2   Changing net exports between China and the United States, 1952–2008 (percentage of total GDP)

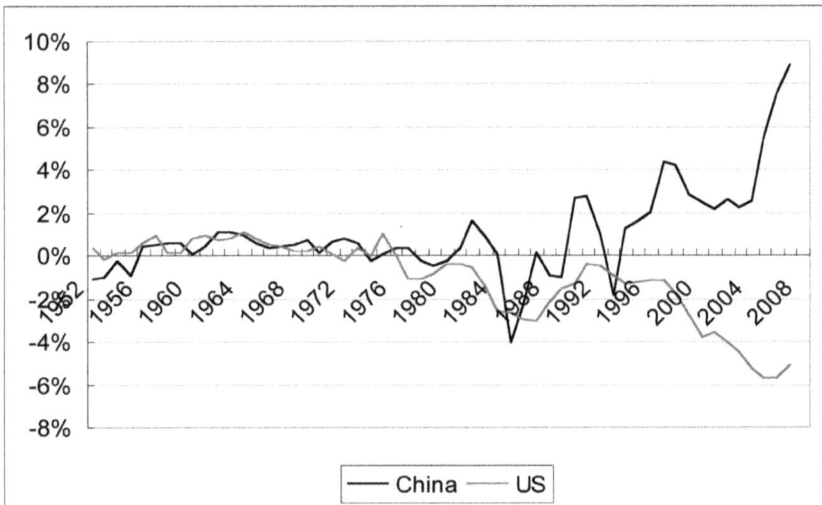

Note: GDP in each country as 100 per cent.

Sources: National Bureau of Statistics (NBS) various years, *China Statistical Yearbook*, China Statistics Press, Beijing; CEIC n.d., *CEIC Database*, CEIC Data Company Limited, <www.ceicdata.com>

This kind of interdependence, however, can no longer be sustained. The US consumption bubble has burst and there must be a major structural adjustment in the United States to increase saving and decrease borrowing and consumption to more sustainable levels. This will mean a contraction of the US commodity market for a long period. The current situation in the world economy indicates that recovery in other major industrialised countries will also follow a long time frame. The Chinese economy therefore has to change its growth pattern to domestic demand-based growth. Unless domestic consumption can be raised sufficiently, the State's stimulus package of CNY4 trillion announced in November 2008 might work only in the short run.

Why consumption is insufficient in China

The modern history of the decreasing consumption rate in China can be divided into two phases. During the central planning period (1952–77), the rate of final consumption in GDP fell from 79 to 65 per cent (NBS 2005). This was a result of forced government saving—that is, using government power to depress wages and the prices of agricultural products and to concentrate resources on government investment in industry. This did not lead to overproduction and insufficiency of consumption demand; on the contrary, there were always supply shortages. This was because, under the centrally planned system of the time, production inefficiency and investment failures ironically acted to remove the potential problem of overcapacity.

Decreases in the consumption rate in the market-oriented reform period (after 1978) were led by a different mechanism. This led in the opposite direction to the contemporary structural imbalance in the United States, but was consistent with that in Western countries before the Great Depression in 1929.

There are several reasons for the decreases in consumption in China. First, as described in the Lewis model (1954), China had an 'unlimited supply' of labour during the reform period. There was continued labour migration from rural to urban sectors. About 140 million rural migrant workers are currently working in urban areas. With total output growing rapidly, the abundant labour supply prevented wages from increasing, which resulted in decreases of both labour shares and household consumption shares in GDP. This trend was moderated only in recent years, due to a reduction of surplus labour in rural areas, but unemployment pressure was reinforced after 2008 by the global financial crisis. From 1985 to 2005, real GDP per capita increased 5 times, whereas the real wage rate in the private sector increased only 3.6 times, and real consumption per capita increased only 3.5 times (NBS 2008).

Second, slower growth of labour wages and faster growth of non-labour incomes resulted in widening income inequality. In this situation, national income is distributed more towards higher-income resident groups, whose saving rate is significantly higher than low-income residents. During the reform period (1978–2005), the income Gini coefficient in China increased from 0.32 to 0.47 (World Bank 2008). The large and widening income inequality automatically results in an increasing share of saving and decreasing share of consumption in GDP. There is no such market mechanism to guarantee that labour income and household consumption will grow in line with output.

Third, while employment and wage determination mechanisms changed from government dominated to the influence of market forces, legislation on labour protection and the development of social security and public service systems lagged behind in China. These institutional innovations, as complements to the market system, were well developed in Europe and North America more than half a century ago. Until 2007, the basic pension insurance and urban medical care insurance systems covered only 201 million and 180 million people, respectively, accounting for only 34 and 30 per cent, respectively, of the urban population. The unemployment insurance system covered only 116 million workers, accounting for 40 per cent of total urban employment. None of these systems covers rural residents. With uncertainties or fear about ageing and future illness, unemployment, and so on, the majority of people are forced to increase their savings.

Fourth, in recent years, the increasing national saving rate has been due mainly to rapid increases in enterprise savings, particularly the savings of state-owned enterprises (SOEs), enterprises operating in natural resources and those with monopolistic power. This is related to the fact that there is no SOE dividend distribution system or a proper taxation system on returns of natural resources—thus, huge undistributed profits are retained in enterprises that have contributed to the high level of investment in China (Fan et al. 2009).

Fifth, in those industries operating in the natural resources sector or that have a natural or state monopoly (or oligopoly)—for example, power generation and supply, telecommunications, banking and insurance, oil and natural gas, tobacco, and so on—a social optimum is not automatically achieved via market competition. Without appropriate regulation and social monitoring, income distribution will deteriorate towards inequality and inequity. Some estimates suggest the income differential between people engaged in state-owned and other sectors is five to 10 times (Wang 2007).

Sixth, governments at the provincial and municipal level have the incentive to promote development of large and capital-intensive firms to achieve higher growth performance—a policy that is unfavourable to small and labour-intensive enterprises. The large bank-dominated financial sector also disadvantages small enterprises in external finance. These reduced employment opportunities and lowered returns to labour therefore contribute to decreases in the consumption rate. According to the two national industrial (economic) censuses in 1995 and 2004, the share of large and medium industrial enterprises in gross industrial output value during this period increased from 43.6 to 60 per cent, and their employment share increased from 33 to 37.7 per cent. Correspondingly, output shares and employment shares of small enterprises decreased from 56.4 to 40 per cent and from 67 to 62 per cent, respectively. The number of small enterprises decreased from 1.83 to 1.35 million, while their employment decreased from 79 to 58 million.[2]

According to Keynesian theory, consumption insufficiency can be supplemented by higher investment leading to expansionary fiscal or monetary policy. As discussed earlier in this chapter, however, after a short period, this investment will lead to an increase in production capacity. Its effect on consumption demand will be restricted to a certain level by the marginal propensity to consume, thus further enlarging the gap between aggregate supply and effective demand. Unless net exports are expanding, economic growth cannot be maintained.

This situation emerged in China over the past decade. In the period 2000–07, the real growth rates of final consumption and urban and rural per capita incomes were lower than the GDP growth rate (Table 8.2). In particular, real consumption growth was slower than GDP growth by 2–5 percentage points in most years, resulting in a reduction in the rate of final consumption in GDP from 62 to 49 per cent. As the other side of the coin, gross saving grew at a much faster rate than GDP growth in most years. Although capital formation grew more rapidly than GDP, it was not as high as that of savings growth in most years, because the existence of overcapacity put limits on opportunities for profitable investment. This indicates an insufficiency of domestic demand. Trends in the loan/deposit ratio in financial institutions also point to low growth in domestic demand.

This ratio decreased from 80 to 67 per cent during the 2000–07 period, indicating accumulation of a large amount of unused financial resources in banks, which could not be fully utilised for investment.

Table 8.2 **Structural imbalance in China: growth of GDP and its components** (per cent)

Year	2000	2001	2002	2003	2004	2005	2006	2007
GDP growth[a]	8.4	8.3	9.1	10.0	10.1	10.4	11.6	13.0
Final consumption	8.4	6.5	6.6	5.3	5.1	8.3	9.1	10.4
Gross saving	2.8	10.8	14.9	18.1	16.2	19.5	18.0	15.4
Capital formation	3.6	11.8	13.9	19.7	15.6	12.4	13.0	12.2
Net export	−7.7	−4.7	32.3	−5.9	27.7	141.5	57.2	33.5
Urban per capita income growth[b]	5.5	9.5	11.1	8.9	7.7	9.6	10.4	12.2
Rural per capita income growth[b]	2.0	4.2	5.0	4.3	6.8	8.5	8.6	9.5
Export growth[c]	27.8	6.8	22.4	34.6	35.4	28.4	27.2	25.7
Final consumption/GDP	62.3	61.4	59.6	56.8	54.3	51.8	49.9	48.8
Loan/deposit[d]	80.3	78.2	76.8	76.4	73.8	67.8	67.2	67.2
Net export/GDP	2.4	2.1	2.6	2.2	2.5	5.4	7.5	8.9

[a] Final consumption, capital formation and net export (of goods and services) are the three components of the GDP-by-expenditure approach (NBS various years); gross saving is defined as GDP–final consumption; their growth rates are deflated by the authors using the implicit GDP deflator of the NBS (various years).

[b] Urban disposable income per capita and rural net income per capita, respectively.

[c] Measured in US dollars in current prices.

[d] The ratio of total loans to total deposits in financial institutions.

Sources: Calculated from National Bureau of Statistics (NBS) various years, *China Statistical Yearbook*, China Statistics Press, Beijing.

The insufficiency of domestic demand pushed firms to expand their exports to overseas markets. Net exports have grown dramatically in recent years, lifting the ratio of net exports to GDP from about 2 to close to 9 per cent between 2001 and 2007.

Data in Table 8.2 indicate an expanding insufficiency of domestic demand in China in recent years, which has been compensated by rapid net export growth. Economic growth was therefore maintained at a high rate of about 10 per cent. This relied on the competitiveness of Chinese products in world markets and also from the over-consumption in the United States.

During the past decade, export growth has remained above 20 per cent. Affected by the financial crisis, it dropped sharply to 4.3 per cent in the year to the fourth quarter of 2008, then to −19.7 per cent in the year to the first quarter of 2009. Exports decreased dramatically in China in 2008–09 (Figure 8.3). The GDP growth rate fell from 13 per cent in 2007 to 9 per cent in 2008—due mainly to lower export growth—and then to 6.1 per cent in the year to the first quarter of 2009, which was the lowest since the 1998 East Asian financial crisis. The recent economic situation indicates that the impact of the global financial crisis will not quickly fade. After the crisis, only a transformation in the growth pattern in China from heavy dependence on external demand to domestic-based demand will provide a basis for continued rapid growth.

Figure 8.3   Falling exports in China amid the economic crisis, 2008–09

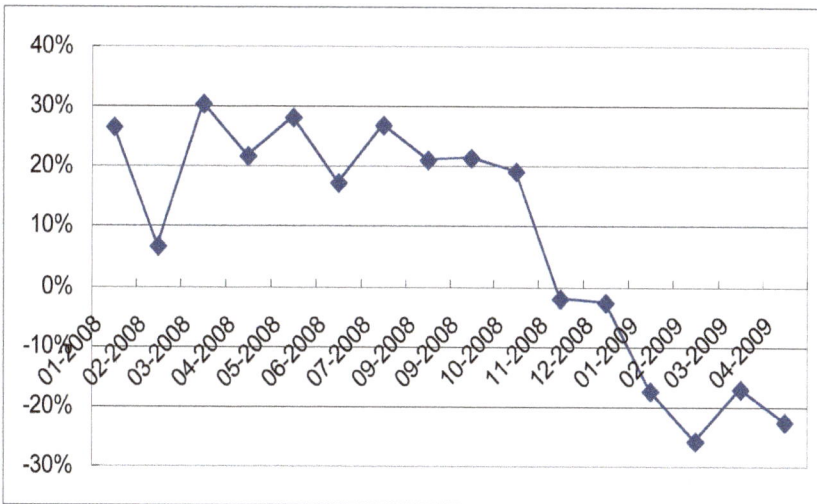

Note: Year-on-year growth rate in US dollars, at current prices.

Source: General Administration of Customs of the People's Republic of China 2009, *Customs Statistical Data*, General Administration of Customs web site, <http://www.customs.gov.cn/>

The Chinese Government in November 2008 announced a CNY4 trillion (US$586 billion) investment package for economic stimulation in 2009–10, accounting for roughly 6 per cent of GDP each year. Although the situation in the international market is still serious, we can expect an increase in the economic growth rate in China in the second half of 2009, and can be quite certain that the Chinese economy will recover from the crisis sooner than the industrialised countries. The question, however, is whether the structural imbalance between saving and consumption in

China can be corrected after the stimulus package has been implemented. If not, the fiscal investment might play a role only in the short run and there will still be a threat of weak demand in the future. The question of whether economic growth can be sustained in the longer term remains unanswered.

The future of the Chinese economy

The above discussion leads to a conclusion that the basic problem for China's economic growth is not a short-run issue; it is the sustainability of rapid growth in the longer term. Sustainable growth has to be based mainly on domestic demand. Therefore the saving–consumption imbalance has to be corrected through some fundamental changes. The most important of these changes are improvements in the social security and public service systems, reforms of the government financial and taxation systems, improvements in the business environment for small enterprises and for employment and acceleration of the urbanisation process. Without such institutional reforms, the demand inefficiency problem will not be solved.

One should note the significant policy adjustment made by the Chinese Government in recent years towards reducing income inequality and improving public services. These include the abolition of the agricultural tax (2004–06), exemption from school fees for the nine-year urban and rural compulsory education system (2006–07), the establishment of an overall rural minimum living allowance system (2006–07) and a rural cooperative medical service system (2006–08), passing into legislation the Labour Contract Law (2008), and so on. These new policies have been effective. As indicated in Table 8.2, consumption growth in 2003–04 was about 5 per cent—only half the economic growth rate. It has increased to 8–10 per cent since 2005, although it is still below the GDP growth rate by more than 2 percentage points. With this trend unchanged, China will continue to suffer from demand insufficiency.

To rebalance the saving–consumption structure and to get the economy growing strongly again, it is necessary to achieve faster consumption growth than GDP growth for a period, so that the final consumption rate can be lifted from the current 49 per cent to about 60 per cent or higher. Household consumption should also be increased from the current 35 per cent, by at least 10 percentage points. A 60 per cent final consumption rate is still significantly lower than the world average—78 per cent in 2006

(World Bank 2008)—but might be enough to offset the negative impact of the world economic crisis.

To rebalance the saving–consumption structure, the following additional policy adjustment and reforms are essential.

First, the current incomplete and regionally segmented social security systems should be unified nationwide and expanded to cover all urban residents in a relatively short period. At the current level of economic development, this system could provide only a minimum level of security to everyone. Supplemental social security and commercial insurance in different regions should be encouraged, especially for the better-developed regions and higher-income residents; however, the unified system will insure all people's basic security, including the 140 million 'floating' rural workers in urban areas. The system should be gradually extended to cover rural residents.

Second, public services in education and health care should be further improved. Upgrading the current nine-year compulsory education to a 12-year system will not be an unaffordable burden, but will provide great returns to the nation in the future. In particular, secondary vocational education and job training programs should be further developed.

Third, low-rent government housing is now provided only to small numbers of low-income urban residents. It can be expanded in the coming years for all low-income families, including rural–urban migrant workers. The current government-subsidised 'affordable housing' is not really affordable for low-income people and actually benefits some middle or higher-income people. These government resources should be redirected entirely to building low-rental housing for low-income families.

Fourth, further financial sector reform is needed to lower the threshold for the development of non-state—especially small—financial institutions. It is particularly important for the finance and development of the small enterprise sector and the creation of employment opportunities.

Fifth, sectors with a state monopoly should be reformed. Market competition should be extended further and the regulatory and monitoring systems should be improved.

Sixth, the government finance and taxation systems should be reformed to impose a resource tax, to establish a dividend distribution system for SOEs, to rearrange central–regional fiscal relations to enable provincial, municipal and local governments to perform their functions, to unify the return distribution system for land selling and to improve the regulation and monitoring systems for the management of public resources—in particular, to make them more transparent and accountable.

With more balanced income distribution and saving–consumption growth, China can expect sustainable economic growth in the long run.

References

CEIC 2009, *CEIC Database*, CEIC Data Company Limited, <www.ceicdata.com>

Fan, G., Wei, Q. and Liu, P. 2009, Internal–external balance and fiscal-taxation reform in China, Unpublished manuscript.

General Administration of Customs of the People's Republic of China 2009, *Customs Statistical Data*, General Administration of Customs web site, <http://www.customs.gov.cn>

Keynes, J. M. 1936, *General Theory of Employment, Interest and Money*, Macmillan, London.

Lewis, W. A. 1954, 'Economic development with unlimited supplies of labor', *Manchester School of Economic and Social Studies*, vol. XXII (May), pp. 139–91.

Marx, K. 1867, *Das Kapital: Kritik der politischen oekonomie. Volume I*, [Chinese translation 1975], People's Publisher, Beijing.

—— 1895, *Das Kapital: Kritik der politischen oekonomie. Volume III*, [Chinese translation 1975], People's Publisher, Beijing.

National Bureau of Statistics (NBS) 2005, *China Statistical Yearbook 2005*, China Statistics Press, Beijing.

—— 2008, *China Statistical Yearbook 2008*, China Statistics Press, Beijing.

—— various years, *China Statistical Yearbook*, China Statistics Press, Beijing.

Roach, S. 2008, Keynote speech to China Development Forum, Beijing.

United States Bureau of the Census 1975, *Historical Statistics of the United States: Colonial times to 1970*, parts 1–2, United States Bureau of the Census, Washington, DC.

Wang, X. L. 2007, 'Grey income and income inequality in China', [in Chinese], *Comparative Studies*, vol. 38, China CITIC Press, Beijing.

World Bank 2008, *World Development Indicators 2008*, The World Bank, Washington, DC.

Endnotes

1. This is under the assumption of simple linear production technology. If we assume a technology with diminishing marginal products of capital and labour, the drop in demand for capital goods will be even greater.

2. The authors have recalculated the 1995 data to exclude household firms in the industrial sector, so that the data series is made consistent with the 2004 data. Still, there are some differences in data definition between the two censuses; therefore the data are not fully comparable. These comparisons show only the direction and an approximate scale of the changes during this period.

State-owned enterprises in China
Reform dynamics and impacts

9

Xiao Geng, Xiuke Yang and Anna Janus

Introduction

Large-scale SOE reform in China has been going on since 1978. In spite of the Chinese Government's efforts towards privatisation and its commitment to market-oriented development, SOEs remain a dominant part of the Chinese economy, especially among certain strategically important sectors, such as infrastructure construction, telecommunications, financial services, energy and raw materials. The question of how this apparent paradox can be resolved—and what the explanation might imply for our understanding of China—is the main focus for this chapter. Many questions arise in this context: should the Chinese Government continue its trend of privatising SOEs or should it continue to keep control of the largest and most important SOEs? Is there a set of implicit objectives in government policies that can explain China's SOE reform dynamics in the past and predict future trends?

SOE reform in China has been unique in many ways. Unlike the abrupt approach to privatisation adopted in Russia, which was followed by a collapse of the economies in all former Soviet Union partner countries in the last decade of the twentieth century, the more gradual approach taken in China has entailed a steady expansion of SOE assets and profits, as well as an accumulation of power and influence among SOEs. Unlike in India, which has to cope with high urban unemployment and poor industrial infrastructure, in China, the privatisation of SOEs has coincided with large-scale improvement of infrastructure and still relatively low urban unemployment.

This chapter reviews the relative performance of large and medium-sized enterprises during the reform period in a comprehensive and systematic way in order to reveal possible underlying patterns and trends. For this purpose, we have used three sets of data: sector-level annual survey data for China's large and medium-sized industrial enterprises from 1995 to 2005, collected by the National Bureau of Statistics; firm-level survey data for China's top-500 enterprises, published by the China Enterprise Confederation; and the Fortune Global 500 data published by *Fortune Magazine*. For our analysis, we have used the novel approach of grouping SOEs by sector into two categories: the competitive and the strategic markets. This distinction was made based on the specific characteristics of the industry sectors. The competitive market contains sectors that relate to the manufacturing of consumer products. Sectors in this market have undergone intensive privatisation. The strategic market contains sectors such as infrastructure construction, financial services, energy and raw materials, where there are still government-imposed market entry barriers. Many government documents and research papers have cited such a distinction when discussing industrial policy, although there has been no official classification of which industries belong to competitive markets and which to strategic markets. The distinction we make in this chapter helps us unveil an implicit objective function behind the facts of SOE transformation in China. The analytical framework in this chapter also highlights the impacts of reforms on enterprise performance as well as on the Chinese economy and society. The results of this study show a comprehensive picture of SOE transformation and provide a useful foundation for consideration of future reforms.

We begin with a review of the advancement of SOE transformation since the beginning of the reforms and an assessment of the current state of SOEs in China. We then explore the characteristic dynamics of SOE transformation in the main part of our chapter. Possible policy implications are then outlined.

Progress of SOE reforms in China

Background of SOE reform

Under heavy influence from the Soviet Union, China gave birth to the SOEs about 50 years ago after the establishment of the People's Republic of China and the socialist industrialisation that came soon after. In less than 10 years, China nationalised virtually all private industrial enterprises during the 1950s. Before 1978—the year that marked the beginning of market-oriented transformation—China operated its SOEs under a centrally planned economy. Since 1978, Chinese authorities have initiated intensive reforms and privatisation of SOEs. At the macro level, the SOE reforms can be seen as a strategic adjustment of the nationalised and centralised economy towards a more market-oriented economy; at the micro level, the reforms are intended to transform the Chinese SOEs into modern corporations. Specifically, SOE reforms fall into three successive phases.

The first phase, from 1978 to 1984, concentrated on increasing managerial autonomy in order to motivate the Chinese SOEs to pursue profit and growth. By loosening its hold on the planned economy, the Chinese Government to some degree began to weaken the link between the State and enterprises. Managers were essentially allowed to sell surplus production at market prices for a profit, once the planned quotas for production were met. The most important innovations during this period were the delegation of managerial autonomy from government bureaucracy to enterprise managers and the introduction of a dual-price system (the existing planned price for within-the-quota output and the new market price for above-the-quota output).

The second phase, from 1985 to 1993, focused on separating company ownership and management by introducing a 'contract responsibility' system. Managers signed a contract with the relevant government agencies and became the legal representatives of the SOE, consequently being held responsible for the company's profits and losses. The idea of reform during this period was to transform SOEs into truly independent economic entities that were responsible for their own profits and losses, as well as to establish independent legal entities that shared certain rights and obligations. The result was that the management teams tended to pursue short-term interests rather than long-term profitable growth because they had the rights only to operate SOEs but no clear property rights. The main problem of the 'responsibility system' is that the managers can easily share profits with the government and employees but are not practically capable of assuming losses and liabilities that might follow from their managerial decisions, since they do not own any significant amount of assets or property.

The third phase, starting from 1993 and continuing into the present, emphasised transforming SOEs into modern corporations. The main elements of reform during this period include the policies of 'grasping the large and letting go the small', severing the link between the State and labour, as well as changing the State's position towards shareholders under mixed ownership (state and non-state ownership). During this period, privatisation took place on a large scale, notably among small SOEs. Some of the largest SOEs are even being listed on the young Chinese stock markets and the Hong Kong Stock Exchange, usually with the State still holding about two-thirds of the shares in the listed companies.

Current state of Chinese SOEs

Even after more than two decades of market-oriented reforms, SOEs still play a prominent role in the Chinese economy. To examine the most relevant trends, our focus here will be on SOEs among large and medium-sized enterprises in China.

In 2005, there were 3999 SOEs among all large and medium-sized industrial enterprises (25 per cent of the total), centralising assets of RMB6.09 trillion (58 per cent of the total) and generating a total profit of RMB268 billion (48 per cent of the total) (Table 9.1).

Table 9.1 **Structure and performance of SOEs in large and medium-sized industrial enterprises, 2005**

Ownership	No. SOEs	Assets (RMB billion)	Profit (RMB billion)	ROA (%)
State	3,999	6,090	268	4.40
Collective	1,331	343	23	6.62
Private	5,584	1,110	68	6.13
Foreign	5,272	2,880	203	7.05
Total	16,186	10,423	562	5.39

ROA = return on assets

Source: National Bureau of Statistics (NBS) 2005, *China Statistical Yearbook 2005*, China Statistics Press, Beijing.

Table 9.2 **Structure and performance of top-500 Chinese enterprises in 2007, by ownership** (per cent)

Ownership	No. SOEs	Assets	Profit	Employees	Taxes	ROA
State	69.8	93.6	87.9	89.3	92.7	1.4
Collective	5.8	4.2	2.2	2.4	1.7	0.8
Private	17.8	1.7	7.1	7.0	3.9	6.1
Foreign	6.6	0.5	2.8	1.3	1.7	8.5

ROA = return on assets

Source: *A Report on the Development of China's Enterprises 2007*, Enterprise Management Publishing House, Beijing, Chapter 12, p. 88.

In 2007, of the top-500 Chinese enterprises, an astounding 69.8 per cent were SOEs, accounting for 94 per cent of asset value and creating 88 per cent of the total profit (Table 9.2). SOEs are not only economically dominant, they are still socially relevant too, employing 89.3 per cent of the workforce and contributing 92.7 per cent of overall taxes.

In 2007, of the top-500 Chinese manufacturing enterprises, almost 50 per cent were SOEs, creating 61 per cent of the total profit (Table 9.3).

Table 9.3 **Structure and performance of top-500 Chinese manufacturing enterprises in 2007, by ownership** (per cent)

Ownership	No. SOEs	Profit	ROA
State	49.8	61.1	3.2
Collective	7.8	7.8	6.2
Private	29.4	21.4	6.4
Foreign	13.0	9.7	7.9

ROA = return on assets

Source: *A Report on the Development of China's Enterprises 2007*, Enterprise Management Publishing House, Beijing, Chapter 13, p. 126.

In 2007, of the top-500 Chinese service-sector enterprises, SOEs were even more dominant, accounting for 94 per cent of assets, 92 per cent of profit and 61 per cent of the number of firms (Table 9.4).

Table 9.4 **Structure and performance of top-500 Chinese enterprises in the service industry in 2007, by ownership** (per cent)

Ownership	No. SOEs	Assets	Profit	ROA
State	61.4	93.6	92.4	0.8
Collective	11.4	5.4	1.1	0.2
Private	23.2	0.8	5.3	5.3
Foreign	4.0	0.1	1.2	8.3

ROA = return on assets

Source: *A Report on the Development of China's Enterprises 2007*, Enterprise Management Publishing House, Beijing, Chapter 14, p. 137.

Meanwhile, Chinese SOEs are also becoming a globally noticeable force. In 2007, there were 22 Chinese SOEs listed in the Fortune Global 500 and China ranked sixth in the number of firms by country. The contributions of the 22 Chinese SOEs in the Fortune Global 500 include employment of 13 per cent of the workforce, 3.6 per cent of overall profit and 3.8 per cent of total revenue (Table 9.5).

Table 9.5   Structure and performance of Fortune Global 500 in 2007, by country (per cent)

Country	No. firms	Assets	Revenue	Profit	No. employees	ROA
United States	32.4	25.5	35.1	38.5	34.1	2.7
Japan	13.4	9.4	11.5	7.0	9.4	1.3
France	7.6	10.9	8.7	7.4	9.7	1.2
Germany	7.4	9.5	8.8	5.7	8.9	1.1
Britain	6.6	12.1	7.4	8.3	6.1	1.2
China	4.4	4.7	3.8	3.5	13.0	1.4

ROA = return on assets

Source: 'Fortune Global 500', *Fortune Magazine*, 23 July 2007.

In addition, the Chinese SOEs accounted for three of the top-five largest employers in the world in 2006 (Table 9.6) and three of the top-five enterprises in Asia in terms of revenue (Table 9.7).

Table 9.6   Top-five enterprises in Asia in 2006, by revenue

Company	Country	Revenue ($million)
Toyota Motors	Japan	204,746.4
Sinopec	China	131,636
China National Petroleum	China	110,520.2
State Grid	China	107,185.5
Honda Motors	Japan	94,790.5

Source: 'Fortune Global 500', *Fortune Magazine*, 23 July 2007.

Table 9.7   Top-five biggest employers in the world, 2006

Company	Country	No. employees
Wal-Mart Stores	United States	1,900,000
State Grid	China	1,504,000
China National Petroleum	China	1,086,966
US Postal Service	United States	796,199
Sinopec	China	681,900

Source: 'Fortune Global 500', *Fortune Magazine*, 23 July 2007.

For the SOE reforms in the past 30 years, however, revenues and profits have consistently run ahead of deeper enterprise transformation such as improvement of operating efficiency and enhancement of industrial productivity. The return on assets (ROA) of Chinese SOEs in the top-500 Chinese enterprises was only 1.4 per cent in 2007—lagging far behind non-state enterprises (NSEs) in China, such as private-owned enterprises

(6.08 per cent) and foreign-funded enterprises (8.48 per cent) (Table 9.2). As for return on equity (ROE), it is only 10.07 per cent for the heavily SOE-dominated top-500 Chinese enterprises—performing far worse than the Fortune Global 500 average of 16.13 per cent (Table 9.8).

Table 9.8   Performance of top-500 Chinese and global companies (per cent)

	ROA	ROE
Top-500 Chinese enterprises	1.82	10.07
Fortune Global 500 companies	1.79	16.13

ROA = return on assets

ROE = return on equity

Sources: *A Report on the Development of China's Enterprises 2007*, Enterprise Management Publishing House, Beijing; 'Fortune Global 500', *Fortune Magazine*, 23 July 2007.

Clearly, apart from increasing revenues and profits, Chinese SOEs still show major deficiencies in regard to efficiency and productivity. As a major economic force in China, they are also quickly becoming more relevant on a global scale. There appears therefore to be a continuing need for reform and enhanced policies for SOEs in China. In order for China's economic transformation to be successful, we have to recognise accurately what is happening in the Chinese SOEs. For this purpose, this chapter attempts to shed some light on the underlying characteristics of SOE reform in China.

The dynamics of SOE reform in China

Our analytical approach

In order to highlight the special characteristics of SOE reform in China, this chapter uses sector-level annual survey data from China's large and medium-sized industrial enterprises during 1995–2005, which are collected at the firm level and maintained at the National Bureau of Statistics (NBS) in China. The sector-level data allow us to compare enterprise performance across ownership, industry and time. The NBS survey covers all of the large and medium-sized industrial enterprises in 38 sectors (Appendix 9.1). In addition to differentiating firms by ownership and by sector (as other studies have done), this chapter groups the 38 sectors into two overall categories: the strategic market and the competitive market (Appendices 9.2 and 9.3). The strategic market, including the sectors of infrastructure construction, energy and raw materials, has been providing critical infrastructure support for the Chinese national economy, whereas the competitive market, including sectors related to personal services and the manufacturing of consumer products, is essential to improving the living standards of the Chinese people. Such a distinction allows us to systematically interpret reform processes and to derive considerations and strategies for future SOE reform.

Special characteristics of SOE reform in China

The transformation of SOEs has been characterised on the one hand by a rapid decline in the number of SOEs and on the other hand by a steady accumulation and expansion of state-owned assets as well as profits in large and medium-sized industrial enterprises.

The number of Chinese SOEs in large and medium-sized industrial enterprises was 15 107 in 1995 and diminished to 3999 in 2005—a loss of 73.5 per cent—and the number of all industrial SOEs fell from 118 000 in 1995 to 27 500 in 2005, a loss of 76.7 per cent (Table 9.9). The sharp decrease in the number of SOEs shows how dramatically privatisation has taken place in the course of reforms.

Table 9.9   The number of industrial SOEs in China, 1995–2005

Year	No. industrial SOEs (all sizes)	No. industrial SOEs (large and medium-sized)
1995	118,000	15,107
2000	53,500	9,144
2005	27,500	3,999

Sources: National Bureau of Statistics (NBS) 1995, *China Statistical Yearbook 1995*, China Statistics Press, Beijing; National Bureau of Statistics (NBS) 2000, *China Statistical Yearbook 2000*, China Statistics Press, Beijing; National Bureau of Statistics (NBS) 2005, *China Statistical Yearbook 2005*, China Statistics Press, Beijing.

The state-owned assets in large and medium-sized industrial enterprises, however, steadily accumulated from RMB3.89 trillion in 1995 to RMB6.09 trillion in 2005 (Table 9.10), with a compound annual growth rate of 4.6 per cent for 10 years. At the same time, the profit generated from large and medium-sized state-owned industrial enterprises also soared—from RMB70.8 billion in 1995 to RMB268 billion in 2005, with a compound annual growth rate as high as 14.2 per cent—indicating that the privatisation and transformation of SOEs during this period contributed to a dramatic increase in state-owned profits and assets, which enhanced the government's financial, political and social net asset value.

Table 9.10 Assets and profits of SOEs in large and medium-sized industrial enterprises

Year	Assets (RMB billion)	Profit (RMB billion)	ROA (%)
1995	3890	70.8	1.82
2000	4640	87.4	1.88
2005	6090	268	4.40

ROA = return on assets

Sources: National Bureau of Statistics (NBS) 1995, *China Statistical Yearbook 1995*, China Statistics Press, Beijing; National Bureau of Statistics (NBS) 2000, *China Statistical Yearbook 2000*, China Statistics Press, Beijing; National Bureau of Statistics (NBS) 2005, *China Statistical Yearbook 2005*, China Statistics Press, Beijing.

Starting with these observations, we explore two key hypotheses about SOE reform in China.

Hypothesis 1

SOEs are more likely to be privatised when they are losing profit in the competitive market.

If we examine the competitive market and the strategic market separately (Table 9.11), we can see that the number of SOEs in the competitive market has diminished dramatically from 12 128 in 1995 to 1975 in 2005 (a loss of 83.7 per cent). However, the amount of state-owned assets in the competitive market remained relatively stable (falling from RMB1819 billion in 1995 to RMB1423 billion in 2005).

Table 9.11 The number and performance of SOEs in the competitive market

Year	No. SOEs	Assets (RMB billion)	Profit (RMB billion)	ROA (%)
1995	12,128	1,819	9	0.51
2000	6,872	1,902	7	0.38
2005	1,975	1,423	27	1.89

ROA = return on assets

Sources: National Bureau of Statistics (NBS) 1995, *China Statistical Yearbook 1995*, China Statistics Press, Beijing; National Bureau of Statistics (NBS) 2000, *China Statistical Yearbook 2000*, China Statistics Press, Beijing; National Bureau of Statistics (NBS) 2005, *China Statistical Yearbook 2005*, China Statistics Press, Beijing.

At the same time, the change in the number of SOEs in the strategic market was less extreme—from 2979 in 1995 to 2024 in 1995 (a loss of only 32 per cent)—yet there was a remarkable increase in state-owned assets, from RMB1.99 trillion to RMB4.66 trillion (Table 9.12).

Table 9.12 The number and performance of SOEs in the strategic market

Year	No. SOEs	Assets (RMB billion)	Profit (RMB billion)	ROA (%)
1995	2,979	1,985	62	3.10
2000	2,272	2,642	80	3.03
2005	2,024	4,664	241	5.17

ROA = return on assets

Sources: National Bureau of Statistics (NBS) 1995, *China Statistical Yearbook 1995*, China Statistics Press, Beijing; National Bureau of Statistics (NBS) 2000, *China Statistical Yearbook 2000*, China Statistics Press, Beijing; National Bureau of Statistics (NBS) 2005, *China Statistical Yearbook 2005*, China Statistics Press, Beijing.

Looking more closely at the competitive market (Table 9.11), it is striking to see that the ROA of SOEs was as low as 0.5 per cent in 1995, 0.4 per cent in 2000 and 1.9 per cent in 2005—lagging far behind the ROA achieved by SOEs in the strategic market, which was 3.1 per cent in 1995, 3.0 per cent in 2000 and 5.2 per cent in 2005 (Table 9.12). The ROA of SOEs in the competitive market was also significantly lower than the ROA of NSEs—4.6 per cent in 1995, 6.26 per cent in 2000 and 7.04 per cent in 2005 (Table 9.14).

The above empirical evidence shows privatisation has been rather instrumental in the abandonment of less-profitable and less-efficient SOEs and thus reducing financial, social and political liabilities arising from loss-making SOEs.

Hypothesis 2

When SOEs are profitable in the strategic market, their sector's state monopoly is more likely to be maintained.

Looking more closely at the strategic market, the number of SOEs has remained relatively stable during the reform period, while the number of assets accumulated in the strategic market has soared remarkably. Moreover, the strategic market was also immensely profitable, with a rise in total profit from RMB61.5 billion in 1995 to RMB241.2 billion in 2005 (Table 9.12). Enterprises in the strategic market had an average ROA of 5.17 per cent in 2005 compared with 1.89 per cent in the competitive market. The government's strong grip on the strategic market is obvious from the proportion of state-owned assets to total assets in the respective sectors. In the strategic market, state-owned assets accounted for 56 per cent of total assets, while in the competitive market the number was only 15 per cent in 2005 (Table 9.13). The strategic market comprises various sectors in which SOEs still hold monopolies, such as infrastructure and energy, and it becomes evident from our analysis that SOEs in this market have been consistently maintained. From the view of the government, reforms of SOEs in the strategic market have led to an increase in profit and asset value and a strengthening of social and political assets.

Table 9.13 Total assets in the strategic and competitive markets in 2005 (RMB billion)

	State-owned assets	Total assets	State-owned assets (%)
Total	6,086.7	17,632.5	34.5
The strategic market	4,663.7	8,338.9	55.9
The competitive market	1,423	9,293.6	15.3

Source: National Bureau of Statistics (NBS) 2005, *China Statistical Yearbook 2005*, China Statistics Press, Beijing.

General implications

If we combine the preceding observations from the competitive market and the strategic market, we can see how SOE reforms have left the government fundamentally better off. In the competitive market, the number of less-efficient and less-profitable SOEs was dramatically reduced, while in the strategic market SOEs were guarded and profits soared. At the same time, this course of reforms has significant wider implications.

Impact on NSEs: infrastructural support and price controls

SOE reforms have successfully created room for non-state enterprises (NSEs) to grow. Assets in NSEs have soared from RMB1264.6 billion in 1995 to RMB11 545.8 billion in 2005, with profit rising from RMB58.2 billion in 1995 to RMB812.6 billion in 2005 (Table 9.14).

The dominance of SOEs in China's strategic market has contributed to this success in two distinct ways. On the one hand, SOEs still hold state monopolies over critical sectors such as infrastructure. By centrally coordinating and pursuing its efforts in these regards, the Chinese Government has managed to provide an extensive and ever-growing infrastructure network as one of the pillars of overall economic growth.

Table 9.14 Performance of NSEs in large and medium-sized industrial enterprises

Year	Assets (RMB billion)	Profit (RMB billion)	ROA (%)
1995	1,264.6	58.2	4.60
2000	3,584.2	224.4	6.26
2005	11,545.8	812.6	7.04

ROA = return on assets

Sources: National Bureau of Statistics (NBS) 1995, *China Statistical Yearbook 1995*, China Statistics Press, Beijing; National Bureau of Statistics (NBS) 2000, *China Statistical Yearbook 2000*, China Statistics Press, Beijing; National Bureau of Statistics (NBS) 2005, *China Statistical Yearbook 2005*, China Statistics Press, Beijing.

The growth in infrastructure is outstanding: in the area of transportation routes, the length of railways in operation extended from 59 700 kilometres in 1995 to 77 100km in 2006 (up 28 per cent). The length of highways extended from 1.16 million km in 1995 to 3.46 million in 2006 (up 200 per cent) and the length of civil aviation routes extended from 1.13 million km in 1995 to about 2.11 million km in 2006 (up 87 per cent). Postal delivery routes, which were about 1.9 million km in length in 1995, extended to 3.4 million km at the end of 2006 (up 79 per cent). As for telecommunications, the capacity of mobile telephone exchanges extended from 8 million subscribers in 1995 to 610 million subscribers in 2006 (up 7525 per cent), and broadband subscriber ports extended from 18 million ports in 2003 to 65 million ports in 2006 (up 260 per cent) (see Appendices 9.4–7 for details on infrastructure growth).

Another channel through which the dominant position of SOEs in the strategic market has contributed to NSE growth is by upholding price controls. Since SOEs still hold monopolies in these strategically relevant sectors, the prices of energy, water and resources are kept artificially low. On the one hand, this serves Chinese consumers. On the other, private and other non-state enterprises also benefit notably from this favourable price environment.

The implicit subsidisation of the private sector, however—including many foreign-invested enterprises—through lower than market prices in key inputs implies that China is subsidising global consumers of made-in-China products. It has also attracted many energy-intensive and environmentally harmful industrial activities to China. On the whole, the price controls that followed from the tight control by the government of SOEs in the strategic market have led to significant hidden social costs. It will be interesting to see how long China can sustain the price control and the implicit subsidies to domestic and international firms and consumers.

Distorted distribution of wealth

SOE transformation has so far increased state-owned assets and profits. The resulting wealth distribution seems unbalanced, as state-owned assets are centralised within the strategic market. While about 51 per cent of all SOEs are included in the strategic market, the assets accumulated here amount to RMB4664 billion, or 77 per cent of total state-owned assets in large and medium-sized industrial enterprises. At the same time, profit generated from SOEs in the strategic market amounts to RMB241 billion, which equals 90 per cent of the total profit generated from large and medium-sized SOEs (Table 9.15).

Table 9.15 Structure and performance of SOEs in strategic and competitive markets, 2005 (per cent)

	Total	Strategic market	Competitive market
No. SOEs	100	51.61	49.39
Assets	100	76.62	23.38
Profit	100	89.97	10.03

Source: National Bureau of Statistics (NBS) 2005, *China Statistical Yearbook 2005*, China Statistics Press, Beijing.

The centralisation of assets and profits in the strategic market and the strengthened monopoly position of SOEs in the most profitable sectors of the Chinese economy, as well as the low efficiency and low productivity of SOEs, all indicate a distorted allocation of wealth. This is prone to hinder innovation and entrepreneurship in China's largest companies and most important sectors, as well as encumbering enterprise efficiency and industrial productivity.

Impact on China's consumption and savings

Retaining profitable SOEs in the strategic market also has major implications for China's macroeconomic balance. Since SOE dividends are not paid out to shareholders, a major source of wealth and income is held back. As a result, household consumption is about only 37 per cent of GDP and household income is about 45 per cent of national income (Table 9.16). High savings held by SOEs and the government (through high taxation) are among the key reasons for China's low consumption rate and large current account surplus.

Table 9.16 China's household income and consumption, 2007

	(RMB billion)	Percentage of GDP
Household income	11,198	45
Household consumption	9,332	37

Note: Household income is estimated using data on per capita income of rural and urban households multiplied by the respective population estimates.

Source: National Bureau of Statistics (NBS) 2008, *China Statistical Yearbook 2008*, China Statistics Press, Beijing.

Concentration of SOEs among top-500 Chinese companies

After several stages of reform, Chinese SOEs still dominate among large enterprises in China to a remarkable degree. SOEs account for 70 per cent of the Chinese top-500 enterprises, 94 per cent of assets and 88 per cent of profits. The Chinese SOEs also contribute 93 per cent of the taxes generated from, and employ 89 per cent of the total workforce in, the Chinese top-500 enterprises (Table 9.2). Although the Chinese SOEs perform worse than non-state enterprises such as collective-owned enterprises, private-owned enterprises and foreign-funded enterprises, they still dominate among large manufacturing enterprises. In the manufacturing sector, SOEs account for about 50 per cent of firms, contributing 61 per cent of the total profit generated from the top-500 Chinese manufacturing enterprises (Table 9.3). In the service sector, SOEs account for 61 per cent of firms, 93 per cent of assets and 92 per cent of profits among the top-500 Chinese enterprises in the service industry (Table 9.4).

Even globally, Chinese SOEs are becoming more and more significant. The number of Chinese enterprises in the Fortune Global 500 increased from 15 in 2005 to 22 in 2007 and China ranked sixth in 2007 in the number of firms by country (Table 9.17).

Table 9.17 The number of Chinese enterprises in the Fortune Global 500

Year	No. of Chinese enterprises
2005	15
2006	19
2007	22

Note: All of the Chinese enterprises in the Fortune Global 500 are SOEs.

Source: 'Fortune Global 500', *Fortune Magazine*, 23 July 2007.

Some policy implications

To address the apparent shortcomings of past SOE reforms, we propose full privatisation as part of a large-scale reform of China's financial sector.[1] Reforms should focus on limiting the role of the State and increasing the global competitiveness of Chinese enterprises. We present several recommendations for such a scenario:

- all large SOEs under central or local-government control should be listed within a short period—that is, five to 10 years
- for SOEs that are already listed, state ownership should be reduced to a minority shareholder level—for example, below 30 per cent—within three to five years
- state-owned shares should be limited to less than 50 per cent for all new initial public offerings (IPOs)
- listed SOEs should be required to have a plan to further reduce state ownership—for example, to below 30 per cent—within three to five years after their IPO.

Majority state ownership is neither necessary to represent the interests of the State nor advantageous in improving the competitiveness of the listed company. The interest of the State can still be maintained through one golden share that gives the State veto power against any decisions by the board that are potentially harmful to the national interest or national security.

Summary and conclusion

By using various statistical data, this chapter examines the transformation of SOEs during the reform period from 1995 to 2005, which has been characterised on the one hand by a sharp decline in the number of firms and on the other hand by a steady accumulation of state-owned assets. The results of this study show that it is the competitive market where there is a sharp decline in the number of SOEs and the strategic market where there is a steady accumulation of state-owned assets. We have shown how Chinese SOEs are more likely to be privatised when they are losing profit. When they are more profitable, their sector's monopoly position is more likely to be strengthened, which leads us to the conclusion that the privatisation of SOEs in China has been driven by an implicit objective of the government to maximise financial, social and political assets and minimise financial, social and political liabilities.

Moreover, we point out that this specific course of reform has affected China's macroeconomic environment in a number of ways. NSEs have benefited from the continuing monopoly position of SOEs in the strategic market in the sense that they can take advantage of a vast system of basic infrastructure, as well as of lasting price controls on energy and resources. The over-concentration of SOEs in the strategic market seems to have served specific government purposes to bolster the nation's economic growth. Low efficiency and productivity in these sectors still hinder innovation and entrepreneurship in China's largest companies and in China's most important sectors. Apart from this domestic problem of a distorted distribution of wealth, the global impacts of the ever-growing Chinese SOEs will not be ignored abroad. Therefore, there will be a further demand for transformation of the Chinese SOEs with pressure coming from domestic consumers and politics, as well as from international competition and international politics.

References

A Report on the Development of China's Enterprises 2007, Enterprise Management Publishing House, Beijing.

'Fortune Global 500', *Fortune Magazine*, 23 July 2007.

National Bureau of Statistics (NBS) 1995, *China Statistical Yearbook 1995*, China Statistics Press, Beijing.

—— 2000, *China Statistical Yearbook 2000*, China Statistics Press, Beijing.

—— 2005, *China Statistical Yearbook 2005*, China Statistics Press, Beijing.

—— 2008, *China Statistical Yearbook 2008*, China Statistics Press, Beijing.

Ten policy recommendations to build Shanghai into a top international financial center within a decade, Brookings-Tsinghua Center Working Paper, Brookings-Tsinghua Center, Beijing.

Endnotes

1. See *Ten policy recommendations to build Shanghai into a top international financial center within a decade*, Brookings-Tsinghua Center Working Paper, Brookings-Tsinghua Center, Beijing.

Appendix 9.1 List of industry codes and the full industry name

06   Coal mining and dressing (CMD)

07   Petroleum and natural gas extraction (PNGE)

08   Ferrous metals mining and dressing (FMMD)

09   Non-ferrous metals mining and dressing (NFMMD)

10   Non-metal minerals mining and dressing (NMMD)

13   Food processing (FPc)

14   Food production (FPd)

15   Beverage production (BP)

16   Tobacco processing (TP)

17   Textile industry (TI)

18   Garments and other fibre products (GOFP)

19   Leather, furs, down and related products (LFDRP)

20   Timber, bamboo, cane, palm fibre and straw (TBCPFS)

21   Furniture manufacturing (FM)

22   Papermaking and paper products (PPP)

23   Printing and recording medium reproduction (PRMR)

24   Cultural, educational and sporting goods (CESG)

25   Petroleum processing and coking (PPC)

26   Raw chemical materials and chemicals (RCMC)

27   Medical and pharmaceutical products (MPP)

28   Chemical fibre (CF)

29   Rubber products (RP)

30   Plastic products (PP)

31   Non-metal mineral products (NMP)

32   Smelting and pressing of ferrous metals (SPFM)

33   Smelting and pressing of non-ferrous metals (SPNFM)

34   Metal products (MP)

35   Ordinary machinery manufacturing (OMM)

36   Special purposes equipment manufacturing (SPEM)

37   Transport equipment manufacturing (TEM)

39   Electric equipment and machinery (EEM)

40   Electronic and telecommunications equipment (ETE)

41   Apparatus and instruments (AI)

42   Cultural, office machinery and other manufacturing (COMOM)

43   Recycling industry (RI)

44   Electric power, steam and hot water (EPSHW)

45   Gas production and supply (GPS)

46   Tap water production and supply (TWPS)

Appendix 9.2 List of sectors in the strategic market

06   Coal mining and dressing (CMD)

07   Petroleum and natural gas extraction (PNGE)

08   Ferrous metals mining and dressing (FMMD)

09   Non-ferrous metals mining and dressing (NFMMD)

10   Non-metal minerals mining and dressing (NMMD)

16   Tobacco processing (TP)

25   Petroleum processing and coking (PPC)

27   Medical and pharmaceutical products (MPP)

32   Smelting and pressing of ferrous metals (SPFM)

33   Smelting and pressing of non-ferrous metals (SPNFM)

44   Electric power, steam and hot water (EPSHW)

45   Gas production and supply (GPS)

46   Tap water production and supply (TWPS)

Appendix 9.3 List of sectors in the competitive market

13 Food processing (FPc)

14 Food production (FPd)

15 Beverage production (BP)

17 Textile industry (TI)

18 Garments and other fibre products (GOFP)

19 Leather, furs, down and related products (LFDRP)

20 Timber, bamboo, cane, palm fibre and straw (TBCPFS)

21 Furniture manufacturing (FM)

22 Papermaking and paper products (PPP)

23 Printing and recording medium reproduction (PRMR)

24 Cultural, educational and sporting goods (CESG)

26 Raw chemical materials and chemicals (RCMC)

28 Chemical fibre (CF)

29 Rubber products (RP)

30 Plastic products (PP)

31 Non-metal mineral products (NMP)

34 Metal products (MP)

35 Ordinary machinery manufacturing (OMM)

36 Special purposes equipment manufacturing (SPEM)

37 Transport equipment manufacturing (TEM)

39 Electric equipment and machinery (EEM)

40 Electronic and telecommunications equipment (ETE)

41 Apparatus and instruments (AI)

42 Cultural, office machinery and other manufacturing (COMOM)

43 Recycling industry (RI)

Appendix 9.4 Length of transportation routes (10 000km)

Year	Length of railways in operation	Length of national electrified railways	Length of highways	Length of expressways	Length of navigable inland waterways	Length of civil aviation routes	Length of international aviation routes	Length of petroleum and gas pipelines
1995	5.97	0.97	115.70	0.21	11.06	112.90	34.82	1.72
1996	6.49	1.01	118.58	0.34	11.08	116.65	38.63	1.93
1997	6.60	1.20	122.64	0.48	10.98	142.50	50.44	2.04
1998	6.64	1.30	127.85	0.87	11.03	150.58	50.44	2.31
1999	6.74	1.40	135.17	1.16	11.65	152.22	52.33	2.49
2000	6.87	1.49	140.27	1.63	11.93	150.29	50.84	2.47
2001	7.01	1.69	169.80	1.94	12.15	155.36	51.69	2.76
2002	7.19	1.74	176.52	2.51	12.16	163.77	57.45	2.98
2003	7.30	1.81	180.98	2.97	12.40	174.95	71.53	3.26
2004	7.44	1.86	187.07	3.43	12.33	204.94	89.42	3.82
2005	7.54	1.94	334.52	4.10	12.33	199.85	85.59	4.40
2006	7.71	2.34	345.70	4.53	12.34	211.35	96.62	4.82

Appendix 9.5 Number of berths in major coastal ports

Year	Total			For productive use			For non-productive use	
	Length of quay line (km)	No. berths (unit)	10,000-tonne class	Length of quay line (km)	No. berths (unit)	10,000-tonne class	Length of quay line (m)	No. berths (unit)
2003	281	2,562	650	257	2238	650	24,008	324
2005	379	3,641	769	341	3110	769	37,951	531
2006	418	3,804	883	382	3291	883	35,257	513

Appendix 9.6 Postal delivery routes ('000 km)

Year	Length of postal routes	Highway routes	Railway routes
1995	1,886	819	183
1996	2,119	917	184
1997	2,363	874	186
1998	2,854	931	190
1999	2,979	989	190
2000	3,073	1,070	185
2001	3,103	1,074	180
2002	3,081	1,113	178
2003	3,270	1,137	191
2004	3,336	1,195	196
2005	3,406	1,230	200
2006	3,369	1,231	205

Appendix 9.7 Main communication capacity of telecommunications

Year	Capacity of long-distance telephone exchanges (circuit, thousands)	Capacity of local-office telephone exchanges (10 000 lines)	Capacity of mobile telephone exchanges	Length of long-distance optical cable lines ('000 km)	Broadband subscribers port of Internet (10,000 ports)
1995	3,519	7,204	797	107	-
1996	4,162	9,291	1,536	130	-
1997	4,368	11,269	2,586	151	-
1998	4,492	13,824	4,707	194	-
1999	5,032	15,346	8,136	240	-
2000	5,635	17,826	13,986	287	-
2001	7,036	25,566	21,926	399	-
2002	7,730	28,657	27,400	488	-
2003	8,694	35,083	33,698	594	1,802
2004	12,630	42,347	39,684	695	3,578
2005	13,716	47,196	48,242	723	4,875
2006	14,423	50,280	61,032	722	6,486

Economic transition and labour market integration in China 10

Prema-chandra Athukorala, Kyoji Fukao and Tangjun Yuan

Introduction

China's rise as a major economic power in the past three decades has been underpinned by large transfers of labour from the rural to the urban economy and a significant reallocation between state-owned and non-state sectors within the latter. Since the early 1980s, more than 100 million people have left their native villages to work in the cities—the largest peacetime movement of people in history.[1] In addition, public enterprise reforms have added more than 40 million workers to the private sector labour supply. In recent years, there have been growing concerns in China policy circles about whether this easy phase of economic transition fuelled by surplus labour is rapidly coming to an end (Garnaut and Huang 2006; Hausmann et al. 2006; Siebert 2007; Islam and Yokoda 2006). This concern is based on steep wage increases in the urban formal sector, as revealed by Chinese official wage data, and scattered cases of labour scarcity in rapidly growing coastal provinces reported in the business press. The purpose of this chapter is to contribute to this debate by examining employment and wage trends in China in the context of continuing structural changes and labour market transition in the past three decades.

There is a large literature on labour market performance in China in the reform period.[2] The overwhelming majority of the existing studies have, however, focused, in a repetitive fashion, on particular micro-aspects of labour market performance. It is not uncommon in this literature to examine a particular issue (such as whether migrant workers are poorly paid relative to permanent city dwellers) in isolation and make policy inferences, ignoring the fact that the issue under discussion is an integral part of the continuing process of transitional growth, not a structural phenomenon. Very few attempts have been made to offer an overall picture of the evolving labour market conditions and their implications for the future growth trajectory and for national development policy. Filling this gap in the literature is important because the evolving labour market conditions and policies affecting labour allocation have a profound impact on the growth process and the economic wellbeing of the nation. If the economy is rapidly moving away from the initial surplus labour conditions, there is a clear national need for greater emphasis on setting the stage for sustained growth through capital deepening and technical progress. On the other hand, if surplus labour conditions persist, contrary to what the readily available data suggest, a policy shift in that direction could run counter to the objective of achieving rapid, equitable growth. Apart from its relevance for China's national development policy, a systematic analysis of China's labour market situation is also essential for informing the contemporary debate about the role of China in the evolving international economic order.

The analytical framework for the study is provided by the celebrated Lewis model of economic growth with unlimited supplies of labour (hereafter, the 'Lewis model') (Lewis 1954, 1958, 1979), which has been used extensively, with appropriate modifications, in analysing the process of modern economic growth in Japan and the newly industrialising economies in East Asia (for example, Minami 1973, 1986; Fields 1994; Ranis and Fei 1975; Ranis 1993). The model starts with the assumption of a closed dual economy with a 'modern' (capitalist) sector and a 'subsistence' (traditional) sector characterised by surplus labour.[3] In the modern sector, profit maximisation rules and labour is paid the value of its marginal product, as postulated in neoclassical economics. In the subsistence economy, the wage rate is determined institutionally at or near the subsistence level along the tradition of classical economics. The modern sector can hire workers at a fixed wage rate, which is set slightly above the subsistence rate to compensate for the higher costs of living in the modern sector compared with the subsistence economy. Given the ample availability of labour at this wage rate, capital formation and technical progress in the modern sector do not raise wages but increase the share of profits in the national income. Suppose that some 'disturbance', such as a policy regime shift from a planned to a market economy (as occurred in China in the late 1970s) or technical change that increases industrial efficiency, triggers an expansion of production in the modern sector. As output expands, profits increase while wages remain constant, leading to a continuous upward shift in the demand for labour. The growth process continues as a positive feedback process—increased profits, reinvested profits, further industrial expansion and further employment expansion—up to the point where the surplus labour pool in the subsistence sectors is depleted. This is the famous 'Lewis turning point'. From then on, wages in the two sectors begin to move towards maintaining parity and the economy begins to look very much like an industrialised one. After the turning point is reached, the dualistic nature of the economy disappears and the subsistence sector becomes a part of the modern economy in which the wage rate and per capita income continue to rise along the upward-sloping labour supply curve.

The model can be extended to the international sphere without changing its basic structure (Kindleberger 1967; Ranis and Fei 1975; Lewis 1979). An open economy provides the setting for a neoclassical response to factor endowments and relative factor prices. For the surplus labour economy, this means greater opportunities for output expansion through the export of goods that are intensive in unskilled labour. The combination of modern industrial technology, low wages and a highly elastic labour supply therefore produces a high rate of profit, translated into a high growth rate through increased capital accumulation. Foreign capital is also attracted by the high profit rate, thus speeding up transitional growth towards the turning point. After reaching the turning point, domestic firms begin to look for cheap labour beyond the country's borders by bringing in cheap immigrant labour or relocating their factories to countries where labour is plentiful and cheap.

Several qualifications of the Lewis model should be mentioned briefly (Rosenzweig 1988). It has often been pointed out that the 'dual economy' assumption is rather restrictive and unrealistic, given that labour markets are often fragmented. Another criticism is that the real labour market conditions in most developing economies do not warrant the assumption of a perfectly elastic labour supply in the subsistence economy. For our purposes, these criticisms of the model's micro-foundation are not disturbing ones; the intended purpose of the Lewis model, and the purpose to which we put it here, is to provide a *macro-theoretical framework* to analyse the role of labour supply in economic transformation from a historical perspective. In studying dynamic transitional growth, the assumption of a unique duality and perfectly elastic labour supply is merely for analytical convenience. If the economy is 'fragmented—irrespective of the number of parts, then the simplifying assumption to make is dualism' (Basu 1997:152). Regarding the elasticity of labour supply, 'we need not make a fettish of "infinite" elasticity; "very large" would do just as well for our purpose' (Lewis 1979:218).

A systematic quantitative appraisal of labour market conditions in China is hampered by the paucity of data on many key variables and the poor quality of the available data. There are no data available, for example, on the skills composition of workers or the wages of agricultural and urban unskilled workers and published data on urban employment do not single out migrant workers, which is essential for a systematic analysis of the existence of excess labour supply in the economy. At the same time, there are also important issues of data quality and consistency, which largely reflect the remaining legacies of the statistical system that evolved in the command economy. A major limitation is the excessive focus of Chinese published statistics on urban industrial workers to the near exclusion of detailed data on the more numerous manufacturing employees working outside the administrative boundaries of cities. Even within the cities, data collection and reporting remain concentrated on the rapidly declining state-owned and urban collective-owned manufacturing enterprises, giving short shrift to the thriving, growing, dynamic private manufacturing sector (Banister 2005a, 2005b). Difficulties also arise from technical issues—notably, the growing institutional complexities of the Chinese economy—and from the politicisation of economic data, especially at the provincial and local levels (Rawski and Xiao 2001).

Given these data problems, what we aim to do in this chapter is to undertake an exploratory analysis of the broader contours of recent developments in Chinese labour markets with a view to inform the policy debate and to help explore avenues for further research. The empirical core of the chapter consists of a careful analysis of the overall labour market conditions and wage trends using readily available official data, while paying attention to their limitations, and an econometric analysis of wage determination using hither-to-unexploited data from a recent household survey. Where relevant, we also draw on the existing microeconomic literature to identify key aspects of labour market performance as they relate to the debate about the description of surplus demand conditions.

Section two of this chapter sets the stage for the ensuing analysis by providing an overview of the initial labour market conditions and the key elements of labour market reforms. The third section examines labour supply and deployment patterns in the reform era with a focus on changing surplus labour conditions. Section four probes the apparent inconsistency between rapid growth in aggregate urban wage rates and the prevailing labour market conditions. Section five summarises the key findings and policy inferences.

Initial conditions, reforms and labour mobility

On the eve of reforms, China's economy, as it had evolved over four decades of central planning, was a classic example of a dualistic, surplus-labour[4] economy (Eckstein 1977; Putterman 1992). Stringent controls on the migration of labour from the countryside to urban areas meant that most rural labour was bottled up in relatively low-productivity farming and small-scale rural industry. When the People's Republic was formed, there was considerable open unemployment in Chinese cities and industrial centres and a great deal of underemployment in rural areas. These labour market conditions existed even during the period of most rapid industrialisation in the 1950s and persisted through most of the 1960s. Therefore, unlike in Russia, in China, there was no need to draw on the reservoir of labour in the countryside. Moreover, the State enforced barriers to rural–urban migration in order to preserve urban amenities for the intended beneficiaries. In the 1950s, the government established the *hukou* system of household registration, confining people to the village or city of their birth, to ensure enough agricultural labour to produce sufficient grain to support the industrial and urban sectors (Cheng and Selden 1994). Under this policy, rural and urban markets became totally segmented, with much of the labour assigned to its place of work. Also, to the extent that rationing was more pervasive, workers could not obtain housing in the place they moved to unless the move was authorised.

Since the early 1980s, China has gradually reduced institutional barriers to internal migration (Meng 2000; Tao 2006). With the introduction of the household responsibility system during the 1970s and early 1980s, farmers had more freedom to allocate their labour to off-farm activities. The government responded by relaxing its rigid regulations on labour deployment in rural areas. In 1983, farmers were permitted to engage in transportation and marketing of their products beyond local markets; the government also permitted the setting up of cooperative ventures and their employment of labour. These initiatives set the stage for the rapid development of rural labour markets. Fast-growing town and village enterprises (TVEs) soon became the initial destinations for migrant workers, absorbing a large number of farmers freed by rising labour productivity on the farms (Garnaut and Ma 1996).

After broadening of the reforms to the urban sector and the creation of special economic zones in the second half of the 1980s, farmers were allowed to work in cities under the condition that they provided their own staples.

Subsequently, gradual dismantling of the food rationing/coupon system facilitated migration by enabling individuals to buy food at market prices. Since the early 1990s, various measures have been introduced to further relax the *hukou* system and to encourage greater rural to urban labour mobility (Naughton 2007:Ch.8). The central and local governments have introduced various measures to encourage labour mobility between rural and urban areas and across regions. Some cities have adopted a selective-migration policy, issuing permanent residency to migrants who pay a fee, invest in local businesses or who buy expensive housing in the city. From 2001, in most small towns, minimum requirements for receiving the local *hukou* were that the applicant had a permanent source of income and legal housing locally. In addition, the lifting of restrictions on house ownership, changes to employment policies, the lifting of rationing and the expansion of the urban non-starter sector have made it easier for migrant workers to live in cities. Increased commercialisation of the urban housing system, rapid expansion of the urban private sector and the rapidly evolving migration network linking cities and villages have made it easier for rural migrants to seek employment in cities.

Wage reforms in the urban economy began in the early 1980s by introducing a flexible labour management strategy under which urban job-seekers were allowed to find jobs with the State, in collectives or in private enterprise. The adoption of this recruitment system (known in China as the 'three channels of employment combined') marked a significant departure from the labour deployment patterns in the planned economy era. A labour contract system introduced in 1983 provided firms with more autonomy in hiring workers on short-term contracts. The traditional tenure arrangement in state-owned enterprise (SOE) employment began to crack from about 1993, when SOE managers were allowed to lay-off redundant workers. This gave rise to a new employment arrangement called *xiagang*, or furlough, under which workers were permitted to retain ties with their firms without reporting to work and remain entitled to receive small stipends and fringe benefits (Rawski 2003:23).

In 1994, the government embarked on reforms of the SOEs. Because of privatisation (mostly of small and medium-scale enterprises) and mergers and closures of loss-making ventures, the number of state-controlled firms dropped from 300 000 a decade ago to 150 000 in 2005 (Bergsten et al. 2006:23–4). This contraction in the number of SOEs, coupled with downsizing and restructuring of the existing SOEs, resulted in a dramatic decline in SOE employment—from a peak of 113 million people in 1995 to 65 million in 2005—augmenting the urban labour supply (Naughton 2007:Ch.8).

In sum, the economic reforms of the past two decades have gradually relaxed restrictions on labour mobility across sectors and industries in the Chinese economy. The labour market is, however, still highly segmented, with various obstacles to labour mobility between the urban and rural areas and the formal and the informal sectors. In particular, there are still serious labour market distortions related to the *hukou* system and the provision of pensions, medical and unemployment benefits. A key feature of *hukou* is that registration is for a specific location and for a specific status—either urban or rural. Only those with urban residency permits—popularly called 'urban *hukou*'—have the right to live permanently in cities. Since the 1980s, access to *hukou* has been substantially liberalised, but the system is still in place and possession of a permit makes a difference. The wealthy or highly educated can obtain *hukou* and can move their *hukou* from towns or small cities to a large city; however, it is not easy for the majority of citizens to obtain *hukou* (Wu and Trieman 2004; Liang and Ma 2004; World Bank 2005). Despite significant reforms in the past 15 years, the SOE sector—in which employment and remuneration practices are far from being subject to market discipline—still provides employment to nearly one-fifth of the urban labour force.

Labour supply and employment

China embarked on market-oriented reforms at a time when its population growth had begun to decline as a result of the rigid implementation of the one-child policy in the early 1970s. The average annual population growth rate declined from 1.4 per cent during 1985–95 to 0.75 per cent during 1995–2007 (Table 10.1). China's current population is 1.32 billion people and, based on current trends, it is expected to reach a peak at about 1.5 billion by 2025 (Tao 2006:Table 8.2).[5] The working-age population (people aged between fifteen and sixty-four)—the potential labour force—has grown much faster than the total population, producing a so-called 'population dividend', as birth rates decline and the number of young adults increases more rapidly than the numbers of dependent children and dependent elders. The labour force has increased even faster—from about 501 million workers in 1985 to 788 million in 2007—reflecting a persistent increase in the labour force participation rate (from 72 per cent to 88 per cent). During 1995–2007, the annual average growth of the working-age population was 1.1 per cent compared with 0.75 per cent growth in the total population. The working-age population is projected to increase from the current level of 925 million to 1.018 billion in 2025.

Table 10.1 China: population statistics, 1985–2005

Year	Total population (million)	Labour force		Urban population	
		Million	Population share (%)	Million	Population share (%)
1985	105,851	50,112	47.3	11,882	23.7
1986	107,507	51,546	47.9	12,639	24.5
1987	109,300	53,060	48.5	13,435	25.3
1988	111,026	54,630	49.2	14,100	25.8
1989	112,704	55,707	49.4	14,601	26.2
1990	114,333	65,323	57.1	17,252	26.4
1991	115,823	66,091	57.1	17,805	26.9
1992	117,171	66,782	57.0	18,338	27.5
1993	118,517	67,468	56.9	18,884	28.0
1994	119,850	68,135	56.9	19,425	28.5
1995	121,121	68,855	56.8	19,995	29.0
1996	122,389	69,765	57.0	21,264	30.5
1997	123,626	70,800	57.3	22,592	31.9
1998	124,761	72,087	57.8	24,041	33.4
1999	125,786	72,791	57.9	25,317	34.8
2000	126,743	73,992	58.4	26,800	36.2
2001	127,627	74,432	58.3	28,031	37.7
2002	128,453	75,360	58.7	29,458	39.1
2003	129,227	76,075	58.9	30,833	40.5
2004	129,988	76,823	59.1	32,081	41.8
2005	130,756	77,877	59.6	33,479	43.0
2006	131,448	78,343	59.6	57,706	43.9
2007	132,129	78,881	59.7	59,379	44.9
Memo item: average annual growth (%)					
1985–95	1.36	3.33		5.4	
1995–2007	0.75	1.13		4.3	
1985–2007	1.02	2.1		4.8	

Sources: National Bureau of Statistics (NBS) various years, *China Statistical Yearbook*, China Statistics Press, Beijing.

Employment expansion in China has not kept pace with the growth in the labour force. Total rural employment (which presumably included a significant number of underemployed workers, as discussed below) remained virtually stagnant at about 490 million during the past 15 years. Employment expansion in the emerging private sector in the urban economy—in foreign-invested enterprises (joint ventures and fully owned foreign firms) and local private firms (including urban informal sector employment)—has been impressive: total employment in these firms increased from 65 million in 1990 to nearly 182 million between 1990 and 2007 (Table 10.2). Total employment in the urban economy has, however, grown at a much slower rate—from 170.4 to 293.5 million—because of massive contraction in employment in the SOE sector. Total employment in SOEs declined persistently—from 103.5 million in 1990 to 64.2 million in 2007. The urban employment elasticity of economic growth—that is, the percentage increase in employment linked to a 1 per cent increase in gross domestic product (GDP)—remains low, fluctuating between 0.1 and 0.2 during 1990–2001 (Brooks and Tao 2003).

Table 10.2 Labour force and employment (millions)

	1985	1990	1995	2000	2001	2002	2003	2004	2005	2006	2007
Labour force	501	653.2	688.5	739.9	744.3	753.6	760.8	768.2	778.8	782.4	786.5
Total employment	498.7	647.5	680.7	720.9	730.3	737.4	744.3	752.0	758.3	764.0	769.9
Urban employment	128.1	170.4	190.4	231.5	239.4	247.8	256.4	264.8	273.3	283.1	293.5
State-owned enterprises	89.9	103.5	112.6	81	76.4	71.6	68.8	67.1	64.9	64.3	64.2
Collectively owned enterprises[a]	33.2	35.5	31.5	15.0	12.9	11.2	11.73	10.9	10.0	9.4	8.9
Foreign-funded enterprises	0.1	0.7	5.1	6.4	6.7	7.6	4.5	5.6	6.9	8.0	9.0
Limited-liability corporations	..	..	..	..	..	..	12.6	14.4	17.5	19.2	20.8
State-holding corporations	..	..	..	..	..	..	5.9	6.2	7.0	7.4	7.9
Privately funded enterprises	0.8	6.7	20.6	34	36.6	42.7	25.5	29.9	34.6	39.5	45.8
Residual	4.9	23.1	16.9	81.6	91.6	96.4	145.9	151.2	157.0	161.9	165.5
Rural areas	370.7	477.1	490.3	489.3	490.9	489.6	487.9	487.2	484.9	480.9	476.4
Township and village enterprises	69.8	92.7	128.6	128.2	130.9	132.9	135.7	138.7	142.7	146.8	150.9
Privately owned enterprises	..	1.1	4.7	11.4	11.9	14.1	17.5	20.2	23.7	26.3	26.7
Self-employed	305.7	14.9	30.5	29.3	26.3	24.7	22.6	20.7	21.2	21.5	21.9
Residual	288.4	368.4	326.4	320.4	321.8	318	312.1	307.7	297.3	286.3	276.9

.. not available

[a] includes cooperative units

Source: National Statistical Bureau (NBS) various years, *China Statistical Yearbook*, China Statistics Press, Beijing.

Surplus labour in the urban economy

The combination of natural population increase and rural-to-urban migration has resulted in continued additions to the urban labour supply. Also, restructuring and downsizing of SOEs—located mostly in urban areas—has led to massive lay-offs. As discussed, employment growth in the emerging private sector, though impressive, has not kept pace with the increase in the urban labour force. Consequently, China's cities now confront large-scale open unemployment.

The official (registered) urban unemployment rate published by the National Bureau of Statistics (NBS),[6] which remained within the narrow margin of 2.3 to 2.6 per cent in the 1990s, increased to 4.3 per cent in 2003 and then declined slightly to 4 per cent in 2007 (this amounted to 8.6 million unemployed workers) (Figure 10.1). Data on provincial-level unemployment from the same source generally show higher unemployment rates in recent years in labour-sending interior provinces (such as Sichuan, Guizhou, Yunnan and Ningxia) than in rapidly growing coastal provinces (such as Beijing, Guangdong, Hainan and Guangxi) (Table 10.3). There are, however, strong reasons to believe that the official data grossly understate the level of unemployment—for several reasons. First, the data-reporting system covers only the age range sixteen–fifty for men and sixteen–forty-five for women. Second, a large number of workers laid off from SOEs are still regarded as employed by their former enterprises. Third, many unemployed people do not have incentives to register themselves at the local employment service agencies because they do not qualify for social security payments or do not have the required qualifications to find employment through such formal mechanisms. Fourth, unemployed people without urban residency status (migrants) are automatically excluded from the registration system, and therefore the bulk of the 'floating population'—which forms a large and growing segment of the urban labour force—is not captured in these data.

Table 10.3 Registered unemployment rates by province, 1995–2005
(per cent)

	1990	1995	2000	2001	2002	2003	2004	2005	2006	2007
China average	2.5	2.9	3.1	3.6	4.0	4.3	4.2	4.2	4.1	4.0
Northern provinces										
Beijing	0.4	0.4	0.8	1.2	1.4	1.4	1.3	2.1	2.0	1.8
Tianjin	2.7	1.0	3.2	3.6	3.9	3.8	3.8	3.7	3.6	3.6
Hebei	1.1	2.2	2.8	3.2	3.6	3.9	4.0	3.9	3.8	3.8
Shanxi	1.2	1.4	2.2	2.6	3.4	3.0	3.1	3.0	3.2	3.2
Inner Mongolia	3.8	3.8	3.3	3.7	4.1	4.5	4.6	4.3	4.1	4.0
North-eastern provinces										
Liaoning	2.2	2.7	3.7	3.2	6.5	6.5	6.5	5.6	5.1	4.3
Jilin	1.9	2.0	3.7	3.1	3.6	4.3	4.2	4.2	4.2	3.9
Heilongjiang	2.2	2.9	3.3	4.7	4.9	4.2	4.5	4.4	4.4	4.3
Eastern provinces										
Shanghai	1.5	2.6	3.5		4.8	4.9	4.5	..	4.4	4.2
Jiangsu	2.4	2.1	3.2	3.6	4.2	4.1	3.8	3.6	3.4	3.2
Zhejiang	2.2	3.2	3.5	3.7	4.2	4.2	4.1	3.7	3.5	3.3
Anhui	2.8	3.1	3.3	3.7	4.0	4.1	4.2	4.4	4.3	4.1
Fujian	2.6	2.6	2.6	3.8	4.2	4.1	4.0	4.0	3.9	3.9
Jiangxi	2.4	2.1	2.9	3.3	3.4	3.6	3.6	3.5	3.6	3.4
Shandong	3.2	3.2	3.2	3.3	3.6	3.6	3.4	3.3	3.3	3.2
Central and southern provinces										
Henan	3.3	2.6	2.6	2.8	2.9	3.1	3.4	3.5	3.5	3.4
Hubei	1.7	3.1	3.5	4.0	4.3	4.3	4.2	4.3	4.2	4.2
Hunan	2.7	3.8	3.7	4.0	4.0	4.5	4.4	4.3	4.3	4.3
Guangdong	2.2	2.6	2.5	2.9	3.1	3.6	2.7	2.6	2.6	2.5
Guangxi	3.9	3.6	3.2	3.5	3.7	3.4	4.1	4.2	4.2	3.8
Hainan	3.0	4.2	3.2	3.4	3.1	4.1	3.4	3.6	3.6	3.5
South-western provinces										
Chongqing	..	..	3.5	3.9	4.1	4.4	4.1	4.1	4.0	4.0
Sichuan	3.7	3.7	4.0	4.3	4.5	4.0	4.4	4.6	4.5	4.2
Guizhou	4.1	5.9	3.8	4.0	4.1	4.1	4.1	4.2	4.1	4.0
Yunnan	2.5	2.9	2.6	3.3	4.0	3.5	4.3	4.2	4.3	4.2
North-western provinces										
Shaanxi	2.8	3.5	2.7	3.2	3.3	3.8	3.8	4.2	4.0	4.0
Gansu	4.9	5.5	2.7	2.8	3.2	4.4	3.4	3.3	3.6	3.3
Qinghai	5.6	7.4	2.4	3.5	3.6	3.5	3.9	3.9	3.9	3.8
Ningxia	5.4	6.4	4.6	4.4	4.4	3.0	4.5	4.5	4.3	4.3
Xinjiang	3.0	..	3.8	3.7	3.7	2.9	3.5	3.9	3.9	3.9

.. not available

Source: National Bureau of Statistics (NBS) various years, *China Labour Yearbook*, China Statistics Press, Beijing.

Figure 10.1 Registered unemployment rate in urban areas

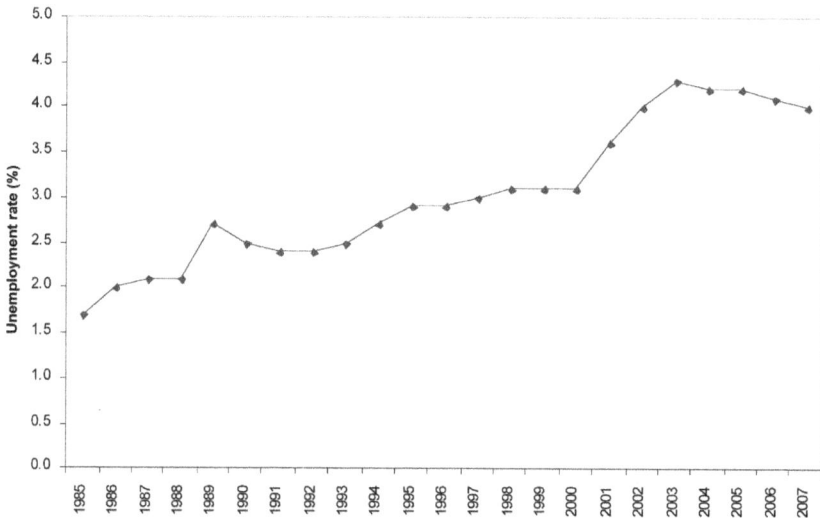

Source: National Bureau of Statistics (NBS) various years, *China Labour Yearbook*, China Statistics Press, Beijing.

According to estimates based on data from the Survey of Population Changes (SPC) conducted by the National Census Bureau (NCB) (which is based on the International Labour Organisation's recommended definitions of employment/unemployment and is not subject to the limitations discussed above), the urban unemployment rate rose from 3.4 per cent in 1995 to 7.7 per cent in 2000 and then declined slightly to a bit above 6 per cent in 2002 and 2003 (Tao 2006:Table 8.6). A survey conducted by the Institute of Population and Labour Economics of the Chinese Academy of Social Sciences between September 1996 and January 2002 in five major cities (Fuzhou, Shanghai, Shenyang, Xian and Wuhan) has come up with an average unemployment rate of 8 per cent (about 15 million people), with rates as high as 14 per cent in some localities (Hu 2007).

Unemployment in rural areas

At the end of the planned economy era in 1978, 71 per cent of the workforce was involved in agriculture. The absolute number of agricultural workers reached a peak of 391 million in 1991, and it has since been in a long, steady decline. By 2001, 33 per cent of rural employment was non-farm related and half of the income in rural areas was generated by non-farm activities (Cooper 2006). The share of agricultural employment in total employment has, however, been consistently and significantly higher than the share of agriculture in GDP. Most of the workers in agricultural pursuits are essentially underemployed; according to official estimates, more than 130 million rural people lack sufficient land or employment opportunities to guarantee their livelihoods (World Bank 2005). In addition to farmers who are underemployed, open rural unemployment has also risen in rural China in recent years. The rural unemployed includes farmers who have been dispossessed though land requisitions, workers who are laid off from TVEs and rural cadres and teachers who are laid off on account of continuing tax reforms and local government restructuring (Tao 2006:527–8).

No data on rural employment and production are available for a systematic quantification of surplus labour in the rural economy in China. A recent study by the Organisation for Economic Cooperation and Development (OECD 2003) has come up with some tentative estimates comparing the average labour productivity of non-agriculture with that of agriculture. When the average production of non-agricultural industries was used as a benchmark, rural hidden unemployment was found to be as high as 275 million people. When the benchmark was set at a more modest level of one-third of the productivity of non-agricultural workers, the estimate came down to 150 million people.

The mere presence of surplus labour does not, however, imply that this labour is readily available for urban employment. This is because migration decisions depend on economic and non-economic considerations. A study of the migration behaviour of rural people in Sichuan Province (the most populous and predominantly rural province in China) finds that although migration yields a large monetary premium, rural people will choose to stay in rural areas rather than migrate under current regulations and conditions (Zhao 1999). According to this study, the major deterrent to migration is the lack of safety during transition and in destination cities as well as forced separation from families and the unavailability of suitable housing in destination cities, primarily because, under the *hukou* system, migrants do not have legal rights to reside permanently in cities. An important implication of the findings of this study, which has also been confirmed by a number of subsequent studies (as surveyed in Zhao 2005), is that the number of migratory workers would be higher in the absence of artificial barriers to migration.

Wage trends

We have observed in the previous section that surplus labour conditions remain in the Chinese economy. Are the trends and patterns of wage behaviour in the Chinese economy consistent with the predictions of the Lewis model? If not, how can we explain the 'Chinese wage puzzle'?

Data on real wage behaviour in the urban sector compiled from NBS sources are plotted in Figure 10.2. It is evident that real wages in all three ownership categories—SOEs, collectively owned firms and private-sector firms[7]—remained virtually stagnant well into the mid-1990s (Figure 10.2). Since then, there has been a persistent increase across the board.

Figure 10.2 Growth of real urban wages[a] by ownership of firms, 1986–2005 (three-year moving averages, centred on the current year)

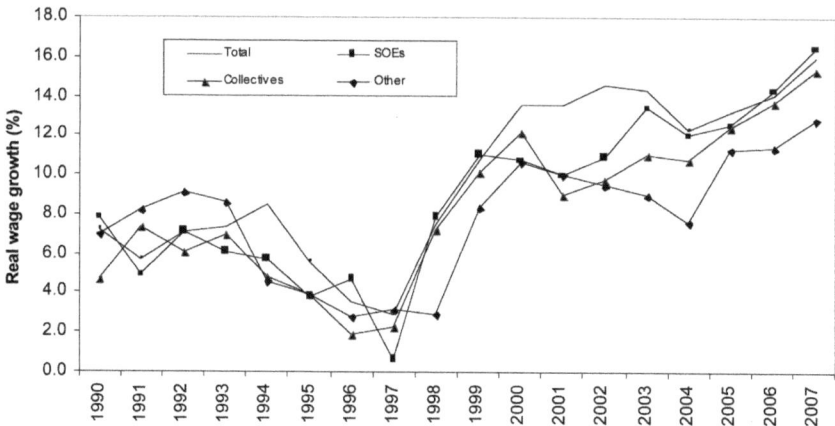

[a] nominal wage deleted by the consumer price index (CPI) (1990 = 100)

Sources: Based on data compiled from National Bureau of Statistics (NBS) various years, *China Labour Yearbook*, China Statistics Press, Beijing; and National Bureau of Statistics (NBS) various years, *China Statistical Yearbook*, China Statistics Press, Beijing.

It is important to note that data on urban wages could give a distorted picture of the labour market conditions faced by rural workers seeking employment in the urban economy by incorporating changes in output and, therefore, the skill mix (Ranis 1995:514). Also, the data tend to be biased by embodying a significant wage premium for workers employed by multinational affiliates and large domestic firms. A more meaningful analysis therefore requires data on unskilled-worker wages or wages of rural migrant workers engaged in the urban informal sector. Apart from these general limitations of the urban wage data, Chinese official urban wage data are particularly problematic because they cover only the upper strata of urban labour markets. Moreover, the magnitude of the bias arising from this omission has presumably increased over time with the sharp increase in rural–urban migration in the past two decades.

These limitations notwithstanding, a careful analysis of official wage data disaggregated by ownership and at the provincial level does point to the fragility of any inferences based on the aggregate series. To comment first on data by ownership categories, among these, the wage growth of SOEs has outpaced that of the urban collective sector and private firms (where wage setting is relatively more market based) by a significant margin. During 1995–2007, the real wage rate of SOEs grew at an average annual rate of 11.2 per cent compared with 7.4 per cent for private firms and 8.3 per cent for collective firms. The SOE wage bill includes additional payments in the form of pensions, health care and housing (Zhu 2002). Moreover, since late 1990, SOE workers' salaries and wages have been periodically and substantially increased as part of the expansionary macroeconomic policy of the government (Rawski 2003). The growth of non-SOE real wages (estimated by purging the SOE wage rate using the employment share weight) for the period 1995–2007 turns out to be 7.1 per cent compared with the average rate of 11.5 per cent recorded in the reported series.

Data on real urban wages at the provincial level (covering all provinces for which data are readily available) from the same source are reported in Table 10.4. The data show a significant increase in real wages across all provinces from about the mid-1990s. This overall pattern does not, however, tell us anything definitive about labour market tightening. There is reason to believe that wages in different sectors generally move together, even in situations in which labour is in 'surplus' in the sense that the marginal product is zero. 'Surplus' workers in the traditional economy are usually involved in activities in which work and income are shared and hence workers' compensation is related to the average product, not to marginal product. When workers are drawn from the traditional sector into the modern sector, therefore, wages can increase throughout the economy, even when surplus labour conditions continue to prevail in the traditional sector.

Table 10.4 Real wages (monthly) by province (RMB at 1985 prices)[a]

Year	Hebei	Henan	Hunan	Jiangsu	Sichuan	Shanghai	Anhui	Shandong	Qinghai	Guangdong	Fujian	Jilin
1985	1,075	1,015	1,059	1,135	992	1,416	950	1,110	1,719	1,393	1,059	1,081
1986	1,200	1,099	1,159	1,245	1,089	1,589	1,059	1,256	1,805	1,469	1,167	1,152
1987	1,223	1,122	1,211	1,294	1,100	1,647	1,069	1,263	1,793	1,494	1,132	1,198
1988	1,255	1,098	1,162	1,298	1,086	1,650	1,053	1,328	1,716	1,491	1,115	1,188
1989	1,141	1,024	1,070	1,169	1,013	1,631	989	1,220	1,545	1,453	1,081	1,091
1990	1,258	1,140	1,169	1,271	1,091	1,716	1,084	1,321	1,587	1,630	1,242	1,119
1991	1,299	1,199	1,196	1,337	1,168	1,796	1,095	1,342	1,597	1,847	1,344	1,135
1992	1,411	1,315	1,268	1,539	1,217	2,068	1,170	1,426	1,607	2,064	1,458	1,186
1993	1,514	1,389	1,351	1,734	1,248	2,274	1,248	1,532	1,676	2,245	1,581	1,233
1994	1,703	1,486	1,408	1,880	1,310	2,405	1,346	1,710	1,872	2,465	1,773	1,387
1995	1,709	1,563	1,383	1,921	1,285	2,540	1,425	1,725	1,834	2,506	1,843	1,455
1996	1,743	1,604	1,365	1,969	1,311	2,673	1,456	1,777	1,924	2,591	1,986	1,646
1997	1,814	1,644	1,387	2,078	1,354	2,785	1,525	1,857	1,947	2,702	2,209	1,674
1998	1,885	1,866	1,422	2,390	1,418	2,940	1,699	2,052	2,184	2,903	2,501	1,952
1999	2,318	2,063	1,536	2,692	1,756	3,398	1,850	2,308	2,488	3,267	2,807	2,176
2000	2,576	2,327	1,661	3,015	2,025	3,613	1,971	2,639	2,768	3,939	3,066	2,443
2001	2,876	2,639	1,981	3,484	2,349	4,162	2,219	2,958	3,464	4,500	3,526	2,670
2002	3,339	3,055	2,259	3,970	2,685	4,540	2,635	3,385	3,797	5,184	3,925	3,056
2003	3,644	3,525	2,488	4,582	3,024	5,163	2,948	3,699	3,950	5,780	4,186	3,350
2004	4,038	3,769	2,754	5,128	3,256	5,565	3,446	4,070	4,297	6,211	4,386	3,611
2005	4,320	4,062	3,059	5,551	3,407	5,867	3,809	4,442	4,562	6,386	4,490	3,908
2006	4,751	4,515	3,378	6,310	3,753	6,498	4,357	4,871	4,854	6,991	4,747	4,248

Year	Hebei	Henan	Hunan	Jiangsu	Sichuan	Shanghai	Anhui	Shandong	Qinghai	Guangdong	Fujian	Jilin
2007	5174	4847	3745	6946	3984	6927	4954	5338	5217	7350	4916	4588
Memo item: average annual growth rates												
1985–95	4.94	4.55	2.85	5.63	2.74	6.12	4.27	4.68	0.8	6.19	5.88	3.14
1995–2007	9.1	9.6	8.0	10.7	9.1	8.5	10.6	9.2	8.4	8.9	8.2	9.7
1985–2007	7.3	7.4	5.7	8.5	6.4	7.5	7.9	7.2	5.1	7.7	7.2	6.9

[a] nominal wage deflated by provincial CPI

Sources: Compiled from National Bureau of Statistics (NBS) various years, *China Labour Yearbook*, China Statistics Press, Beijing; and National Bureau of Statistics (NBS) various years, *China Statistical Yearbook*, China Statistics Press, Beijing.

So what is important is the relative rate of wage growth and the differences in relative wage levels. The data in fact point to vast differences in the magnitude of wage growth across provinces. Wage growth in rapidly growing coastal provinces (such as Guangdong, Shanghai and Guangxi) has been much faster than in labour-sending interior provinces (such as Sichuan, Gansu and Qinghai). A comparison of the real wages of Sichuan (by far the largest source of migrant labour) and Guangdong (the fastest-growing and most labour-absorbing province) illustrates this point (Figure 10.3). In the late 1980s, there was not much difference between the wage levels in the two provinces. During the next 15 years, the growth rate of wages in Guangdong was almost twice as fast as that in Sichuan.

Figure 10.3 Real wages[a] in Sichuan and Guangdong Provinces, 1985–2007 (CNY at 1990 prices)[b]

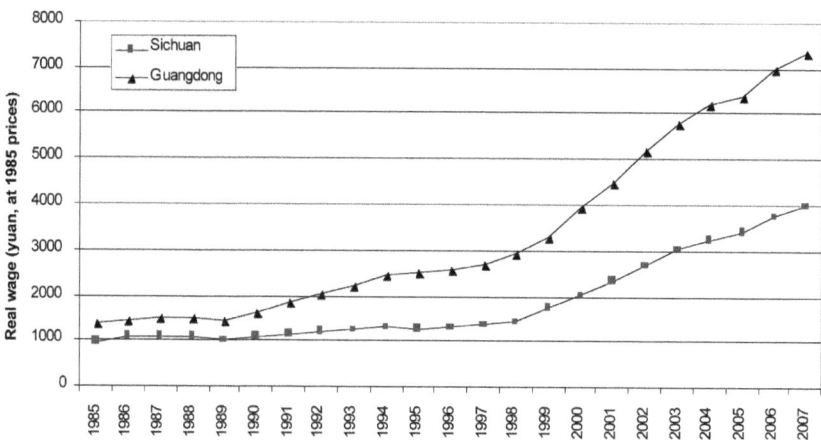

[a] nominal wage (yuan) deflated by the regional CPI (1990 = 100)
[b] average annual growth rates—for Sichuan: 5.63 (1985–95), 10.7 (1995–2007) and 8.5 (1985–2007), for Guangdong: 6.19 (1985–95), 8.9 (1995–2007) and 7.7 (1985–2007)

Sources: Based on data compiled from National Bureau of Statistics (NBS) various years, *China Labour Yearbook*, China Statistics Press, Beijing; and National Bureau of Statistics (NBS) various years, *China Statistical Yearbook*, China Statistics Press, Beijing.

So far, we have examined the trends and patterns of urban wages using official data from the *China Labour Yearbook*. We now turn to examining the official data on the wages of workers in TVEs available from another official source, *Town and Village Enterprise Yearbook*.[8] Presumably, TVE data better reflect labour market conditions facing urban unskilled workers than with the aggregate wage series or wages relating to workers in other types of firms (Banister 2005b; Cooper 2006). Apparently, virtually all of China's manufacturing enterprises and factories located outside strict city limits are lumped together under the category 'town and village enterprises' (TVEs). Foreign and domestic manufacturers who are eager to keep down their costs (such as requirements to pay social insurance and other welfare obligations) and statistical requirements prefer their factories to be classified as rural or TVE. The majority of TVEs (about 94 per cent) are located in 'rural areas' (by the official definition) and they employ largely unskilled rural workers whose employment decisions are presumably closely tied to agricultural income.

Real annual wages of workers in urban private enterprise and TVEs for the period 1987–2005 are compared in Figure 10.4. During this period, the average real wages of TVE workers rose at only an annual rate of 5.5 per cent compared with 6.5 per cent growth in urban private enterprises. More importantly, the data indicate that the vast wage gap between TVEs and urban enterprises has widened in recent years. During 2000–05, the average TVE wage rate amounted to 65 per cent of that in urban private firms. According to provincial-level data (not reported here, for brevity), these gaps are much wider in rapidly growing costal provinces than in the labour-sending interior provinces (Table 10.5). It seems that China's labour market conditions enable firms to achieve significant cost advantages by manipulating the existing institutional procedures to achieve TVE status.

Figure 10.4 Real manual wages[a] in urban private firms and TVEs, 1989–2005 (CNY at 1985 prices)

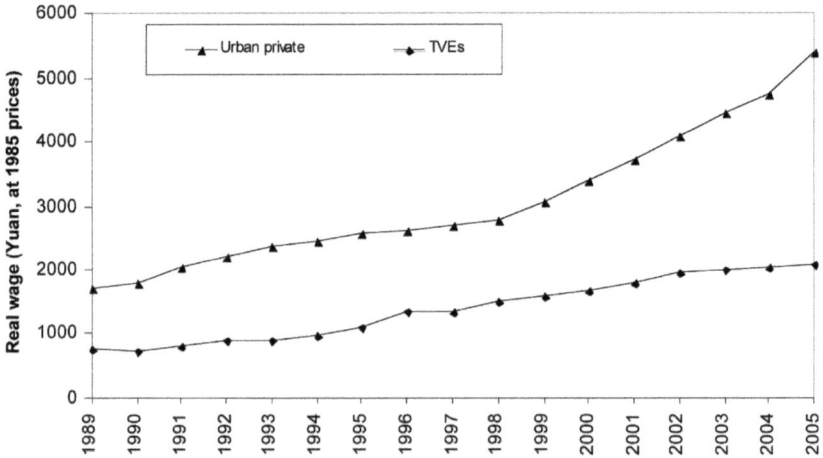

[a] nominal wage (yuan) deflated by the regional CPI (1985 = 100)

Sources: Based on data compiled from National Bureau of Statistics (NBS) various years, *China Labour Yearbook*, China Statistics Press, Beijing; National Bureau of Statistics (NBS) various years, *China Statistical Yearbook*, China Statistics Press, Beijing; National Bureau of Statistics (NBS) various years, *Town and Village Enterprise Yearbook*, China Statistics Press, Beijing.

Table 10.5 Average wage in TVEs relative to average wages in urban private firms (per cent)

Province	1994–95[a]	2004–05[a]	Province	1994–95[a]	2004–05[a]
Beijing	69.6	82.0	Henan	102.0	71.0
Tianjin	85.7	119.6	Hubei	87.9	87.0
Hebei	103.3	75.9	Hunan	90.0	74.6
Shanxi	93.8	106.2	Guangdong	77.5	73.2
Inner Mongolia	101.2	95.0	Guangxi	90.0	68.2
Liaoning	101.8	85.4	Hainan	81.2	73.8
Jilin	129.9	69.4	Sichuan	83.0	53.4
Heilongjiang	115.6	85.5	Guizhou	63.2	70.1
Shanghai	67.3	74.2	Yunnan	72.5	56.5
Jiangsu	88.2	87.0	Shaanxi	82.9	64.8
Zhejiang	89.4	67.1	Gansu	56.7	58.7
Anhui	112.4	91.7	Qinghai	69.6	42.5
Fujian	105.9	66.5	Ningxia	61.1	48.1
Jiangxi	107.7	76.1	Xinjiang	76.5	52.3
Shandong	84.2	68.2	National average	81.6	74.2

[a] two-year average

Sources: Based on data compiled from National Bureau of Statistics (NBS) various years, *China Labour Yearbook*, China Statistics Press, Beijing; National Bureau of Statistics (NBS) various years, *China Statistical Yearbook*, China Statistics Press, Beijing; National Bureau of Statistics (NBS) various years, *Town and Village Enterprise Yearbook*, China Statistics Press, Beijing.

The discussion so far suggests that even the official data when analysed at the disaggregate level suggest significant continuing duality and surplus labour conditions in the Chinese labour market. The few available studies that have looked specifically at the relative wages of unskilled and migrant workers provide further support for this inference. For instance, a study of wage behaviour in Guangdong Province found that between 1992 and 2002, the real wages of migrant workers had hardly risen (Qin 2003). Using a survey of residents in Hubei Province (a major labour-sending province), Zhu (2002) found, after controlling for skill differences, that the wages of workers who had migrated to the city were almost twice as high as those workers who had remained in the countryside. In a survey of the floating population in Shanghai Province, Meng and Zhang (2001) found a clear division between the floating population and local residents both in terms of work conditions and wages. In a recent study, Meng and Bai (2007) examined wage patterns of unskilled workers during the five-year period from 2000–04 using a unique data set extracted from the payrolls of seven large manufacturing factories in Guangdong Province. A simple comparison of wages showed that the real wages of production workers increased at an average annual rate of only 3.5 per cent compared with a rate of more than 6 per cent for the total sample of workers. Once education, period of employment and other variables that could affect wage levels had been controlled for, the average annual growth rate for the unskilled workers turned out to be negative or near zero.

Functional share of labour in value added

How have the surplus labour conditions in the Chinese economy been reflected in the functional distribution of income in domestic manufacturing in China? The data on the labour share in value added plotted in Figure 10.4 provide important insight into this issue. Overall, the patterns shown by the data are quite consistent with the Lewisian prediction of persistence of high profits in the modern sector in a surplus labour economy.

In the mid-1990s, labour received about half of total industrial value added. This share declined persistently to about 40 per cent by 2006. The disaggregated data clearly suggest that the aggregate wage share is heavily influenced by the functional distribution of income in SOEs, whose employment practices have continued to be influenced by non-market considerations. The wage share in private enterprises (encompassing foreign-invested and domestic private enterprises, which generally operate under competitive conditions) in 1999 was 22 per cent (compared with 34 per cent for SOEs) and it declined sharply during the ensuing years, reaching 12 per cent in 2006. Although remarkably low by the standards of mature industrial countries, these figures are consistent with the evidence available about the functional distribution of income in the late 1940s through to the early 1960s in Hong Kong, when labour-intensive growth there was fuelled by a massive influx of workers (refugees) from the Chinese mainland (Chow and Papanek 1981; Athukorala and Manning 1999). Some recent firm-level studies of Chinese manufacturing performance have also reported estimates that corroborate the private-sector wage shares reported in Figure 10.5 (Bergsten et al. 2006:Ch.3; Fukao et al. 2007).

Figure 10.5 Wage share in industrial value added by ownership category, 1995–2007

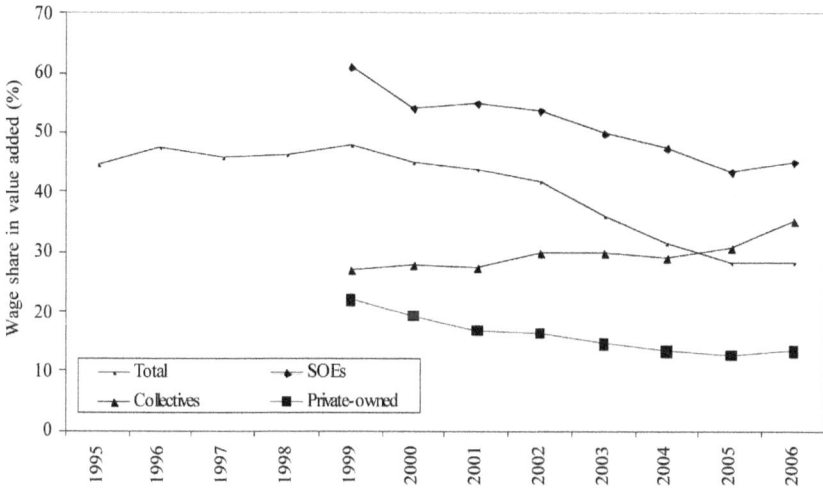

Source: Based on data compiled from *CEIM Database*.

Of course, the degree of elasticity of labour supply is not the sole determinant of the functional distribution of income.[9] For instance, during the early transitional period, when wages were relatively stable, the labour share in value added could decline (increase) whenever its average productivity increased (decreased). If technological change is biased in a labour-saving direction—that is, a change contributing to slower labour absorption—labour productivity will increase, leading to a decline in the labour share in value added and a less equitable pattern of family income distribution (Fei et al. 1985; Minami 1973). The contrasting patterns in labour share in value added among the three ownership categories are, however, not supportive of such an alternative inference; as we have noted, the labour share of value added of private-sector enterprises has been much lower and has declined faster over the years compared with SOEs, even though total labour absorption in the former has increased at a much faster rate. All in all, the data seem to suggest that surplus labour conditions in China remain highly favourable for private sector industrial expansion, notwithstanding some reported isolated cases of labour scarcity.

Concluding remarks

China's dramatic economic expansion, fuelled by massive domestic labour surpluses, has not yet run out of steam. There is still considerable room for moving unskilled workers out of agriculture into more productive economic activities in the modern sector. In addition, rural–urban labour migration in the past two decades and labour shedding by the SOE sector have given rise to a significant additional reserve of workers within the urban sector.

Absorbing these labour surpluses in a gainful way is vital for maintaining the growth momentum of the economy and for poverty reduction. This calls for further labour market reforms to remove institutional constraints on labour mobility. It is also vital to avoid politically popular, but economically counterproductive policies that artificially increase the cost of hiring workers. In this context, the government's plan to create a universal employment insurance scheme and introduce retirement pensions and other social security provisions—as well as the already implemented Labour Contract Law—could be premature. The best social protection that the government can provide the poor is opportunities for gainful employment—and greater labour market flexibility and enhanced labour mobility are essential prerequisites for achieving this objective.

Given the environmental considerations and infrastructure problems associated with massive rural–urban migration, there is a strong case for renewed emphasis on rural development—in particular, in initiatives to spread industrialisation dynamism to the countryside. In this, China might find important policy lessons in the Taiwanese experience of promoting rural non-agricultural activities as part of a balanced growth process in the 1960s and 1970s. A key factor behind Taiwan's highly publicised 'growth with equity' outcome was that its industrialisation patterns clearly avoided the customary relative (somewhat absolute) decline in rural non-agricultural activities—increasingly, in food processing. Rural non-agricultural activities were not competed out of existence by favoured urban industries and services (Ranis 1993). While the current emphasis of the Chinese Government on higher education is justifiable from a long-term perspective, the existing surplus-labour conditions in the countryside call for an even greater emphasis on primary education.

References

Athukorala, P. and Manning, C. 1999, *Structural Change and International Migration in East Asia: Adjusting to labour scarcity*, Oxford University Press, Melbourne and Oxford.

Banister, J. 2005a, 'Manufacturing employment in China', *Monthly Labor Review*, July, US Bureau of Labor Statistics, pp. 11–29.

—— 2005b, 'Manufacturing earnings and compensation in China', *Monthly Labor Review*, August, US Bureau of Labor Statistics, pp. 22–40.

Basu, K. 1997, *Analytical Development Economics*, MIT Press, Cambridge, Mass.

Bergsten, C. F., Gill, B., Lardy, N. R. and Mitchell, D. 2006, *China: The balance sheet*, Public Affairs, New York.

Brooks, R. and Tao, R. 2003, *China's labour market performance and challenges*, IMF Working Paper, no. WP/03/210, International Monetary Fund, Washington, DC.

Cheng, T. and Selden, M. 1994, 'The origin and social consequences of China's *hukou* system', *China Quarterly*, vol. 139, pp. 644–68.

Chow, S. C. and Papanek, G. 1981, 'Laissez-faire, growth and equity—Hong Kong', *Economic Journal*, vol. 91, no. 263, pp. 466–85.

Cooper, R. N. 2006, *How integrated are Chinese and Indian labour into the world economy?*, Background paper for *Dancing with Giants: China, India and the global economy*, The World Bank, Washington, DC.

Eckstein, A. 1977, *China's Economic Revolution*, Cambridge University Press, Cambridge.

Fei, J. C. H. and Ranis, G. 1997, *Growth and Development from an Evolutionary Perspective*, Basil Blackwell, Oxford.

Fei, J. C. H., Ohkawa, K. and Ranis, G. 1985, 'Economic development in historical perspective: Japan, Korea and Taiwan', in K. Ohkawa, G. Ranis and L. Meissner (eds), *Japan and the Developing Countries: A comparative analysis*, Basil Blackwell, Oxford, pp. 35–64.

Fields, G. S. 1994, 'Changing labor market conditions and economic development in Hong Kong, the Republic of Korea, Singapore and Taiwan, China', *World Bank Economic Review*, vol. 8, no. 3, pp. 395–414.

Fukao, K., Ito, K., Kabe, S., Liu, D. and Takeuchi, F. 2007, Are Japanese firms failing to catch up in localisation? An empirical analysis based on affiliate-level data of Japanese firms and a case study of automobile industry in China, Draft paper, Institute of Economic Research, Hitotsubashi University, Tokyo.

Garnaut, R. and Huang, Y. 2006, 'Continued rapid growth and the turning point in China's development', in R. Garnaut and L. Song (eds), *The Turning Point in China's Economic Development*, Asia Pacific Press, Canberra, pp. 12–34.

Garnaut, R. and Ma, G. 1996, 'The third revolution', in R. Garnaut, G. Shatian and G. Ma (eds), *The Third Revolution in the Chinese Countryside*, Cambridge University Press, Cambridge.

Hausmann, R., Lim, E. and Spence, M. 2006, *China and the global economy: medium-term issues and options, a synthesis report*, Centre for International Development Discussion Paper, no. RWP06-029, John F. Kennedy School of Government, Harvard University, Cambridge, Mass.

Hu, A. 2007, *Economic and Social Transformation in China: Challenges and opportunities*, Routledge, London.

Islam, N. and Yokoda, K. 2006, 'An initial look at China's industrialization in light of the Lewis growth model', *East Asian Economic Perspectives*, vol. 17, no. 2, pp. 103–32.

Kindleberger, C. P. 1967, *Europe's Postwar Growth: The role of labour supply*, Harvard University Press, Cambridge, Mass.

Lewis, A. W. 1954, 'Economic development with unlimited supplies of labour', *Manchester School*, vol. 22, no. 2, pp. 139–91.

—— 1958, 'Unlimited labour: further notes', *Manchester School*, vol. 26, no. 1, pp. 1–32.

—— 1979, 'Dual economy revisited', *Manchester School*, vol. 47, no. 3, pp. 211–29.

Liang, Z. and Ma, Z. 2004, 'China's floating population: new evidence from the 2000 census', *Population and Development Review*, vol. 30, no. 3, pp. 467–88.

Meng, X. 2000, *Labour Market Reforms in China*, Cambridge University Press, Cambridge.

Meng, X. and Bai, N. 2007, 'How much have the wages of unskilled workers in China increased: data from seven factories in Guangdong', in R. Garnaut and L. Song (eds), *China: Linking markets for growth*, Asia Pacific Press, Canberra, pp. 151–74.

Meng, X. and Zhang, J. 2001, 'The two-tier labor market in China—occupational segregation and wage differentials between urban residents and rural migrants in Shanghai', *Journal of Comparative Economics*, vol. 29, no. 3, pp. 485–504.

Minami, R. 1973, *The Turning Points in Economic Development: Japanese experience*, Konokuniya, Tokyo.

—— 1986, *The Economic Development of Japan: A quantitative study*, Macmillan, London.

National Bureau of Statistics (NBS) 2005, *Chain Labour Statistics Yearbook*, China Statistics Press, Beijing.

—— various years, *China Labour Yearbook*, China Statistics Press, Beijing;

—— various years, *China Statistical Yearbook*, China Statistics Press, Beijing;

—— various years, *Town and Village Enterprise Yearbook*, China Statistics Press, Beijing.

Naughton, B. 2007, *China's Economy: Transition and growth*, MIT Press, Cambridge, Mass.

Organisation for Economic Cooperation and Development (OECD) 2003, *Migration and Labour Markets in Asia 2002*, Organisation for Economic Cooperation and Development, Paris.

Putterman, L. 1992, 'Dualism and reform in China', *Economic Development and Cultural Change*, vol. 72, no. 6, pp. 712–23.

Ranis, G. and Fei, J. C. H. 1975, 'Growth and employment in the open dualistic economy: the case of Taiwan and Korea', *Journal of Development Studies*, vol. 11, no. 2, pp. 32–63.

Ranis, G. 1995, 'Another look at the East Asian miracle', *World Bank Economic Review*, vol. 9, no. 3, pp. 509–34.

Rawski, T. G. 2003, 'Recent development in China's labour economy', in K. Nakagane and T. Kojima (eds), *Restructuring China: Party, society and after the reform and opening door*, The Tokyo Bunko, Tokyo, pp. 16–47.

Rawski, T. G. and Xiao, W. 2001, 'Symposium on Chinese economic statistics: introduction', *China Economic Review*, vol. 13, no. 4, pp. 361–72.

Rosenzweig, M. R. 1988, 'Labour markets in low-income countries', in H. B. Chenery and T. N. Srinivasan (eds), *Handbook of Development Economics. Volume 1*, North Holland, Amsterdam.

Shi, L. and Sato, H. (eds) 2006, *Unemployment, Inequality and Poverty in Urban China*, Routledge, London.

Siebert, H. 2007, 'China: coming to grips with the new global player', *World Economy*, vol. 30, no. 6, pp. 883–922.

Tao, R. 2006, 'The labor market in the People's Republic of China: developments and policy challenges in economic transition', in J. Felipe and R. Hasan (eds), *Labour Markets in Asia: Issues and perspectives*, Palgrave Macmillan, London, pp. 503–58.

World Bank 2005, *China: integration of national product and factor markets—economic benefits and policy recommendations*, World Bank Report, no. 31973-CHA, The World Bank, Washington, DC.

Wu, X. and Treiman, D. J. 2004, 'The household registration system and social stratification in China, 1955–1996', *Demography*, vol. 41, no. 2, pp. 363–84.

Zhao, Y. 1999, 'Labor migration and earnings differences: the case of rural China', *Economic Development and Cultural Change*, vol. 47, no. 4, pp. 767–82.

Zhao, Z. 2005, 'Migration, labour market flexibility, and wage determination in China: a survey', *The Developing Economies*, vol. XLIII, no. 2, pp. 285–312.

Zhu, N. 2002, 'The impact of income gap on migration decision in China', *China Economic Review*, vol. 13, nos 2–3, pp. 210–30.

Endnotes

1. Data reported in this paper, unless otherwise stated, come from the *China Statistical Yearbook* (NBS various years).

2. Zhao (2005) provides a comprehensive survey of this literature up to about 2003. For more recent collections of papers, which also provide extensive listing of the related literature, see Shi and Sato (2006).

3. In many applications of the Lewis model, the 'subsistence sector' has been treated as conterminous with 'agriculture'. This alternative terminology is misleading; it ignores unemployed and underemployed labour in the small-scale non-agricultural and informal sectors, which form part of the labour reserve (Lewis 1958).

4. Surplus labour exists when roughly the same level of output can be maintained by a smaller labour force with some organisational reform and very little investment.

5. Based on population projections by the China Population Information Centre.

6. According to the definition used by the NBS, unemployed people are men in the group aged sixteen–fifty and women in the group aged sixteen–forty-five who hold urban residential permits (urban *hukou*), are able to work, are unemployed but willing to be employed in non-agricultural activities and are registered at the local employment services agencies.

7. Collectively owned firms include various enterprises with collective ownership of means of production such as enterprises run by townships and villages, collective enterprises run by cities, counties and towns and neighbourhood companies. Private-sector firms ('other ownership units') cover purely local companies, foreign-invested enterprises (joint ventures, fully foreign-owned firms and firms owned by entrepreneurs from Hong Kong, Macau and Taiwan) (NBS 2005).

8. In the Chinese national data-reporting system, TVEs are treated as part of the rural economy and therefore the wages of workers employed in these enterprises are not covered in the reported urban wages data.

9. The labour share in value added in industrial activity (wB/Y, where w is the wage rate, B is the size of the industrial labour force and Y is industrial value added) is equal to the ratio of the real wage to average industrial labour productivity (w/ρ, where $\rho = Y/B$ = average labour productivity).

Flying geese within borders
How does China sustain its labour-intensive industries?

11

Cai Fang, Dewen Wang and Qu Yue

Introduction

In explaining how the current financial crisis happened, most studies are looking for the root causes in the prevailing financial institutions and credit system. And, since the crisis broke out in the United States and was channelled to other countries' financial systems and the real economy through financial, industrial and trade links, most countries have chosen to claim this crisis as an external shock imposed on their economies. Viewing the current crisis through the lens of economic history, however, we can see that the impacts of economic crises differ among countries, among regions and sectors within a country and even among enterprises within a sector. Whereas a crisis can be said to result from external sources, the degree of the shocks will be dependent on certain domestic conditions such as the pattern of growth, the state of the industrial structure, the stage of development and the technological structure and operational mechanisms of enterprises. In this regard, one needs to go beyond the framework by which the business cycles are explained simply by the operation of the monetary and credit systems and seek to find the root causes of crises from the point of view of the real economy, looking especially at what happens to the industrial structure. As one of a few economists who made a contribution to the interpretation of the business cycle from the angle of the real economy, Schumpeter (1961:Ch.6) pointed out that there were some real opportunities for economic development in an economic crisis.

While there have been no symptoms of crisis in its financial system—which is connected but not integrated with those in the United States and Europe—China has suffered from a severe economic slowdown and unemployment, because of a fall in exports brought about by the global financial crisis and the internal imbalance between consumption and investment in the domestic economy. Our observation that the impacts of the financial crisis on the real economy differ from region to region, from sector to sector and from enterprise to enterprise is consistent with Schumpeter's opinion of economic crises (Cai 2009). This is because Schumpeter does not see economic development as a smooth movement, but a process of jumps with tempestuous fluctuations. That is, the business cycle is built within the process of economic development. In Schumpeter's opinion (1961:Ch.6, 1976:Ch.7), economic development is driven by the invention and production of new consumer goods, the new methods of production or transportation, the new markets and the new forms of industrial organisation that enterprises create. This kind of innovation, however, proceeds in unevenly distributed intervals and emerges discontinuously in groups or swarms. Innovative new enterprises appear side-by-side with old enterprises and try to take their place and eventually replace them. As an adaptation, the changes in development conditions caused by the competition between the new and old enterprises act as and take the form of a business cycle—known as a process of 'creative destruction'. As a result, more and more new enterprises follow and imitate the innovation of the early enterprises, impelling an economy to boom. Because the economic boom is pushed partly by the latecomer enterprises, which are progressively less qualified in innovation, and the old enterprises' struggle for survival, the economic crisis eventually comes and is in turn followed by recession.

Furthermore, in a financial crisis, the degree of shocks and the time lag between economic recovery and employment recovery depend on the characteristics of a country's growth pattern, industrial structure and the countermeasures implemented by the government to tackle the negative impacts of the crisis. In the process of economic recovery and subsequent growth, there can be a phenomenon known as a 'jobless recovery'— that is, a time lag between the end of the recession and the time when employment finally rises above the level at the end of the recession. In explaining the reason for the jobless recovery after the 1990–91 recession, the prevailing propositions agree that it had to do with the adjustments made by industries and/or enterprises during the economic slowdown. To cope with the shocks brought about by economic crisis, enterprises are forced to strengthen their competitiveness in the market by cutting costs or restructuring, for example, and as a consequence, industrial structural adjustment takes place at a faster speed and takes a more radical form. First of all, enterprises often try to replace workers with robots and machinery in order to enhance labour productivity and reduce the costs of production. As a result, the numbers of workers needed for the same unit of production falls. Second, relatively labour-intensive industries shift abroad to adjust domestic production to its changing underlying comparative advantage. While international competitiveness can be sustained, the domestic structure of industries becomes more capital intensive. Third, as a result of all the adjustments mentioned above, the changes in the industrial structure modify the skills demanded of workers. While workers adjust their human capital to meet the changes in the skills demanded, structural unemployment can increase, because the match between employees who want to find jobs and employers who want to hire workers takes time.

Due to the close link between the Chinese and global economies, some factors that help reduce unemployment can lurk in the process of economic recovery. Before the financial crisis hit China, export-oriented enterprises—located mostly in the coastal provinces—had already begun suffering from labour shortages and wage inflation (Cai 2008). It was no accident therefore that the enterprises hit most severely by the crisis were those with rising costs of production. According to the 'flying geese' paradigm, labour-intensive industries are expected to transfer to other developing countries, where business can reduce costs of production by hiring workers at much lower costs. If one applies an extended theoretical framework of flying geese—namely, a model containing overall explanations of industrial transfer among localities—and combines it with Schumpeter's paradigm of creative destruction to analyse the characteristics of regional development in China, we can conclude that the comparative advantage in labour-intensive industries will be sustained in the Chinese economy as a whole.

Mainly thanks to the contributions made by Akamatsu (1962), Okita (1985), Vernon (1966) and Kojima (2000), the theoretical model of flying geese has experienced stages of formation and extension, eventually becoming an integrated theoretical framework interpreting industrial transfer among regions.[1] This model was created to depict how Japan—as a latecomer in development—could catch up with more advanced countries through an integrated process of moving from imports, via import substitution, to exports, and it later became a widespread notion for interpreting and understanding the development pattern of East Asian economies. That is, the production of labour-intensive goods has shifted from Japan—the leading goose—in turn to the four Asian tigers of South Korea, Taiwan, Singapore and Hong Kong, to Association of South-East Asian Nations (ASEAN) countries and to the coastal provinces of China as a result of the dynamic changes of the underlying comparative advantages in the region.

The major propositions of the extended version of this theory can be summarised as follows. First, it firmly holds its original idea that in responding to the relative change in comparative advantage, industries containing different intensities of production factors will transfer among economies. Second, flying geese-like industrial transfer is related to the characteristics of the life cycle of products (Vernon 1966), which implies its pertinence to the dynamics of comparative advantage. Third, its scope of explanatory power has been extended to foreign direct investment (FDI)—namely, its flow follows a pattern similar to that of trade among countries (Kojima 2000). Finally, the great variety in countries' and regions' stages of development, resource endowments and heritage is seen as critical reasoning with which to build such links between them (Okita 1985:21).

Industrial transfers depicted by the flying-geese pattern are directly engendered by changes in dynamic comparative advantage. That is, as a country's per capita income increases, its resource endowment changes over time. When advanced countries upgrade their industrial structure— say, from labour-intensive to capital-intensive industries—the latecomers can take over the industries washed out by the former and receive foreign investment to those industries. Changing paths of comparative advantage and forms of the flying-geese model, however, are not the same between small and large economies. This is because a small economy is characterised by the homogeneity of its resource endowment and hence its industrial structure. Once its comparative advantage changes, the economy as a whole enters a new stage of development. In contrast, a large economy is characterised by heterogeneity in its resource endowment and its industrial structure among different regions. While some regions move to a new stage of development, the development stage of others might remain unchanged. Therefore, the flying-geese pattern means industrial transfer among independent economies for a small economy, but industrial transfer among different domestic regions within an individual economy for a large country.

In a financial crisis, understanding this regional pattern of industrial structure requires combining the flying-geese model with relevant theory of the business cycle. According to Schumpeter, during times of economic crises, there is a greater chance than otherwise to form a process of creative destruction—namely, production factors can be recombined, old patterns of growth can be replaced by new ones, new technologies wash out the old technologies and productivity improvement contributes a larger and larger role to economic growth. It is obvious that intense changes in the industrial structure are the by-product of economic crises, and the acceleration of industrial transfers among regions can be given impetus on the way out of the crisis. Given the characteristics of previous regional patterns of economic growth in China, we expect to see the central-western regions—or in a broader sense, the regions that were not major engines of China's economic growth in previous years—obtain faster rates of productivity and output growth, so that they are bound to catch up with their advanced eastern counterparts and sustain the further development of China's labour-intensive industries.

The rest of this chapter is organised as follows. Section two depicts and summarises the characteristics of the regional pattern of industrial evolution in China. Section three estimates the contribution of total factor productivity (TFP) to manufacturing by region and reveals the possibility that the provinces in the central and western regions will become major drivers of China's growth. Section four calculates the real labour costs of manufacturing by region, exploring the opportunities that central and western regions will receive from the reallocation of labour-intensive industries. Section five concludes and draws policy implications by responding to some of the questions about the potential for China's economic growth and international competitiveness.

The spatial characteristics of industrial evolution

The past 30 years of rapid growth in the Chinese economy have some outstanding spatial characteristics. For a long time, China's growth has been driven by its coastal regions. Thanks to their geographical advantages, the migration of abundant cheap labour from central and western regions and, most of all, favourable and preferential government policies, the eastern provinces have been successfully receiving transferred industrial opportunities and FDI and gaining competitiveness in international markets. While the central and western provinces have gained their share more or less through spill-over effects, they have begun to catch up quickly since the beginning of this century. As a result, China's economic growth has been much more balanced than in the past since the beginning of this century. On the other hand, some serious structural shortcomings still exist—related partly to China's stage of development and partly to the incomplete nature of institutional reform.

First, thanks to its longstanding dual economy characterised by the existence of an unlimited supply of labour, China's economic growth has benefited from its significant demographic dividend, it has avoided the phenomenon of diminishing return to capital and has broken the 'Young–Krugman curse'.[2] On the one hand, it has also been trapped in a pattern in which economic growth is driven mainly by inputs of capital and labour and less by technological advancement, industrial upgrading and productivity enhancement (Cai 2008). Such a growth pattern is embodied in the heavy dependence of growth on demands created by export and investment and not by domestic consumption, which has been insufficient. The other manifestation of this pattern is the overwhelming share of government revenue and enterprises' profits in national income, which leaves an extremely small part for residents' income in total national income.

Second, the regional disparities in economic development existing during the reform period have formed a path-dependent sequel. That is, the implementation of the strategy of coastal development, while spurring the economic growth in eastern provinces, has locked in a regional pattern of industrial allocation, preventing the eastern and central-western regions from upgrading their industries and leading to regions' industrial structure deviating from their comparative advantages. The over-active government intervention in economic activities, while filling the gap of entrepreneurship at the early stage of market maturity, creates no adequate incentives for regions to upgrade their technological and industrial structures. In the entire reform period, central and local governments have been deeply involved in regional economic development, not only by artificially depressing prices of land and other local resources in order to create favoured policies for attracting more foreign investment and ambitiously planning local industrial structures based on maximising regional gross domestic product (GDP), but by being directly involved in negotiating over and participating in some projects. Owing to such a close relationship between local governments and regional economic activities and the heavy reliance of government budgets on a small group of enterprises and projects with overwhelmingly large scales, local governments' industrial policies have been captured by vested interests in these industries and enterprises. Protected enterprises continually receive fiscal subsidies, physical assistance, monopoly status and other institutional rents and, as a result, the allocation of factors of production is continuously distorted and entrepreneurs are no longer capable of judging the changes in relative scarcities of production factors and hence comparative advantage dynamics. In short, when expected innovation is replaced by rent-seeking activities, the process of industrial upgrading is postponed and an outmoded growth pattern gives way to inertia.

The transformation of the economic growth pattern, which has been preached by the central government for a very long time, is in its nature a process of creative destruction. Because of the reasons described above, however, Chinese enterprises have little incentive to play their part in transforming the current pattern of economic growth—or, in other words, they do not feel that transformation through creative destruction is financially or physically affordable. As a result, the inevitability of such a transformation of the growth pattern—as required to maintain sustainable economic growth—through upgrading technologies and industries in the long term takes the form of regional leapfrogging. Given the variety of geographical features and economic endowments in China's regions, and particularly the characteristics of regional competition led by fiscal decentralisation (Jin et al. 2005), while the advanced regions are reluctant to upgrade their growth pattern, the latecomer regions will start building their industrial structure rapidly by leapfrogging, as a substitution for the trudging method of industrial upgrading undertaken in the advanced regions. This type of industrial upgrading, due to the existence of the wave phenomenon (Lin 2007), tends to depart from or overrun the requirement of changes in comparative advantage.

Using the example of manufacturing in three Chinese regions—the Pearl River Delta region, the Yangtse River Delta region and some old industrial bases such as the north-eastern provinces—Figure 11.1 illustrates such a unique mode of industrial upgrading. It shows that instead of the theoretically expected smooth process of industrial upgrading in the country as a whole, there has been an alternative pattern in which newly emerged regions have jumped to an industrial structure with higher-graded manufactures, whereas the industrial structure of the early developed regions remains little changed.[3] The Pearl River Delta region, for example, started its industrialisation with processing trades based on external orders and formed an unskilled or semi-skilled labour-intensive industrial pattern. It is generally believed that the industrial structure in this region has not changed significantly despite its experiences with wage inflation and labour shortages in recent years. Instead, the more technology-intensive industries are emerging in the Yangtse River Delta region, which relies more on skilled workers in production. In the meantime, as the result of the boosting of old industrial bases, north-eastern provinces and other regions have developed their equipment-manufacturing sectors, which are more capital intensive.

Figure 11.1 Leapfrogging pattern of regional growth in China

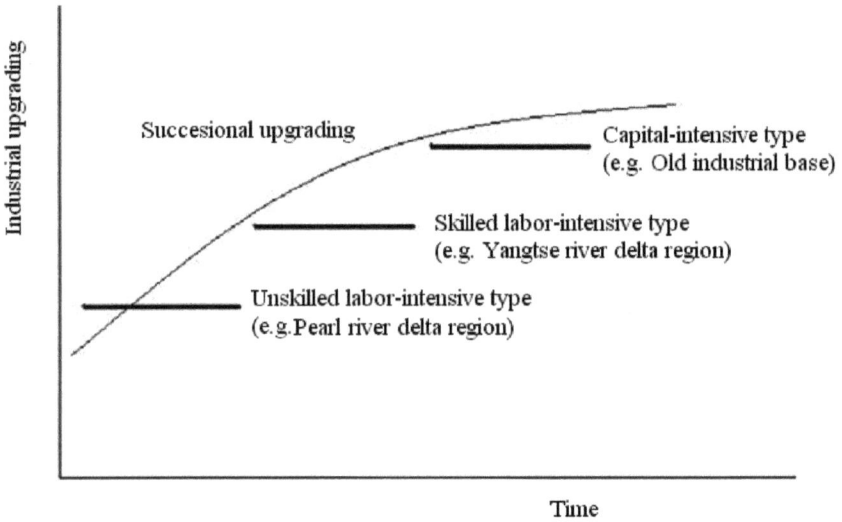

Such a pattern of regional development and industrial structural change is to some extent the outcome of government intervention in regional economic growth. It also reflects the need for industrial upgrading and the transformation of the growth pattern as it is required now. Therefore, this leapfrogging type of regional development can be seen as a variant form of the required upgrading and transformation because it is indeed accompanied by enhancement of productivity and it does not necessarily reflect the changing features of comparative advantage among regions. The mass migration of labour from central and western regions to eastern regions, the wave phenomenon in the process of industrial upgrading and the price distortion of production factors lead to the separation of revealed comparative advantage from the real resource endowments in those regions.

Estimating total factor productivity by region

Total factor productivity (TFP) is often used to evaluate economic performance and the quality of growth in a country (region or industry). It has two components: allocative efficiency and technological efficiency (Lau and Yotopoulos 1971; Barro 1999). In China, regional competition has caused large differences in growth performance and TFP across regions. The developing areas might have plenty of room to realise more rapid technological progress through technological diffusion and spill-over. In contrast, leading areas have formed mature industrial structures in the process of their growth and will have to face the constraints of high adjustment costs and the shocks of creative destruction—probably leading to their technological progress being temporarily or permanently locked at a certain level.

In terms of growth accounting (Solow 1957), economic growth can be decomposed into two sources: factor accumulation and TFP advancement. Capital and labour are two important factors of production in economic activities, and growth can benefit from their accumulation, but they are not the major determinants of growth—due to the law of marginal diminishment. In growth accounting equations, TFP is measured by the Solow residual, which accounts for the effects of total output not caused by inputs and is considered to be the most important driving force for growth in the long run.

Economic activities can be viewed as a process of production by means of various inputs, in which output (Y) is a production function of TFP (A), capital (K), labour (L) and intermediate input (I)—that is, $Y = F(A,K,L,I)$. Intermediate input is an essential part of industrial production and often contains technological progress attached to capital goods, so it can be categorised as a type of production factor. According to the theory of TFP, output growth can be decomposed into two parts: changes in the accumulation of capital, labour and intermediate inputs, and changes in technological progress. Based on the Cobb-Douglas (CD) production function equation, the source of output growth has the following three components: $g_Y = g + \alpha * g_K + \beta * g_L + \gamma * g_I$, in which g_Y represents output growth and g_K, g_L, g_I represent the growth of capital, labour and intermediate input, respectively. α, β, λ are elasticities of capital, labour and intermediate input, respectively. If technological progress is Hicks-neutral, g measures TFP. Its formula is as in Equation 11.1.

Equation 11.1

$$g = g_Y - \alpha * g_K - \beta * g_L - \gamma * g_I$$

This chapter utilises the data for manufacturing firms that include all state-owned enterprises (SOEs) and non-state-owned enterprises with annual revenue greater than CNY5 million from 2000 to 2007. It covers the manufacturing enterprises in 31 provinces (cities and autonomous areas). The number of manufacturing enterprises was about 150 000 in 2000 and

2001 and 160 000 in 2002, 180 000 in 2003, 250 000 in 2004 and 2005, close to 280 000 in 2006 and more than 310 000 in 2007.

In order to compare changes in TFP by region, we divide 31 provinces (cities and autonomous areas) into six regions: South China coastal region (including Guangdong, Fujian and Hainan), East China coastal region (including Shanghai, Jiangsu and Zhejiang), North China coastal region (including Beijing, Tianjin, Hebei and Shandong), the North-East region (including Liaoning, Jilin and Heilongjiang), the Central region (including Shanxi, Anhui, Jiangxi, Henan, Hubei and Hunan) and the Western region (including Inner Mongolia, Guangxi, Chongqing, Sichuan, Guizhou, Yunnan, Tibet, Shaanxi, Gansu, Qinghai, Ningxia and Xinjiang).

This chapter will estimate the production function to obtain the elasticities of capital, labour and intermediate inputs, and then calculate annual growth and the contribution of TFP to regional economic growth. When estimating the production function, the industrial gross output value is chosen as the output variable, net fixed assets as the capital variable, the employment number as the labour variable and the value of intermediate input products as the intermediate input variable. Among these, the industrial gross output value is deflated using the output price index. Net fixed-asset values equal the original fixed-asset value minus depreciation and plus newly added fixed assets. Net fixed-asset values are also deflated using the fixed-assets price index to calculate the stock of capital. The employment number is the number of workers employed at the end of the year. Intermediate input is also deflated using the price index for raw materials.

The regression equation of output on capital, labour and intermediate input is given in Equation 11.2.

Equation 11.2

$$\ln Y_{ji} = a_j + \alpha_j \ln K_{ji} + \beta_j \ln L_{ji} + \gamma_j \ln I_{ji} + \mu_t D_t + \mu_n N_n + \mu_m M_m + e_j$$

In this equation, $j = 1,2,...,6$ represents six areas; i represents individual enterprise; D, N, M are the dummy variables of years, provinces and industries. μ is the coefficient of dummy variables; t, n, m are the number of years, provinces and industries and e is the error term. $a_j, \alpha_j, \beta_j, \gamma_j, \mu_t, \mu_n, \mu_m$ are the parameters to be estimated. Based on the data for manufacturing enterprises, the regression results are reported in Table 11.1.

The regression results show that statistic values of capital, labour and intermediate input variables are significant at 1 per cent and their coefficients are consistent with theoretical expectation. The elasticity values of capital, labour and intermediate input, however, vary across regions. Among them, the elasticity values of capital range between 0.012 and 0.039, those of labour range between 0.057 and 0.1, and those of intermediate input range between 0.812 and 0.910. Summing the elasticity coefficients of capital, labour and intermediate input falls between 0.951 and 0.993 in six regions—close to 1—indicating the existence of constant returns to scale for the production function. The values of the goodness of fit from six regression equations are 0.90–0.97, showing the results have a good power for explanation.

We can calculate the growth rates of TFP in six regions by using the results of the above coefficients (Table 11.2). From 2000 to 2007, all three coastal regions saw a faster growth of output than the North-East, Central and Western regions, with an annual rate of more than 22 per cent. The growth rate of output in the Central region was close to that in the coastal regions. The North-East and Western regions had a lower growth rate of output—standing at 19.74 per cent and 21.38 per cent, respectively. The accumulation of factors varied significantly from region to region. The growth rates of capital, labour and intermediate input are much higher in coastal regions than in the North-East, Central and Western regions. The East China coastal region topped the growth rate of capital, followed by North China and then South China. The North-East region had the slowest growth rate of capital. In contrast, the South China coastal region had the fastest labour growth rate, followed by East China and North China coastal regions. The North-East region even had a negative growth rate of labour. Changes in growth rates of labour input from six regions are very much in line with the observed reality. That is, many jobs have been created in the coastal regions through high-speed growth in the industrial sector. North China had the highest growth rate of intermediate input, followed by East China while the North-East region was the lowest.

Table 11.1 Regression results of gross output values in log form

	ln(Capital)		ln(Labour)		ln(Intermediate input)		Constant		Observations	R^2
South China coastal	0.03	(68.62)[a]	0.091	(125.1)[a]	0.867	(1429.17)[a]	0.764	(101.33)[a]	274,109	0.95
East China coastal	0.023	(93.85)[a]	0.061	(152.2)[a]	0.909	(2644.23)[a]	0.68	(213.13)[a]	577,948	0.97
North China coastal	0.033	(48.35)[a]	0.085	(80.84)[a]	0.847	(1161.80)[a]	1.013	(148.04)[a]	271,732	0.92
North-East region	0.018	(20.17)[a]	0.057	(39.97)[a]	0.894	(804.92)[a]	0.861	(88.22)[a]	96,914	0.94
Central region	0.039	(47.39)[a]	0.1	(80.82)[a]	0.812	(904.56)[a]	1.132	(136.09)[a]	215,713	0.90
Western region	0.012	(16.28)[a]	0.061	(50.16)[a]	0.910	(1043.96)[a]	0.756	(71.87)[a]	157,645	0.95

[a] represents significance at 1 per cent

Notes: For simplicity, the coefficients of dummy variables of years, industries and provinces are deleted; the absolute values of z statistics are in parentheses.

Source: Authors' estimations.

Table 11.2 Growth and contribution of total factor productivity

Growth rate (%)	Output	Capital	Labour	Intermediate input	TFP
South China coastal	22.51	14.07	12.87	18.81	4.60
East China coastal	23.84	18.17	11.59	20.17	4.38
North China coastal	24.28	14.77	5.26	20.95	5.60
North-East region	19.74	8.08	−0.05	15.82	5.46
Central region	22.98	12.32	2.00	19.86	6.17
Western region	21.38	10.34	1.05	18.76	4.13
Contribution rate (%)					
South China coastal	100.0	1.88	5.21	72.47	20.45
East China coastal	100.0	1.75	2.96	76.91	18.37
North China coastal	100.0	2.01	1.84	73.09	23.06
North-East region	100.0	0.74	−0.02	71.63	27.65
Central region	100.0	2.09	0.87	70.20	26.84
Western region	100.0	0.58	0.30	79.82	19.30

Source: Authors' estimations.

It is interesting that the TFP growth rates in the South and East China coastal regions are similar to that of West China, but lower than that of the North China, North-East and Central regions. Among all regions, the Central region had the highest TFP growth rate (6.17 per cent) and the Western region had the lowest TFP growth rate, of 4.13 per cent—2 percentage points lower than the former. Higher TFP growth rates in the North-East and Central regions can be attributed largely to innovation from industrial upgrading and technological diffusion in these two regions and therefore their achievement of faster technological progress. Such empirical evidence illustrates the evolved characteristics of China's industrial structure, as discussed earlier, and the mismatched outcome between factor endowments and comparative advantage. In contrast, despite faster output growth driven by an export-oriented economy, coastal regions are lagging behind in terms of the TFP growth rate, which means that the efforts in transforming the growth pattern in coastal regions through innovation and industrial upgrading are lagging behind the requirement for changes in dynamic comparative advantage.

The above results also demonstrate that, apart from the contributions of intermediate input (70–80 per cent in six regions), TFP is an important source of China's industrial growth—contributing between 18 and 28 per cent. The TFP contributions in the North-East, Central and Western regions are much higher than in coastal regions. The North-East region topped the TFP contribution with 27.7 per cent, followed by the Central region with 26.8 per cent. The East China coastal region had only 18.4 per cent TFP contribution—the lowest among all regions. Relatively speaking, the contribution of capital ranged from 0.58–2.1 per cent and the contribution of labour ranged from –0.02–5.2 per cent. Our micro-data and subregional analysis, however, do not capture the reallocation effects of factors through regional mobility and the accumulation effects of human capital and changes in the intensities of working time in production.

Opportunities for the central and western regions to catch up

The task of transforming the growth pattern requires a switch from the present track of regional development to one conforming with the comparative advantages of the regional economies. China's regions are at different stages of development and hence the difference in resource endowments is not smaller than that among countries. Therefore, the flying-geese model that previously explained industrial transfers and investment flows among countries could be fully applied to predict the path of regional shifts in economic activities among the Chinese regions. The expected scenario of creative destruction to cope with the financial crisis provides opportunities to realise the objective. The relationship among regions within a country, however, has fundamental differences from that among countries. When we employ the flying-geese theory to predict and analyse industrial transfers among regions, some distinguishing features among the eastern and central-western regions should be borne in mind.

While there are still large differentials in prices of production factors, due to their relative scarcity among the Chinese regions, the degrees of the relative differences in prices of production factors differ, because of the variation of mobility of each factor of production. First of all, with regard to land—an immobile factor of production—while its relative price has substantially increased in coastal areas, where industries are concentrated, it remains relatively low in central and western areas. Second, thanks to the improved mobility of labour migration, relative prices of labour have largely converged among regions (Cai et al. 2007), though the regional difference in wage rates still exists. Third, though capital is a highly mobile factor of production, its relative prices are far from equalised among regions, because of the existence of various kinds of institutional constraints (World Bank 2005).

Such regional differences in relative prices of factors of production—as one of the factors determining performances in attracting FDI and therefore industrial development—are consistent with development levels and the extent of outward orientation among the Chinese regions—namely, descending from eastern, central and western regions (Cai 2009). Figure 11.2 demonstrates such a characteristic of export levels among regions. The current distribution of industries and export-oriented production to a large extent reflects the outcomes of the spatial reallocation of factors of production after China's period of reform and opening up. For instance, the overwhelming proportion of manufacturing workers in coastal sectors come from migrants flowing from central and western regions. That indicates that while the interior provinces hold advantages in cheap labour, the coastal areas have so far had the most efficient allocation of resources.

Figure 11.2 Regional distribution of export value of manufacturing goods (CNY billion)

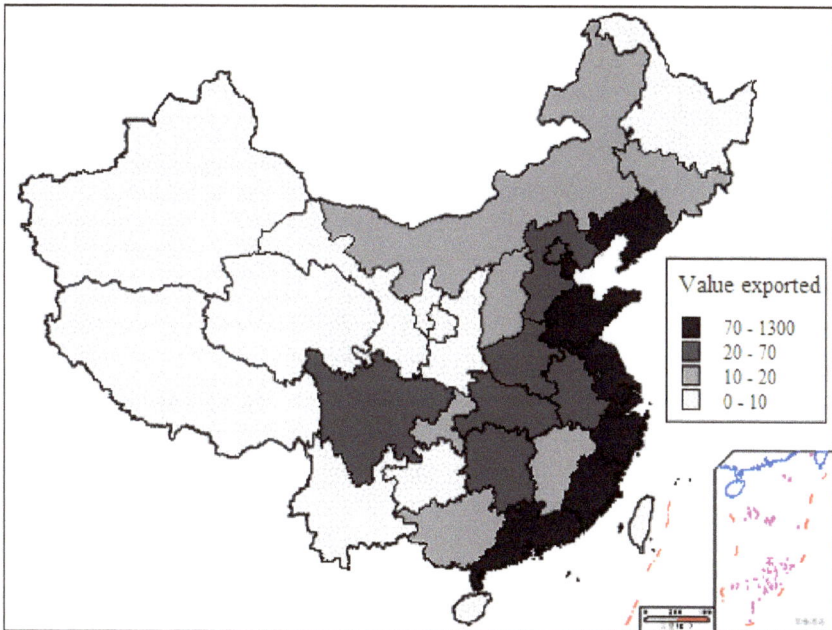

Sources: State Council 2006, *China Economic Census Yearbook 2004*, The First National Economic Census Leading Group Office, State Council, China Statistics Press, Beijing.

To answer the question of whether or not the central and western regions are ready to receive the transfer of labour-intensive industries from eastern regions, one needs to investigate the relative changes in potential for labour productivity among regions. In the period of successful reform and rapid growth, cheap labour was believed to be the major reason for the competitiveness of China's manufacturing products. As wages rise, however, observers tend to believe that China is losing its comparative advantage in the manufacture of labour-intensive products and that the new producers of manufacturing products, and thus foreign investment, will tend to move to other developing countries with lower labour costs (for example, AlixPartners 2009). Since the wage rise is real, the question needing an answer is whether the enhancement of labour productivity will be faster than the rise of wage rates in China as a whole and in different Chinese regions. Assertions and misgivings about China losing comparative advantage in manufacturing dominated by labour-intensive industries are beneath methodological accuracy, because the factors determining comparative advantage in labour-intensive industries include labour costs and labour productivity. Considering both factors—namely, dividing the wage rate by the productivity of labour—we can obtain a better indicator to reflect the real cost of labour used in industries: the unit labour cost (Van Ark 2008). The smaller the magnitude of this indicator, the lower will be the costs of labour employed to produce the same volume of products.

While workers' compensation pushes up labour costs—thus lowering the competitive advantage in labour-intensive industries—the improvement of labour productivity counteracts the negative effects of wage rises on competitiveness and therefore sustains comparative advantage in labour-intensive industries. In past years, the growth of average productivity represented by per capita GDP has been no less than the increase in wages. Compared with both industrialised countries and newly emerging market economies, China's performance in this regard is superior (The Conference Board 2009). To complement the above oversimplified comparison, based on the same data set of manufacturing enterprises explained in section three, we can estimate the average productivity of labour and the marginal productivity of labour for six regions between 2000 and 2007 and compare the results of labour productivity performance with workers' compensation, which includes wages, income in kind and social security benefits enterprises paid to employees.

After estimating the production functions for the country as a whole and for six regions categorised, we use Equations 11.3 and 11.4 to calculate marginal and average productivities of labour, respectively.

Equation 11.3

$$MPL = \frac{\partial Y}{\partial L} = \frac{\beta \times Y}{L}$$

Equation 11.4

$$APL = \frac{Y}{L}$$

The estimated results are listed in Table 11.3, which shows the changing trends of labour compensation and two indicators of labour productivity in 2000 and 2007. Because the average productivity of labour contains the contribution of other factors (such as capital and intermediate inputs) to output, it is bigger than the marginal productivity of labour in volume. Those two indicators of productivity also tend to diverge.

From the table, we can clearly see that in the first years of this century, wage rises and labour productivity enhancement in China's manufacturing sectors have not been increasing at the same rate. That is, although wage rates increased rapidly, labour productivity increased much faster, which offset the effects of wage inflation on labour costs and actually lowered the unit labour costs in the sectors concerned. No matter how one compares with the marginal or the average productivity of labour, the calculated unit labour costs—the ratio of workers' compensation to labour productivity—declined by more than 30 per cent, or more than 5 per cent annually.

Table 11.3 Compensation and labour productivity of China's manufacturing, 2000–07

	2000	2001	2002	2003	2004	2005	2006	2007	Annual growth (%)
Magnitude (CNY thousand per person)									
Compensation	11.48	12.25	13.09	14.08	15.35	16.96	20.74	22.02	9.75
MPL	12.31	14.44	16.65	19.93	22.29	25.09	28.91	34.3	15.76
APL	163.07	191.35	220.63	264.06	295.33	332.44	383.01	454.52	15.77
Unit labour costs									
Compensation/MPL	0.933	0.848	0.786	0.707	0.689	0.676	0.718	0.642	–5.20
Compensation/APL	0.07	0.064	0.059	0.053	0.052	0.051	0.054	0.048	–5.25

Note: Compensation here is the average—namely, the sum of wages, income in kind and social security benefits paid by enterprises divided by total employees.

Source: Authors' own calculations.

Having grasped the overall picture of labour costs in the country as whole, we are in a position to look further into the different trends in wages and labour productivity among the six regions categorised. Those differences in real labour costs can be large, based on theoretical expectation, because of the diversities in resource endowments, institutional environments and, most of all, development levels among the regions. If that assumption can be proven, the systematic transfer of labour-intensive industries from coastal to interior provinces instead of to other countries should be a realistic strategy to sustain comparative advantage in the industries in China. Table 11.4 shows the results of calculation on workers' compensation and the marginal productivity of labour for six Chinese regions.

As shown in Table 11.4, the levels and changing trends of wages and labour productivity differ significantly among regions, which is expected, based on observation of the changing regional patterns in the relevant years. For example, the south-eastern coastal areas held relatively high wage rates but relatively slower growth rates of labour productivity, which made those areas disadvantageous in unit labour costs, whereas the rest of the regions had lower wage rates and faster growth of labour productivity and more advantageous labour costs. While 2003 was a turning point for the speedy wage rises in all regions, and the increase in labour productivity was even faster, the unit labour costs actually declined, except in the South China coastal area. In general, the central and western regions performed extraordinarily well in reducing labour costs. Given the potential of productivity gains in those areas and the trend of backflow of labour migration that tends to enlarge the supply of labour in the regions, the bigger advantages in labour costs can be expected. With the central and western regions moving towards industries based on their comparative advantages in labour, labour-intensive industries will be sustained within China.

Table 11.4 Compensation and marginal productivity of labour by region

	2000	2001	2002	2003	2004	2005	2006	2007	Annual growth
Compensation (CNY thousand per worker)									
South China coastal	13.20	13.32	14.69	14.89	15.71	17.46	21.27	25.69	10.0
East China coastal	13.93	14.12	15.25	16.20	16.49	18.41	20.27	22.08	6.8
North China coastal	11.14	10.99	11.89	12.77	15.19	16.65	18.16	20.01	8.7
North-East China	10.80	11.86	13.38	14.52	16.66	16.97	19.80	23.49	11.7
Central China	8.61	11.39	10.41	11.48	13.52	14.18	15.87	18.87	11.9
Western China	10.87	11.08	12.39	13.81	15.81	16.64	19.37	20.93	9.8
MPL (CNY thousand per worker)									
South China coastal	18.21	20.58	22.31	24.72	24.93	24.85	27.79	32.51	8.6
East China coastal	13.66	15.2	17.28	20.09	19.14	23.56	26.36	30.41	12.1
North China coastal	14.6	16.63	19.65	24.35	29.64	33.73	39.13	47.02	18.2
North-East China	8.2	10.35	12.15	15.42	18.25	21.08	24.5	29.41	20.0
Central China	11.08	13.12	15.44	18.95	24.4	27.34	33.14	41.93	20.9
Western China	6.72	8.26	9.71	11.57	14.64	16.89	20.63	24.59	20.4
Unit labour cost									
South China coastal	0.72	0.65	0.66	0.60	0.63	0.70	0.77	0.79	1.3
East China coastal	1.02	0.93	0.88	0.81	0.86	0.78	0.77	0.73	−4.7
North China coastal	0.76	0.66	0.61	0.52	0.51	0.49	0.46	0.43	−7.8
North-East China	1.32	1.15	1.10	0.94	0.91	0.81	0.81	0.80	−6.9
Central China	0.78	0.87	0.67	0.61	0.55	0.52	0.48	0.45	−7.6
Western China	1.62	1.34	1.28	1.19	1.08	0.99	0.94	0.85	−8.8

Note: Unit labour cost is the ratio of workers' compensation to the marginal productivity of labour.

Source: Authors' own calculations based on the survey data.

Conclusion

This chapter expounds a unique regional pattern of changes in industrial structure—the leapfrogging type of industrial evolution among the Chinese regions—and it provides an empirical test by estimating TFP by region. Although the newly emerging regions other than the coastal areas have shown faster upgrading of their industrial structure, such trends have not yet changed the potential comparative advantages they hold in labour-intensive industries. From this standpoint, combining Schumpeter's notion of creative destruction with the flying-geese paradigm, one can expect that in the course of tackling the financial crisis, central and western regions will rise to sustain the sources of China's rapid economic growth. At the same time, applying the flying-geese theory to the scenario in which industrial transfer happens not only among countries but among regions within a country with the unique characteristics of a large economy will lead us to conclude that labour-intensive manufacturing will not shift from China to other developing countries in a general way.

It is important to understand the Chinese economy from a regional point of view in that when some regions experience tremendous changes in resource endowments and tend to loose their comparative advantage in labour-intensive industries, other regions can still hold a comparative advantage in those industries. Viewing China as a homogenous economy in spite of the huge diversities among its regions, it is difficult to believe that China will not conform to the pattern of traditional industrial transfer as predicted by the flying-geese model, but will sustain labour-intensive industries and simultaneously ascend to a higher level of industrial chains. For example, a report by the Japanese Ministry of Economy, Trade and Industry is puzzled by the observation that China not only gains comparative advantage in labour-intensive industries, it holds competitiveness in technology-intensive industries such as the information technology sector via FDI (Ahearne et al. 2006). This phenomenon shows precisely the regional heterogeneity among Chinese regions and the large-economy effects of China as a whole, which allow the flying-geese pattern of industrial transfer to come into being within the country.

Industrial upgrading in all regions is a requirement for achieving the economic transformation needed to maintain high growth. For the antecedent order of industrialisation, shifting their industrial structure to a higher level of value chains—namely, from labour to technology-intensive industries—is a natural response to the increases in costs of labour and land. For the central and western regions, carrying on some of the labour-intensive industries vacated by the eastern regions is itself an upgrade in industrial structure and an accomplishment of their own task of transforming the growth pattern as well. It can be expected that after such adjustments in the eastern and central-western regions, the scale of the east's absorption of migrant workers will stabilise, while the incremental labour force shift from agriculture will be employed more in central and western regions. As a result, the industrial structure in the central and western regions will focus more on producing those labour-intensive products that are in conformity with the underlying comparative advantage determined by the relatively abundant labour force.

References

Ahearne, A. G., Fernald, J. G., Loungani, P. and Schindler, J. W. 2006, *Flying geese or sitting ducks: China's impact on the trading fortunes of other Asian economies*, International Finance Discussion Paper, no. 887 (December), Board of Governors of the Federal Reserve System, Washington, DC.

Akamatsu, K. 1962, 'Historical pattern of economic growth in developing countries', *Journal of Developing Economies*, vol. 1, no. 1 (March–August), pp. 3–25.

AlixPartners 2009, AlixPartners introduces new outsourcing tool that determines 'best-cost countries', Press release, AlixPartners web site, <http://www.marketwire.com/press-release/Alixpartners-991044.html>

Barro, R. 1999, 'Note on growth accounting', *Journal of Economic Growth*, vol. 4, no. 2, pp. 119–37.

Cai, F. 2008, *Approaching a triumphal span: how far is China towards its Lewisian turning point?*, UNU-WIDER Research Paper, no. 2008/09, World Institute for Development Economics Research of the United Nations University, Helsinki, Finland.

—— 2009, 'The impacts of financial crisis on manufacture: opportunities for central and western China to catch up', *Economic Perspectives*, no. 2, pp. 4–8.

Cai, F., Du, Y. and Zhao, C. 2007, 'Regional labour market integration since China's World Trade Organization entry: evidence from household-level data', in R. Garnaut and L. Song (eds), *China: Linking markets for growth*, Asia Pacific Press, Canberra, pp. 133–50.

Jin, H., Qian, Y. and Weingast, B. R. 2005, 'Regional decentralization and fiscal incentives: federalism, Chinese style', *Journal of Public Economics*, vol. 89, pp. 1719–42.

Kojima, K. 2000, 'The "flying geese" model of Asian economic development: origin, theoretical extensions, and regional policy implications', *Journal of Asian Economics*, vol. 11, pp. 375–401.

Krugman, P. 1994, 'The myth of Asia's miracle', *Foreign Affairs*, (November–December).

Lau, L. J. and Yotopoulos, P. A. 1971, 'A test for relative efficiency and an application to Indian agriculture', *American Economic Review*, vol. 61, pp. 94–109.

Lin, J. Y. 2007, 'Wave phenomena and rebuilding of macroeconomic theory in developing countries', *Economic Research Journal*, no. 1, pp. 126–31.

Okita, S. 1985, 'Special presentation: prospect of Pacific economies', in Korea Development Institute (ed.), *Pacific Cooperation: Issues and opportunities. Report of the Fourth Pacific Economic Cooperation Conference, Seoul, Korea, 29 April 29 – 1 May*, pp. 18–29.

Schumpeter, J. A. 1961, *The Theory of Economic Development: An inquiry into profits, capital, credit, interest, and the business cycle*, Oxford University Press, New York.

—— 1976, *Capitalism, Socialism and Democracy*, George Allen & Unwin, London.

Solow, R. M. 1957, 'Technical change and the aggregate production function', *Review of Economics and Statistics*, vol. 39, pp. 320–1.

State Council 2006, *China Economic Census Yearbook 2004*, The First National Economic Census Leading Group Office, State Council, China Statistics Press, Beijing.

The Conference Board 2009, *Performance 2009: Productivity, employment, and growth in the world's economies*, The Conference Board, New York, <http://www.conference-board.org/>

Van Ark, B. 2008, *Performance 2008: Productivity, employment, and growth in the world's economies*, The Conference Board, New York, <http://www.conference-board.org/>

Vernon, R. 1966, 'International investment and international trade in the product cycle', *Quarterly Journal of Economics*, pp. 190–207.

World Bank 2005, *Integration of national product and factor markets: economic benefits and policy recommendations*, Report no. 31973-CHA (13 June), Poverty Reduction and Economic Management Unit, East Asia and Pacific Region, The World Bank, Washington, DC.

Young, A. 1992, 'A tale of two cities: factor accumulation and technical change in Hong Kong and Singapore', in O. Blanchard and S. Fischer (eds), *NBER Macroeconomics Annual*, MIT Press, Cambridge, Mass.

Endnotes

1. Kojima (2000) reviewed the evolution of the flying-geese theory in detail.

2. Young (1992) and Krugman (1994) questioned the East Asian miracle because they found that the rapid growth in those economies depended heavily on inputs of capital and labour other than total factor productivity.

3. Here, we take the upgrades of industrial structure to represent transformation of the economic growth pattern, but by no means are the upgrades consistent with the requirement of that transformation.

Impact of economic slowdown on migrant workers

12

Sherry Tao Kong, Xin Meng
and Dandan Zhang

Introduction

The recent global economic downturn has had a significant impact on employment in many countries and the full effect is yet to be felt, with the Organisation for Economic Cooperation and Development (OECD) expecting unemployment rates of about 10 per cent next year. It is noticeable that the economic downturn in China has been relatively mild in so far as economic growth is expected to be in the order of 6 or more per cent. Labour productivity growth, however, has been so significant in China in the past few decades that even a high output growth rate of this level is not sufficient to offset job losses, which are already apparent.

In China, the currently observed employment effect could be a product of three different events: first, the contractionary macroeconomic policies introduced by the government and central bank in 2007 aimed at slowing growth. It is interesting to note that the policy instruments adopted are likely to have the same impact on the economy as the current crisis. The second event was the introduction of the new Labour Contract Law at the beginning of 2008. This policy initiative sizeably increased the cost of unskilled labour and there is evidence that employers have responded by reducing labour inputs. The third event is the reduction in export orders due to the global financial crisis since the second half of 2008. These three events occurred sequentially and their impacts on employment have been borne most heavily by rural–urban migrants, as they form the major labour force for the export and low-cost labour-intensive industries in China. The close relationship between the timing of these events will make it difficult to estimate the contribution of each factor but it is nevertheless useful to bear in mind that the Chinese economic downturn from mid-2008 to early 2009 is the outcome of these combined effects.

Generally speaking, the adverse effects of these three shocks impact most on the same set of people: rural–urban migrants. In 2008, about 130 million rural–urban migrants worked in cities and they accounted for one-third of the total urban labour force. They are heavily involved in export industries and building and construction, both of which have been particularly affected by the downturn. The disproportionate share of the adjustment that is being borne by migrant workers is an important policy issue. Not only should we be concerned about the uneven share of the cost of the economic downturn, the sheer number of migrant workers suggests that if the economic crisis is not handled properly, heavy job losses among migrants could affect economic and social stability.

In this chapter, we address two issues. First, we document the extent of employment loss and its geographic location and industry distribution. Second, we study which types of migrants are bearing most of the brunt of the downturn.

The Rural–Urban Migration in China and Indonesia (RUMiCI) project provides a unique set of data to help understand these issues. The project began in the second half of 2007. As a major part of the research, we surveyed 5000 migrant households in 15 cities. During the process of sampling, interviewing, tracking and re-interviewing this group of migrants, we have accumulated a considerable amount of data to provide a detailed record of what is happening.

The chapter is structured as follows. The next section provides background information on the economic policy environment during the period leading up to and during the economic downturn. Section three discusses the size of the impact on employment and section four examines the type of migrant worker separated from their jobs in 2008 because of the economic downturn. Conclusions are given in the last section.

Background

After double-digit growth in 2006 and, with the trade surplus and foreign reserve both hitting new highs, in 2007, rebalancing the economy moved onto the government's agenda. While in the first half of the year, the main concern was the rapid growth of asset prices (share and property prices), as the consumer price index (CPI) and producer price index (PPI) rallied during the second half of 2007, Chinese policymakers had to take measures to tame the beast of an overheating economy. Lending and deposit rates were lifted six times in 2007 and reserve requirements increased 10 times, reaching the highest levels for more than two decades. At the end of 2007, at the Central Economic Work Conference, the primary policy agenda for the next year remained 'two acts of prevention'—that is, to prevent the economy from overheating and to prevent the current structural inflation from turning into a broad-based one.

Against this macroeconomic background, the most significant reform to employment relations regulation in more than a decade was brewing. The Twenty-Eighth National People's Congress, held in June, formally approved the bill for the new Labour Contract Law, to take effect from 1 January 2008. For the first time, workers in domestic and foreign-owned enterprises, including migrant workers, were entitled to collective consultation, severance payment, a minimum wage and other rights.

The significant implication of this law is, to some extent, reflected in the polarised drafting process since 2006 and the highly contentious debates preceding and following its formal adoption (Cooney et al. 2007). On the one hand, a rise in labour disputes and other social problems undermined social stability and called for the implementation of a national labour law. Furthermore, the Chinese Government has embarked on a development strategy that emphasises industrial upgrading and promotes social harmony. The long-term development agenda for the central government in turn translated into active promotion of innovative service industries, moving up the value scale while at the same time combating pollution at the local level. Proponents of the law argued that a set of regulations aimed at promoting workers' interests—particularly in forms of greater employment security and income protection—was urgently needed and would align with China's development agenda. On the other hand, the law inevitably increased labour costs, limited the flexibility of corporations to structure their employment arrangements and possibly 'over-regulates [the] employment relationship' (Zhao and Lim 2008).

On the ground, sharp reaction from employers had emerged long before the official promulgation of the law. While the drafting process was still under way, some factories were already gearing towards evading responsibility and potential additional costs under the new law. Wang et al. (2009) summarise two coping strategies used by employers. The first is 'creative compliance' (that is, evasion). Employers coerce many employees to resign their posts—thereby forfeiting important seniority claims—and then rehire them as new employees. For example, Huawei Technologies

Company Limited, China's biggest maker of telecommunication network equipment, allegedly encouraged more than 7000 employees to take part in a 'voluntary resignation' scheme at the end of 2007 to avoid the obligation of giving employees who had served more than 10 years permanent positions ('ACFTU: Huawei agrees to suspend controversial employment scheme after union talks', *People's Daily Online*, 2007, <http://english.peopledaily.com.cn/90001/90776/90882/6300313.html>).

The second strategy is reduction in employment, which has a stronger and more immediate implication for migrant workers. Many labour-intensive manufacturers began to shut their factories and shift production to even lower-wage regions of China or South-East Asia. By one account, cited by Wang et al. (2009), 1000 footwear and accessory producers had reduced output or closed shop in Guangdong by early 2008. Some moved to the Chinese hinterland, while others relocated to Vietnam and Burma, where labour was cheaper and legally defenceless. Similarly, after the law took effect, already feeling the pinch of weakening export demand, business owners hurried to shed workers and rearrange work contracts so as to circumvent the new regulations ('Last call for Guangdong shoemakers', *Asia Times Online*, 2008, <http://www.atimes.com/atimes/China_Business/JB05Cb01.html>).

China began 2008 with a growth rate of 13 per cent, a $29.3 billion trade surplus and nearly $2 trillion in foreign reserves. At the time, China's CPI had been increasing since 2002. By February 2008, it had soared by 8.7 per cent on a year-on-year basis (NBS 2009)—a 12-year high. In particular, prices of pork and cooking oil skyrocketed at the beginning of 2008, contributing to an increase of 14.3 per cent in overall food prices in 2008. In response, Chinese policymakers implemented a steady fiscal policy and tightened monetary policy to control the money supply and credit and stabilise expectations of inflation. This was the first time in 10 years that China had enforced a contractionary monetary policy. Aside from rising interest rates and increasing bank reserve requirements, the government also cut easy access to bank loans and reduced credit growth. Banking authorities strictly defined a 'second home' according to the property owned by the families of mortgage applicants rather than just the applicant. This was to control speculative home-buyers pushing up property prices to an artificially high level (Batson 2008). Quota controls on lending by commercial banks were also introduced. The export tax rebate was reduced and the renminbi was allowed to appreciate to balance China's trade surplus.

While the government still feared the economy would overheat, coastal exporters and textile manufacturers were feeling the pinch from rising costs and weakening global demand. Meanwhile, property markets in some cities were softening. The employment impact of the external shock had taken shape. By mid-2008, rising costs and a slowdown in exports contributed to the closure of at least 67 000 factories across China in the first half of the year, forcing labourers to scramble for other jobs or return home to the countryside (Wong 2008; 'China 2008: the global financial crisis', *China Digital Times*, 2008, <http://chinadigitaltimes.net/2008/12/2008-financial-crisis-and-china/>). It was increasingly clear that overheating was no longer the main challenge, and policymakers gradually reduced the magnitude of the threat of inflation. The debate about de-coupling had become irrelevant and China quickly found itself having to refocus on sustaining economic growth amid a global slowdown. Accordingly, the 'two acts of prevention' policy gave way to 'one ensure and one control'—ensuring stable economic growth and controlling inflation. Policymakers halted the yuan's appreciation and boosted tax rebates to help exporters. The People's Bank of China (PBOC) cut interest rates in mid-September 2008, for the first time in six years, foreshadowing the stumble China might have to put up with.

The worldwide economic downturn has undoubtedly occupied centre stage since the last quarter of 2008. China's gross domestic product (GDP) recorded 6.8 per cent growth—unbelievably low by Chinese standards. In November 2008, China's exports declined by 2 per cent, which was the first drop in seven years. More than 600 000 small and medium-sized companies were closed, putting millions of migrants out of work (Ramzy 2009).

To reboot the economy, a CNY4 trillion ($586 billion) stimulus package was unveiled in November. In the same month, the central bank also cut interest rates by 1.08 percentage points and lowered banks' reserve requirements. In addition, a host of policies was subsequently implemented to promote growth and employment through investment and consumption. These included policies such as the value-added tax (VAT) rebate for purchasing machinery and equipment, an increase in the export rebate, a loosening of controls on mortgage loans and the removal of quota controls on lending by commercial banks. Provided with the strong measures of credit expansion, the first quarter of 2009 has already observed a surge in renminbi-denominated loans. It takes time, however, for investment to be translated into output. During the first quarter of 2009, real GDP growth moderated to 6.1 per cent. In January, exports fell 17.5 per cent from a year ago—the biggest percentage decline since October 1998. The weakened export demand foreshadows the troubles ahead for millions of migrant workers who rely on factory jobs.

To gauge the employment impact on migrant workers, one has to take into account the external factors—such as plummeting export demand since late 2008—and the dynamism of domestic policies, as well as the interaction of the two. In particular, in the past two years, China's macroeconomic policies have experienced a roller-coaster ride, from containing an overheating economy to injecting CNY4 trillion to provide a jump-start. Furthermore, the new Labour Contract Law has shaped the labour-intensive sector significantly—independently of the subsequent external shock. Taking into account the major events that have shocked the employment of migrant workers, a set of hypotheses can be derived to set the stage for disentangling the separate impacts of each event:

- regional differences (the Labour Contract Law should be applied across the board, but the export demand shock should affect coastal regions more than interior areas)
- time difference (the Labour Contract Law impacted from 2007 to mid-2008, while this was compounded by the effects of the global recession after mid-2008)
- sectoral difference (the global downturn primarily affects construction and manufacturing).

The size of the adverse employment effect

Existing estimates

How badly did contractionary macroeconomic policies, the new Labour Contract Law and the global financial crisis affect the employment of migrants? Three survey-based estimates have recently revealed a very gloomy picture. One survey, carried out by the Chinese Ministry of Agriculture in January 2009, covered 150 counties in 15 provinces that were known to be major migration sending areas. Based on this survey, about 15.3 per cent of the 130 million migrant workers—20 million—lost their jobs due to the global financial crisis.[1]

Another official survey was conducted by the National Bureau of Statistics (NBS) of China, covering 68 000 rural households in 31 provinces,

857 counties and 7100 villages between the end of 2008 and early 2009. The estimates based on these data show that, in 2008, about 140 million rural migrants worked in cities. By the end of 2008, 50 per cent had returned to their home villages, of which 80 per cent went back to cities after the Chinese New Year, while the remaining 20 per cent decided to stay in their rural hometown. The total effect was therefore that about 10 per cent of the migrant labour force returned to their home village.

The third source of information is a series of small-scale surveys conducted by the Xilu Migrants Survey Group between November 2008 and January 2009. Of the 809 individuals surveyed, 89.5 per cent returned home for the Chinese New Year by 14 January 2008—12 days before Chinese New Year. Some 46 per cent of the returning migrants said that they were returning earlier than usual, of which 76 per cent indicated that it was due to workplace shutdowns, downsizing or they had been forced by their employers to take extended holidays. About 35 per cent of the total number of migrants therefore returned home earlier than usual because of the economic downturn. Of the 89.5 per cent of migrants who returned home before Chinese New Year, 69 per cent indicated that they would definitely be going back to cities after the New Year, 7.2 per cent suggested they would not return to cities, while the remaining 24 per cent were uncertain at the time of the survey.

All three studies seem to indicate a similar size for the adverse impact of the economic downturn. These studies are, however, based primarily on surveys conducted at the sending end and on migrant intensions to return to cities. What really happened has not been revealed in the existing literature. Did they go back to cities and, if so, were they able to find jobs? In this chapter, we use more objective information gathered from the sampling, interviewing, tracking and re-interviewing of a group of migrants in the RUMiCI survey to gauge the size of the adverse impact of the economic downturn on migrant employment.

RUMiCI survey and tracking method

The RUMiCI project is a research collaboration initiated by The Australian National University and Beijing Normal University. The project surveyed three groups of households: 5007 rural–urban migrants who worked in 15 designated cities[2] in 2008; 5000 urban households in the same cities; and 8000 rural households from 10 provinces or metropolitan areas where the 15 cities were located.[3] While the urban and rural household surveys use the existing NBS household survey samples, no available sampling frame exists for rural–urban migrants. Previous migration surveys have normally used a household-based sampling methodology, whereby interviewers in selected urban neighbourhood communities randomly select migrants. The main concern about this sampling method is that only a small proportion of migrants in Chinese cities live within urban neighbourhood communities. A large proportion of them live either in factory dormitories, at the back of the restaurants or construction sites where they work or in surrounding rural suburbs. A sample drawn from urban residential communities might be quite unrepresentative of the migrant population. The RUMiCI research team employs a unique and innovative sampling strategy to address this concern.

Essentially, the survey uses a sampling frame that is based on information collected in a census of migrant workers at their workplaces. More specifically, we divided our sample cities into 500 metre by 500m blocks and randomly selected blocks equal to about 12 per cent of the sample size for each city. Within each block, a census was conducted of all the workplaces within the selected blocks and the questions included the industry type, total number of workers and total number of migrant workers. The data obtained from this census of workplaces were then used as the sampling frame and a simple random-sampling method was used to select our sample of migrant individuals. Once we located the individual migrant, the interview was conducted with his/her household.[4]

From October to December 2007, the project team conducted a block census in the 15 cities. The sampling and surveying were conducted between March and June 2008 after migrants came back to cities from their annual home visit for Chinese New Year. We interviewed 5007 migrant households in the 15 cities. At the time of sampling in March–April 2008, we observed that a sizeable number of workplaces were already shut down, mainly in Dongguan, Shenzhen and Guangzhou. The survey company indicated to us that this was the result of the implementation of the contractionary macroeconomic policy and the new Labour Contract Law.

Because the survey is designed to be a five-year panel, a tracking strategy has been developed. An important feature of the migrant population is a high degree of geographic mobility. This makes tracking very difficult. At the time of the survey, we recorded individuals' work and home addresses and contact details in the cities as well as in their home village. In addition, we recorded phone numbers of three close relatives or friends of the interviewee in case they or their households moved. These are normal tracking strategies adopted by any panel survey. We realised that our sample population was different and their high degree of mobility suggested that these simple tracking designs might need to be enhanced. We therefore developed further tracking incentives. First, each year, we conduct three lottery activities for all our sample respondents. The prize ranges from CNY50–2000 in the first year and will increase each year. The lottery is designed to cover 1.5 per cent of individuals, but if an individual follows the survey for five years the probability of receiving a prize increases to 20 per cent. Only when an individual is successfully tracked can his/her name be entered in the lottery. This information is made available to the interviewees at the time of the interview. We hope this will give respondents an incentive to keep us informed of their whereabouts. Second, we send a present to interviewees' rural home every year before Chinese New Year, hoping to strengthen the link between the interviewees and the project team.

Five months after the first-wave survey (October 2008), we contacted all the respondents to confirm their current contact details so that a gift could be sent to them. At the same time, the first lottery results were revealed. Soon after, in December, and again in February 2009, another two rounds of tracking were conducted.[5] Despite all these efforts, however, the attrition rate for the 2008 survey was very high, which was closely associated with the economic downturn. To compensate for the high attrition rate, a re-sampling based on 2007 census data was carried out before the 2009 survey. It is important to understand, however, the validity of the 2007 census frame after the economic downturn. We revisited 13 per cent of the census blocks (64 blocks) from the original total of 489 blocks surveyed in 2007 to examine whether the workplaces recorded in 2007 had changed their operating status.[6] This small-scale re-census provided us with another set of information to examine whether the original workplace had shut down, changed to a new entity or had not changed. It does not, however, inform us of the degree of downsizing within existing workplaces. It therefore gives us a lower-bound estimation of the impact of the economic downturn.

Estimates of the adverse employment impact using RUMiCI data

Our 2007 census data calculated the number of workplaces and rural migrant workers by city and industry (Table 12.1). Among our sample migrants, 67 per cent were employed in the service and wholesale-retail trade sectors, while 18 per cent worked in the manufacturing industry. The manufacturing industries were heavily concentrated in the coastal regions. In addition, more than 70 per cent of the migrants were employed in eight coast cities (Guangzhou, Dongguan, Shenzhen, Shanghai, Nanjing, Wuxi, Hangzhou and Ningbo). These data give us a starting point in describing the pre-economic downturn employment situation for rural–urban migrants in our sample cities, with which we can compare the post-economic downturn employment data.

Two data sources are used to gauge the post-economic downturn employment situation: the block re-census data and the sample tracking data.

We classify our block re-census workplaces into those that have been shut down and those that have not. We then use this information together with the 2007 census data to draw implications on the proportion of workplaces in each industry within our 2007 census blocks that have shut down, and further use the inverse-probability as a weight to generate an implied shutdown ratio for the city as a whole. In addition, using the 2007 census data for the number of migrants employed in each workplace, we calculate the implied employment impact of these shutdowns. We report the proportion of workplaces being shut down after the economic downturn by city and industry (Table 12.2). In all 15 cities, about 9 per cent of the total number of workplaces had been closed since November–December 2007. Among these cities, Wuhan and Dongguan have the highest proportion of closed workplaces and in both cities almost all industries have been adversely affected. For the 15 cities as a whole, construction, manufacturing and various types of agencies have the highest levels of shutdowns.

Table 12.1 Distribution of workplaces and rural migrants across city and industry: 2007 census data

	Construction	Manufacturing	Education and government organisations	Various types of agencies	Services	Wholesale and retail trade	Total
Number of workplaces:							
Guangzhou	550	2,201	2,699	4,952	54,732	48,863	11,3996
Dongguan	1,344	6,049	1,253	2,108	42,345	50,777	103,876
Shenzhen	1,311	2,639	1,090	2,970	43,150	37,683	88,843
Zhenzhou	1,628	4,379	767	1,404	44,072	35,220	87,471
Luoyang	192	947	414	207	10,049	6,956	18,766
Hefei	1,130	706	477	1,377	30,406	27,298	61,394
Bangbu	42	260	54	91	3412	3,551	7,411
Chongqing	1,280	1,668	756	1,513	54,768	35,219	95,205
Shanghai	2,091	3,772	1,804	9,553	105,370	87,002	209,592
Nanjing	916	1,374	1,168	3,595	55,938	35,880	98,871
Wuxi	914	5,044	914	2,133	27,689	19,633	56,326
Hangzhou	404	1,374	1,159	2,210	36,392	31,421	72,960
Ningbo	274	535	162	635	11,591	9,163	22,360
Wuhan	1,205	4,367	1,857	2,460	62,223	53,036	125,149
Chengdu	1,121	1,033	1,475	6,461	94,695	81,656	186,440
Total	14,404	36,348	16,049	41,667	676,833	563,359	1,348,661

% of employment by industry and city:

	Construction	Manufacturing	Education and government organisations	Various types of agencies	Services	Wholesale and retail trade	Total number of employment
Guangzhou	1.30	23.23	2.88	6.07	40.09	26.43	1,041,502
Dongguan	1.24	26.29	3.23	1.72	12.55	54.97	2,274,729
Shenzhen	7.21	21.81	0.99	2.77	36.32	30.91	949,059
Zhenzhou	21.48	8.21	1.27	1.60	34.49	32.96	434,452
Luoyang	8.33	12.92	2.23	0.52	38.85	37.15	95,874
Hefei	10.10	5.35	1.29	8.94	36.33	37.99	2,939,56
Bangbu	7.91	13.78	0.30	1.44	30.32	46.24	24,859
Chongqing	9.22	4.68	1.24	0.82	48.76	35.28	642,618
Shanghai	8.35	10.85	1.50	11.88	41.29	26.13	1,479,731
Nanjing	16.86	15.86	1.19	10.21	38.16	17.73	672,406
Wuxi	9.40	40.82	2.00	6.03	22.01	19.75	1,024,504
Hangzhou	7.06	17.64	2.48	2.69	36.98	33.15	548,258
Ningbo	26.06	8.99	5.07	10.14	28.21	21.55	216,356
Wuhan	5.17	28.90	3.08	2.88	36.49	23.47	911,481
Chengdu	10.69	3.08	0.57	6.37	45.83	33.45	877,242
Total share of employment	8.36	18.25	2.04	4.68	34.00	32.68	
Total employment	991,995	2,475,530	266,698	667,909	4,282,078	2,802,816	11,487,028

Table 12.2 Distribution of closed workplaces and shutdown rate: 2009 re-census data

Panel A: Number of closed workplaces (weighted by industry-city sampling weight)

City	Construction	Manufacturing	Education and government organisations	Various types of agencies	Services	Wholesale and retail trade	Total no. of shutdown workplaces
Guangzhou	0	0	257	990	5,711	6,261	13,220
Dongguan	672	3,074	501	527	11,934	15,118	31,826
Shenzhen	82	0	0	858	2,123	1,489	4,553
Zhenzhou	814	0	0	0	5,650	4,892	11,356
Luoyang	96	0	0	0	412	598	1,106
Hefei	0	0	238	172	3,062	3,140	6,613
Bangbu	0	0	0	272	991	991	1,263
Chongqing	0	0	0	0	5,353	3,953	9,307
Shanghai	0	0	361	546	6,144	10,741	17,792
Nanjing	0	153	156	1,514	6,978	11,012	19,811
Wuxi	166	1,244	0	711	4,214	4,945	11,279
Hangzhou	101	89	145	0	6,000	5,308	11,643
Ningbo	91	76	0	41	874	1,857	2,940
Wuhan	0	662	929	1,757	25,075	31,389	59,811
Chengdu	140	0	0	0	455	1,884	2,480
Total	2,163	5,297	2,586	7,388	83,985	103,578	204,999

245

Panel B: Shutdown rate (%)

City	Construction	Manufacturing	Education and government organisations	Various types of agencies	Services	Wholesale and retail trade	Total no. of shutdown workplaces
Guangzhou	0.00	0.00	6.25	12.20	8.07	7.31	7.69
Dongguan	36.36	44.93	21.05	23.08	22.14	24.44	24.65
Shenzhen	6.06	0.00	0.00	17.81	4.27	3.25	4.27
Zhenzhou	46.15	0.00	0.00	0.00	10.14	10.47	10.30
Luoyang	50.00	0.00	0.00	0.00	1.69	4.00	2.63
Hefei	0.00	0.00	14.29	6.67	6.01	8.02	6.85
Bangbu	0.00	0.00	0.00	37.50	0.00	9.76	5.17
Chongqing	0.00	0.00	0.00	0.00	6.74	7.01	6.67
Shanghai	0.00	0.00	6.25	3.51	3.77	6.58	4.94
Nanjing	0.00	7.69	6.67	25.81	8.89	11.76	10.80
Wuxi	18.18	21.95	0.00	17.65	11.07	15.81	13.91
Hangzhou	20.00	5.13	5.56	0.00	12.71	12.97	12.11
Ningbo	25.00	6.45	0.00	2.90	5.19	9.09	7.21
Wuhan	0.00	15.15	37.50	62.50	34.62	49.15	40.64
Chengdu	20.00	0.00	0.00	0.00	0.63	2.52	1.57
Total	12.88	11.89	9.14	11.96	9.48	12.20	9.16

Matching the shutdown workplaces with the number of migrant workers hired by these workplaces in November–December 2007, we are able to examine the employment effect of the shutdown. We present the industry and city distribution of the impact of the shutdown on migrant employment for both calculations (Table 12.3). On average, about 13 per cent (or 1.4 million) of the migrants employed in the 15 surveyed cities were affected by the post-economic downturn shutdowns. Among the 15 cities, Dongguan has been hit the worst, with about 34 per cent of its migrant employment affected. The other cities badly affected are Wuxi and Ningbo, which has about 20 per cent of the migrant employment affected by shutdowns. If we believe that the global financial downturn affects mainly cities that are export oriented, we can rank our 15 cities according to their export concentration. Appendix 12.2 provides the proportion of export value to the city level GDP for each of our 15 cities for 2006 and ranks them accordingly. Among them, Shenzhen and Shanghai are ranked first and third. Surprisingly, their levels of migrant employment are among the lowest of the cities affected by the shutdowns, suggesting that perhaps there are factors other than the global financial crisis causing the current economic downturn.

Further, if we examine the industry distribution of the impact, we find that both the traded-goods industry (manufacturing) and the non-traded goods industry (wholesale and retail trade, for example) are affected. For example, in Wuhan, 28 per cent of migrant employment in the wholesale-retail trade sector is affected. From this point of view, it seems that domestic policies and the global financial crisis have had a sizeable impact.

Table 12.3 Proportion of rural migrant employment being affected by shutdown (per cent)

	Construction	Manufacturing	Education and government organisations	Various types of agencies	Services	Wholesale and retail trade	Total proportion of migrants being affected	Total no. of migrants in shutdown workplaces
Guangzhou	0.00	0.00	0.43	28.51	5.18	8.25	5.68	60,400
Dongguan	6.17	70.88	0.00	22.96	14.05	22.38	33.69	766,808
Shenzhen	0.42	0.00	0.00	15.05	2.77	14.25	4.56	41,911
Zhenzhou	2.10	0.00	0.00	0.00	3.59	8.23	3.61	15,886
Luoyang	77.95	0.00	0.00	0.00	0.82	1.85	12.31	8,727
Hefei	0.00	0.00	66.67	0.00	3.32	7.52	4.19	12,348
Bangbu	0.00	0.00	0.00	0.00	0.00	8.78	2.57	523
Chongqing	0.00	0.00	0.00	0.00	1.73	0.78	1.30	7,151
Shanghai	0.00	0.00	13.89	18.23	2.52	2.46	4.17	78,485
Nanjing	0.00	0.00	7.61	66.53	3.94	11.81	10.28	65,426
Wuxi	26.89	29.04	0.00	13.95	3.42	24.02	19.98	188,434
Hangzhou	0.00	3.41	1.05	0.00	8.75	1.90	4.43	20,552
Ningbo	70.42	0.00	0.00	0.12	3.63	10.75	22.33	48,539
Wuhan	0.00	2.16	1.96	95.51	1.51	27.68	9.43	77,173
Chengdu	0.00	0.00	0.00	0.00	0.00	1.30	0.25	1,083
Total	7.87	23.54	2.25	23.78	3.96	15.05	12.64	1,393,447
Total no. of migrants affected	81,969	573,735	5,276	164,157	152,633	415,677	1,393,447	
Total no. of original number of migrants	1,674	6,252	26	2,010	1,547	5,436	16,945	

Note that the shutdown effect is a lower-bound estimate of the extent of the total economic downturn effect on employment. From our re-census data, we are unable to examine the size of the downsizing within the existing workplaces. Our tracking data for the 5007 migrant households surveyed in 2008 could shed some light on this; however, using tracking data to infer the economic downturn effect on employment is quite tricky, as in a normal environment one expects a certain attrition rate. The literature does not provide a benchmark on the issue of what is a normal rate of attrition for an average population in a normal economic environment. Nevertheless, the Household Income and Labour Dynamics in Australia (HILDA) survey and the British Household Panel Survey (BHPS) could serve as such benchmarks. From the first to the second wave, HILDA has an attrition rate of about 13.2 per cent, while the rate for the BHPS is 12.4 per cent (Watson and Wooden 2004). We can therefore regard the 12–13 per cent attrition rate for HILDA and BHPS as a benchmark for an average population in a normal economic environment.

Our sample population, however, has much higher mobility and hence the attrition rate for the average population represented in HILDA and BHPS might not be a suitable benchmark for our purposes. In an industrialised country, the population regarded as highly mobile is the youth group—in particular, young men (for example, Olsen 2005). The attrition rate from wave one to wave two for the group aged twenty to twenty-four in the HILDA survey is 23.4 per cent (Watson and Wooden 2004).

The migrant population represented in our sample, although older with an average age of twenty-eight years, in fact faces a very different institutional environment to that facing youth in industrial countries. Because of the restrictions on accessing formal-sector jobs, social services and a social safety net in cities, migrants have very insecure jobs and, when they are fired, they have no safety net to rely on (Meng 2000; Meng and Manning 2010). They therefore tend to move around much more than an average population or even average youth. Using the data for the year since first migration and the number of cities worked in since first migration, we are able to calculate the average time migrants stay in one city. Among our 2008 sample of the 5007 migrant household heads, the median number of years they stayed for work purposes in one city was three (Figure 12.1). The average annual mobility therefore should be about 33 per cent without the economic downturn. Based on this information, we expect that the normal attrition rate for our sample between the first and second wave in a normal situation without an economic downturn should be about 30 per cent.

Figure 12.1 Kernel density estimate

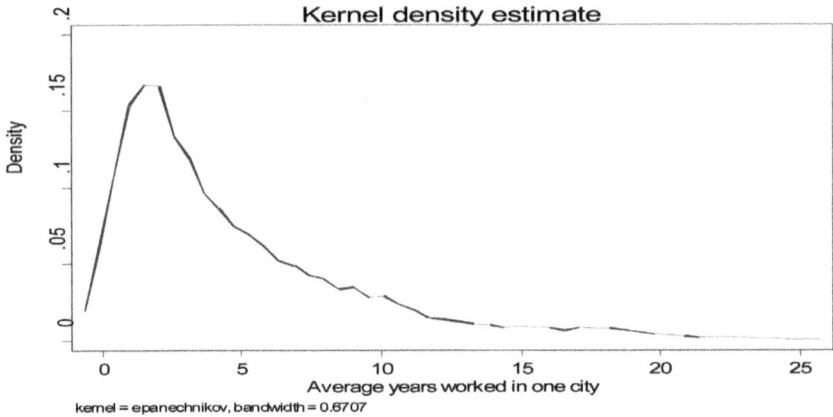

As discussed earlier, in October 2008, December 2009 and February 2009, we tracked our 5007 migrant households three times. Each time, our targeted tracking population was the 5007 original households surveyed. The attrition rate for each of these trackings is reported (Table 12.4). The attrition rate for the first tracking in October 2008 is 34.2 per cent—already exceeding our expectation for a normal economic environment. Two months later, the second tracking resulted in a 39.4 per cent attrition rate with respect to the original 5007 sample households, or an additional 5.2 percentage point loss of our sample. Relative to the 3296 households being tracked in October 2008, the second attrition rate was 16.7 per cent. Finally, just before we embarked on the second-wave survey, the third tracking recorded an attrition rate of 48.8 per cent with respect to the original sample (an additional 14.6 percentage points relative to the first tracking), or 24.9 per cent with respect to the second tracked sample of 3035 households. This final tracking gives us an attrition rate that is 18.8 percentage points higher than our expected attrition for a normal economic environment. This could serve as an upper-bound estimation of the employment effects of the economic downturn.

Table 12.4 Attrition rates for the three trackings

	First (October)	Second (December)	Third (February)
As % of original sample	34.17	39.38	48.77
As % of last tracked sample		16.76	24.89
As % of first tracking tracked sample			32.55
Total sample	5,007	5,007	5,007
Total sample tracked last time		3,296	3,035
Total sample tracked current time	3,296	3,035	2,565

The industry and city distributions for the total lost sample from the third tracking (February 2009) are reported (Table 12.5). All the cities had lost more than 30 per cent of the original sample in the third tracking. Among the total lost sample, cities that had lost more than 50 per cent of the sample were Guangzhou, Dongguan, Nanjing, Hangzhou, Ningbo and Wuhan. Although most of these cities are in the coastal region, where export industries are concentrated, except for Wuhan, the cities with the highest and third-highest export concentration levels—Shenzhen and Shanghai—are not among this list. It is also interesting to see that Nanjing and Ningbo have extremely high rates of attrition—more than 10 percentage points higher than Dongguan, whose export concentration exceeds the former two cities by a large margin.

Table 12.5 Proportion of migrants not being found in the February 2009 tracking by city and industry

City	Construction	Manufacturing	Education and government organisations	Various types of agencies	Services	Wholesale and retail trade	Total % not being tracked	Total no. of migrants not being tracked
Guangzhou	45.45	53.45	64.71	53.85	52.94	58.18	54.89	400
Dongguan	50.00	52.63	0.00	66.67	49.02	41.94	50.17	301
Shenzhen	50.00	43.66	25.00	34.88	36.25	29.17	36.75	302
Zhenzhou	61.19	34.78	33.33	37.50	53.76	24.79	41.43	350
Luoyang	50.00	68.42	60.00	75.00	52.17	31.18	44.50	200
Hefei	50.91	36.36	56.52	27.27	37.80	29.36	38.04	350
Bangbu	57.89	60.00	42.86	0.00	42.50	42.42	45.73	200
Chongqing	46.34	32.00	71.43	38.89	42.26	34.96	40.00	400
Shanghai	55.32	63.33	17.65	55.00	53.88	38.66	49.10	503
Nanjing	76.47	69.33	78.57	0.00	69.06	67.35	70.00	400
Wuxi	15.79	41.11	0.00	0.00	31.75	45.00	34.67	200
Hangzhou	71.79	50.48	35.29	37.50	49.67	44.74	50.25	400
Ningbo	69.35	68.00	0.00	60.00	62.67	48.28	62.00	200
Wuhan	65.79	60.68	38.89	50.00	52.48	52.50	55.53	400
Chengdu	59.26	60.00	27.78	56.25	53.97	39.64	49.75	401
Total	59.23	53.33	38.74	42.93	50.76	39.87	48.75	5,007

Among the six industry groups, construction, manufacturing and services lost more than 50 per cent of the original sample, of which the impact on manufacturing industries can be tied directly to the global financial crisis due to its export intensity, whereas this might not be the case for the construction and service industries. The high attrition rate across the board for different cities and the fact that the non-tradable sectors (construction and services) are hit equally hard are suggestive of the fact that the impact on migrant employment comes not only from the global financial crisis but is a combined effect of domestic macroeconomic policies and external shocks.

Who has borne the brunt of the economic downturn?

Another interesting issue to examine is who, among the rural–urban migrants, has been affected the most by the economic downturn. In this section, we utilise our 2008 survey data combined with the tracking records to investigate this issue.

In the 2008 survey, we collected a rich set of information about the households and individual migrants. Using these data, we are able to identify the individual and household characteristics of the group, which we are unable to record in each of the three trackings. We estimate the linear-probability model of whether a household is tracked in each of the three trackings. The independent variables include household and household head characteristic variables, such as household size, the age of the household head, his/her gender, marital status, years of schooling, year since migration, number of cities he/she has worked in since first migrating, the household head's 2008 job descriptions (workplace size, whether the workplace was in the manufacturing or construction sector and whether the individual was self-employed) and a subjective variable indicating whether, if the policy allowed, the household would like to stay in the city forever. In addition, we include a group of city-level dummy variables. The estimated results are reported (Table 12.6).

Table 12.6 Regression results on probability of being tracked in each of the three trackings

	Being tracked (Oct. 2008)	Being tracked (Oct. 2008)	Being tracked (Feb. 2009)
Age	0.019	0.020	0.015
	(0.005)[c]	(0.005)[c]	(0.005)[c]
Age^2/100	−0.024	−0.026	−0.022
	(0.006)[c]	(0.006)[c]	(0.007)[c]
Dummy for males	0.022	0.011	0.038
	(0.015)	(0.015)	(0.016)[b]
Dummy for married	0.047	0.037	0.036
	(0.022)[b]	(0.022)[a]	(0.023)
No. of household members	0.019	0.029	0.048
	(0.009)[b]	(0.009)[c]	(0.009)[c]
Years of schooling	0.012	0.016	0.015
	(0.003)[c]	(0.003)[c]	(0.003)[c]
Year since first migration	0.003	0.005	0.007
	(0.001)[b]	(0.001)[c]	(0.001)[c]
No. of cities worked in since first migrated	−0.009	−0.007	−0.008
	(0.003)[c]	(0.003)[b]	(0.003)[b]
If allowed, will stay in city forever	0.038	0.032	0.035
	(0.014)[c]	(0.014)[b]	(0.015)[b]
Working in manufacturing industry	−0.063	−0.057	−0.065
	(0.020)[c]	(0.020)[c]	(0.021)[c]
Working in construction industry	−0.103	−0.096	−0.145
	(0.025)[c]	(0.026)[c]	(0.026)[c]
Self-employed	0.058	0.031	0.014
	(0.041)	(0.041)	(0.042)
Dongguan	−0.111	0.061	0.048
	(0.036)[c]	(0.037)[a]	(0.038)
Shenzhen	0.064	0.260	0.210
	(0.036)[a]	(0.037)[c]	(0.037)[c]
Zhenzhou	0.230	0.275	0.131
	(0.035)[c]	(0.036)[c]	(0.037)[c]
Luoyang	0.108	0.185	0.102
	(0.041)[c]	(0.042)[c]	(0.043)[b]
Hefei	0.103	0.301	0.150
	(0.035)[c]	(0.036)[c]	(0.037)[c]
Bangbu	0.186	0.272	0.048
	(0.042)[c]	(0.042)[c]	(0.043)
Chongqing	0.212	0.234	0.128
	(0.033)[c]	(0.034)[c]	(0.035)[c]

	Being tracked (Oct. 2008)	Being tracked (Oct. 2008)	Being tracked (Feb. 2009)
Shanghai	0.097	0.213	0.036
	(0.032)[c]	(0.032)[c]	(0.033)
Nanjing	0.095	0.158	−0.136
	(0.033)[c]	(0.034)[c]	(0.035)[c]
Wuxi	0.062	0.239	0.220
	(0.041)	(0.042)[c]	(0.043)[c]
Hangzhou	0.085	0.147	0.048
	(0.033)[b]	(0.034)[c]	(0.035)
Ningbo	0.118	0.021	−0.039
	(0.041)[c]	(0.042)	(0.043)
Wuhan	0.036	0.114	−0.027
	(0.034)	(0.034)[c]	(0.035)
Chengdu	0.157	0.285	0.038
	(0.034)[c]	(0.034)[c]	(0.035)
Firm size	Yes	Yes	Yes
Observations	4897	4897	4897
R-squared	0.07	0.09	0.09

[a] significant at 10 per cent;

[b] significant at 5 per cent;

[c] significant at 1 per cent

Note: Standard errors in parentheses.

We find that the results are largely consistent across the equations for three different sets of tracking data. In general, age has a positive effect on being tracked, but it reaches the peak about thirty-five to forty. By age fifty-five, the probability of being tracked reduces to the same level as that for those aged sixteen (Appendix 12.1). Males, married individuals and migrants who have other family members living in the same cities with them are more likely to be tracked. In addition, those who have a higher education level and longer migration experience are more likely to be tracked, while those who often change places and those who do not want to stay in the city forever, even if allowed to, are less likely to be tracked. These results are quite intuitive. If we believe that attrition, to a certain extent, indicates the adverse employment impact of the economic downturn, the above results can be read as showing that individuals who are single, not in the primary working-age group, are less educated and have less migration experience are more likely to be adversely affected by the economic downturn. These findings are largely consistent with the literature on unemployment in most countries (for example, Devine and Kiefer 1991; Svejnar 1999).

With respect to employment, it seems that those who worked in the manufacturing and construction industries in 2008 were more likely to have left their previous job than those who worked in tertiary industries. The effect is much stronger for the construction industry than for the manufacturing industry, especially in the third tracking, where the effect on a construction job is twice as high as that on a manufacturing job. Working in the construction sector in 2008 increases the probability of having left that job by February 2009 by 15 per cent, while the probability of leaving a manufacturing job is 7 per cent. Neither self-employment nor firm size has an effect on leaving the job.

Conditional on all the above variables, relative to Guangzhou, almost all cities have a higher probability of being tracked, except Dongguan in October 2008. By the second and third tracking, Dongguan has a higher probability of being tracked, while the probability for Nanjing has dropped dramatically to below Guangzhou's level.

Conclusion

In this chapter, we use a unique set of data from the RUMiCI project to investigate the employment impact of the economic downturn on rural–urban migrants. We find that, on average, the total effect of the economic downturn has adversely affected 13–19 per cent of jobs for rural–urban migrants. These estimates are higher than those in the existing literature using data from migrant sending regions, which estimate that about 10–15 per cent of migrants are affected by the economic downturn.

We also find that the group of migrants whose jobs are most likely to be affected by the economic downturn is the one comprising those who would normally be affected in any economy. These are the people who are less educated, single, not in the primary age group and have less migration experience.

Our analysis indicates that job loss is not confined to the export-concentrated coastal regions. The majority of cities in our sample have had significant jobs losses. In fact, two of the top export-concentrated cities—Shenzhen and Shanghai—have had a low level of job loss relative to their interior counterparts.

We also find that job loss is not confined to export-manufacturing industries. Indeed, the non-traded goods sectors—construction, retail and wholesale—are where most job losses occur.

We interpret the widespread nature of this job loss, and the heavy incidence of job losses outside the export industries, to indicate that job losses in China are primarily a response to factors other than the decline in export markets. In particular, tight monetary policy in the past few years was important at the start of the current downturn and the introduction of the new Labour Contract Law could also be responsible. Of course, as the economy responds to the global financial crisis, this pattern of job loss could change and the loss of jobs in the export sector, at least in relative terms, could become more important.

References

Batson, A. 2008, 'China aids home buyers to curb impact of slump', *Wall Street Journal*, 24 October 2008.

Cooney, S., Biddulph, S., Kungang, L. and Zhu, Y. 2007, 'China's new Labour Contract Law: responding to the growing complexity of labour relations in the PRC', *UNSW Law Journal*, vol. 30, no. 3, pp. 788–803.

Devine, T. J. and Kiefer, N. M. 1991, *Empirical Labor Economics: The search approach*, Oxford University Press, Oxford.

Olsen, R. J. 2005, 'The problem of respondent attrition: survey methodology is key', *Monthly Labor Review*, February 2005, pp. 63–70, <http://www.bls.gov/opub/mlr/2005/02/art9full.pdf>

Svejnar, J. 1999, 'Labor markets in the transitional Central and Eastern European economies', in O. Ashenfelter and D. Card (eds), *Handbook for Labor Economics. Volume 3B*, Elsevier, North-Holland, pp. 1809–2858.

Wang, H., Appelbaum, R. P., Degiuli, F. and Lichtenstein, N. 2009, 'China's new Labour Contract Law: is China moving towards increased power for workers?', *Third World Quarterly*, vol. 30, no. 3, pp. 485–501.

Watson, N. and Wooden, M. 2004, *Assessing the quality of the HILDSA survey wave 2 data*, HILDA Project Technical Paper Series, no. 5/04, Melbourne University, Melbourne.

Wong, E. 2008, 'Factories shut, China workers are suffering', *New York Times*, 14 November 2008.

Zhao, L. and Lim, T. S. 2008, *China's new Labour Contract Law: belated convent to better protection of workers*, EAI Background Brief, no. 378, 10 April 2008, East Asian Institute, National University of Singapore.

Appendix 12.1

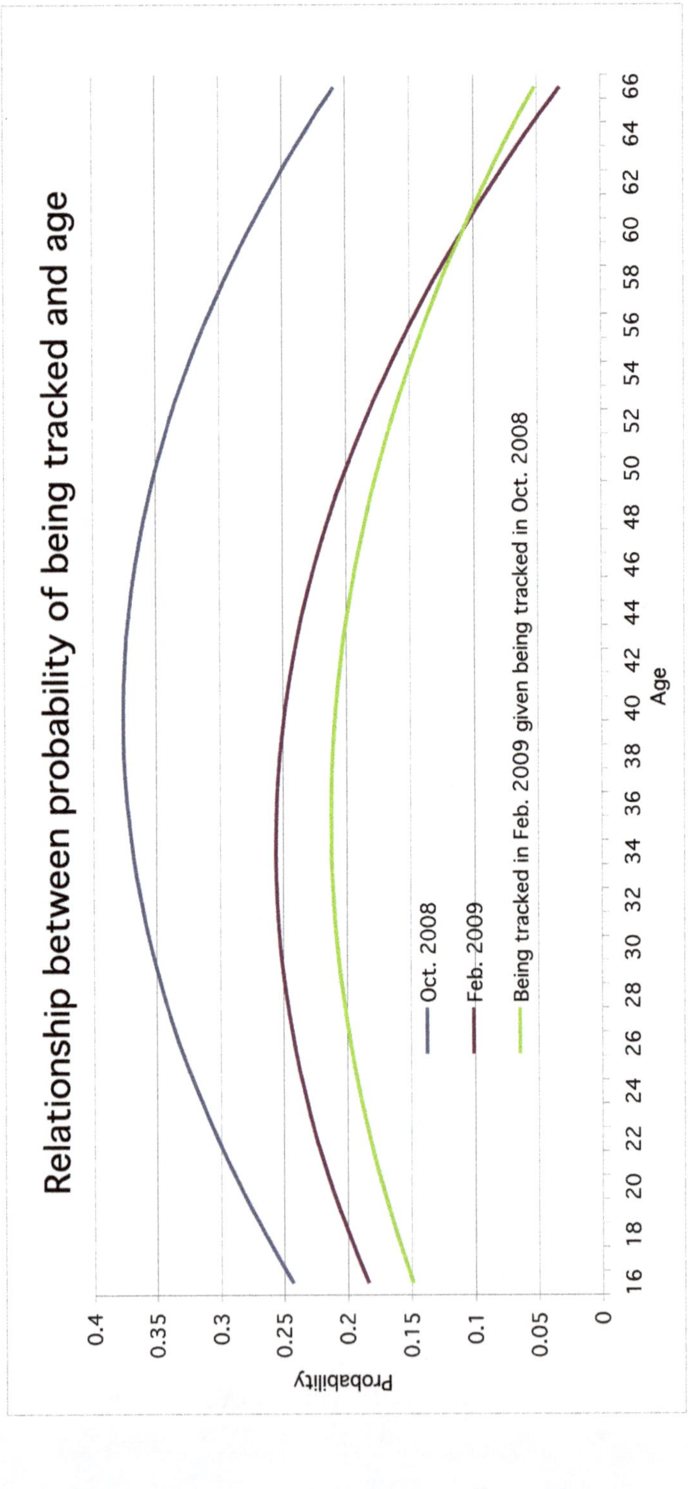

Relationship between probability of being tracked and age
Probability
0.4
0.35
0.3
0.25
0.2
0.15
0.1
0.05
0
16 18 20 22 24 26 28 30 32 34 36 38 40 42 44 46 48 50 52 54 56 58 60 62 64 66
Age
Oct. 2008
Feb. 2009
Being tracked in Feb. 2009 given being tracked in Oct. 2008

Appendix 12.2 GDP and import–export values by city

	Local GDP (10,000 yuan) (2005 price)	Import value (10,000 US$)	Export value (10,000 US$)	Export value (10,000 yuan) (1US$ = 7.8 yuan)	Import–export total value in US$	Import–export total value in Yuan 1 = 7.8	Total import–export value as % of total GDP	Total export value as % of GDP	Ranking of export orintation
Shenzhen	57,703,731	10,130,300	13,610,800	106,164,240	23,741,100	185,180,580	3.21	1.84	1
Dongguan	26,008,962	3,684,467	4,737,640	36,953,592	8,422,107	65,692,434.6	2.53	1.42	2
Shanghai	102,676,400	11,391,624	11,357,306	88,586,986.8	22,748,930	177,441,654	1.73	0.86	3
Ningbo	27,836,308	1,344,136	2,877,052	22,441,005.6	4,221,188	32,925,266.4	1.18	0.81	4
Hangzhou	33,625,701	1,268,100	2,622,800	20,457,840	3,890,900	30,349,020	0.90	0.61	5
Wuxi	32,338,000	1,775,332	2,143,980	16,723,044	3,919,312	30,570,633.6	0.95	0.52	6
Nanjing	27,749,700	1,416,982	1,736,491	13,544,629.8	3,153,473	24,597,089.4	0.89	0.49	7
Guangzhou	59,182,610	3,138,448	3,237,713	25,254,161.4	6,376,161	49,734,055.8	0.84	0.43	8
Hefei	10,449,800	146,922	340,723	2,657,639.4	487,645	3,803,631	0.36	0.25	9
Wuhan	25,705,814	423,464	377,750	2,946,450	801,214	6,249,469.2	0.24	0.11	10
Chengdu	24,445,849	281,183	414,116	3,230,104.8	695,299	5,423,332.2	0.22	0.13	11
Chongqing	34,425,600	211,821	335,192	2,614,497.6	547,013	4,266,701.4	0.12	0.08	12
Zhengzhou	19,257,908	70,872	180,763	1,409,951.4	251,635	1,962,753	0.10	0.07	13
Louyang	12,875,311	25,986	78,075	608,985	104,061	811,675.8	0.06	0.05	14
Bangbo	3,532,800	2,526	24,913	194,321.4	27,439	214,024.2	0.06	0.06	15

Endnotes

1. These data were released by Xiwen Chen, the Director of the Chinese Communist Party's Office on Rural Policy, during a news conference in Beijing on 2 February 2009.

2. The 15 cities are Shanghai, Guangzhou, Shenzhen, Dongguan, Nanjing, Wuxi, Hangzhou, Ningbo, Wuhan, Chongqing, Chengdu, Hefei, Bangbu, Luoyang and Zhengzhou.

3. The RUMiCI project is funded by the Australian Research Council, the Australian Agency for International Development (AusAID) and the Ford Foundation.

4. For detailed information regarding sampling methodology, see <http://rumici.anu.edu.au/>

5. The 2009 Chinese New Year was 26 January. Normally, migrant workers return to their rural home village for Chinese New Year and come back to the city about 15–20 days afterwards. Our last tracking, therefore, was conducted after 15 February 2009, when the majority of migrant workers had come back to cities.

6. The total number of blocks in the census in 2007 and the number of blocks in the re-census in 2009 are listed in Appendix 12.1.

Global implications of China as a manufacturing powerhouse

13

Huw McKay and Ligang Song

This study examines the nature and consequences of China's rise to the centre of world economic affairs through manufacturing-led development. The first half of the nineteenth century was characterised by the diffusion of Britain's new industrial strategy to Continental Europe; the second half featured the ascent of the United States to global prominence, before it then rose to pre-eminence in the first half of the twentieth century. The second half of the twentieth century saw first Japan and then the East Asian region rise to global relevance. In turn, the first half of the twenty-first century will be substantially shaped by China's continuing engagement with a strategy of manufacturing-led development.

The first section of this chapter provides historical context for a balanced consideration of Chinese and global prospects. We argue that the current wave of industrial and technological diffusion in the early twenty-first century, led by China, while differing from waves in the past in some ways, has fundamental points of reference that are readily explicable under the strategic framework we employ. The analysis presents a key finding: genuine powerhouses 'make room for themselves' through rising competitiveness, the exploitation of their own resource endowment and domestic market development.

We see China diverting from its current industrialisation path—which exhibits a modest but not overwhelming bias towards external demand— to a strategy of domestic market integration and internally driven development. This reorientation will be shaped by the unique constraints that China faces relative to its predecessors.

A major attendant theme is that the current trajectory of industrialisation will have to be altered when China becomes more actively engaged in dealing with structural issues at home and abroad against the background of the unwinding of global imbalances. This issue, which is the major subject of section two, has profound implications for Chinese economic strategy.

The third section discusses the potential economic impact of climate change on the future pattern of growth in China. The basic question here is to what extent will any Chinese commitment to low carbon growth alter the future structure of the Chinese and global economies? The issue is significant as the earlier adopters of industrial strategies were not subject to any such constraint on growth. Further, China's relatively recent engagement with a manufacturing-led growth path, and its immense backwardness before this engagement, means that the middle phase of industrialisation—characterised by rapidly growing emission intensities and continuing increases in global market share—is still ahead of it. This is an uncomfortable reality for China and the world.

With the prospect that a global framework for emissions mitigation will move forward strongly in the next few years, coupled with the observation that conflict between manufacturing-led growth and the health of the biosphere is already starkly evident in China, such constraints could become increasingly binding.

The answers provided to each of these questions are conditional and preliminary. It is clear that to achieve a benign outcome, China itself will be required to adjust enormously. As such adjustments are made more easily at low levels of development, however, where the capital stock is still being rapidly built up from a modest base and strategy could be regarded as fluid, we are guardedly optimistic about China's prospects for and its ability to find its own space in the increasingly crowded global economy.

China's emergence in comparative historical context

The historical diffusion of the manufacturing-led strategy

The history of the world economy since the final quarter of the 1700s can be seen as a continuous but fluctuating process of technological diffusion conditioning the emergence of manufacturing-led national development strategies (Snooks 1999). Descriptive analyses of this process abound, with a chronological advance through the initial construction of long-run time series (Kuznets 1930; Clark 1940; Bairoch 1982), attempts at systematic taxonomy (Chenery et al. 1986; Gerschenkron 1962; Rostow 1971), accounting for growth and studying its convergence (Solow 1957; Denison 1967; Baumol 1986; Abramovitz 1986; Dowrick and Ngyuen 1989) and the eventual synthesis of these threads into turn-of-the-millennium global-level analysis (Maddison 2001).[1] The efforts of these scholars, supplemented by the efforts of specialists concentrating on the time paths of individual countries, have provided an empirical basis for the study of long-run structural change at the national, regional and global levels.

A country's long-term growth pattern is determined by its choice of economic strategy, which is endogenous to decisions on saving and investment and is informed by the supply of labour and non-labour inputs and the state of indigenous technological attainment. Strategic direction will also be steered, to varying degrees, by the nature of the international system of the time, most directly through the cross-border availability of technology to allow 'leapfrogging' (Gerschenkron 1962; Brezis et al. 1991), but also through the more prosaic channels of goods, services, capital and labour flows. These choices and their outcomes will determine the productivity growth premium a country can achieve and hence the absolute and relative standard of living that it can attain.

The key feature of world history since the Industrial Revolution has been the spread of the overarching strategy of technological progress from the pioneering zones to those regions with the ambition and drive to engage with and eventually join the core. This strategic transition has been associated with dynamic competition for global leadership and a fluid distribution of economic gravity. China's formidable rise as a manufacturing powerhouse is the latest example of this continuing process.

In addition to a consideration of the usual macroeconomic variables, we have assembled long time series of urbanisation rates, infrastructure investment, metal and energy intensity and automobile penetration to add a practical edge to the discussion. These indicators have been shown to contain substantial information on the development process (Song and Yu 2007; McKay 2008b) and are essential metrics for assessing the scale of global adaptation to the emergence of a new powerhouse.

The basics: how China compares[2]

China began its rise to global prominence from a very low base. In terms of the productivity frontier, which we define as the highest realised gross domestic product (GDP) per capita level of a major nation at any point in time, China was extremely backward when it initially engaged with the world. (Here we use the raw national accounts measure of GDP, with all its weaknesses.) The relative output per person of the United States, Japan, South Korea and China in their respective sample periods can be compared

(Figure 13.1). In 1980, Chinese productivity was just 2.1 per cent of the frontier. That compares with 20 per cent for Japan in 1950 (and 26 per cent in 1900), 11 per cent for South Korea in 1960 and 75 per cent for the United States in 1870. As of 2008, nearly three decades on, the Chinese enjoy per capita output just below 13 per cent of the frontier, as represented by the United States. That is close enough to the position of South Korea at the beginning of its high-growth era, a little more than half the level of post-World War II Japan and exactly half of the relative Japanese level in 1900. On this basis, we can safely classify China's industrialisation as immature in terms of the relative rise in living standards it has achieved.

Figure 13.1 Relative output per capita (years from the start of modern industrial development)

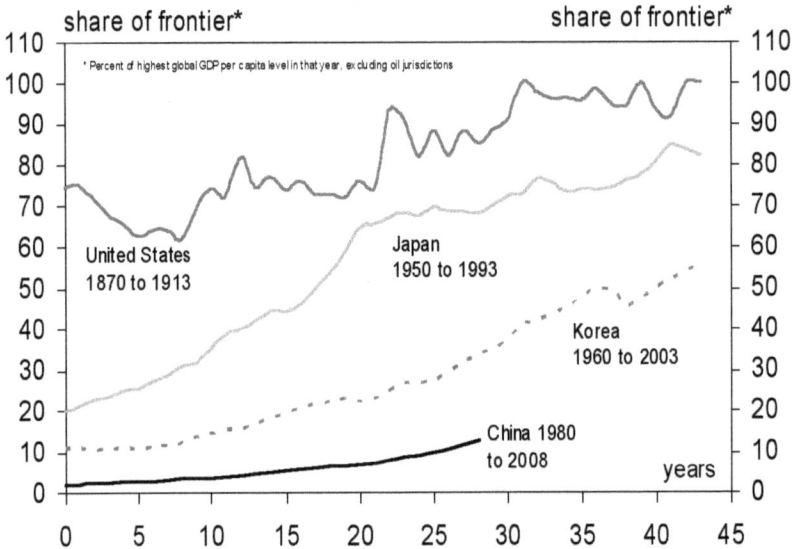

Sources: For China, International Monetary Fund (IMF) 2009, *World Economic Outlook Database*, April, International Monetary Fund, Washington, DC, <http://www.imf.org/external/pubs/ft/weo/2009/01/weodata/>; others, Maddison, A. 2009, *Historical Statistics of the World Economy: 1–2006AD*, March update, Groningen Growth and Development Centre, Groningen, The Netherlands, <http://www.ggdc.net/maddison/>

Equally, China's GDP per capita level in absolute terms is still well short of the levels associated with the deceleration of latecomer growth and a peak in the industrial value-added share of output. This point is somewhere in the area between US$10 000 and US$15 000 per capita in purchasing power parity (PPP) terms (Garnaut et al. 2008; Perkins and Rawski 2007; McKay 2008b). China attained a PPP GDP per capita level of US$5962 in 2008 and, on current projections by the International Monetary Fund (IMF), it will not reach the $10 000 per capita level until 2014. That said, China is an outlier in the sample with a high industrial value-added share before its policy of engagement, a relic of the self-sufficiency ethic and the pervasive price distortions that underpinned the pre-1978 economy. We return to this point in section three.

In terms of urbanisation levels, about one-fifth of the Chinese population lived in urban settings in 1980—a level reached in Japan by the late 1920s, by South Korea in 1950 and by the United States in 1860. China's urbanisation level advanced to about 45 per cent in 2008—equivalent to Japan in the mid-1950s, South Korea about the time of the first oil shock and the years immediately before World War I in the United States. China is set to converge with the global average of about 60 per cent in 2030 on projections by the United Nations (UN 2007). The United States reached that level about the end of World War II, Japan in the mid-1960s and South Korea in the mid-1980s (Figure 13.2).

Figure 13.2 Long-run rates of urbanisation

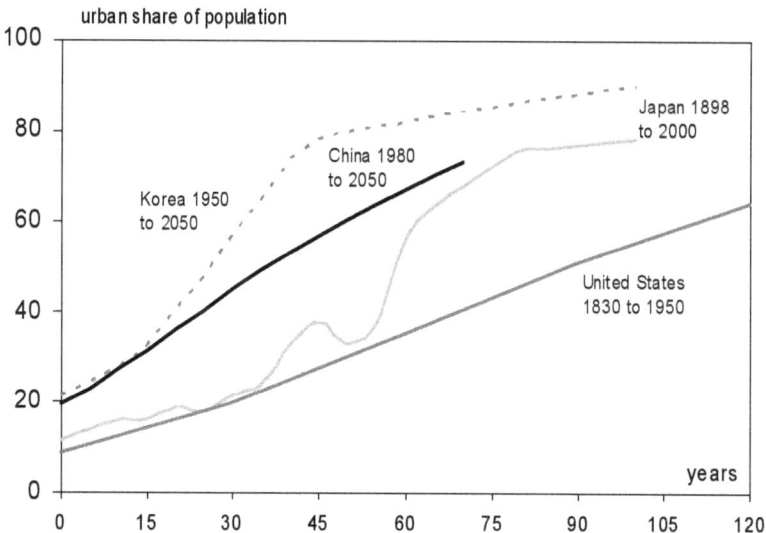

Sources: Figures for China, South Korea, Japan and the United States from 1950 from United Nations (UN) 2007, *World Urbanization Prospects: The 2007 revision*, United Nations, New York, < http://www.un.org/esa/population/publications/WUP2005/2005WUP_DataTables2.pdf >; for Japan before 1950, from Japanese Statistics Bureau 2009, *Historical Statistics of Japan*, Japanese Statistics Bureau, Tokyo, < http://www.stat.go.jp/english/data/chouki/index.htm >; for the United States before 1950, from United States Bureau of Statistics (USBS) various years, *Statistical Abstract of the United States*, United States Bureau of Statistics, Washington, DC.

China has maintained a higher investment share than our sample group. Gross capital formation has been on average 38 per cent of GDP since 1978, with a peak of 44.5 per cent in 1993 (Table 13.1). China's high investment share has been funded with an extraordinary supply of savings, averaging 41 per cent of GDP for the period, with a peak of 53 per cent in 2008.

Table 13.1 Investment to GDP ratios during rapid industrialisation periods

Year	Japan	Year	South Korea	Year	China	Years	United States
1898	12.6	1963	13.4	1978	38.0	1869–78	24.0
1905	12.6	1968	27.0	1983	34.4	1879–88	25.0
1919	16.0	1973	25.6	1988	38.2	1889–98	29.0
1931	16.5	1978	33.1	1993	44.5	1899–1908	29.0
1938	27.6	1983	29.0	1998	37.1		
1954	20.9	1988	31.4	2003	41.2		
1961	35.2	1993	35.7	2008	43.5		
1970	39.8	1998	25.0				
1980	32.8	2003	30.0				
1990	33.1						

Notes: Japanese figures up to 1961 are gross fixed capital formation; all other figures are gross capital formation—that is, they include inventories.

Sources: For China and South Korea, World Bank n.d., *World Development Indicators*, The World Bank, Washington, DC; for Japan for 1961 onwards, World Bank n.d., *World Development Indicators*, The World Bank, Washington, DC, and for 1898–1961, Ohkawa, K. and Rosovsky, H. 1968, 'Postwar Japanese growth in historical perspective: a second look', in L. Klein and K. Ohkawa (eds), *Economic Growth: The Japanese experience since the Meiji era*, Richard D. Irwin Inc., Homewood, Ill., Tables 1–7, p. 22; for the United States, Gallman, R. E. 2000, 'Economic growth and structural change in the long nineteenth century', in S. E. Engerman and R. E. Gallman (eds), *The Cambridge History of the United States. Volume II: The long nineteenth century*, Cambridge University Press, New York, Table 1.14, p. 50.

Despite the large proportion of expenditure devoted to capital formation since 1978, China still invests far less per capita than the comparator nations. Chinese investment per capita was about 2 per cent of the high-income level of the Organisation for Economic Cooperation and Development (OECD) countries in 1978. That compares with 4.8 per cent for South Korea in 1960. By this time, Japan was already investing 27 per cent *more* per capita than the high-income group—on its way to twin peaks of 238 per cent in 1970 and 1991. By 2007, China had just moved beyond 10 per cent of the high-income OECD level of capital spending per capita. Suffice to say that China's capital stock is still very shallow in relative terms.[3]

Turning now to infrastructure provision, in terms of roads, the experience of China looks very similar to that of Japan between the late 1800s and the mid-1920s (Figure 13.3). South Korea kept pace with the other two for the first 25 years or so, before the Chinese and Japanese investments in roads really took off. The United States was off the pace in the road stakes (taking data from 1900–30), but it led the way in railway investment (data from the last 30 years of the 1800s). China has been a notable laggard in the area of railways (Figure 13.4), although the indications are that the next few years will see a major investment in transcontinental trunk lines and intra-city commuter systems.

Figure 13.3 Investment in infrastructure: roads

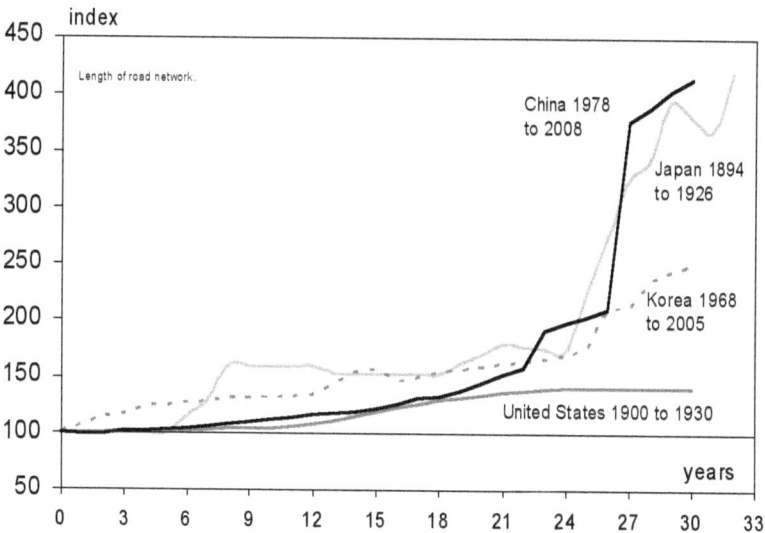

Sources: For China and Korea, CEIC n.d., *CEIC Database*, CEIC Data Company Limited, <www.ceicdata.com>; for Japan, Japanese Statistics Bureau 2009, *Historical Statistics of Japan*, Japanese Statistics Bureau, Tokyo, <http://www.stat.go.jp/english/data/chouki/index.htm>; for the United States, United States Federal Highway Administration (USFHA) 2008, *Highway Statistics 2007*, United States Federal Highway Administration, <http://www.fhwa.dot.gov/policyinformation/statistics/2007/vmt421.cfm>

Figure 13.4 Investment in infrastructure: railways

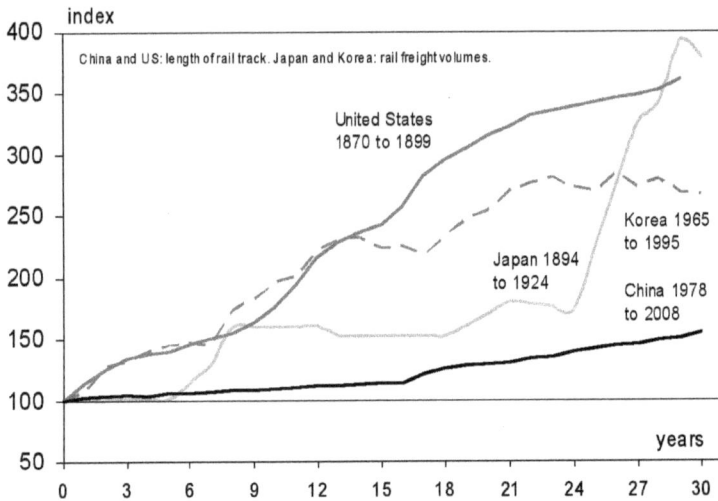

index

China and US: length of rail track. Japan and Korea: rail freight volumes.

United States
1870 to 1899

Korea 1965
to 1995

Japan 1894
to 1924

China 1978
to 2008

years

Sources: For China and Korea, CEIC n.d., *CEIC Database*, CEIC Data Company Limited, <www.ceicdata.com>; for Japan, Japanese Statistics Bureau 2009, *Historical Statistics of Japan*, Japanese Statistics Bureau, Tokyo, <http://www.stat.go.jp/english/data/chouki/index.htm>; for the United States, Fishlow, A. 2000, 'Internal transportation in the nineteenth and early twentieth centuries', in S. E. Engerman and R. E. Gallman (eds), *The Cambridge History of the United States. Volume II: The long nineteenth century*, Cambridge University Press, New York, pp. 543–642.

Where resource intensity is concerned, in absolute terms China remains at the low end of the spectrum in per capita terms, although relative to its own income level consumption is quite high. Compared with US steel output per capita in 1900, China was at just 27 per cent in 1978 (Figure 13.5). China did not surpass the United States' 1900 level until the early years of the current decade, although it has since accelerated to more than 300 per cent of this benchmark.

As far as total commercial energy use is concerned, China was self-sufficient in the aggregate until the early years of the current decade. The United States was self-sufficient in petroleum products until 1957 (Bairoch 1993:61), by which time the country already had 327 cars per 1000 residents—on the way to a peak of 547 in 1988. Japan attained the 1957 US level of auto penetration in the late 1990s. It took South Korea until 2006 to reach this level. In 2006, China had just 18 cars per 1000 residents—up from just eight in 2002—yet it was already consuming more than double its annual domestic supply of approximately three million barrels a day of crude oil. The predictable rise in Chinese per capita consumption of resources will put a great deal of pressure on the global supply complex.

Figure 13.5 Long-run steel output per capita

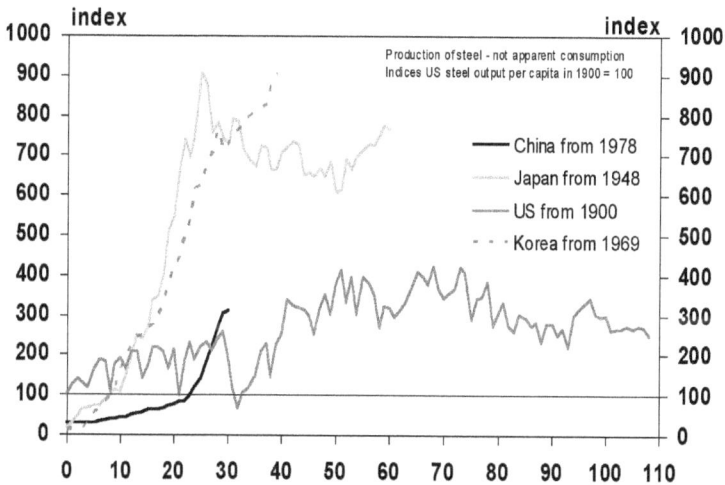

Production of steel - not apparent consumption
Indices US steel output per capita in 1900 = 100

China from 1978
Japan from 1948
US from 1900
Korea from 1969

Sources: For China and Korea, International Iron and Steel Institute updated using CEIC n.d., *CEIC Database*, CEIC Data Company Limited, < www.ceicdata.com >; for Japan, Japanese Statistics Bureau 2009, *Historical Statistics of Japan*, Japanese Statistics Bureau, Tokyo, < http://www.stat.go.jp/english/data/chouki/index.htm >; for the United States, United States Geological Survey (USGS) various years, *Minerals Yearbooks*, United States Geological Survey, < http://minerals.usgs.gov/minerals/pubs/ >; population data from the sources cited above for individual countries.

The overall picture from this succinct survey of China's relative development position is that on most measures it is still well short of the point where, based on relevant historical precedents, it can be expected to:

• experience decelerating growth
• experience decelerating demands for capital formation
• see resource intensity diminish.

Definitions of strategy: outward orientation versus export dependency

The preceding section sought to describe the broad contours of China's development position relative to nominated comparators. This section will delve deeper to isolate the strategic differences between the nations in the group that has produced the outcomes detailed above.

A simple but effective way of differentiating between strategies is to track trends in global market shares. An economy that maintains an average export share of GDP will expand its share of global exports by the same fraction as it expands its share of global output. Extending the logic, an economy expanding its share of global exports faster than its share of global GDP is betraying an outward bias and vice versa.

Keeping these relationships in mind, consider Figure 13.6. A balanced economy replicating the global average structure will have a scatter that describes a 45 degree line, moving along that schedule as its rate of growth moves from above to below the global average. The curves described by our sample countries are highly instructive regarding the development of economic strategies that in turn determine structure.

Figure 13.6 Global export and GDP shares

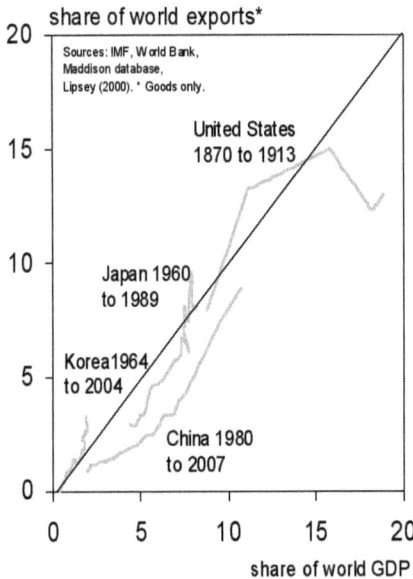

Sources: Merchandise export shares after 1960 are compiled from information in the World Bank n.d., *World Development Indicators*, The World Bank, Washington, DC; US data are from Lipsey, R. E. 2000, 'US foreign trade and the balance of payments, 1800–1913', in S. E. Engerman and R. E. Gallman (eds), *The Cambridge History of the United States. Volume II: The long nineteenth century*, Cambridge University Press, New York, Table 15.1, p. 688; world GDP shares are from Maddison, A. 2009, *Historical Statistics of the World Economy: 1–2006AD*, March update, Groningen Growth and Development Centre, Groningen, The Netherlands, <http://www.ggdc.net/maddison/>, World Bank n.d., *World Development Indicators*, The World Bank, Washington, DC and International Monetary Fund (IMF) 2009, *World Economic Outlook Database*, April, International Monetary Fund, Washington, DC, <http://www.imf.org/external/pubs/ft/weo/2009/01/weodata/>

For the case of the United States in the second half of the nineteenth century, the data argue very strongly that its emergence was associated with a balanced strategy that neither ignored nor prioritised exports. Indeed, the observations for 1870, 1880 and 1890 in Figure 13.6 are near enough to the 45-degree line that we might classify the US strategy as close to a neutral one regarding the prevailing global structure. It is only between 1900 and 1913 that a decisive preference between external and internal demand can be seen—and that shift is decisively in the direction of the domestic economy. That is consistent with our knowledge of the major investments in domestic market integration that occurred during the previous century and the diffusion of the victorious North's industrialisation strategy across the continent in the post-bellum era.

The situation in the United States is a prime example of a large nation making room for its own industrial rise through the integration and then exploitation of internal markets. While external demand and foreign capital were certainly not trivial for US industrial development in the middle decades of the nineteenth century, they were becoming something of a footnote by the beginning of the twentieth. The United States would go on to take advantage of its domestic mega-market by developing mass-production techniques and enjoying the associated economies of scale. The successful application of this strategy eventually led to its domination of the global consumer durables industries until well into the second half of the twentieth century (Snooks 1997:384–90).

The growing competitiveness of US industry manifested itself in a rising share of manufactures in exports and a falling share of manufactures in imports (Table 13.2). The failures of Latin America's import-substitution policies, which go against comparative advantage (Lin 2008), have led economists to be suspicious of declining import shares in industrial economies. A declining import share in manufactures is, however, absolutely consistent with outward orientation if global export shares are also rising in the same areas. As competitiveness is absolute vis-a-vis local and foreign markets, there is no reason to differentiate between displacing imports and making inroads internationally. Both are positive functions of development. We will call the displacement of imports through rising competitiveness 'dynamic substitution' to distinguish it from discredited strategies of activist import substitution.

Table 13.2 Dynamic substitution in the United States, 1820–1913

Percentage	Raw materials		Semi-manufactures		Manufactures	
shares of...	Exports	Imports	Exports	Imports	Exports	Imports
1820	59.6	5.5	9.6	7.3	5.8	56.4
1830	62.7	7.9	6.8	7.9	8.5	57.1
1840	67.9	12.2	4.5	11.2	9.8	44.9
1850	62.2	7.5	4.4	14.9	12.6	54.6
1850–58	60.3	8.7	4.1	13.2	12.6	52.5
1859–68	41.3	13	5.3	13.1	15.7	42.3
1869–78	44.1	15.7	4.7	12.8	15.9	34.6
1879–88	34.2	20.6	4.8	14.5	15.1	30.9
1889–98	32.9	24.7	7	13.9	17.1	26.7
1899–1908	29.2	33	11.9	16.6	24.6	25
1904–13	32.3	34.6	14.8	17.7	28.3	24.1

Source: Lipsey, R. E. 2000, 'US foreign trade and the balance of payments, 1800–1913', in S. E. Engerman and R. E. Gallman (eds), *The Cambridge History of the United States. Volume II: The long nineteenth century*, Cambridge University Press, New York, Table 15.10, p. 702.

The United States, Japan and South Korea have each experienced periods when imports have fallen as a share of GDP. Further, through their phases of rapid industrialisation, dynamic substitution and a rising share of manufactures in exports were both evident. Each economy moved from running trade deficits to trade surpluses on the back of these trends. These developmental forces are most pronounced in the experiences of Japan and the United States, where there are more historical data to consider (Tables 13.2 and 13.3).

Table 13.3 Dynamic substitution in Japan, 1876–1940

Exports	Food	Materials	Semi-manufactures	Manufactures	Other
1876–80	38.1	11.1	41.6	4.7	4.5
1894–98	15.1	10.7	44.3	26.5	3.4
1911–15	10.8	7.9	49.5	30.4	1.4
1921–25	6.4	6	47.8	38.6	1.2
1936–40	9.9	4.3	26	57.4	2.4
Imports	Food	Materials	Semi-manufactures	Manufactures	Other
1876–80	13.5	3.7	27.2	52.1	3.5
1894–98	23.2	22.5	18.2	34.1	2
1911–15	11.7	52.2	18.3	17.1	0.7
1921–25	14.1	49.3	18	17.9	0.7
1936–40	8.7	51.1	25.7	13	1.5

Source: Baba, M. and Tatemoto, M. 1968, 'Foreign trade and economic growth', in L. Klein and K. Ohkawa (eds), *Economic Growth: The Japanese experience since the Meiji era*, Richard D. Irwin Inc., Homewood, Ill., Table 6.8, p. 177.

It is a common misconception that Japan was dependent on export growth through its rapid development phase. That was not the case. The economy was oriented outward but it was not export dependent. Again, the scatter plot is instructive. Figure 13.6 shows the Japanese economy advancing its share of both world GDP and world exports for two decades from 1960 on a trajectory parallel to the 45-degree line but firmly in the GDP segment. Only then does the curve turn north, implying that export shares continued to rise, but Japan had ceased to make material progress on the GDP axis. The curve then crosses the 45-degree line and enters the export segment of the figure space. This kinked curve hints at a major turning point for the economy that was not helpful for its relative advancement.

The Chinese economy initially moved decisively in the direction of expanding its share of world GDP faster than its share of exports in the 1980s. The economy then shifted course, with a mild bias towards exports pushing the curve back towards the 45-degree line from 1990 or so. The finishing point is, however, still comfortably in the GDP segment, indicating that the recent bias towards exports has been a relative rather than an absolute phenomenon.

The importance of inward foreign direct investment (FDI) (Chen 2007), the rise of the component trade (Athukorala and Yamashita 2008) and the associated dominance of foreign-funded firms in Chinese trade activity combine to inflate the importance of 'headline' exports to aggregate income. Figure 13.7 adjusts for this factor by separating foreign-funded firms from indigenous ones. The outcome is stark. Indigenous firms have made respectable progress in export markets, but their efforts look feeble relative to foreign-funded firms, as shown by the rapidly widening wedge between the two curves. Clearly, the attitudes of multinational manufacturers to China as a production and assembly base explain a material proportion of the emerging skew we observed in the Chinese curve in Figure 13.6.

Figure 13.7 China's adjusted world export share

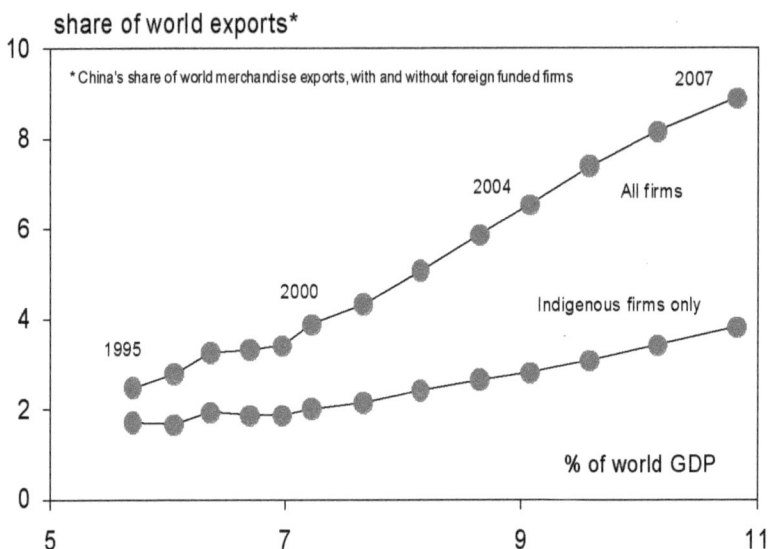

Sources: The foreign share of Chinese exports calculated from CEIC n.d., *CEIC Database*, CEIC Data Company Limited, <www.ceicdata.com> For global export and output shares: merchandise export shares after 1960 are compiled from information in World Bank n.d., *World Development Indicators*, The World Bank, Washington, DC; World GDP shares are the International Monetary Fund (IMF) 2009, *World Economic Outlook Database*, April, International Monetary Fund, Washington, DC, http://www.imf.org/external/pubs/ft/weo/2009/01/weodata/

The nature of the next kink in China's strategic curve will have major implications for the balance of the global economy and for China's long-run economic outcomes. If China were to go successfully down the route pursued by the United States in the late nineteenth century—seeking to make room for itself through developing and integrating its potential internal mega-market—it will continue to advance for decades to come. If China follows the post-1980 Japanese example—which entailed expanding its export market share from an already high base—its rate of relative gains will be lower, and they will exhaust sooner.

The evidence as stated argues that China has so far avoided moving too far down this economic cul-de-sac, although we revisit this theme at a sectoral level in section two and will qualify this finding at that time. On the other hand, efforts at domestic integration, proxied by the strength in inter-regional growth spill-overs, are still nascent (Golley and Groeneweld 2007). The rhetoric of the Chinese administration indicates that it understands these dynamics very well. In a complex world, however, it is not enough to choose the correct path from those observable in the historical record. Enacting structural change from above, in the absence of effective price signals across all relevant factor markets (Huang 2009), is no straightforward matter. Concerns about environmental impacts and food and resource security are also impinging on strategic options. The continuing adjustments required to address the real and financial imbalances evident in the world economy today are also a constraint. We now consider in turn these major factors that will feed in to strategic economic calculus in China in the long run.

Imbalances in the world economy and China's future trajectory

The emergence of major trade and financial imbalances between regions has been the key characteristic of the global economy in the current decade (Figure 13.8). In the real economy, these imbalances are inherently transpacific in nature, with the petro-economies thrown in. In the financial arena, the imbalances have a transatlantic bent. This separation is due to the uniqueness of China's interaction with the world. It has achieved a position of major relevance in terms of the real economy, with global shares of output, trade, emissions and commodity consumption that rank it as a tier-one power. On the other hand, it has a financial system and a framework of exchange arrangements that presently disallow it from achieving equivalent heft in the financial sphere, with the intermediation of real economy imbalances left by default to the financial systems of the industrialised countries. Given China's relatively low income per capita level, it is the undeveloped financial system that is perhaps less surprising.

It is against this backdrop of imbalances that China, and the other major nations and regions, must seek to alter the composition of their economic activity and eventually their balance sheets. The intense distress experienced across the globe as the financial de-leveraging process accelerated in the second half of 2008 (Devlin and McKay 2008) and the uneven signs of stabilisation observed since have not reduced the enormity of the challenge. Indeed, one might argue that in the industrialised countries, policy has been designed to avoid structural adjustment, rather than to embrace it.

Figure 13.8 Global imbalances: current account balances as a share of world GDP at PPP weights

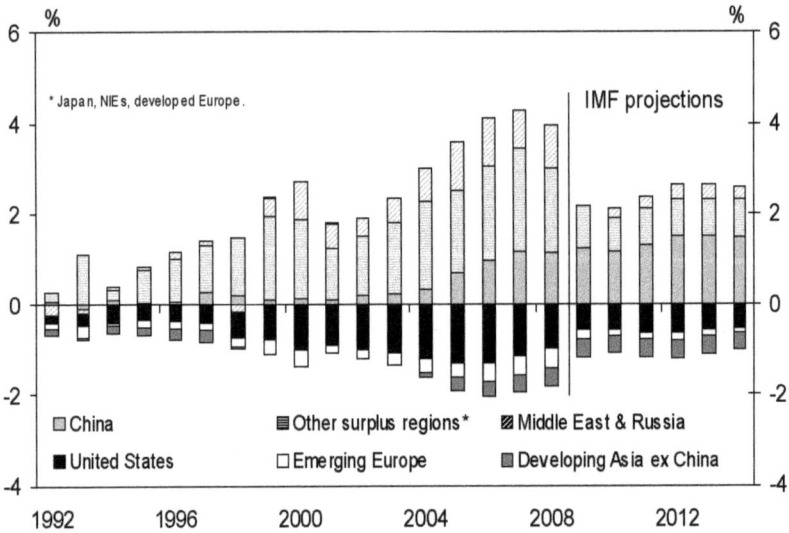

Sources: All underlying data and projections from International Monetary Fund (IMF) 2009, *World Economic Outlook Database*, April, International Monetary Fund, Washington, DC, <http://www.imf.org/external/pubs/ft/weo/2009/01/weodata/>, translated to shares of world GDP by the authors.

From a fundamental point of view, transpacific imbalances in the real economy boil down to a low rate of savings relative to investment in the United States and the opposite scenario in East Asia. Some analysts focus on the latter phenomenon, colloquially called the 'savings glut', and ascribe it catalytic force (Bernanke 2005; Cooper 2005). More subtly, a related theory apportions the 'blame' for the volume of capital flowing from emerging markets to the United States to the underlying theme of asymmetrical financial development (Caballero et al. 2008). Some focus rather narrowly on the pursuit of exchange rate stability in East Asia, linking the consequent foreign exchange reserve accumulation to export-driven strategies and mercantilist motivations (Dooley et al. 2003; Aizenman and Lee 2005). Others offer a more balanced approach and argue for significant adjustments from both deficit and surplus regions (Lee et al. 2004; Roubini and Setser 2005; IMF 2005:68–124).

Looking at China specifically, none of the unilateral prescriptions seems compelling in the least. Principally, they underwhelm as they fail to identify the drivers of the spectacular rise in the Chinese savings rate since the early years of this decade, which has simultaneously accommodated a historically high investment share of GDP and an enormous current account surplus. Relative to the somewhat predictable decline in the US savings rate in an era of loose fiscal (Roubini and Setser 2005; Brookings Institution 2004) and monetary (Taylor 2008) policy, in tandem with a social policy that encouraged the broadening of home ownership beyond its 'natural' perimeter, the Chinese experience needs significant explanation.

The Governor of the People's Bank of China has argued (Zhou 2008:1) that China's high savings ratio, and that of East Asia more generally, is related to 'tradition, cultural, family structure, and demographic structure and stage of economic development'. In Zhou's view, when the tangible factors of demography and development level are accounted for, but large unexplained differentials in savings rates are apparent—as in, say, East Asia vis-a-vis Latin America or Japan vis-a-vis the United States—culture must play a role in explaining these gaps.

Cross-country studies of savings rates emphasise their strong persistence/inertia, positive relationships to income per capita levels, credit, GDP growth and the terms of trade, weak relationships with rates of return and precautionary motivations, and negative relationships with the strength of social safety nets, the fiscal position and the dependency ratio (Loayza et al. 2000; IMF 2005:Ch.2). The Chinese savings rate has, however, consistently recorded outcomes well in excess of the predictions generated by cross-country frameworks, even before the recent jump (Kuijs 2006; IMF 2005:Box 2.1, pp. 96–7).

The Zhou approach—to attribute residual savings to cultural factors—is insufficient. While it is a convenient explanation for the persistence of relatively high savings rates in East Asia across time, it does not provide a suitable explanation for the jump in savings in the current decade. Complicating matters further, as Zhou himself points out later in the same speech, households—the sector seemingly most likely to define cultural norms—have maintained their savings as a share of GDP at a relatively stable level since the late 1990s. The rise in aggregate Chinese savings has been dominated by a major increase in the gross corporate savings rate, with some moderate assistance from an improving fiscal position (Kuijs 2006; Zhou 2008:3; Anderson 2006:6; IMF 2005:Box 2.1, pp. 96–7; Figure 13.9). The key to understanding the remarkable rise in Chinese savings, and the ultimate impact this phenomenon has had on inflaming the state of global imbalances, seems to lie with the corporate sector.

Figure 13.9 Net financial investment by sector, China, 1992–2006

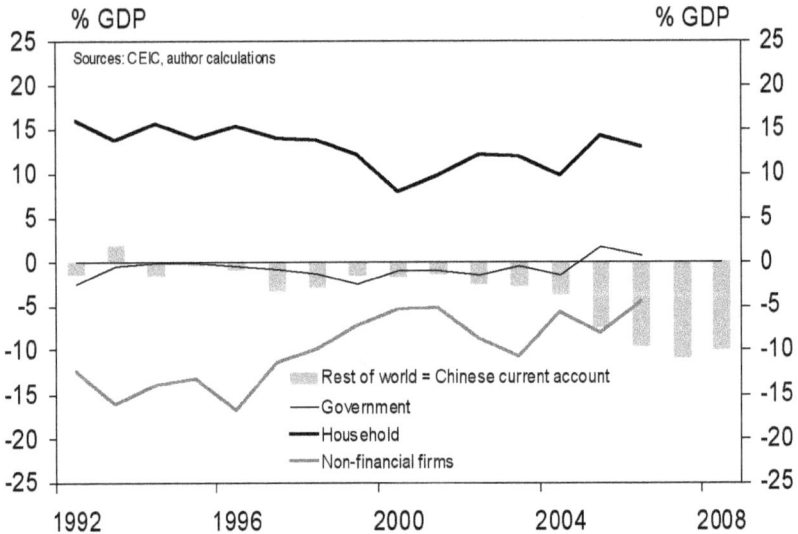

Source: Calculated from data in China's Flow of Funds accounts, accessed via CEIC n.d., *CEIC Database*, CEIC Data Company Limited, <www.ceicdata.com>

Identifying the corporate sector as the major contributor to the alteration of the savings story seems to reject the cultural hypothesis. Something more tangible is needed to explain this distinctive behaviour of firms. As it happens, the rise in corporate savings is readily explicable in economic terms. In brief, it is a function of excess capacity in heavy industry, coupled with the ability of Chinese firms to overcome this impediment, which is negative for profit margins, by expanding the volume of their sales through large market share gains at home and abroad. This development is the major discontinuity that explains the extraordinary rise in the Chinese current account balance since 2004.

Consider Figures 13.10, 13.11 and 13.12 as a sequence. The first illustrates developments in the profitability of the corporate sector since 1985. There is a strong and intuitive relationship between the profit share of GDP and industrial profit margins[4] for the majority of the period. The relationship has broken down since 2004, however, with the profit share of GDP rising sharply, but profit margins essentially stable. The last development is a predictable outcome of the re-emergence of excess capacity in heavy industry after rapid investment growth in the early years of the decade. The former is a puzzling outcome that needs further explanation.

Figure 13.10 Excess capacity driving excess profits?

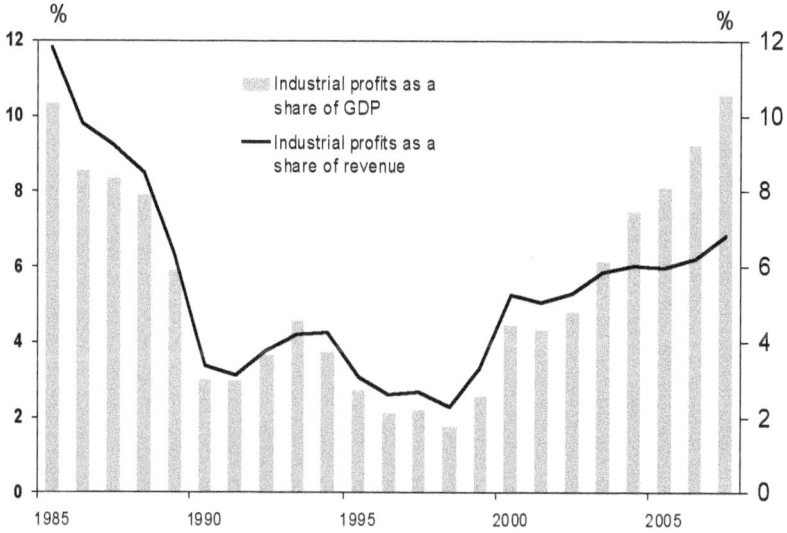

Source: All measures calculated from underlying data sourced via CEIC n.d., *CEIC Database*, CEIC Data Company Limited, <www.ceicdata.com>

Figure 13.11 Excess capacity in heavy industry requires market share gains at home and abroad

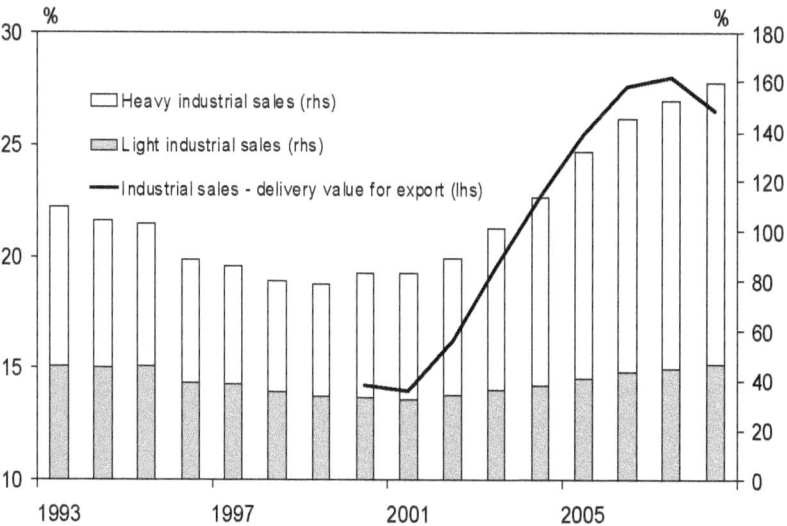

Source: All measures calculated from underlying data sourced via CEIC n.d., *CEIC Database*, CEIC Data Company Limited, <www.ceicdata.com>

Figure 13.12 Decomposing China's trade balance by broad sector

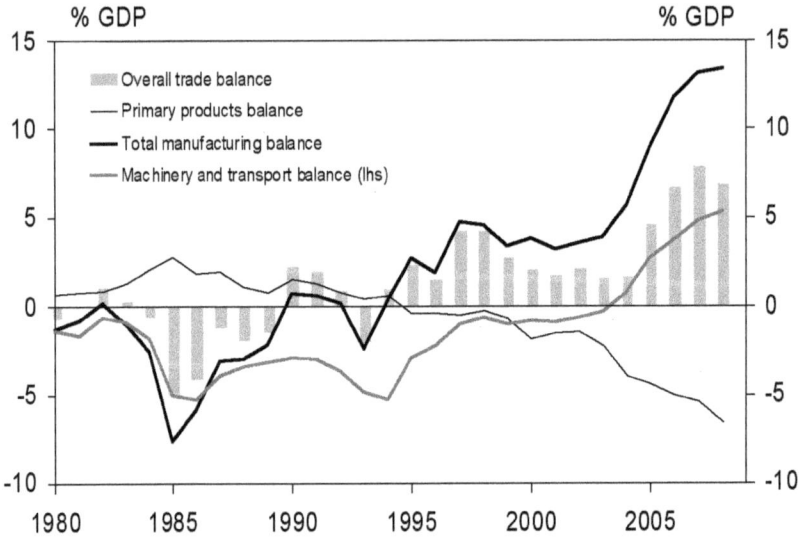

Source: All measures calculated from underlying data sourced via CEIC n.d., *CEIC Database*, CEIC Data Company Limited, < www.ceicdata.com >

Applying logic to this combination of circumstances, it is not difficult to deduce that when profit *levels* are rising but profit *margins* are not, an increase in the volume of sales must be substituting for the latter to achieve the former. Figure 13.11 illustrates this dynamic. Further, it highlights that it has been heavy industry that has provided the bulk of the increase in sales relative to GDP.[5] This has been mirrored by a rise in the share of exports in industrial sales. Clearly, excess capacity provides the vehicle for a large increase in the volume of output and external demand provides an outlet for its sale. Increasing domestic market share at the expense of imports will produce a similar result at the aggregate level.

The end result of these trends has been a pronounced widening of the trade balance (Figure 13.12). Consistent with our identification of heavy industry as the major source of excess capacity in the current business cycle, it is the sectoral trade position of machinery and transport equipment that has contributed the most to the shift in the aggregate balance, moving from a *deficit* of 5.3 per cent of GDP in 1994 to a *surplus* of 5.3 per cent of GDP in 2008. That has assisted the overall manufacturing goods balance to improve by a spectacular 15.8 per cent of GDP since 1993. While this has naturally brought with it large demands for imported resources (a deterioration of 7 per cent of GDP in the primary products balance over the equivalent period), this has done little to curb the dramatic widening of the overall external imbalance.

Anderson (2006:8) has described this process as the cyclical 'expropriation' of market share by Chinese firms at home and abroad. It is this aspect of China's growth path that is imposing structural adjustments elsewhere. China's current account balance represented 1.1 per cent of world GDP in 2008—a rise of about 1 per cent since the middle 1990s. The IMF's formal projections of the future development of global imbalances to 2014 (Figure 13.8) indicates that China's current account balance as a share of world GDP will increase slowly from the 2008 level to about 1.5 per cent.

Thinking about this projection carefully, we can ascertain that a moderation in China's current account relative to domestic GDP is assumed, as the Chinese economy will be increasing its share of the global output over this period. This view is consistent with underlying assumptions of stable household and corporate savings relative to GDP, but deteriorating public savings, consistent with the announced fiscal expansion. The adjustments expected elsewhere, however, are much more significant.

What can we infer from this? First, it would seem that these projections assume that structural changes are more likely to be imposed on the rest of the world by China, rather than the reverse. Second, it also implicitly assumes that the savings-investment conditions prevailing in China in 2008 are a reasonably stable constellation of affairs. From the foregoing discussion, we know that for these assumptions to be validated by events, Chinese heavy industry will have to keep expropriating external and domestic market share to keep profit levels high despite low margins, allowing aggregate savings to remain at a level consistent with a very large current account surplus. Alternatively, domestic and global demand for heavy industrial output could rise so rapidly that current capacity levels become more reasonable in a short timeframe.[6] It is rarely courageous to forecast the status quo—but this could be one of those circumstances.

To this point of the chapter, there has been no consideration of the reasons behind the re-emergence of excess capacity in the present business cycle phase. Our view is that rapid investment growth in heavy industry is directly related to the inefficient allocation of capital by the financial system—an allocation that is against China's present comparative advantage (Lin 2008). The preferential access to bank funding enjoyed by state-owned enterprises (SOEs); the lack of diversity in financial assets that gives banks preferential access to private savings; the prevalence of SOEs in the heavy-industrial sectors of the economy; the fragmented nature of heavy industry, in terms of geographical and industrial concentration; weak corporate governance and the historical absence of a dividend payment requirement for SOEs that jointly enable high retained earnings and their inefficient reinvestment; and the differential incentives of central and local administrators all contribute to an outsized share of investment funds being devoted to the addition of heavy-industrial capacity.

There are a number of options available to policymakers to improve the quality of resource allocation by the financial system. Many have already been taken, such as the move away from policy lending to commercial decision making, share market listings, the introduction of foreign expertise through equity injections, the introduction of foreign competition via WTO accession requirements and the encouragement of the corporate bond market. The acceleration of each of these trends, further progress on interest rate liberalisation (Song 2005), the deepening of inter-bank money markets and the further development of domestic accounting, legal and credit rating frameworks should all contribute positively to the future quality of savings allocation.

Financial system development is intimately associated with exchange rate regime choice, the design of exchange arrangements and the tools available for enacting monetary policy (McKay 2007; Prasad et al. 2005; Dobson and Masson 2009). Despite contrary evidence presented by the modelling community (for example, Lee et al. 2004), exchange rate adjustment in the surplus regions is often put forward as the key fulcrum in the imbalances story. Our view is that China's exchange rate regime choice has contributed to the current degree of imbalances as a central cog in the elaborate, path-dependent institutional structures that combine to produce a misallocation of resources internally, which manifests itself as an unwieldy external surplus. Given space constraints, we will go no further on this subject, referring the reader to the references above.

It is improvement in the quality of the financial sector's aggregate decision making that will catalyse a move back to a more balanced economic structure in China. A stronger, more competitive financial system could precipitate market-based adjustment profiles in areas such as the retirement of excess capacity in heavy industry, concentration in industries where fragmentation is a concern and improved access to credit for the private sector generally and for small and medium-sized enterprises in particular.

A more productive allocation of investment funds between the coastal provinces and the central and western zones could also be forthcoming—a development that would do much to further the process of provincial convergence that seems the most likely future source of rapid economic growth. That brings us back to a point from the historical analysis of section one. Recall that Chinese economic strategy in the reform era was characterised as outward oriented but domestically led, with an emerging bias in the direction of external demand adduced only in the most recent run of annual observations. That fits nicely with the analysis of sectoral savings trends that highlighted the increasing importance of market share gains at the expense of foreign producers to alleviate excess capacity in heavy industry. We asserted that 'the nature of the next kink in China's strategic curve will have major implications for the balance of the global economy and for China's long-run economic outcomes'.

The United States created its own space in the global economy through the optimisation of internal strengths, while Japan's economic ascent exhausted when it deviated from a balanced strategy in the direction of export dependence. The implications for China are clear. Inefficient resource allocation has, over time, created large imbalances in China's domestic economy.

As the economy itself has grown, and its integration with the world has accelerated, these domestic imbalances have progressively spilled over into issues of a global scale. The China of today is not just making its own space—it is expropriating the place of others through the extraordinary growth of its heavy industrial capacity.

Carbon constraints on growth and China's future trajectory

A further major factor that will do much to determine the future course of Chinese industrialisation will be its response to the conflict between its current growth model and the biosphere—at the local, national, regional and global levels. While a 'Kuznetsian' inverse U-shaped relationship between certain measures of emissions per capita and developmental progress are apparent in cross-sectional empirical studies (Grossman and Krueger 1995), implying that China will at some point achieve a position where the marginal benefits of environmental amenity will exceed the perceived costs, the foregoing analysis has emphasised that China is still some way from the cluster of aggregate developmental trigger points. China's status as a global manufacturing powerhouse has thrust it to the forefront of the global debate on low carbon growth. Indeed, the world seems increasingly reluctant to let China find a congenial moment of its own choosing to tackle this fundamental issue.

The daunting task China faces if it is to achieve an emissions reduction target consistent with global mitigation efforts is comprehensively described by Stern (2008) and Garnaut (2008). As climate change is global in its origins and in its impacts, an effective response must therefore be organised globally, indicating that no major emitter can be excluded from a solution.

The awkward reality is that the rather compressed time frame for reaching an ambitious global emissions reduction target does not square with the development position of the Chinese economy. The current phase of China's industrialisation is characterised by a relatively high share of activity in the manufacturing sector, where high energy intensities prevail. The prevalence of heavy industrial activity growth in the current cycle was highlighted in section two. This sector was associated with the rapid rise in China's external surplus. It has also been the major source of emissions accelerating in recent years (Figure 13.13).

Figure 13.13 Total fossil fuel emissions of the major economies, 1751–2006 (1000 metric tonnes)

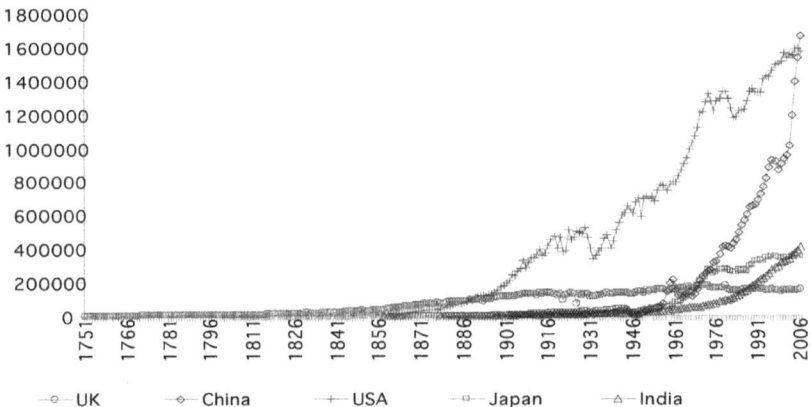

Source: All data from the Carbon Dioxide Information Analysis Center, *Fossil-Fuel CO$_2$ Emissions*, <http://cdiac.ornl.gov/trends/emis/meth_reg.html>

Rapid manufacturing-led growth is expected to persist for some time, whether one focuses solely on the projected increase in China's per capita income or other macroeconomic indicators such as auto penetration, metal and energy intensity, capital stock per capita or the level of urbanisation. The last is expected to rise from 45 per cent now to 60 per cent in 2020 and 73 per cent in 2050 (Figure 13.2). Given the strength of the underlying forces working against emissions reduction under the 'conventional' Chinese growth model, the model itself might have to give. An industrialisation path that achieves growth at the expense of profound environmental degradation is a finite strategy. Structural change in China is thus a prerequisite for a successful global program of emissions control.

Three questions stand out. First, what will be the practical and effective means through which China can confront this challenge of maintaining growth while reducing the emissions intensity of the economy? Second, to what extent will the adoption of a low-carbon growth model alter the pattern of industrialisation by prioritising energy intensity and changing the energy mix? Third, to what extent will a concerted effort to meet an ambitious global carbon emissions reduction target constrain Chinese economic growth? In other words, can China cheat economic gravity and decouple its carbon emissions increase from economic growth in the next chapter of its industrialisation?

The United States and China are two of the largest carbon emitters in the world. Together, they are responsible for about 40 per cent of the world's greenhouse gas emissions. The sheer size of these two economies obviously contributes strongly to this dominant share of emissions output, but at 33 per cent of world GDP at PPP weights, there is still some explaining to do.

China has joined the top ranks of emitters in a very short time. It took only about 30 years for China to climb from a relatively low base to the same level of emissions reached by the United States over more than a century. China's future trend of emissions—whether measured by total, by intensity or per capita—will depend on the composition and level of growth the economy generates through the next phase of industrialisation.

We contend that China will be encouraged to adjust due to rational self-interest, communicated by internal and external voices. It has certain strategic choices before it as it seeks to reorient its structural frameworks to incorporate both rapid economic growth and emissions reduction.

These choices can be inferred from the simplicity of the well-known Kaya identity (Kaya 1990).[7] The identity shows that there are four factors that contribute to a country's total carbon emissions: population, output per capita, the energy intensity output and the carbon intensity of the energy mix. Demographic variables are essentially set. China is also on track to achieve the official target of quadrupling 2000 per capita income by 2020. This too will drive a continual increase in carbon emissions in the next decade or so. This is the developmental gravity that macro-strategy must lean heavily against.

In the context of the current discussion, the other two factors in the Kaya identity—namely, energy intensity and the energy mix—deserve special attention.

China has to rely primarily on lowering energy intensity and changing the energy mix to confront the challenge of emissions control. Both have strategic implications for future economic growth and the structure of the economy.

There are three commonly cited basic factors that determine the changes in a country's energy intensities in production over time. These are the structural adjustment towards high value-added production and the service sector, technological advancement to increase factor productivity and energy pricing to encourage the more efficient use of resources in production and consumption. Shifts in underlying comparative advantage will be crucial in determining the nature of structural change. We argue here that this process can be accelerated when a country is compelled to comply with emissions mitigation requirements, triggering the need to replace old, energy-intensive activities with new, environmentally friendly pursuits, while reassessing the conventional modes of production in the industrial sector. Private entrepreneurship, a competitive environment and strategic government leadership in the fields of pricing reform, innovation and education will all contribute positively to the development of low carbon growth. That is even before we mention the extremely powerful force of technological leapfrogging (Brezis et al. 1991) precipitated by diffusion through FDI and other forms of knowledge transfer—both tacit and concrete.

It is expected that technological diffusion through international cooperation on emissions adaptation and mitigation will help lower China's energy intensities in a significant way. China is relatively well endowed with a skilled labour force. According to the theory of Nelson and Phelps (1966), this is a key channel whereby the rate of technological diffusion can be raised.[8] Needless to say, government policies and market and regulatory institutions are playing important roles in influencing the ways that energy prices work. In the case of China, allowing the pricing of energy products to gravitate upwards according to their true market values will be conducive to the further improvement of energy efficiency and the associated declines in intensity.

The historical experience of the fully industrialised countries of today demonstrates a certain pattern with respect to changing energy intensities through the various stages of development (Figure 13.14). This provides a point of reference for assessing the Chinese case.

Figure 13.14 Long-run energy intensities of the major industrial countries, 1840–1990

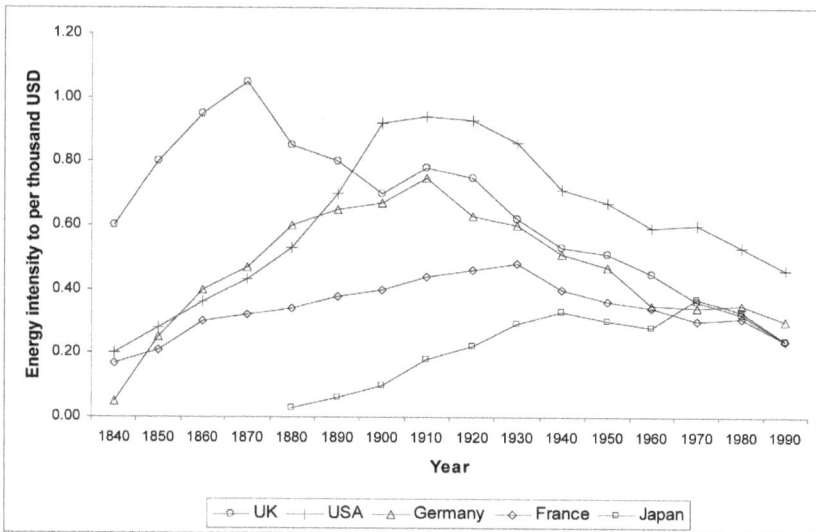

Source: Data estimated from Nishioka, S. 2008, 'A Japanese climate policy based on science, equity and cooperation', *Asia-Pacific Review*, vol. 15, no. 1, pp. 1–11, Figure 3.

The pattern of energy intensity in these countries shows a number of points of commonality. First, energy intensities rise in the early phases of industrialisation before peaking about the times when shares of industrial workers in the total labour force and industrial value added in total GDP reach high levels (for example, the United Kingdom in the 1870s and the United States in the 1910s).[9] Second, peak energy intensities fell consistently with each successive wave of industrialisation, indicating accumulated technological advancement and diffusion, with a substantial beneficial impact on the latecomers. Third, energy intensities tended to converge to a relatively low level after the process of industrialisation was completed, reflecting the accelerated pace of economic integration, especially among the industrialised countries. The study by Wing (2008) shows that the declining energy intensity of the US economy is due mainly to industrial structural adjustment, with both inter and intra-industry structural change leading to energy-efficiency improvements across the whole economy.

With this historical pattern of change in energy intensity in mind, we observe that China has been making progress in lowering the energy intensity of its GDP. This measure has now been falling since the late 1970s to a significantly lower level in 2005[10] (Garnaut 2008:Fig. 3.4; and Figure 18.1 in this book). The high level of energy intensities in the 1970s was due to the distinctive characteristics of industrialisation under the centrally planned system in which

> China built an exceedingly energy-intensive and economically inefficient industrial structure…and economic resources were directed out of agriculture and into energy-intensive heavy industries like steel and cement. This had the effect that industry's share of economic output grew from 18 to 44 per cent, while the amount of energy required to produce each unit of economic output tripled. (Hallding et al. 2009:62)

This suggests that the observed pattern of energy intensity of Chinese production is not attributable solely to the normal course of industrialisation. It is also closely linked to the way in which the central planning system worked. The system itself ran against all three factors we have just identified—namely, it was rigid regarding structural change, sluggish in technological change and diffusion and, more importantly, fixed in pricing resources, with the predictable outcome of enormous price distortions in energy products and materials.

The reform carried out during the past 30 years has fundamentally transformed the planning system into a market system, but historical legacies remain, such as state monopoly in some key industries and administrative energy prices. Such legacies explain a large portion of the existing structural problems and the inefficient utilisation of resources. The Chinese economy is therefore characterised by the high resource costs per unit of output and the relatively high elasticities of energy and electricity consumption in comparison with mature industrialised countries (Figures 13.15 and 13.16).

Figure 13.15 Elasticity of Chinese energy and electricity consumption, 1990–2007

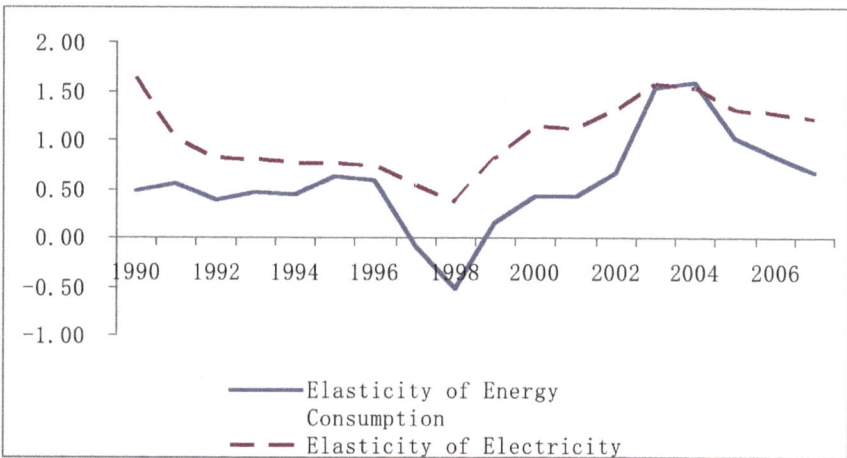

Source: All data from National Bureau of Statistics (NBS) various years, *China Statistical Yearbook*, China Statistics Press.

Figure 13.16 International comparison of energy consumption elasticities, selected countries, 2006[11]

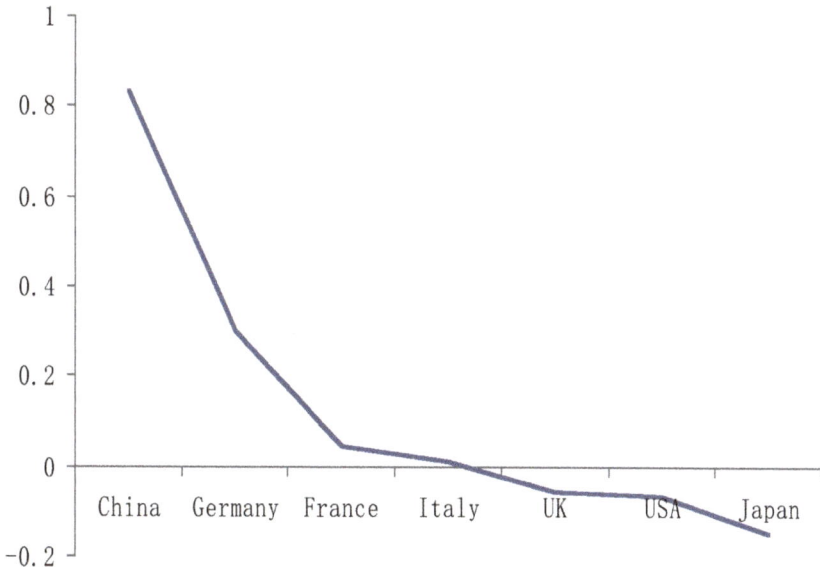

Source: Plotted using the data taken from National Bureau of Statistics (NBS) 2008, *China Statistical Yearbook 2008*, China Statistics Press, Beijing.

This implies that for China to continue to drive down its energy intensities, it is crucial to deepen institutional reform. This would drive progress on structural change, technological advancement and diffusion at the most fundamental level by establishing a market-based pricing system for resources. If China is to transit through the next phase of industrialisation with relatively low energy intensities, reform of the pricing system is paramount. In the current decade, Chinese demand has been the major factor in a historically significant rise in commodity prices. Chinese users of these materials are, however, in many cases sheltered from the price rises that they have themselves done so much to produce. This perverse situation should be corrected without delay.

There is huge potential for China to narrow its technological gap with mature industrialised economies. This statement holds particularly strongly in the areas of green technologies. A concerted effort to procure flows of environmentally sound technology would enable China to quicken the pace of industrial structural change. In the first instance, immense gains can be predicted from a focus on technological transfer (and the retirement of old 'smoke-stack' capacity) in the energy-intensive industrial sectors such as iron and steel, base metals processing, power generation and chemicals. Technological advancement and more efficient use of energy (including coal) are needed to reconcile the twin objectives of growth and emissions reduction.

If a wholesale effort is launched in these areas, China will catch up more quickly and could even rise to leadership in the application of green technologies, given the economies of scale that would be associated with their use in China's projected mega-market, its strong foundation of human capital and, more importantly, the administrative determination to adopt a new model for economic growth. This is because China basically satisfies those conditions that must hold if introduction of a new technology is to lead to a leapfrogging process (Brezis et al. 1991).[12]

The realisation of the 'leapfrogging' process is also important in that it helps China avoid 'locked-in effects' in its major industrial sectors. This malignant effect on efficiency emerges when large-scale energy infrastructure development is only 'a simple replication of conventional technology' in the accelerated phase of industrialisation (Zhuang 2008:96). More simply, China should avoid over-investing in old technology and should move assertively to ensure that new additions to the capital stock satisfy the basic condition of the 'most energy efficient' technology available anywhere in the world. If that fundamental creed is adopted, a new pattern of industrialisation in China characterised by a shift towards producing more high-valued products driven by innovation and technology advancement could emerge. While some observers are pessimistic about China 'locking in' inefficient energy production capacity (Rosen and Houser 2007), others are more sanguine (Rawski 2008)—in line with our view.

The success of Chinese and other developing countries' endeavours for emissions reduction also hinges on whether industrialised countries transfer technology and finance to these countries. It is therefore critical that global efforts combating climate change formalise the proposition that the pace of technological diffusion between industrialised and developing countries must accelerate. Such diffusion is a critical assumption for achieving conditional convergence in the latest generation of orthodox growth models (Barro and Sali-i-Martin 2004). This indicates that industrialised countries have a crucial role to play in determining the future growth trajectories of China and its developing peers. The provision of the global public good of responding to climate change, and broadening the degree of success in the global convergence of living standards, centres on the development and diffusion of advanced technology.

Alterations to the energy mix will also help reduce China's total carbon emissions. An increasing share of renewable energy in its total energy consumption (the share is expected to reach 15 per cent by 2020) is a promising trend, but there is no quick fix. The biggest challenge is that China is essentially a coal-driven economy. Coal accounted for 70 per cent of the total primary energy consumption in China during the period 1995–2005 (Song and Sheng 2007) and the share will remain unchanged for the foreseeable future. China accounts for almost two-fifths of the world's total coal consumption, which is more than the United States, Russia and India combined. 'With a lifecycle of about 50 years the huge investments in coal fired power today will have considerable impact on the climate well into the middle of the century' (Hallding et al. 2009:71). Carbon capture and storage (CCS) technology, which has huge potential in China once the underlying concept reaches the point of widespread commercial application, is the major hope. Improvements in other technologies, such as coal washing and dust precipitation, will begin to reduce the carbon intensities of the economy at the margin (Shi 2008).

Considering the issue of whether dealing with emissions reduction will materially compromise Chinese growth rates requires complex scenario analysis over long periods. One approach to this question is to estimate the costs of inaction, which could be high, thus negatively affecting the economy (Stern 2007; Garnaut 2008).

Fankhauser and Tol (2005) make the following points with respect to the possible impact of climate change on economic growth. First, 'negative climate change impacts are likely to reduce the rate of economic growth, but [are] unlikely to reverse a long-term path of increasing per capita income'. Second, 'climate change will always have a negative effect on the absolute capital stock, and the capital–labour ratio is also certain to decrease if agents are allowed to change their saving behaviour'. Third, 'as a result of climate change some sectors will grow faster than others, thereby changing the size and composition of GDP...such changes in the structure of an economy could have an impact on its long-term growth potential' (Fankhauser and Tol 2005:13). The last point is consistent with the argument for enhancing structural change and technological advancement in the process of dealing with carbon emissions. If successful, this could become a new source of economic growth, especially in renewable and low-carbon industries, as huge amounts of investment will be made in these segments.[13]

Industrialisation and globalisation have already turned China into a global manufacturing powerhouse. As we have noted, a large portion of China's global market share gains are attributable to the activities of foreign-funded firms. This has been the outcome of the working of China's underlying comparative advantage. This raises the issue of whether China's total carbon emissions should be examined in terms of production or should emissions consumed by an end user outside China be netted out. It seems that the latter calculation makes China less uncomfortable. The real issue, however, is to what extent the pursuit of a low-carbon growth strategy will alter the way that underlying comparative advantage works in efficiently determining China's pattern of trade. Imposing a cap on carbon emissions will disproportionately affect energy-intensive industries by increasing their costs of production and reducing their competitiveness. This should quicken the pace of industrial structural adjustment, which will otherwise take much more time to complete following the conventional industrialisation path.

On the other hand, underlying comparative advantage will shift more quickly towards producing and trading those industrial goods that are more energy efficient and less pollution intensive. As argued by Hallding et al. (2009:105), the 'green leap forward' for Chinese industries, when it occurs, is likely to eliminate, or sharply diminish, the net export of embedded carbon. Moving towards more domestic consumption-driven growth, thereby bringing domestic demand more in line with domestic supply—a necessary condition for resolving global imbalances (as argued in section two)—will accelerate the pace of such an adjustment.

To conclude, there is a fair chance that China will demonstrate a different pattern of industrialisation from its major predecessors. As China rises inexorably towards the per capita income thresholds associated with developmental turning points, it is being presented with a challenge faced by none of its forebears: the requirement that it adopt a low-carbon growth strategy. Any alternative to a low-carbon strategy would essentially preclude it from reversing its emissions growth path in a fashion timely enough for the world to avoid 'dangerous' climate change. The new strategy will be shaped by the imperative that the growth rate of carbon emissions is substantially lower than that of GDP. This can be done only through decisive progress on lowering the energy intensity of output and an associated shift in the energy mix towards renewables and cleaner applications of fossil-fuel sources.

If a substantial reduction of emissions consumption elasticities is successfully achieved, growth might not necessarily be compromised. Studies looking at China's long-term growth potential anticipate a deceleration in the second half of the next decade, even without incorporating assumptions related to mitigation regimes (Perkins and Rawski 2007; He et al. 2007; McKay 2008b). Any sustained effort to reduce excess capacity in heavy industry, and to reduce fragmentation in key sectors such as steel and automobiles, will be positive for long-run productivity growth and for emissions control.

It should also be noted that China's transition towards a low-carbon growth economy faces many uncertainties, such as incentive problems, the capacity of China's manufacturing industry to respond to the demand for introducing low-carbon technology, the incomplete reform of the energy market and the lack of appropriate institutions and policy mechanisms aimed at increasing energy efficiency and lowering carbon intensities. Success will require not only a commitment from China, but intensive international collaboration in technology and finance.

Conclusions

China's emergence as a manufacturing powerhouse has altered the distribution of power in the world economy in irreversible fashion. The first half of the twenty-first century will be shaped substantially by the nature of China's continuing engagement with a strategy of manufacturing-led development.

Our historical analysis has highlighted that China is still well short of the point in its developmental process where its growth might be reasonably expected to slow or the energy, resource and carbon intensity of growth to recede. On the other hand, structural adjustment within China and without the associated unwinding of imbalances could produce somewhat lower rates of economic growth for the next few years. A global environment in which carbon constraints become increasingly binding will produce a similar effect in the short run.

To take a benign view of long-run growth prospects, we argue that China must 'make its own space' by pursuing an internally led growth model that develops along emission-friendly lines. China has the great advantage of backwardness—in terms of both technological attainment and depth of capital stock. Given this starting point, we view future strategy as fluid rather than path dependent.

One profitable strategy that China might employ would be to approximate the incredibly fruitful mass-market integration efforts of the United States that eventually elevated it to its position of global primacy. The re-emergence of excess capacity in Chinese heavy industry, serious questions about the medium term ability of other major regions to accommodate further large gains in Chinese market share and the stark conflict between the contemporary style of industrial development and the health of the biosphere indicate strongly that now is the time to catalyse the required adjustment and reform processes that will underpin sustainable long-run prosperity.

References

Abramovitz, M. 1986, 'Catching up, forging ahead and falling behind', *The Journal of Economic History*, vol. XLVI, no. 2 (June), pp. 385–406.

Aizenman, J. and Lee, J. 2005, *International reserves: precautionary versus mercantilist views, theory and evidence*, Working Paper 05/198, International Monetary Fund, Washington, DC.

Anderson, J. 2006, 'Rebalance this', *UBS Investment Research*, 12 December.

Athukorala, P.-C. and Yamashita, N. 2008, 'Global production sharing and US–China trade relations', in L. Song and W. T. Woo (eds), *China's Dilemma: Economic growth, the environment and climate change*, Asia Pacific Press and Brookings Institution Press, Canberra and Washington, DC, pp. 59–89.

Baba, M. and Tatemoto, M. 1968, 'Foreign trade and economic growth', in L. Klein and K. Ohkawa (eds), *Economic Growth: The Japanese experience since the Meiji era*, Richard D. Irwin Inc., Homewood, Ill., pp. 162–96.

Bairoch, P. 1982, 'International industrialisation levels from 1750 to 1980', *The Journal of European Economic History*, vol. 2, pp. 269–333.

—— 1993, *Economics and World History: Myths and paradoxes*, University of Chicago Press, Chicago.

Barro, R. J. and Sala-i-Martin, X. 2004, *Economic Growth*, Second edition, The MIT Press, Cambridge, Mass.

Baumol, W. 1986, 'Productivity growth, convergence and welfare: what the long run data show', *The American Economic Review*, vol. 76, no. 5 (December), pp. 1072–85.

Bernanke, B. 2005, The global savings glut and the US current account deficit, The Sandridge Lecture, Virginia Association of Economics, Richmond, Va., March.

Brezis, E., Krugman, P. and Tsiddon, D. 1991, *Leapfrogging: a theory of cycles in national technological leadership*, NBER Working Paper 3886, National Bureau of Economic Research, Cambridge, Mass.

Brookings Institution 2004, *Event summary: restoring fiscal sanity while we still can*, Brookings Institution, Washington, DC, <http://www.brookings.edu/opinions/2004/0518budgetdeficit.aspx>

Caballero, R. J., Farhi, E. and Gourinchas, P.-O. 2008, 'An equilibrium model of "global imbalances" and low interest rates', *American Economic Review*, vol. 98, no. 1 (March), pp. 358–93.

Cappiello, L. and Ferrucci, G. 2008, *The sustainability of China's exchange rate policy and capital account liberalisation*, ECB Occasional Paper Series, no. 82 (March), European Central Bank, Frankfurt am Main, Germany.

Carbon Dioxide Information Analysis Center n.d., *Fossil-Fuel CO_2 Emissions*, <http://cdiac.ornl.gov/trends/emis/meth_reg.html>

CEIC n.d., *CEIC Database*, CEIC Data Company Limited, <www.ceicdata.com>

Chen, C. 2007, 'Foreign direct investment in China: trends and characteristics after WTO accession', in R. Garnaut and L. Song (eds), *China: Linking markets for growth*, Asia Pacific Press, Canberra, pp. 197–224.

Chenery, H., Robinson, S. and Syrquin, M. 1986, *Industrialisation and Growth: A comparative study*, Oxford University Press, Oxford.

Clark, C. 1940, *The Conditions of Economic Progress*, Macmillan, London.

Cooper, R. N. 2005, *Living with global imbalances: a contrarian view*, Policy Brief, no. 5-3 (November), Peterson Institute for International Economics, Washington, DC.

Denison, E. 1967, *Why Growth Rates Differ: Postwar experience in nine Western countries*, Brookings Institution, Washington, DC.

Devlin, W. and McKay, H. 2008, 'The macroeconomic implications of financial de-leveraging', *Economic Roundup*, issue 4, pp. 47–75.

Dobson, W. and Masson, P. R. 2009, 'Will the renmimbi become a world currency?', *China Economic Review*, vol. 20, pp. 124–35.

Dooley, M., Folkerts-Landau, D. and Garber, P. 2003, *An essay on the revised Bretton Woods system*, NBER Working Paper, no. 9971, National Bureau of Economic Research, Cambridge, Mass.

Dowrick, S. and Nguyen D. T. 1989, 'OECD economic growth in the post-war period: catch-up and convergence', *American Economic Review* vol. 79, no. 5 (December), pp. 1010–30.

Fankhauser, S. and Tol, R. S. J. 2005, 'On climate change and economic growth', *Resource and Energy Economics*, vol. 27, pp. 1–17.

Fishlow, A. 2000, 'Internal transportation in the nineteenth and early twentieth centuries', in S. E. Engerman and R. E. Gallman (eds), *The Cambridge History of the United States. Volume II: The long nineteenth century*, Cambridge University Press, New York, pp. 543–642.

Gallman, R. E. 2000, 'Economic growth and structural change in the long nineteenth century', in S. E. Engerman and R. E. Gallman (eds), *The Cambridge History of the United States. Volume II: The long nineteenth century*, Cambridge University Press, New York, pp. 1–56.

Garnaut, R. 2008, *Climate Change Review Report*, Cambridge University Press, Cambridge.

Garnaut, R., Howes, S., Jotzo, F. and Sheehan, P. 2008, *Emissions in the Platinum Age: the implications of rapid development for climate change mitigation*, Garnaut Review Working Paper, Revised draft, 2 May 2008, <www.garnautreview.org.au>

Gerschenkron, A. 1962, *Economic Backwardness in Historical Perspective*, Harvard University Press, Cambridge, Mass.

Golley, J. and Groeneweld, N. 2007, 'Domestic market integration and inter-regional growth spillovers', in R. Garnaut and L. Song (eds), *China: Linking markets for growth*, Asia Pacific Press, Canberra, pp. 176–96.

Golley, J. and Tyers, R. 2006, 'China's growth to 2030: demographic change and the labour supply constraint', in R. Garnaut and L. Song (eds), *The Turning Point in China's Economic Development*, Asia Pacific Press, Canberra, pp. 203–26.

Grossman, G. and Krueger A. 1995, 'Economic growth and environment', *Quarterly Journal of Economics*, vol. 110, no. 2, pp. 353–77.

Hallding, K., Han, G. and Olsson, M. 2009, *A Balancing Act: China's role in climate change*, The Commission on Sustainable Development, Stockholm.

He, J., Li, S. and Polaski, S. 2007, 'China's economic prospects 2006–2020', *Carnegie Papers*, no. 83, April.

Huang, Y. 2009, China's subsidised prosperity: the great ascendancy and structural risks, Unpublished manuscript.

International Monetary Fund (IMF) 2005, 'Global imbalances: a savings and investment perspective', *World Economic Outlook*, September, International Monetary Fund, Washington, DC, pp. 91–124.

—— 2009. *World Economic Outlook Database*, April, International Monetary Fund, Washington, DC, <http://www.imf.org/external/pubs/ft/weo/2009/01/weodata/>

Japanese Statistics Bureau 2009, *Historical Statistics of Japan*, Japanese Statistics Bureau, Tokyo, <http://www.stat.go.jp/english/data/chouki>

Kaya, Y., 1990, 'Impacts of carbon dioxide emission control on GDP growth: Interpretation of proposed scenarios', paper presented at IPCC Energy and Industry Subgroup Response Strategies Working Group, Paris, France.

Klein, L. and Ohkawa, K. (eds) 1968, *Economic Growth: The Japanese experience since the Meiji era*, Richard D. Irwin Inc., Homewood, Ill.

Kuijs, L. 2006, *How will China's saving–investment balance evolve?*, World Bank Policy Research Working Paper, no. 3958 (July), The World Bank, Washington, DC.

Kuznets, S. 1930, *Secular Movements in Production and Prices*, National Bureau for Economic Research, Boston.

Lee, J.-W, McKibbin, W. J. and Yung, C. P. 2004, *Trans-Pacific trade imbalances: causes and cures*, Lowy Institute Issues Brief, September, Lowy Insitute, Sydney.

Lin, J. Y. 2008, 'Rebalancing equity and efficiency for sustained growth', in L. Song and W. T. Woo (eds), *China's Dilemma: Economic growth, the environment and climate change*, Asia Pacific Press and Brookings Institution Press, Canberra and Washington, DC, pp. 90–109.

Lipsey, R. E. 2000, 'US foreign trade and the balance of payments, 1800–1913', in S. E. Engerman and R. E. Gallman (eds), *The Cambridge History of the United States. Volume II: The long nineteenth century*, Cambridge University Press, New York, pp. 685–732.

Loayza, N., Schmidt-Hebbel, K. and Serven, L. 2000, 'Saving in developing countries: an overview', *The World Bank Economic Review*, vol. 14, no. 3, pp. 393–414.

McKay, H. 2007, 'Reforming China's exchange arrangements: monetary and financial sovereignty, sequencing and the foreign exchange market', in R. Garnaut and L. Song (eds), *China: Linking markets for growth*, Asia Pacific Press, Canberra, pp. 290–315.

—— 2008a, *Asian industrialisation: a strategic analysis with a memorandum on the Australian response*, Global Dynamic Systems Centre Working Papers, no. 4 (June), Global Dynamic Systems Centre, Canberra.

—— 2008b, *Metal intensity in comparative historical perspective: China, North Asia, the United States and the Kuznets curve*, Global Dynamic Systems Centre Working Papers, no. 6 (September), Global Dynamic Systems Centre, Canberra.

Maddison, A. 2001, *The World Economy: A millennial perspective*, Organisation for Economic Cooperation and Development, Paris.

—— 2009, *Historical Statistics of the World Economy: 1–2006AD*, March update, Groningen Growth and Development Centre, Groningen, The Netherlands, <http://www.ggdc.net/maddison/>

National Bureau of Statistics (NBS) 2008, *China Statistical Yearbook 2008*, China Statistics Press, Beijing.

—— various years, *China Statistical Yearbook*, China Statistics Press, Beijing.

Nelson, R. R. and Phelps, E. 1966, 'Investment in humans, technological diffusion, and economic growth', *American Economic Review*, vol. 56 (May), pp. 69–75.

Nishioka, S. 2008, 'A Japanese climate policy based on science, equity and cooperation', *Asia-Pacific Review*, vol. 15, no. 1, pp. 1–11.

Ohkawa, K. and Rosovsky, H. 1968, 'Postwar Japanese growth in historical perspective: a second look', in L. Klein and K. Ohkawa (eds), *Economic Growth: The Japanese experience since the Meiji era*, Richard D. Irwin Inc., Homewood, Ill., pp. 3–35.

Perkins, D. H. and Rawski, T. G. 2007, *Forecasting China's Economic Growth to 2025*, <http://post.economics.harvard.edu/faculty/perkins/papers/Chapter20.pdf>

Prasad, E., Rumbaugh, T. and Wang, Q., 2005, *Putting the cart before the horse? Capital account liberalization and exchange rate flexibility in China*, IMF Policy Discussion Paper, PDP/05/01, International Monetary Fund, Washington, DC.

Rawski, T. G. 2008, Can China sustain rapid growth despite flawed institutions?, Paper presented to the Sixth International Symposium of the Centre for China–US Cooperation, University of Denver, Colorado, 30–31 May.

Rosen, D. H. and Houser, T. 2007, *China Energy: A guide for the perplexed*, May, Peterson Institute for International Economics, Washington, DC.

Rostow, W. W. 1971, *The Stages of Economic Growth: A non-communist manifesto*, Oxford University Press, New York.

—— 1978, *The World Economy: History and prospect*, Macmillan, London.

Roubini, N. and Setser, B. 2005, Will the Bretton Woods 2 regime unravel soon? The risk of a hard landing in 2005–06, Paper prepared for Federal Reserve Bank of San Francisco and University of California at Berkeley symposium Revived Bretton Woods System: A new paradigm for Asian development, 4 February.

Shi, X. 2008, 'Can China's coal industry be reconciled with the environment?', in L. Song and W. T. Woo (eds), *China's Dilemma: Economic growth, the environment and climate change*, Asia Pacific Press and Brookings Institution Press, Canberra and Washington, DC, pp. 367–91.

Snooks, G. D. 1997, *The Ephemeral Civilisation: Exploding the myth of social evolution*, Routledge, London.

—— 1999, *Global Transition: A general theory of economic development*, Macmillan, London.

—— 2009, *Climate mitigation or technological revolution? A critical choice of futures*, Global Dynamic Systems Centre Working Papers, no. 10 (February), Global Dynamic Systems Centre, Canberra.

Solow, R. M. 1957, 'Technical change and the aggregate production function', *Review of Economics and Statistics*, vol. 39, no. 3 (August), pp. 312–20.

Song, L. and Yu, S. 2007, 'China's demand for energy: a global perspective', in R. Garnaut and L. Song (eds), *China: Linking markets for growth*, Asia Pacific Press, Canberra, pp. 225–47.

Song, L. 2005, 'Interest rate liberalisation in China and the implications for non-state banking', in Y. Huang, A. Saich and E. Steinfeld (eds), *Financial Sector Reform in China*, Harvard University Asia Center, Cambridge, Mass., pp. 111–30.

Stern, N. 2007, *The Economics of Climate Change: The Stern review*, Cambridge University Press, Cambridge and New York.

—— 2008, 'The economics of climate change', *American Economic Review: Papers & Proceedings*, vol. 98, no. 2, pp. 1–37.

Taylor, J. B. 2008, The financial crisis and the policy responses: an empirical analysis of what went wrong, Keynote address at the Bank of Canada, Ottawa, November.

Trebilcock, C. 1986, *The Industrialisation of the Continental Powers 1780–1914*, Longman, London.

United Nations (UN) 2007, *World Urbanization Prospects: The 2007 revision*, United Nations, New York, <http://www.un.org/esa/population/publications/WUP2005/2005WUP_DataTables2.pdf>

United States Bureau of Statistics (USBS) 1901, *Statistical Abstract of the United States 1900–01—Twenty-Third Number, Prepared under direction from the Secretary of the Treasury*, United States Bureau of Statistics, Washington, DC, <http://www2.census.gov/prod2/statcomp/documents/1900-01.pdf>

United States Federal Highway Administration (USFHA) 2008, *Highway Statistics 2007*, United States Federal Highway Administration, <http://www.fhwa.dot.gov/policyinformation/statistics/2007/vmt421.cfm>

US Federal Reserve 2009, *Flow of Funds Accounts*, United States Federal Reserve <http://www.federalreserve.gov/releases/z1/>

United States Geological Survey (USGS) various years, *Minerals Yearbooks*, United States Geological Survey, <http://minerals.usgs.gov/minerals/pubs/>

Wing, I. S. 2008, 'Explaining the declining energy intensity of the US economy', *Resource and Energy Economics*, vol. 30, pp. 21–49.

Zhang, J., Gao, X. and Li, H. 2007, *Global Economic Evolution: Structure, logic and China factor*, The Renmin University Press, Beijing.

Zhou, X. 2008, On savings ratio, Address to the High Level Conference, Central Bank of Malaysia, Kuala Lumpur, 10 February 2009, <http://www.bis.org/review/r090327b.pdf>

Zhuang, G. 2008, 'How will China move towards becoming a low carbon economy', *China & World Economy*, vol. 16, no. 3, pp. 93–105.

Endnotes

1. The citation of a single work for these authors is an obvious understatement. The work of quantitative economic history is by its very nature a labour of decades. It is assumed that readers will be familiar with their broad contributions and will forgive a lean attitude to referencing in this context.

2. This section includes large amounts of data derived from a great many sources. To assist readability in the text, referencing will be kept to a minimum.

3. According to the study by CEIC and Goldman Sachs (2005), in 2004, capital stocks per worker in the United States, Japan and China were US$149 000, US$177 000 and US$2600, respectively (calculated using 1984 prices).

4. We define industrial profit margins as the share of profits in total sales.

5. The fact that industrial sales exceed GDP by a large margin should not be alarming, as sales are a gross concept that does not control for intra and inter-industry transactions and import content. GDP, as a value-added concept, avoids this double-counting problem.

6. Of course, our analysis implies that from a long-run structural perspective, Chinese domestic demand will catch up to supply in the heavy industrial field. However, that long-run view does not exclude the possibility of pronounced cyclical deviations between the two, such as the current episode.

7. The Kaya identity is defined as CO_2 emission = population*(GDP/population)*(energy/GDP)*(CO_2/energy).

8. This is because greater human availability of human capital reduces a country's costs of adopting sophisticated techniques or equivalently raises the return to this adoption of new technology (Barro and Sala-i-Martin 2004).

9. In 1870, the United Kingdom accounted for 32 per cent of world total industrial output. Its energy consumption was five times that of the United States and Germany, six times that of France and 155 times that of Russia (Zhang et al. 2007).

10. PPP GDP levels are used in compiling this measure. Improvement is less pronounced under other measurement regimes.

11. Note that these elasticities are based on local currency values of GDP and energy consumption.

12. These conditions include that the difference in wage costs between the leading nation and potential challengers is large, experience in the old technology becomes rapidly obsolete and the new technology must ultimately offer the possibility of substantial productivity improvement over the old (Brezis et al. 1991).

13. For example, it is reported that worldwide investment in renewable energy has grown by 65 per cent a year since 2004 and is projected to reach US$600 billion a year by 2020 (*The China Daily*, 5 May 2009).

China's textile and clothing trade and global adjustment 14

Will Martin

The year 2009 is proving to be a remarkable one in many respects. One of the most important of these from a trade perspective has received very little attention. This is the first year in half a century in which the world has not had a system of quotas to slow the growth of exports of textiles and clothing from developing countries in general, and particularly from China. That these quotas have been abolished seems remarkable given the intensity of the support for these quotas in earlier periods. Perhaps even more remarkable is the fact that they disappeared almost without trace in 2009, without evidence of the major disruption against which they were long seen as a bulwark. Have world textile-trade policymakers finally found the virtue they have long sought, but whose realisation they often seemed to defer (Reinert 2000)?

Quotas against exports of textiles and clothing from developing countries were introduced on a large scale in the 1960s, based on precedents of quotas used to slow the seemingly inexorable growth in exports of textiles and clothing from Japan in the 1930s. The quotas of the 1960s were partial in coverage, focusing on only textiles and clothing made from cotton, and from a relatively limited set of countries. As is frequently the case with quantitative restrictions, one set of restrictions begot another. In this case, the restrictions on cotton textiles created incentives for suppliers to use synthetics and other fibres, including such previously—and since—obscure fibres as ramie. As a result of these spill-over effects, a complex web of quotas covering a wide range of textile fibres was introduced under the Multi-Fibre Arrangement (MFA) in the 1970s and progressively tightened during the 1980s and early 1990s.[1]

In principle, these quotas were intended to grow over time so that trade in textiles and clothing could return to a system regulated under World Trade Organisation (WTO) rules involving tariffs, rather than quotas. The quotas and rates of quota growth over time were negotiated under bilateral agreements that applied over extended periods. Because neither the level of the quotas nor their rates of growth responded to shifts in supply and/or demand, the protective effect of these quotas varied considerably across suppliers and with time. The resulting export barriers were a particularly serious problem for countries such as China that had quotas that were low relative to productive potential, and grew at rates that were low relative to the underlying growth in export supply. In this situation, the prices of scarce quotas could become very large relative to the net value of these exports. Given the importance of labour-intensive manufactured exports in labour-intensive countries such as China (Lin 2009), these quotas posed particular problems for developing countries attempting to develop through the expansion of labour-intensive exports.

In this short chapter, we first consider the evolution of the quotas on exports of textiles and clothing from China. Then, we look at the evidence available on the protective impacts of these quotas. Finally, we consider some of the implications of their abolition for the markets for clothing and textiles, and for China's balance of agricultural trade.

The quotas on textiles and clothing

The quotas implemented under the MFA, and the Uruguay Round Agreement on Textiles and Clothing that succeeded it, were imposed after bilateral consultations between the importer and the exporter for particular products. These negotiations covered the size of the initial quotas and their rate of growth. The quotas were administered by the exporter, which was—perhaps because of the initially grey-area status of 'voluntary export restrictions' under General Agreement on Tariffs and Trade (GATT) rules— allowed to keep any quota rents associated with the quotas. Importers could potentially have imposed quotas against non-members of the GATT/ WTO and kept the quota rents themselves, but they generally chose to follow similar procedures for members and non-members.

Large countries such as China were more likely to attract attention as their exports grew and hence to find themselves with limits that were small relative to their production potential. Perhaps for the same reason, China's exports of textiles and clothing were subjected to lower growth rates than most other developing-country exporters. Another factor contributing to differences in quota growth rates during the period after 1994 was the Agreement on Textiles and Clothing under the Uruguay Round, which phased out the quotas on some products and increased the growth rates of the remaining export quotas from 1995 to 2004, before their planned elimination in 2005. As is evident from Table 14.1, China's quota growth rates in the US market for the decade to 2004–05 were particularly low relative to those of other countries. The fact that China was not a member of the GATT/WTO until 2001 also meant that China lacked access to mechanisms for challenging decisions about restrictions on her exports of textiles and clothing.

Table 14.1 Quota enlargement under the Agreement on Textiles and Clothing, 1994–2004 (percentage change for the full period)

	Textiles		Clothing	
	European Union	United States	European Union	United States
Bangladesh	n.a.	168	n.a.	168
China	50	33	38	41
Hong Kong, China	16	37	22	17
India	50	141	79	116
Indonesia	83	134	117	133
South Korea	70	37	38	12
Pakistan	79	139	119	150
Sri Lanka		134	204	132
Philippines		134	112	119
Thailand	59	127	116	123
Taiwan, China	34	22	24	4
Total	62	93	54	67

n.a. not available

Note: Based on quotas and growth rates in effect at the beginning of the implementation period.
Source: International Textile and Clothing Bureau, Geneva.

Since the textile and clothing export quotas were scarce, they became valuable assets. While quotas were allocated in a variety of ways, trade between enterprises was allowed, with prices quoted widely, including through web sites such as <www.chinaquota.com>. The tradability of these quotas ensured that the opportunity cost of using a quota to export was broadly similar across enterprises. Since a quota had to be purchased— or the opportunity to sell a quota forgone—the quotas acted like an export tax in raising the cost of exporting textiles and clothing. With data on the cost of quotas and the export quota-inclusive price of exports, it became possible to estimate meaningful export tax equivalents for these quotas. Given the dynamism of China's underlying export growth, her limited and slow-growing quotas for textile and clothing exports frequently translated into very high, and rising, export tax equivalents of these quotas.

Using data on the prices of quota and the (quota price-inclusive) export unit values for a range of developing-country suppliers, Martin et al. (2004) estimate the export tax equivalents of quotas on exports of clothing from China to the European Union to have averaged 54 per cent in 2002–03 and 36 per cent on exports to the United States. These are high rates of export tax equivalent and could be expected to divert exports from China to other, non-restricted markets and to reduce exports overall. Two other notable features of the table are that, first, many exporters had zero or very low export barriers; given the size of their quotas, they were essentially unrestricted. Another feature was that the lower-income developing countries, such as China, India and Pakistan, had much higher tariff equivalents than the newly industrialising countries, which had largely lost comparative advantage in these products.

Table 14.2 Estimated export tax equivalents of quotas in key supplying regions, 2002–03 (per cent)

	Textiles		Clothing	
	European Union	United States	European Union	United States
Bangladesh[a]	n.a.	0.0	n.a.	20.4
India	1.0	3.0	20	20
Pakistan[a]	9.4	9.8	9.2	10.3
China[a]	1.0	20.0	54.0	36.0
Hong Kong, China[a]	2.1	0.0	12.3	2.3
Sri Lanka	1.0	0.0	0.0	7.0
Other East Asia[b]	1.0	0.0	3.0	7.0
Newly industrialising economies[c]	1.0	0.0	0.3	2.5

n.a. not available

[a] denotes an estimate based on quota price information

[b] based on Indonesia, Philippines and Thailand

[c] South Korea and Taiwan, China

Note: Other estimates interpolated from quota utilisation data.

A key feature of the export tax equivalents in Table 14.2 is the very high values on exports of clothing from China to the United States and the European Union. A surprising feature is the very low apparent barrier to exports of textiles from China to the European Union. Another important feature of the table is the apparently very high barriers on exports of clothing from Bangladesh to the United States and the relatively high barriers on textiles and clothing from Pakistan. The broad pattern of export tax equivalents appears to be similar to that contained in the Global Trade Analysis Project (GTAP) model (Nordas 2004:25), except that the GTAP numbers show an export tax equivalent of 20 per cent on textile exports into the European Union. The overall similarity of the estimates is reassuring given that these are central to any analysis of the implications of liberalisation, and that the GTAP estimates are derived using a completely different methodology—the gravity-model approach used by Francois and Spinanger (2000).

The policies of quota phase-out and export quota expansion under the Agreement on Textiles and Clothing (WTO 1995) could have been key influences on the export tax equivalents. A major objective of this agreement was to progressively return these sectors to normal market disciplines by a combination of accelerated growth in quotas and progressive abolition of quotas during the phase-out period up to 1 January 2005. The phasing out of quotas was not generally regarded as successful in achieving significant liberalisation because the quotas phased out were largely those in which developing countries had no comparative advantage. Given the diversity of China's textile and clothing industry, however, it would have provided opportunities from unrestricted expansion in some products.

The high growth rates of quotas in many suppliers after the acceleration in their growth rates under the Agreement on Textiles and Clothing (Table 14.1) undoubtedly contributed to the relatively low average export tax equivalents observed in countries such as Pakistan, Sri Lanka, the Philippines and Thailand. In contrast, the low growth of China's export quotas contributed to the emergence of high export tax equivalents on these exports by restricting their growth relative to the underlying shift in the supply of these exports. Effectively, this stored up adjustment that could otherwise have occurred smoothly during the 10-year phase-out period to the end of the quota phase-out. The low growth rates in mature exporters such as Hong Kong and South Korea were sufficient because these economies were rapidly losing comparative advantage in these products.

The average export tax equivalents of the quotas presented in Table 14.2 have the advantage of having been built up from information about the prices of quotas for particular product categories and the quota premium-inclusive unit values of exports. This has the advantage of allowing us to examine the differences in the export tax equivalents of quotas across products and over time. The 36 per cent average export tax equivalent for China's exports to the United States involved positive export taxes on

62 per cent of clothing products, with export tax equivalents ranging up to 192 per cent (on women's knit shirts) (Martin et al. 2004). As shown in Appendix Table 14.1, many other popular clothing items, such as men's and boys' cotton trousers, also had very high export tax equivalents, making the impact of reform very sensitive to the treatment of individual categories—as well, of course, as raising the efficiency cost of the regime relative to a system involving more uniform rates of distortion.

The abolition of the export quotas on textile and clothing quotas imposed under the MFA was effective only for GATT members. This meant that quotas on China's exports could have been continued, perhaps indefinitely. As part of China's WTO accession package in 2001, China negotiated that the quotas against her exports would also be phased out by 2005. China was also to benefit from the abolition of quotas on some products and higher growth rates of quotas on products still under quotas. The accession agreement, however, introduced the possibility of these quotas being replaced by special textile 'safeguard' measures during the period 2005–08.

Under Paragraph 242 of the *Report of the Working Party on China's Accession to the WTO*, other members were entitled to impose safeguard quotas against China during the period 2005–08. In mid-2005, the European Union reached an agreement with China that allowed the former to impose such quotas on selected products from China between 2005 and 2007 (EC 2005a, 2005b). In November 2005, the United States and China signed a memorandum of understanding allowing the United States to impose similar quotas against China between 2006 and 2008 (Governments of the United States of America and of the People's Republic of China 2005). The European Commission made relatively minor revisions to its agreement in September 2005 to deal with unexpectedly large quantities of products in transit. The working party report allows all WTO members to impose these sanctions—irrespective of whether they previously imposed quotas—and some other countries have imposed quotas against China, although the European Union and the United States are by far the most important markets to have imposed these quotas.

The accession agreement specified that the special safeguard quotas were to be based on imports in 12 of the preceding 14 months and that the quotas should grow by at least 7.5 per cent per annum (WTO 2001). These quotas would have been very cumbersome to use, particularly because they could last no longer than one year at a time. Perhaps because of this, the two major importers chose to negotiate larger quotas and higher growth rates than could potentially have been imposed under this provision of China's accession agreement. The quotas imposed by the United States are compared with the levels of the corresponding quotas in 2004—the last year of the Agreement on Textiles and Clothing (Table 14.3).

A striking feature of Table 14.3 is just how much the quotas increased for the products that were covered by the post-Agreement on Textiles and Clothing safeguards imposed under the accession agreement. Many of these products—and particularly Categories 338/339, 349/649 and 666—were subject to particularly high export tax equivalents, as is evident from Appendix Table 14.1. Much of the increase in the quotas shown in Table 14.3 is the result of the pent up need for adjustment associated with having low rates of quota growth in China—one of the most dynamic exporters in the world and the largest exporter whose exports were growing the most rapidly. Some of the quotas, however—on products such as knit fabric and special-purpose fabric, which had not previously been subject to tightly restrictive quotas—seemed to suggest the emergence of new sensitivities in the US market. The US agreement specified growth rates of 12.5 per cent for most products in 2007 and 2008, allowing significantly more than the minimum 7.5 per cent growth rate specified in China's accession agreement.

The EC agreement with China also involved substantial increases in the levels of the quotas and in the growth rates for the products covered by the quotas (Table 14.4). In the case of the European Commission, the initial increases in the levels of the quotas averaged about 220 per cent, with increases in subsequent years of 10 or 12.5 per cent per annum. It appears likely that, as in the United States, in the European Commission, the increases between 2004 and 2006 would have been large enough to substantially reduce the adjustment pressures resulting from the low growth rates in China's pre-accession textile and clothing export quotas.

Table 14.3 Quotas imposed by the United States on exports from China

Category	Description	Units	2006 quota	2004 quota	Growth 2006 vs 2004 (%)
200/301	Thread	kg	7,529,582	3,610,544	108.5
222	Knit fabric	kg	15,966,487		
229	Special-purpose fabric	kg	33,162,019		
332/432/632T	Cotton, wool, man-made fibre socks	DPR	64,386,841	42,433,990	51.7
338/339	Cotton knit shirts	doz.	20,822,111	2,523,532	725.1
340/640	Men's and boys' woven shirts	doz.	6,743,644	2,345,946	187.5
345/645/646	Sweaters	doz.	8,179,211	1,030,348	693.8
347/348	Men's and boys' cotton trousers	doz.	19,666,049	2,421,922	712.0
349/649	Brassieres	doz.	22,785,906	1,094,132	1,982.6
352/652	Underwear	doz.	18,948,937	5,276,745	259.1
359S/659S	Swimwear	kg	4,590,626	750,959	511.3
363	Cotton terry towels	doz.	103,316,873	24,773,109	317.1
638/639	Men's and boys' man-made fibre knit shirts	doz.	8,060,063	2,712,680	197.1
647/648	Man-made fibre trousers	doz.	7,960,355	2,974,238	167.6
666	Other man-made fibre furnishings	kg	964,014	573,372	68.1
847	Trousers, shorts, silk, etc.	doz.	17,647,255	1,452,972	1,114.6
	Weighted average, 2005 weights				573

Note: Growth rate weighted by import value shares.

Sources: <www.cpb.gov www.chinaquota.com>; <www.otexa.itc.gov>

Table 14.4 Adjustments in China's textile export quotas to the European Community

Cat.	Product	Unit	2004 quota	2005 quota	2006 quota	Increase 2006–04 (%)	Growth rate (%)
2	Cotton fabric	tonne	30,556	49,060	61,948	103	12.5
4	T-shirts	1,000	126,808	501,289	540,204	326	10
5	Pullovers	1,000	39,422	231,047	189,719	381	10
6	Men's trousers	1,000	40,913	336,372	338,923	728	10
7	Blouses	1,000	17,093	74,094	80,493	371	10
20	Bed linen	tonne	5,681	14,028	15,795	178	12.5
26	Dresses	1,000	6,645	24,649	27,001	306	10
31	Brassieres	1,000	96,488	217,984	219,882	128	10
39	Table linen	tonne	5,681	10,966	12,349	117	12.5
115	Flax yarn	tonne	1,413	4,494	4740	235	10
Value share weighted total						218	

Sources: European Commission (EC) 2005a, 'Commission regulation (EC) no. 1084/2005', *Official Journal of the European Commission*, l. 177/19, 8 July 2005; European Commission (EC) 2005b, 'Commission regulation (EC) no. 1478/2005', *Official Journal of the European Commission*, l. 263/3, 12 September 2005.

What has happened? Some key changes

As noted in Elbehri et al. (2003), one likely impact of quota abolition is an increase in the share of China and other quota-restricted exporters in the restricted markets. This reflects the fact that a primary effect of the quotas is to cause the more strongly restricted exporters to have low shares in the restricted markets and correspondingly high shares in unrestricted markets (Yang et al. 1997). Removal of highly restrictive export quotas can be expected to cause a large decline in the landed price of imports under these circumstances simply because exporters no longer have to use up expensive quotas whenever they export to restricted markets. The increase of imports in volume terms into the formerly restricted market is likely to be particularly sharp. The increase in value terms might be smaller because of the fall in the landed price of imports. As long as the demand for exports of an individual country is strongly price responsive, however, the value share of a country whose export quotas are being eliminated can be expected to increase. The share of China in the US market changed around the time of quota abolition (Table 14.5), as it did for the European Union-27 (Table 14.6).

Table 14.5 China's value shares of US textile and clothing markets (per cent)

Year	Textiles		Clothing	
	Share	Growth rate	Share	Growth rate
1999	11.9	11.9	13.2	3.9
2000	12.2	15.0	13.3	15.4
2001	12.9	1.7	14.0	3.9
2002	15.8	35.3	15.1	8.7
2003	19.9	35.3	16.9	19.2
2004	22.3	27.0	19.0	19.8
2005	26.9	31.8	26.4	46.9
2006	29.6	14.8	29.4	15.4
2007	31.8	10.1	33.6	16.9
2008	34.1	2.9	34.7	0.2
2009	35.9	−14.9	39.4	1.6

Source: COMTRADE, except for 2009, which were estimated using Otexa data for the first quarter of 2009.

Table 14.6 Changes in China's value shares of EU-27 textile and clothing markets (per cent)

Year	Textiles		Clothing	
	China's share	Growth rate	China's share	Growth rate
2001	12.5	1.2	21.8	4.4
2002	14.5	16.0	23.8	15.8
2003	16.7	32.4	25.2	27.6
2004	19.1	36.3	26.9	25.1
2005	23.4	25.3	35.3	43.4
2006	25.6	21.7	35.0	12.6
2007	27.1	21.0	38.3	24.0
2008	29.8	12.5	42.8	23.4

Source: Import data from COMTRADE.

A striking feature of Table 14.5 is the dramatic increase in China's share of the US markets for textiles and apparel during the quota-abolition period. China's share of imports began to grow in earnest in 2002, after China's WTO accession, with the introduction of higher growth rates, the elimination of some quotas and with more rigorous multilateral disciplines on the introduction of new quotas. The rate of growth in China's market share, however, increased substantially in 2005, when the quotas were initially lifted on all exports, but subsequently reimposed, at a higher level, as 'safeguards' against China's exports. One factor contributing to the surge in exports in 2005 might have been the expectation that quotas would be reimposed in future years, combined with the expectation that quotas would be allocated within China based on the traditional system.[1] With past performance playing a major role in quota allocation, firms had an incentive and an opportunity to expand their exports during the period that quotas did not apply so that they could earn quota allocations for future years. This growth in market share continued in subsequent years, with China's share of clothing imports to the United States rising to almost 40 per cent in 2009. This increase was in the order of magnitude predicted by Nordas (2004), whose simulation modelling suggested that China's share of the US market for apparel might reach 50 per cent.

Turning to the results for the European Union presented in Table 14.6, we also see large increases in China's share of the import market. The results presented in Table 14.2 indicate that China's share of the textile import market has increased to two and a half times its original level, while China's import share in clothing has roughly doubled. These increases were much higher than the estimates of Nordas (2004), whose simulation estimates suggested only a marginal increase in China's share of the EU textile market and an increase from 18 per cent to 29 per cent in its share of the clothing market.

Many observers have concluded that dramatic increases in China's share in the US and EU markets would cause policymakers in these countries to use contingent protection measures such as anti-dumping and safeguards. Bown's (2009) database on contingent protection suggests that this has not, as yet, occurred for textile and clothing products in general, although there has been considerable use of these measures for upstream products such as polyester staple fibre. Perhaps the customised nature of most shipments of apparel means that the long-feared use of anti-dumping measures to replace the quotas will not take place and the textile and garment sectors will quietly return to being regulated under a pure tariff regime.

Table 14.7 China's share of developing-country exports of textiles and clothing (per cent)

	World	United States and European Union	Other
1999	36.3	18.1	67.0
2000	38.6	19.2	68.9
2001	38.8	19.5	69.4
2002	39.7	21.2	70.0
2003	40.9	23.1	70.7
2004	42.4	25.3	70.4
2005	47.1	32.3	70.9
2006	48.2	34.1	71.3
2007	49.5	37.1	69.7
2008	47.4	39.5	66.8

Source: COMTRADE data extracted from WITS.

Too much emphasis on what happens in the US and EU markets could, however, be somewhat misleading. From the point of view of other developing-country exporters, what matters is their share of world markets for textiles and clothing, rather than their shares in the US and EU markets. The evolution of China's share of exports of textiles and clothing from developing countries has been examined (Table 14.7). The first column of the table shows these exports relative to exports from all developing countries. The second shows China's share of developing-country exports to the US and EU markets and the third shows China's share in markets other than the United States and the European Union.

The second column shows the very rapid growth in China's share of exports seen in the previous tables. China's share in markets other than the United States and the European Union has, however, been essentially static. Overall, China's share of developing countries' total exports has grown from 36 per cent to 47 per cent in the decade from 1999 to 2008. While this is a rapid increase in share, it seems likely to be considerably less alarming to competitors than the doubling of China's share in the US and EU markets alone.

One key question underlying this table is whether the increase in China's share reflects in part the extraordinary growth in China's economy, and in overall exports, or whether it reflects something more specific to the textile sector. One measure that provides some insights into this question is the revealed comparative advantage (RCA) index. This measure adjusts for growth in overall exports by expressing the share of the good of interest in total exports of the country relative to the same good's share in world exports, or the exports of another reference group. The RCA indexes for China relative to world exports (Table 14.8) reveal a steady downward trend in China's RCA for textiles, clothing and for textiles and clothing combined. Given that abolition of the export quotas against China was essentially the only reduction in the trade barriers facing China brought about by China's accession to the WTO (Ianchovichina and Martin 2004), one might have expected an increase in China's RCA for textiles and clothing. The continuing downward trend in China's RCA for these products suggests that other powerful forces—such as an accumulation of the factors used intensively in other exports or technological advances in other export sectors—are outweighing the effects of this liberalisation on China's export mix. This is consistent with the observation in Dimaranan et al. (2007) that China's list of top-25 exports is dominated by products such as computers and components and includes very few textile and clothing products. As noted by Martin and Manole (2008), however, and in the World Bank's *Global Economic Prospects 2004*, many other developing countries have also been expanding their exports of non-traditional products very rapidly. When China's RCA is calculated relative to exports from only developing countries other than China, as in the final column of Table 14.8, the decline in this RCA disappears.

The decline in the RCA for China's clothing exports from 5 to 3 over 13 years translates into a decline of about 4 per cent per annum in the share of clothing exports in China's total exports. Given the phenomenally high growth rate of China's total exports for this period (19 per cent on average), even China's exports of textiles and clothing are still growing extremely rapidly in absolute terms. If, however, the growth rate of China's overall exports should decline, such a strong shift in comparative advantage would substantially reduce the growth rate in the volume of China's exports.

Table 14.8 China's revealed comparative advantage

	Textiles[a]	Clothing[a]	Textiles and clothing[a]	Textiles and clothing[b]
1995	2.8	5.0	3.9	2.6
1996	2.6	5.1	3.9	2.9
1997	2.4	5.0	3.8	2.8
1998	2.3	4.7	3.6	2.5
1999	2.4	4.6	3.6	2.5
2000	2.4	4.6	3.6	2.7
2001	2.4	4.2	3.4	2.5
2002	2.4	3.9	3.2	2.4
2003	2.5	3.7	3.2	2.3
2004	2.5	3.5	3.1	2.3
2005	2.6	3.5	3.1	2.5
2006	2.6	3.7	3.2	2.9
2007	2.5	3.6	3.2	2.8
2008	2.5	3.0	2.8	2.9

[a] calculated relative to world exports
[b] calculated relative to exports from developing countries other than China

One key feature of the expansion of China's exports of textiles and clothing during the period of quota abolition has been rapid growth in China's imports of fibres, textiles and clothing, particularly from developing countries. In the period from 1995 to 2008, China's imports of these goods from developing countries grew by 14 per cent per annum, while imports of these goods from all sources rose by only 3.7 per cent per annum. Imports of cotton grew by 7 per cent per annum from all sources, but by 9.6 per cent per annum from developing countries. As noted by Martin et al. (2004), the growth of imports of inputs into the textile and clothing sector can be an important source of welfare gains to other developing countries, particularly to countries such as Pakistan, for which textile exports are hugely important, and for cotton exporters.

Conclusions

This study concludes that the quota regimes imposed under the MFA and the Agreement on Textiles and Clothing imposed very restrictive barriers against the expansion of textile and clothing exports from China. This restrictiveness was a consequence of the small initial quotas on China's exports, the low rates of growth permitted under these arrangements and the fact that quota phase-out and quota growth increases allowed to other countries under the Uruguay Round agreement did not apply to China until after its accession to the WTO in 2001.

China's WTO accession agreement allowed for textile safeguards that could apply between 2005 and 2008, after the quotas had been abolished for other WTO members. While many feared that these would be used in a very restrictive manner, their introduction appears to have involved a very substantial liberalisation of the market, with the quota levels and their growth rates both being much higher than under the earlier quota regimes.

China's exports of textiles and clothing to the United States and the European Union increased rapidly after 2001, and particularly rapidly in 2005 and subsequent years. China's shares of these markets grew dramatically—frequently doubling in less than a decade. China's global export shares in textiles and clothing grew much less rapidly, since much of the expansion of these exports could arise from redirection of exports from other markets to the formerly restricted markets of the United States and the European Union. It turns out that China's share of total global exports has also been growing, but much more slowly than her exports to the United States and the European Union. In fact, the evidence suggests that China's underlying comparative advantage in textiles and clothing is declining relative to global exports because of China's astoundingly successful expansion of other exports, particularly of products such as computers and components.

References

Bown, C. 2009, *Global Antidumping Database*, Version 5.0 Beta, May, Brandeis University, The Brookings Institution and The World Bank (Development Research Group), <http://people.brandeis.edu/~cbown/global_ad/>

Dimaranan, B., Ianchovichina, E. and Martin, W. 2007, 'Competing with giants: who wins, who loses?', in L. A. Winters and S. Yusuf (eds), *Dancing with Giants: China, India and the global economy*, The World Bank and Institute of Policy Studies, Washington, DC, and Singapore.

Elbehri, A., Hertel, T. and Martin, W. 2003, 'Estimating the impact of WTO and domestic reforms on the Indian cotton and textile sectors: a general equilibrium approach', *Review of Development Economics*, vol. 7, no. 3, pp. 343–59.

European Commission (EC) 2005a, 'Commission regulation (EC) no. 1084/2005', *Official Journal of the European Commission*, I. 177/19, 8 July 2005.

—— 2005b, 'Commission regulation (EC) no. 1478/2005', *Official Journal of the European Commission*, I. 263/3, 12 September 2005.

Francois, J. F. and Spinanger, D. 2000, *Hong Kong's Textile and Clothing Industry: The impact of quotas, the UR and China's WTO accession*, Kiel Institute of World Economics, Kiel, Germany.

Governments of the United States of America and of the People's Republic of China 2005, *Memorandum of Understanding Between the Governments of the United States of America and of the People's Republic of China Concerning Trade in Textiles and Apparel Products*, Office of the US Trade Representative, Washington, DC, <www.ustr.gov>

Ianchovichina, E. and Martin, W. 2004, 'Economic impacts of China's accession to the WTO', in D. Bhattasali, Shantong Li and W. Martin (eds), *China and the WTO: Accession, policy reform and poverty reduction*, Oxford University Press and The World Bank, Oxford and Washington, DC.

Lin, J. L. 2009, *Economic Development and Transition: Thought, strategy and viability*, Cambridge University Press, Cambridge.

Martin, W. and Manole, V. 2008, 'China's emergence as the workshop of the world', in B. Fleisher, N. Hope, A. Pena and D. Yang (eds), *Policy Reform and Chinese Markets: Progress and challenges*, Edward Elgar, Northampton, Mass.

Martin, W., Manole, V. and van der Mensbrugghe, D. 2004, Dealing with diversity: analyzing the consequences of textile quota abolition, Paper presented to the Conference on Global Economic Analysis, Washington, DC, September, <https://www.gtap.agecon.purdue.edu/dresources/download/1845.pdf>

Nordas, H. 2004, *The global textile and clothing industry post the Agreement on Textiles and Clothing*, Discussion Paper no. 5, World Trade Organisation, Geneva.

Reinert, K. 2000, 'Give us virtue, but not yet: safeguard actions under the Agreement on Textiles and Clothing', *World Economy*, vol. 23, no. 1, pp. 25–54.

World Trade Organisation (WTO) 2001, *Draft report of the working party on the accession of China*, WT/MIN(01)/3, World Trade Organisation, Geneva.

Yang, Y., Martin, W. and Yanagishima, K. 1997, 'Evaluating the benefits of abolishing the MFA in the Uruguay Round package', in T. Hertel (ed.), *Global Trade Analysis: Modelling and applications*, Cambridge University Press, Cambridge.

Endnotes

1. The system in use since the late 1990s involved allocating 70 per cent of the quota based on past performance to restricted (70 per cent weight) and unrestricted (30 per cent weight) markets. The other 30 per cent of the quota was allocated through an auction system.

Appendix 14.1

Appendix Table 14.1 Export tax equivalents of clothing quotas in the United States (per cent)

		Bangladesh	China	Hong Kong, China	India	Indonesia	Taiwan, China	Pakistan
237	Playsuits, sunsuits, etc.	4.2	3.2	0.0	0.0	1.1	0.0	0.0
239	Babies' garments and accessories	0.0	35.8	0.0	0.0	0.0	0.0	0.1
330	Handkerchiefs	0.0	0.0	0.0	0.0	0.0	0.0	0.0
331	Gloves and mittens	0.0	112.8	0.0	0.0	0.0	0.0	0.3
332	Hosiery	0.0	0.0	0.0	14.3	0.0	0.0	0.0
333	Men's and boys' suit-type coats	0.0	0.0	0.0	0.0	0.0	0.0	0.0
334	Other men's and boys' coats	22.3	37.3	0.0	0.6	7.8	0.0	3.7
335	Women's and girls' coats	9.1	44.4	0.0	0.2	7.9	0.3	0.2
336	Dresses	11.6	34.3	0.0	1.8	4.5	0.0	2.5
338	Men's and boys' knit shirts	43.9	23.2	0.0	2.2	9.3	9.4	11.1
339	Women's and girls' knit shirts and blouses	44.8	191.4	0.0	2.5	10.3	11.8	8
340	Men's and boys' shirts, not knit	6.7	60.8	0.0	2.6	2.7	0.0	0.6
341	Women's and girls' shirts, not knit	1.9	68.7	0.0	1.1	2.8	0.0	0.3
342	Skirts	43.7	143.5	0.0	1.2	16.5	0.0	0.2
345	Sweaters	0.0	42.3	0.0	0.0	17.5	0.0	0.0
347	Men's and boys' trousers and shorts	73.2	94.2	0.0	4.5	17.9	4.8	31.1
348	Women's and girls' trousers and shorts	74.5	77.2	0.0	4.6	17.8	3.8	36.2
349	Brassieres	0.0	0.0	0.0	0.0	0.0	0.0	0.0
350	Robes, dressing gowns	0.0	0.0	0.0	0.0	0.0	0.0	0.0

		Bangladesh	China	Hong Kong, China	India	Indonesia	Taiwan, China	Pakistan
351	Nightwear and pyjamas	17.0	57.2	0.0	1.8	14.5	0.0	10.4
352	Underwear	6.6	47.9	3.0	0.0	0.0	0.0	13.0
353	Men's and boys' down-filled coats	0.0	0.0	0.0	0.0	0.0	0.0	0.0
354	Women's and girls' down-filled coats	0.0	0.0	0.0	0.0	0.0	0.0	0.0
359	Other cotton apparel	0.0	13.5	3.7	9.0	0.0	0.0	0.4
431	Gloves and mittens	0.0	0.0	0.0	0.0	0.0	0.0	0.0
432	Hosiery	0.0	0.0	0.0	0.0	0.0	0.0	0.0
433	Men's and boys' suit coats	0.0	30.1	0.0	0.0	0.0	0.0	0.0
434	Other men's and boys' coats	0.0	30.5	3.7	0.0	0.0	0.0	0.0
435	Women's and girls' coats	0.0	52.0	1.3	0.0	0.0	0.0	0.0
436	Dresses	0.0	16.2	0.6	0.0	0.0	0.0	0.0
438	Knit shirts and blouses	0.0	34.7	0.7	0.0	0.0	0.0	0.0
439	Babies' garments and accessories	0.0	0.0	0.0	0.0	0.0	0.0	0.0
440	Shirts and blouses, not knit	0.0	0.0	0.0	0.0	0.0	0.0	0.0
442	Skirts	0.0	11.9	1.9	0.0	0.0	0.0	0.0
443	Men's and boys' suits	0.0	40.2	0.0	0.0	0.0	0.0	0.0
444	Women's and girls' suits	0.0	10.7	0.0	0.0	0.0	0.0	0.0
445	Men's and boys' sweaters	0.0	31.0	10.0	0.0	0.0	0.0	0.0
446	Women's and girls' sweaters	0.0	35.3	11.2	0.0	0.0	0.0	0.0
447	Men's and boys' trousers and shorts	0.0	41.6	4.5	0.0	0.0	0.0	0.0
448	Women's and girls' trousers and shorts	0.0	22.7	6.6	0.0	0.0	0.0	0.0
459	Other wool apparel	0.0	0.0	0.0	1.7	0.0	0.0	0.0
630	Handkerchiefs	0.0	0.0	0.0	0.0	0.0	0.0	0.0

		Bangladesh	China	Hong Kong, China	India	Indonesia	Taiwan, China	Pakistan
631	Gloves and mittens	0.0	55.2	0.0	0.0	0.0	0.0	0.1
632	Hosiery	0.0	0.0	0.0	0.0	0.0	0.0	0.0
633	Men's and boys' suit-type coats	0.0	42.1	0.3	0.0	0.0	0.0	0.0
634	Other men's and boys' coats	18.6	21.1	0.5	0.6	27.2	0.0	4.2
635	Women's and girls' coats (doz. 34.50)	25.8	31.0	0.4	0.2	39.0	0.0	0.3
636	Dresses	10.1	17.9	0.4	1.6	3.3	0.0	1.7
638	Men's and boys' knit shirts	6.2	78.6	9.0	0.0	4.3	0.0	10.1
639	Women's and girls' knit shirts and blouses	6.4	56.4	8.5	0.0	3.5	0.0	9.8
640	Men's and boys' shirts, not knit	5.6	49.6	0.6	2.8	3.4	0.0	0.8
641	Women's and girls' shirts and blouses, not knit	1.0	26.3	0.6	0.5	0.0	0.0	0.4
642	Skirts	37.8	85.3	10.2	1.2	0.0	0.0	0.0
643	Men's and boys' suits	0.0	60.1	0.0	0.0	0.0	0.0	0.0
644	Women's and girls' suits	0.0	28.0	0.0	0.0	0.0	0.0	0.0
645	Men's and boys' sweaters	11.4	60.6	4.5	0.0	5.7	0.0	0.0
646	Women's and girls' sweaters	12.1	35.6	4.3	0.0	4.7	0.0	0.0
647	Men's and boys' trousers and shorts	37.9	31.6	4.8	1.7	6.5	0.0	1.4
648	Women's and girls' trousers and shorts	30.7	37.8	8.4	1.8	5.2	0.0	1.7
649	Brassieres	0.0	114.2	0.0	0.0	0.0	0.0	0.0
650	Robes, dressing gowns	0.0	121.2	25.3	0.0	0.0	0.0	0.0
651	Nightwear and pyjamas	15.9	28.5	5.3	0.0	0.0	1.4	11.5
652	Underwear (doz. 13.40)	0.0	26.2	5.6	0.0	0.0	0.0	10.0
653	Men's and boys' down-filled coats	0.0	0.0	0.0	0.0	0.0	0.0	0.0
654	Women's and girls' down-filled coats	0.0	0.0	0.0	0.0	0.0	0.0	0.0

		Bangladesh	China	Hong Kong, China	India	Indonesia	Taiwan, China	Pakistan
659	Other man-made fibre apparel	0.0	9.2	2.3	15.7	0.0	0.0	0.3
831	Gloves and mittens	0.0	0.0	0.0	0.0	0.0	0.0	0.0
832	Hosiery	0.0	0.0	0.0	0.0	0.0	0.0	0.0
833	Men's and boys' suit-type coats	0.0	0.0	0.0	0.0	0.0	0.0	0.0
834	Other men's and boys' coats	0.0	0.0	0.0	0.0	0.0	0.0	0.0
835	Women's and girls' coats	0.0	0.0	0.0	0.0	0.0	0.0	0.0
836	Dresses (doz.)	0.0	0.0	0.0	0.0	0.0	0.0	0.0
838	Knit shirts and blouses	0.0	0.0	0.0	0.0	0.0	0.0	0.0
839	Babies' garments and accessories	0.0	0.0	0.0	0.0	0.0	0.0	0.0
840	Shirts and blouses, not knit	0.0	0.0	0.0	0.0	0.0	0.0	0.0
842	Skirts (doz.)	0.0	0.0	0.0	0.0	0.0	0.0	0.0
843	Men's and boys' suits	0.0	0.0	0.0	0.0	0.0	0.0	0.0
844	Women's and girls' suits	0.0	47.4	0.0	0.0	0.0	0.0	0.0
845	Sweaters, non-cotton vegetable fibres	0.0	13.4	1.0	0.0	0.0	0.0	0.0
846	Sweaters, of silk blends	0.0	2.7	0.5	0.0	0.0	0.0	0.0
847	Trousers and shorts	22.5	0.0	0.0	0.0	0.0	0.0	0.0
850	Robes, dressing gowns, etc.	0.0	0.0	0.0	0.0	0.0	0.0	0.0
851	Nightwear and pyjamas	0.0	0.0	0.0	0.0	0.0	0.0	0.0
852	Underwear	0.0	0.0	0.0	0.0	0.0	0.0	0.0
858	Neckwear	0.0	0.0	0.0	0.0	0.0	0.0	0.0
859	Other apparel	0.0	0.0	0.0	0.0	0.0	0.0	0.0
	Average	20.4	36.1	2.3	1.9	6.4	0.8	10.3
	Memo: % with positive export tax equivalents	31.4	61.6	34.9	34.9	27.9	8.1	32.6

Inflow of foreign direct investment

15

Chunlai Chen

Introduction

The global financial and economic crisis that started in 2008, triggered by the US sub-prime crisis, which began in the summer of 2007, has had an enormous negative impact on the world economy. The growth rate of global real gross domestic product (GDP) dropped from 5.2 per cent in 2007 to 3.2 per cent in 2008. It is expected that the world economy will contract by 1.3 per cent in 2009 (IMF 2009). The current global financial and economic crisis (hereafter 'the current crisis') has also generated a huge negative impact on flows of global foreign direct investment (FDI). World FDI flows declined sharply from a historic high of US$1833 billion in 2007 to US$1449 billion in 2008—a decrease of 21 per cent. As the full impact of the current crisis materialises, world FDI flows are expected to decline further in 2009 (UNCTAD 2009).

As the world's third-largest and fastest-growing economy—and the largest FDI recipient among the developing countries—China is not immune from the current crisis. China's GDP growth rate dropped from 11.4 per cent in 2007 to 9.6 per cent in 2008 and, according to the International Monetary Fund (IMF 2009), China's economy is expected to grow by 6.5 per cent in 2009, although the Chinese Government has set a growth target of 8 per cent for the year. Surprisingly, the current crisis had only a moderate impact on FDI inflows into China in 2008. FDI inflows into China (excluding those into financial sectors—the banking and insurance industries) increased by 24 per cent, from US$75 billion in 2007 to US$92 billion in 2008. As the current crisis worsened in the second half of 2008, however, the negative impact on FDI inflows into China gradually became apparent. Since October 2008, FDI inflows into China have declined for seven consecutive months, compared with the same period a year earlier.

The current crisis has had and will continue to have a negative impact on the world economy and on global FDI flows. What, however, will be the impact of the current crisis on FDI inflows into China? This is the key question that this chapter seeks to answer. The chapter is structured as follows. The next section discusses the mechanism of how the current crisis affects FDI flows by analysing the impact on the magnitude of FDI flows and on different types of FDI. This section provides a theoretical and analytical framework for the analysis in the next section of the impact of the current crisis on FDI inflows into China. Section three first presents a brief introduction to FDI inflows into China for the past three decades and describes the impact of the current crisis up to the first quarter of 2009. It then provides more detailed discussions about the impact of the current crisis on FDI inflows into China by analysing the nature and charactersistics of FDI in China, aiming to predict the impact of the current crisis. Based on the above analysis and discussion, section four provides some estimations for FDI inflows into China in 2009, while section five concludes the chapter.

How the current crisis affects FDI flows

The impact on the magnitude of FDI flows

After a sharp decline in 2001–03, global FDI flows increased rapidly and experienced a period of high growth during 2003–07, reaching a historic high of US$1833 billion in 2007. This trend came to an end in 2008 (Figure 15.1), when global FDI inflows declined by 21 per cent.

The current crisis began in the industrialised countries, although it is spreading rapidly to developing countries. Industrialised countries have therefore been hit directly by the current crisis, while developing countries have been affected indirectly. As a result, FDI inflows into industrialised countries declined sharply from US$1248 billion in 2007 to US$840 billion in 2008—a drop of 33 per cent. In contrast, FDI inflows into developing countries remained stable, increasing by 3.6 per cent, from US$500 billion in 2007 to US$518 billion in 2008 (Figure 15.1).

Figure 15.1 Global FDI inflows (at current prices)

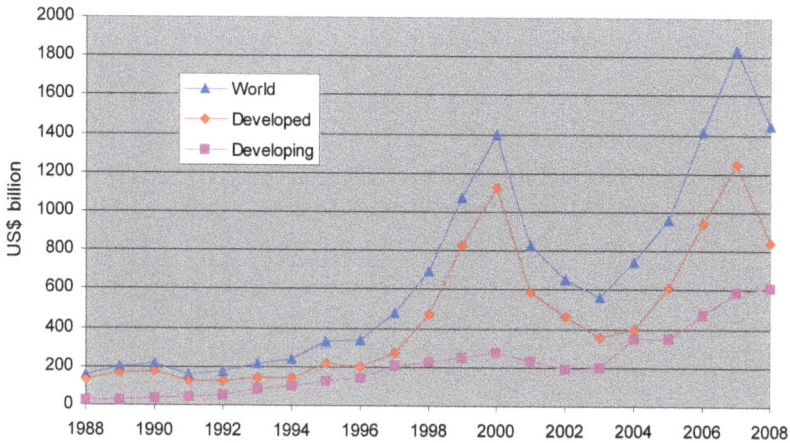

Sources: United Nations Conference on Trade and Development (UNCTAD) various issues, *World Investment Report*, United Nations Publications, New York and Geneva; United Nations Conference on Trade and Development (UNCTAD) 2009, *Assessing the Impact of the Current Financial and Economic Crisis on Global FDI Flows*, United Nations, New York and Geneva, viewed 21 May 2009, <http://www.unctad.org/en/docs/webdiaeia20091_en.pdf>

The current crisis affects FDI flows in three main aspects. It affects multinational enterprises' (MNEs) capacity to invest as a result of reduced availability of finance internally and externally. It affects MNEs' propensity to invest due to gloomy economic and market prospects. And it affects MNEs' risk-taking behaviour through the scaling back of existing investment plans due to a high level of perceived risk and uncertainty (UNCTAD 2009).

First, the environment has deteriorated rapidly across financial markets worldwide and has negatively affected MNEs' capacity to invest as tighter credit conditions and lower corporate profits reduce MNEs' financial resources for investment projects at home and abroad. On the one hand, credit has become less abundant and more expensive. The external funding environment for non-financial companies has deteriorated markedly since mid-2008, making it more difficult for them to invest in foreign operations or to make cross-border merger and acquisition deals. On the other hand, the poor earnings of large companies in a broad range of industries in the United States, Europe and Japan reduce the companies' self-financing capabilities. At the same time, the sharp decline (more than 40 per cent) in stock markets worldwide has reduced MNEs' ability to turn to stock markets for financing purposes and to leverage their cross-border merger and acquisition activities using stock shares (UNCTAD 2009).

Second, the sharp economic recession worldwide, especially in a number of industrial countries such as the United States, Japan, Germany and the United Kingdom, and a heightened appreciation of risk have also reduced MNEs' propensity to invest in further expansion of production capacity domestically and internationally (UNCTAD 2009). According to the latest IMF (2009) forecasts, global output is expected to contract by 1.3 per cent in 2009, and industrialised countries are expected to contract by 3.8 per cent. Deep recessions are forecast for all major industrialised economies. The United States is expected to contract by 2.8 per cent in 2009, the euro area by 4.2 per cent, the United Kingdom by 4.1 per cent, Japan by 6.2 per cent and other advanced economies by 3.9 per cent. As a result, FDI flows in industrialised countries are expected to decline further by a large amount in 2009.

The economic growth for developing economies is expected to slow substantially, from 6.1 per cent in 2008 to 1.6 per cent in 2009. Among the developing economies, those in Asia are expected to grow by 4.8 per cent, which is much lower than the growth rates of 10.6 per cent in 2007 and 7.7 per cent in 2008. Compared with industrialised economies, however, in the Asian developing economies economic growth is more resilient. Therefore, FDI flows in developing economies as a whole are expected to decline in 2009; however, this decline is expected to be moderate.

Third, the current crisis could also affect MNEs' risk-taking behaviour. MNEs' investment plans could be scaled back, especially in industrialised countries, due to a high level of perceived risk and uncertainty, in order to develop resilience to possible worst-case scenarios regarding financial and economic conditions.

Therefore, as the full consequences of the current crisis for MNEs' investment expenditure continue to unfold, there are reasons to expect that global FDI flows will decline further in 2009. Based on information from the UN Conference on Trade and Development (UNCTAD 2009), global FDI flows are expected to decline by 25 per cent in 2009 to about US$1000 billion—driven mainly by a large decline in FDI flows in industrialised countries, while developing countries are expected to witness a moderate decline.

The impact on different types of FDI flows

The current crisis has had and will continue to have a negative impact on global FDI flows. However, the impact differs according to the types and entry modes of FDI.

In terms of the types, FDI can be classified as efficiency seeking (mostly export oriented), market seeking (market oriented) and resource seeking (mostly export oriented). All three types are impacted by the current crisis, but the magnitude of the impact differs for different types of FDI in different locations.

The FDI type most directly affected has been market-seeking projects, especially those aimed at industrialised countries. As industrialised countries are expected to experience negative growth in 2009, MNEs are restraining the launching of new projects aimed at increasing their market-oriented production capabilities. MNEs might, however, remain more committed to capacity expansion in developing countries. This commitment might, however, weaken in 2009 as growth slows in developing countries due to a decline in the value of their exports as a result of weakening external demand from industrialised countries and a fall in commodity and energy prices (UNCTAD 2009).

The impact of the current crisis on efficiency-seeking FDI is more difficult to assess. On the one hand, this type of FDI will suffer globally from the decline in the MNEs' financial capabilities. On the other hand, many MNEs might be compelled by the continuing crisis to restructure their international activities to cut costs and boost overall efficiency. This means they might close or downsize obsolete or non-cost-competitive facilities (often located in industrialised counties); however, they might also open new cost-efficient facilities, especially in developing countries, or shift production facilities from industrialised to developing countries (UNCTAD 2009).[1]

Resource-seeking FDI could suffer, at least in the short run, from the decline in global demand and consequently in prices, with particularly negative effects on resource-rich developing countries. Resource-seeking FDI will, however, rise quickly again once the current recession is over, as rapidly rising global demand triggers imbalances in commodity markets, boosting prices and leading MNEs to launch many new projects.

In terms of the entry modes, FDI can take the form of greenfield investment and cross-border mergers and acquisitions. Greenfield investment is financed by equity capital, reinvested earnings and intra-company loans (between a parent company and a subsidiary). Cross-border mergers and acquisitions can be financed in several ways, including through FDI (the purchase of foreign equity shares at least 10 per cent of the total equity), portfolio equity investments (less than 10 per cent of the total equity), domestically raised capital and capital raised from international capital markets. Therefore, not all cross-border mergers and acquisitions are financed through FDI; however, in industrialised countries, most are.

There is evidence that cross-border mergers and acquisitions have been sharply affected as a direct consequence of the current crisis. Cross-border mergers and acquisitions declined from US$1637 billion in 2007 to US$1184 billion in 2008. This sharp decline was due mainly to the fact that leveraged buy-outs—a common transaction method in mergers and acquisitions—fell considerably due to weakened world stock markets (UNCTAD 2009). The decline in cross-border mergers and acquisitions is of utmost importance for FDI flows, especially for FDI flows in industrialised countries, which are strongly correlated with cross-border mergers and acquisitions.

Greenfield investments seemed to be resilient to the crisis in 2008. According to UNCTAD (2009), at the end of October, the number of greenfield investments since the beginning of 2008 was already more than 13 000, exceeding the level registered for the whole of 2007. The current crisis might, however, have some negative impact on greenfield investments in 2009 as the world recession worsens. Compared with cross-border mergers and acquisitions, however, the impact of the current crisis on greenfield FDI is relatively moderate.

Therefore, in terms of the types of FDI, the current crisis will have more direct negative impacts on FDI inflows into industrialised countries for market-seeking FDI and efficiency-seeking FDI, while the negative impact on FDI inflows into developing countries will be small for market-seeking FDI and moderate for efficiency-seeking FDI. In terms of the entry modes, the current crisis will have more direct negative impacts on cross-border mergers and acquisitions, while the impact on greenfield FDI will be moderate.

The impact of the current crisis on FDI inflows into China

As the largest FDI recipient among the developing countries, China will undoubtedly be affected by the current crisis. What, however, will be the impacts on FDI inflows into China? This section will analyse both the nature of FDI and the special characteristics of FDI in China.

The trend of FDI inflows into China

In the past three decades, China has attracted a large volume of FDI inflows. The growth of FDI inflows into China from 1982 to 2008 can be broadly divided into three phases: the experimental phase from 1982 to 1991; the boom phase from 1992 to 2001; and the post-World Trade Organisation (WTO) phase from 2002 to 2008 (Figure 15.2).

Figure 15.2 FDI inflows into China (at current prices)

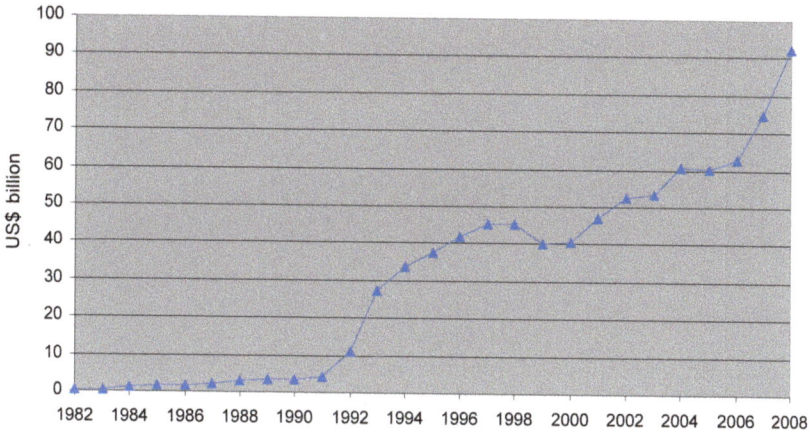

Sources: National Bureau of Statistics (NBS) various issues, *China Statistical Yearbook*, China Statistics Press, Beijing; Ministry of Commerce (MOFCOM) 2009a, 'FDI statistics', *Invest in China*, Ministry of Commerce, Beijing, viewed 21 May 2009, <http://www.fdi.gov.cn/pub/FDI_EN/Statistics/FDIStatistics/default.htm>

During the experimental phase, FDI inflows into China were at low levels but grew steadily. In the second phase, FDI inflows increased very rapidly. FDI inflows into China slowed, however, after 1997 and declined in 1999 and 2000—due mainly to the East Asian financial crisis. Since China's entry into the WTO in 2001, with the implementation of its WTO commitments and broader and deeper liberalisation in trade and investment, China's economy has been growing very rapidly. As a result, FDI inflows into China present an increasing trend—rising from US$47 billion in 2001 to US$75 billion in 2007. In 2008, despite the current crisis and the sharp decline in world FDI, FDI inflows into China increased by 23.58 per cent to reach US$92 billion.[2]

The current crisis has, however, had gradual and progressive negative impacts on FDI inflows into China since the second quarter and especially since October 2008. Based on the quarterly data, FDI inflows into China declined continuously in 2008 (Figure 15.3). FDI inflows into China decreased by 8.9 per cent and by 11.96 per cent in the second and third quarters, respectively, compared with those in the pervious quarters. The negative impact of the crisis on FDI inflows into China started to worsen in October 2008.

Figure 15.3 Quarterly FDI inflows into China (at current prices)

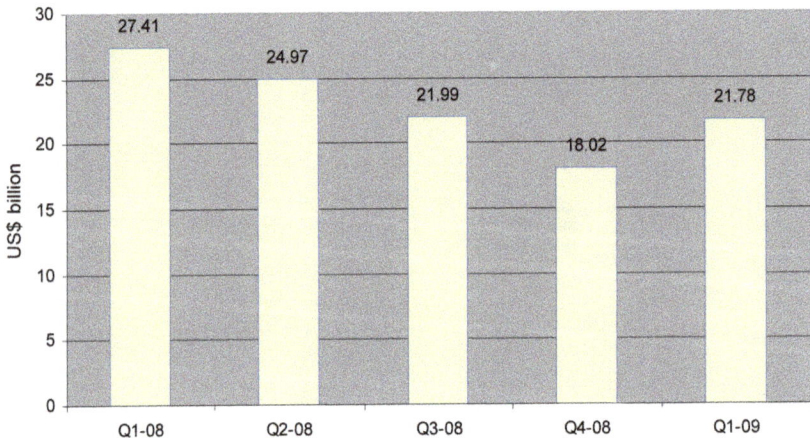

Sources: Ministry of Commerce (MOFCOM) 2009a, 'FDI statistics', *Invest in China*, Ministry of Commerce, Beijing, viewed 21 May 2009, <http://www.fdi.gov.cn/pub/FDI_EN/Statistics/FDIStatistics/default.htm>

In the first quarter of 2009, FDI inflows into China were US$22 billion, increasing 21 per cent from those in the fourth quarter, but still lower than those in the first and second quarters of 2008. It is, however, a positive sign of recovery—from a declining trend for three consecutive quarters to an increasing trend.

The composition of FDI sources in China

FDI in China is overwhelmingly dominated by developing source economies, particularly the Asian newly industrialising economies (NIEs). During the period 1992–2008, developing economies accounted for 77 per cent of the total accumulated FDI inflows into China, while industrialised economies accounted for only 23 per cent. Among the developing economies, Hong Kong is the largest single investor (41 per cent), next is Taiwan (5.86 per cent), South Korea (4.9 per cent), Singapore (4.5 per cent) and ASEAN+4 (1.6 per cent). Among the industrialised economies, Japan (7.5 per cent) and the United States (7 per cent) are the largest investors, while the European Union-15 as a group accounted for 7.2 per cent of the total accumulated FDI inflows into China.[3] Tax havens, for example, Virgin Islands (10.2 per cent), were the immediate source of some investment. These have been counted as developing countries.

There are two interesting points about the annual FDI inflows into China by developing and industrialised economies during the period 1992–2008 (Figure 15.4). First, FDI inflows into China slowed and then declined during 1997–2000. This was caused entirely by the decline of FDI inflows from developing economies due to the East Asian financial crisis. The East Asian financial crisis, which started in 1997 and lasted until the early 2000s, substantially weakened the capacity for outward investment of the Asian developing economies. As a result, FDI inflows into China from these economies declined substantially during 1997–2000. During this period, however, FDI inflows into China from industrialised economies were relatively stable at about US$12 billion.

Second, after China's accession into the WTO, FDI inflows into China increased rapidly, which was almost entirely the result of the large increase of FDI inflows from developing economies—from US$33 billion in 2001 to US$80 billion in 2008, with an annual growth rate of 13 per cent. FDI inflows from industrialised economies, however, increased only marginally during 2002–05, and then declined during 2006–08. As a result, the share of developing economies in total FDI inflows into China increased from 75 per cent in 1992–2001 to 80 per cent in 2002–08, while the share of industrialised economies declined from 25 per cent to 20 per cent in the same period.

Figure 15.4 FDI inflows into China by source economies
(at current prices)

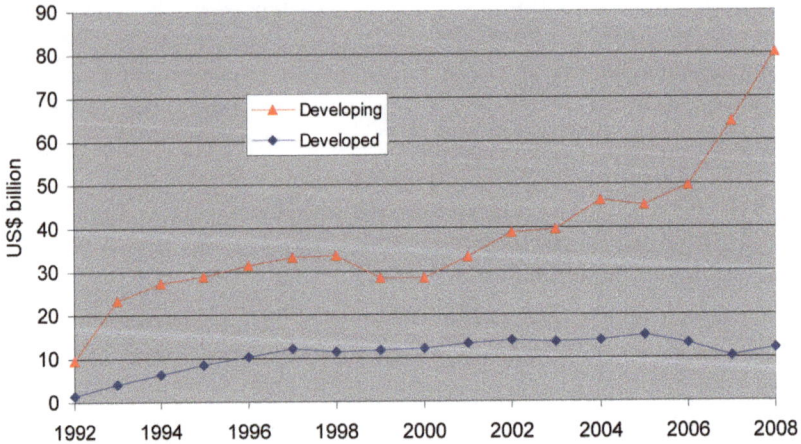

Sources: National Bureau of Statistics (NBS) various issues, *China Statistical Yearbook*, China Statistics Press, Beijing; Ministry of Commerce (MOFCOM) 2009a, 'FDI statistics', *Invest in China*, Ministry of Commerce, Beijing, viewed 21 May 2009, <http://www.fdi.gov.cn/pub/FDI_EN/Statistics/FDIStatistics/default.htm>

Unlike the 1997 East Asian financial crisis, which originated in developing economies and had a significant negative impact on FDI outflows from Asian developing economies, the current crisis began in the industrialised economies—in particular, the United States and the European Union—and this will substantially reduce the outward FDI flows from these economies.

In contrast, Asian economies, particularly the Asian developing economies, are the major sources for China's FDI inflows. As the Asian economies have suffered a lighter impact from the current crisis, their financial institutions are in better position than many of their counterparts in the Western industrialised economies. Although FDI inflows into China from Asian countries could decline moderately in the short term, as the impact of the current crisis recedes, Asian investments will recover and China's FDI inflows from Asian economies, especially Asian developing economies, will resume their robust growth. As a result, the current crisis will have a moderately negative impact on China's FDI inflows.

Figure 15.5 FDI inflows and cross-border mergers and acquisitions in China (at current prices)

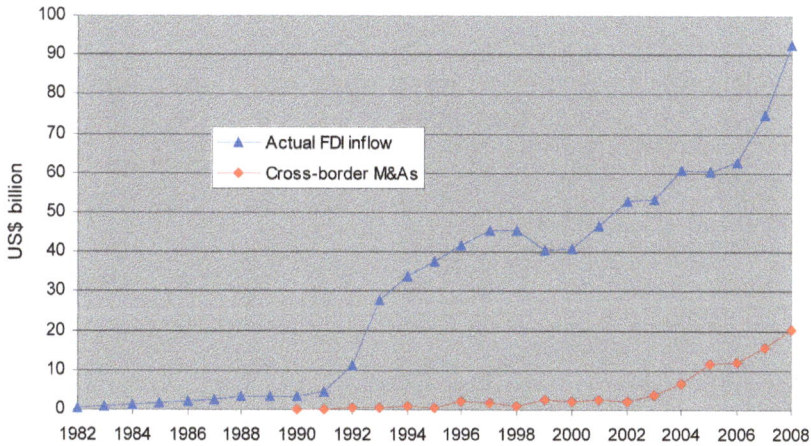

Sources: United Nations Conference on Trade and Development (UNCTAD) 2009, *Assessing the Impact of the Current Financial and Economic Crisis on Global FDI Flows*, United Nations, New York and Geneva, viewed 21 May 2009, <http://www.unctad.org/en/docs/webdiaeia20091_en.pdf>; United Nations Conference on Trade and Development (UNCTAD) various issues, *World Investment Report*, United Nations Publications, New York and Geneva.

The entry modes of FDI in China

FDI in China is overwhelmingly conducted through greenfield investment, which accounts for more than 95 per cent of FDI inflows into China. Cross-border mergers and acquisitions were prohibited in China before 1990. They were allowed in an experimental fashion in the 1990s, and started to increase only after 2002 (Figure 15.5). As not all cross-border mergers and acquisitions are related to FDI—especially for cross-border mergers and acquisitions in developing countries—the importance of cross-border mergers and acquisitions in FDI inflows to China has been very low. FDI inflows and cross-border mergers and acquisitions in China are, however, closely correlated and have moved in the same direction, especially since 2002.

The relative importance of cross-border mergers and acquisitions to FDI inflows has been very low in China compared with the rest of the world. The ratio of cross-border mergers and acquisitions to FDI in the world was about 70 per cent and increased to more than 80 per cent after 2005 (Figure 15.6). In contrast, the ratio of cross-border mergers and acquisitions to FDI in China was below 5 per cent and increased to about 20 per cent after 2005.

Figure 15.6 The ratio of cross-border mergers and acquisitions to FDI in the world and China

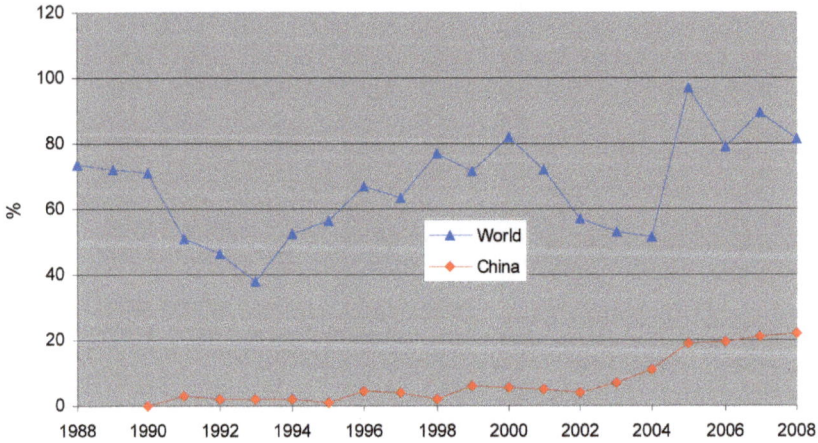

Sources: United Nations Conference on Trade and Development (UNCTAD) various issues, *World Investment Report*, United Nations Publications, New York and Geneva; United Nations Conference on Trade and Development (UNCTAD) 2009, *Assessing the Impact of the Current Financial and Economic Crisis on Global FDI Flows*, United Nations, New York and Geneva, viewed 21 May 2009, < http://www.unctad.org/en/docs/webdiaeia20091_en.pdf >

The current crisis will have a larger negative impact on cross-border mergers and acquisitions than on greenfield investment. Because FDI in China has been overwhelmingly dominated by greenfield investment and cross-border mergers and acquisitions account for only a very small share of total FDI inflows, the current crisis will have a moderately negative impact on FDI inflows into China. There are, however, also a lot of opportunities for cross-border merger and acquisition deals in China. As the Chinese Government further liberalises its policies, the momentum for cross-border mergers and acquisitions in China could remain strong.[4]

Sectoral structure of FDI in China

By the end of 2008, the sectoral distribution of FDI in China was characterised by its concentration in the manufacturing sector. The manufacturing sector attracted 63 per cent of the total FDI inflows into China during the period 1997–2008, the services sector attracted 35 per cent, while the primary sector attracted only 2.5 per cent.[5]

Figure 15.7 FDI inflows into China by sector (at current prices)

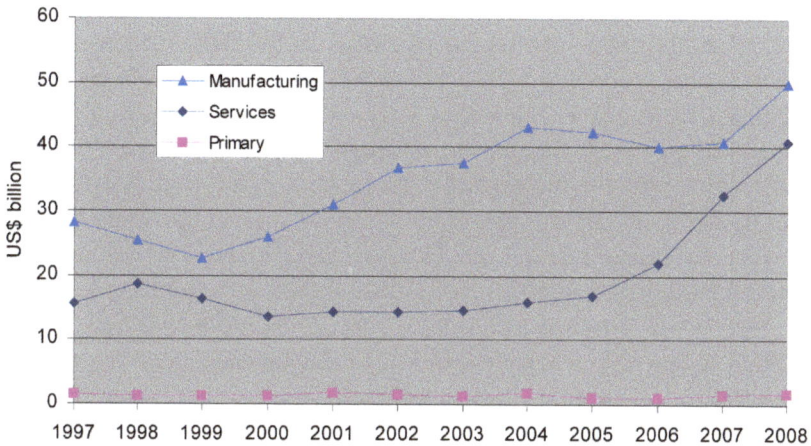

Note: Excluding FDI inflows into the financial sector (banking and insurance industries).

Sources: National Bureau of Statistics (NBS) various issues, *China Statistical Yearbook*, China Statistics Press, Beijing; Ministry of Commerce (MOFCOM) 2009a, 'FDI statistics', *Invest in China*, Ministry of Commerce, Beijing, viewed 21 May 2009, <http://www.fdi.gov.cn/pub/FDI_EN/Statistics/FDIStatistics/default.htm>

The sectoral structure of FDI in China is different to that in the rest of the world, where the services sector accounts for more than 60 per cent of the total global FDI. The sectoral structure of FDI in China has, however, been gradually changing from a heavy concentration in the manufacturing sector towards increasing inflows into the services sector. Although the manufacturing sector continued to receive large amounts of FDI inflows after China's accession into the WTO in 2001, the growth rate of inflows into the manufacturing sector has slowed since 2004 (Figure 15.7). In contrast, FDI inflows into the services sector have increased rapidly since 2005. By 2008, the share of FDI inflows into the services sector increased to 44 per cent, while the share of FDI inflows into the manufacturing sector declined to 54 per cent. FDI inflows into the primary sector have been at a low but relatively stable level.

Undoubtedly, the current crisis will have a negative impact on FDI inflows into China in all three economic sectors. However, the extent of the impact on each sector will be different according to the nature of the FDI.

The manufacturing sector

For the manufacturing sector, in terms of the capital to labour ratio, FDI can be classified into labour-intensive industries, capital-intensive industries and technology-intensive industries. In terms of the market orientation, FDI can be classified into domestic market-oriented FDI (market-seeking FDI) and export-oriented FDI (efficiency-seeking and resource-seeking FDI). In general, FDI in labour-intensive industries in China is aimed mainly at taking advantage of low labour costs in order to reduce production costs and increase competitiveness in the world market. Therefore, FDI in China's labour-intensive industries is mainly export oriented. In contrast, FDI in capital-intensive and technology-intensive industries is mainly looking at the Chinese domestic market, though there has been an increasing trend in exports of some products from these industries (for example, general machines, electronics, electric machines and equipment). Therefore, FDI in China's capital-intensive and technology-intensive industries is mainly market oriented.

In the past three decades, FDI inflows into China's manufacturing sector have gradually shifted from being heavily concentrated in labour-intensive industries, which is mainly export-oriented FDI, towards more investment in capital-intensive and technology-intensive industries, which are mainly domestic market-oriented FDI.

From 1995 to 2006, the share of labour-intensive industries in the industrial composition of FDI firms in the manufacturing sector had declined while the share of capital-intensive industries—especially the share of technology-intensive industries—increased (Figure 15.8). The share of labour-intensive industries declined from 47 per cent in 1995 to 30 per cent in 2006, while the shares of capital-intensive and technology-intensive industries increased from 25 per cent and 27 per cent in 1995 to 31 per cent and 38 per cent in 2006, respectively.

The changing industrial structure of FDI firms—from their high concentration in labour-intensive industries towards more investment in capital-intensive and technology-intensive industries—is clearly an indication that FDI inflows have been increasingly targeting China's huge domestic market. In other words, more than half of the FDI in China's manufacturing sector is domestic market oriented and that share is increasing.

Figure 15.8 Structural changes of FDI firms in manufacturing by total assets

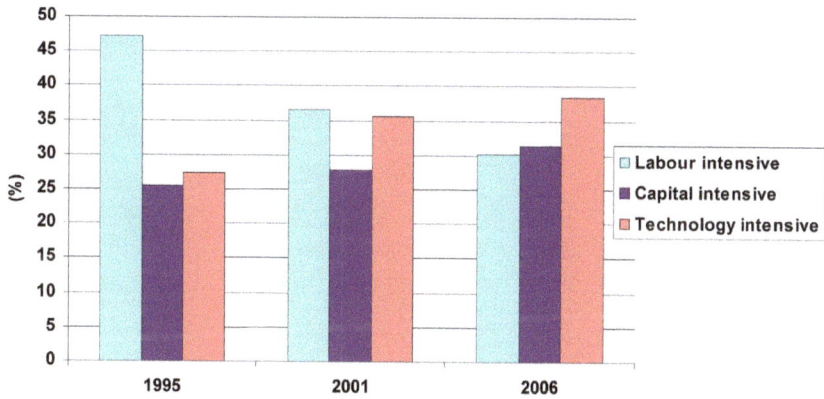

Source: National Bureau of Statistics (NBS) various issues, *China Statistical Yearbook*, China Statistics Press, Beijing.

The current crisis will have a large negative impact on market-seeking FDI in industrialised countries because of the expected negative economic growth there. Market-seeking FDI in developing countries, however, is expected to remain committed because of positive economic growth in 2009. This high economic growth will increase China's domestic market demand and provide good opportunities for market-seeking FDI. Therefore, market-seeking manufacturing FDI inflows into China are expected to experience a moderate decline or remain stable in 2009.

China's labour-intensive industries are quite competitive, with abundant and well-educated human resources and low labour costs, making China one of the most attractive locations for efficiency-seeking and export-oriented FDI. The current crisis will have a two-pronged impact on efficiency-seeking FDI in China. On the one hand, the weakening of the global economy—especially the severe economic recession in industrialised countries—has greatly reduced the external demand for China's exports. This will have a negative impact on FDI inflows into China's labour-intensive industries. On the other hand, to reduce production costs and restructure global production, MNEs might shift their production from industrialised countries to developing countries. Undoubtedly, China will be one of the most attractive locations for efficiency-seeking MNEs' offshore production. Therefore, the current crisis will have some negative impacts on efficiency-seeking FDI inflows into China, but the impact will be moderate.

In the first quarter of 2009, FDI inflows into the manufacturing sector were US$12 billion. This represented a decline of 11.5 per cent from the same period in 2008, but decreasing by only 0.66 per cent from the average quarterly FDI inflows into the manufacturing sector in 2008. Against the general declining trend, in the first quarter of 2009, FDI inflows into some manufacturing industries even increased. For example, FDI inflows into the communication equipment, computer and other electronic equipment industry increased by 11.5 per cent; into the medical and pharmaceutical industry, they increased by 10.3 per cent; and into the general-purpose machinery industry, they increased by 6.2 per cent. FDI inflows into China's manufacturing sector are expected to remain relatively stable with a moderate decline in 2009.

The services sector

FDI inflows into China's services sector were about 32 per cent of total FDI inflows during 1997–2006 and increased to about 44 per cent in 2007–08. Among the services sector, FDI inflows into the real estate industry accounted for about 35 per cent during 1997–2006. In 2007 and 2008, FDI inflows into the real estate industry increased rapidly to about 50 per cent of the total FDI inflows into the services sector. Therefore, the sharp increase in FDI inflows into the services sector during 2007–08 was driven mainly by the large increase in inflows into real estate.

The large increase of FDI inflows into the real estate industry in recent years has two main causes. First, some foreign investors aimed to take advantage of the booming housing market in China, where house prices skyrocketed in the past couple of years. Second, some foreign investors were speculating on a sharp appreciation of the Chinese currency against the US dollar in order to make windfalls from the change in exchange rates. Obviously, such FDI inflows are not only speculative in nature, they are unstable. Therefore, the current crisis will have a large negative impact on such FDI. In fact, compared with the same period in 2008, in the first quarter of 2009, FDI inflows into the real estate industry declined sharply, by 38 per cent, which accounted for 61 per cent of the total decline of FDI inflows into the services sector. As a result, FDI inflows into other service industries declined only 12 per cent in the first quarter of 2009 compared with the first quarter of 2008, but actually increased slightly compared with the average quarterly FDI inflows in 2008.

FDI inflows into China's services sector are mainly domestic market oriented. Although the value of China's services exports has been increasing since 2002, the share of services in China's total exports has been about 10 per cent and has shown a declining trend since 2003. Manufactured exports have grown more rapidly. The current crisis has had a large negative impact on FDI flows into the services sector, especially in financial industries such as banking and insurance, in industrialised countries. The impact of the current crisis on FDI inflows into the services sector in developing countries, however, should be relatively moderate because of the higher economic growth and the market-oriented nature of FDI in this sector. Therefore, it is expected that, except for the real estate industry, FDI inflows into China's other services sector will be relatively stable in 2009. If the Chinese economy recovers in the second half of 2009, the real estate industry will regain its attractiveness to FDI. Overall, FDI inflows into China's services sector could witness a relatively large decline in 2009, driven mainly by the decline in FDI inflows into the real estate industry.

The primary sector

FDI inflows into China's primary sector have been very low but relatively stable at about 2.5 per cent. They have been constrained more by institutional and policy factors than by economic factors. China's agricultural land tenure system and the traditional pattern of small-scale family-based agricultural production have greatly limited the inflows of agricultural FDI with large-scale production and advanced technologies. Therefore, China will not attract large amounts of FDI inflows into its agricultural sector without fundamentally changing its land tenure system and dramatically reforming the traditional farming pattern. China's FDI policies for mining industries are relatively restricted. According to China's *Industrial Guideline for Foreign Direct Investment* (amended in 2007), FDI is either restricted or prohibited in most mining industries, except for coal (excluding special coal), petroleum, natural gas, iron ore and manganese. Therefore, unless China liberalises its FDI policies for the mining industries, there will not be a large increase in FDI inflows. Consequently, the current crisis will have a marginal impact on FDI inflows into China's primary sector.

Prospects for FDI inflows into China

The current crisis has greatly reduced global economic growth, particularly in the industrialised countries. As a result, external demand for China's exports has been negatively affected. The external demand for China's exports has been a very important component of China's high economic growth. The contribution of net exports to China's GDP growth was, on average, about 20 per cent during 2005–07. Apart from the direct contribution of exports to China's economic growth, there have been a lot of indirect economic activities generated by the export sector. For example, large portions of local services and local investment are connected with export industries, whose employees also generate multiplier effects in the economy.

One of the major risks to China's economic recovery from the current crisis and its overall economic growth lies in the external side and China could undergo long-term economic and structural adjustments given the fact that its major trading partners—the United States, Japan and the European Union—could take three to five years to come out of recession.[6] Therefore, a full recovery of China's economy will depend on developments in the world economy, particularly the advanced economies.

In the first quarter of 2009, China's exports continued to fall—by 20 per cent—compared with the same period in 2008. The negative impact on exports was much more severe for foreign-invested enterprises (FIEs). The exports of FIEs decreased by 23 per cent in the first quarter of 2009, compared with the same period in 2008. Undoubtedly, this will have a negative impact on the ability of labour-intensive and export-oriented manufacturing industries to attract FDI inflows.

While the current crisis will continue to generate negative impacts on FDI inflows into China, various positive factors are also at work and will attract inflows in 2009 and coming years.

There are a number of reasons why MNEs might remain committed to investing in China. First, China's overall investment environment is quite competitive. Relatively efficient public services, good infrastructure, a large and rapidly growing domestic market, abundant and well-educated human resources, low labour costs and macroeconomic and political stability—make China one of the most attractive locations for FDI.

China, as the largest developing and fastest growing economy, has remained attractive to FDI, particularly to market-seeking FDI. As economic prospects continue to deteriorate in industrialised countries, investors will favour the relatively more profitable options available in developing countries. A survey by the US–China Business Council in March 2009 revealed that 88 per cent of foreign businesses in China were profitable, 81 per cent had a higher profit margin in China than elsewhere and 89 per cent selected China as their first-time investment location ('China's FDI decline slows in March', *Xinhuanet*, viewed 21 May 2009, <http://news.xinhuanet.com/english/2009-04/14/content_11181782.htm>).

China's abundant and relatively well-educated labour force and its low labour costs remain attractive to labour-intensive and export-oriented FDI projects. China's labour-intensive products are mostly daily consumer goods, which have a relatively low elasticity of demand. Therefore, the negative impact of the economic recession on demand for China's labour-intensive products is relatively small compared with luxury consumer goods. In April 2009, although China's total exports continued to decline by 5.5 per cent from March, exports of some major labour-intensive products actually increased. For example, exports of textiles and clothing increased by 7.6 per cent, furniture increased by 2.7 per cent, footwear increased by 3.8 per cent, suitcases and handbags increased by 22.4 per cent and toys increased by 18 per cent (MOFCOM 2009b). This is a good sign that exports of labour-intensive products will lead the overall recovery of China's exports and it is also a positive signal to efficiency-seeking FDI to increase investment in China's labour-intensive industries. Therefore, China will continue to attract efficiency-seeking FDI inflows, including the diversion of efficiency-seeking FDI from industrialised and other developing countries.

China has implemented a series of favourable FDI and trade policies that will have a positive impact on FDI inflows. China decentralised FDI approval rights in March 2009 and provincial authorities now have the right to approve FDI projects of less than US$100 million. China has increased the tax rebate for exports six times since 2008 for some export products. As a result, the comprehensive tax rebate reached 12.4 per cent.[7]

China has been arranging currency swaps with trading partners to bypass the US dollar in trade settlements. These swap accords allow overseas central banks to sell the renminbi to local importers who want to buy Chinese goods. Since mid-December 2008, China has signed currency swap contracts worth RMB650 billion (US$95.6 billion) with central banks in Hong Kong, South Korea, Malaysia, Belarus, Indonesia and Argentina. In April 2009, the Chinese State Council gave the green light to five major trade cities—Shanghai, Guangzhou, Shenzhen, Zhuhai and Dongguan—to use the renminbi as an option to settle international trade deals. A similar arrangement has been proposed for exporters in Guangxi and Yunnan in southern China, who will be allowed to use the renminbi to settle trade with Association of South-East Asian Nations (ASEAN) members from 2009. These arrangements will benefit manufacturers and traders at home and abroad by reducing their exposure to exchange rate volatility, increasing liquidity in foreign trade and reducing consumer burdens ('Yuan edges into place as international trade currency', *Xinhuanet*, viewed 21 May 2009, <http://news.xinhuanet.com/english/2009-04/16/content_11194529.htm>).

China has also implemented a series of concrete measures to facilitate trade, especially exports—for example, by supporting small and medium-sized enterprises (SMEs) to explore international markets, especially new markets in emerging economies, which will cover 80 000 SMEs in 2009; adjusting processing trade category lists, by dropping 27 categories from the prohibited list and 1730 categories from the restricted list; and improving trade facilitation by reducing red tape in customs procedures (MOFCOM 2009b). These policy changes are necessary to deal with the current crisis, increase exports and boost economic growth, which will have a positive impact on attracting FDI inflows.

Conclusion

The current crisis has severely affected the world economy as well as global FDI flows. As the impacts of the continuing crisis unfold, the global economy is expected to shrink by 1.3 per cent and global FDI flows are expected to decline by 25 per cent in 2009. As the third-largest economy in the world and the largest FDI recipient among the developing countries, China is not immune to the current crisis. Its economic growth is expected to decline from a high of more than 10 per cent annually in the past decade to about 8 per cent (the level set by the Chinese Government) or 6.5 per cent (forecast by the IMF) in 2009. FDI inflows into China have also been negatively affected by the crisis, especially since October 2008. Compared with the sharp decline of global FDI inflows, however, the negative impact of the current crisis on FDI inflows into China has been moderate. Why have FDI inflows into China been resilisent and what will be the impact of the current crisis on inflows in 2009?

Industrialised countries have been hit directly by the current crisis, while developing countries have been affected only indirectly. As a result, FDI inflows into China from industrialised economies—particularly from the United States and the European Union—will decline by a relatively big margin, but FDI inflows from developing economies, particularly from the Asian developing economies, are expected to decline only moderately. Because about 80 per cent of FDI inflows into China come from developing economies, the overall negative impact of the current crisis on FDI inflows into China will be moderate.

The current crisis will have a larger negative impact on cross-border mergers and acquisitions than on greenfield investment. On the one hand, leveraged buy-outs—a common transaction method in cross-border mergers and acquisitions—have fallen considerably due to weakened world stock markets. On the other hand, the deterioration of the external funding environment has also made it more difficult for MNEs to make cross-border merger and acquisition deals. In contrast, the impact of the current crisis on greenfield FDI projects has been limited. Because more than 95 per cent of FDI inflows into China are greenfield investments, the negative impact of the current crisis on overall FDI inflows into China is therefore expected to be moderate.

The current crisis will have a moderately negative impact on FDI inflows into China's manufacturing sector, mainly on efficiency-seeking manufacturing FDI. The impact of the current crisis on FDI inflows into the services sector will be larger than that on FDI inflows into the manufacturing sector; however, most of the negative impact will be on FDI inflows into the real estate industry. FDI inflows into the other service industries are expected to remain stable. Finally, the impact of the current crisis on FDI inflows into the primary sector will be marginal given the institutional and policy factors affecting FDI inflows in the primary sector in China.

This study therefore estimates that FDI inflows into China will most likely be about US$85 billion in 2009—a moderate decline of 8 per cent from 2008.

References

International Monentary Fund (IMF) 2009, 'Crisis and recovery', *World Economic Outlook*, April 2009, International Monentary Fund, Washington, DC, viewed 21 May 2009, <http://www.imf.org/external/pubs/ft/weo/2009/01/pdf/text.pdf>

Ministry of Commerce (MOFCOM) 2009a, 'FDI statistics', *Invest in China*, Ministry of Commerce, Beijing, viewed 21 May 2009, <http://www.fdi.gov.cn/pub/FDI_EN/Statistics/FDIStatistics/default.htm>

—— 2009b, Regular news conference, Ministry of Commerce, Beijing, 15 May 2009, viewed 21 May 2009, <http://www.mofcom.gov.cn/aarticle/ae/ah/200905/20090506252069.html>

National Bureau of Statistics (NBS) various issues, *China Statistical Yearbook*, China Statistics Press, Beijing.

United Nations Conference on Trade and Development (UNCTAD) 2009, *Assessing the Impact of the Current Financial and Economic Crisis on Global FDI Flows*, United Nations, New York and Geneva, viewed 21 May 2009, <http://www.unctad.org/en/docs/webdiaeia20091_en.pdf>

—— various issues, *World Investment Report*, United Nations Publications, New York and Geneva.

Endnotes

1. One such example is Pacific Brands, an Australian multinational textile and clothing company, which has closed its production in Australia and is shifting its manufacturing operations to China for price reasons ('Pac Brands exits Australian manufacturing', *Sydney Morning Herald*, 25 February 2009, viewed 21 May 2009, <http://business.smh.com.au/business/pac-brands-exits-australian-manufacturing-20090225-8hei.html>).

2. The data do not include FDI inflows into the financial sector (banking and insurance industries).

3. Calculated from NBS (various issues); MOFCOM (2009a). Note: calculations are based on 2000 constant US dollar prices.

4. One example is the acquisition deal proposed by the Coca Cola Company to buy China Huiyuan Juice Group Limited for US$2.4 billion in early 2009—although the Ministry of Commerce of China rejected the deal.

5. Data for real FDI inflows by sector are not available before 1997. Calculations are based on 2000 constant US dollar prices.

6. In 2007, the United States, the European Union and Japan accounted for 19.14 per cent, 18.19 per cent and 8.38 per cent, respectively, of China's total exports. In aggregate, these three major trading partners accounted for 45.71 per cent of China's total exports in 2007.

7. The full tax rebate for exports is 17 per cent.

Chinese foreign direct investment in the Australian resource sector

16

Peter Drysdale and Christopher Findlay

The appetite for resources in the rapidly growing Chinese and Indian markets before the global financial crisis drove escalating interest in resource investment worldwide (Streifel 2006; ABARE 2008). These economies have now emerged themselves as major players in overseas resource investment and development. The global economic crisis has not dampened China's appetite for investment in Australia's resource sector and the shortage of international capital has further enhanced the attractiveness of investment alliances with Chinese partners.

North American and European investment dominated the international resource industry in its early days, often through vertically integrated operations that incorporated the supply of metal products to industrial-country markets. This pattern of development changed remarkably about 40 years ago as Japan emerged as a major consumer of imported minerals and energy (Drysdale 1970). At the time, Japanese end users had little capacity to invest in the huge projects overseas that were needed to service procurement of the resources to fuel Japan's rapid industrialisation (Crawford et al. 1978). This was the era in which the emergence of the huge independent suppliers of resources to Japan and eventually to the rest of East Asia laid the foundations for the strength and competitiveness of the Australian minerals industry and Australia's leading minerals companies. They became leading world suppliers to the international market of a whole range of products, including iron ore, coal, bauxite, alumina, aluminium, copper, nickel, natural gas and uranium (Drysdale 1988).

China and India offer opportunity on a scale that already dwarfs established markets in Japan and the rest of Asia for the expansion of resource supplies from Australia. As in the past, realising the opportunity will depend not only on gearing up investment from Australian and foreign firms who are already significant players in the international resource business, it will encourage and require a large injection of additional capital from new investors—foreign and domestic (Albanese 2008; Kloppers 2008).

Australia has perhaps the most efficient mining sector in the world. This is due importantly to its openness to foreign investor competition and participation, because that brings with it, and fosters, the technology, management know-how and market links that are essential ingredients in the development of a world-class, internationally competitive industry. Australia therefore has a long record, and a strong policy regime, characterised by openness towards foreign investment in its resource industries, despite the fact that, by one measure, Australia is ranked among the most restrictive among Organisation for Economic Cooperation and Development (OECD) countries in its treatment of foreign direct investment (FDI) more generally (Stoeckel 2008; Kearney 2007).[1] There was some retreat from openness to investment in the resource sector that created uncertainties about the resource investment climate during the last global resource boom in the 1970s (McKern 1976; Caves 1978; Hanratty 1996). The change in policy tone was encouraged by a big shift in the relative price of resource goods in those years and reflected the emergence of a measure of resources nationalism. Although the period of retreat was relatively short lived, consumers sought alternative supplies elsewhere and Australia lost some market share As markets eased, Australian policy towards foreign investment in the resource and energy sector opened up once again.

The collapse of commodity prices, coinciding with a sharp global recession, has not seen the abatement of interest by Chinese and some other investors in Australian resources this time around. Indeed, established and aspiring producers have turned to Chinese investors for equity and financial support as bank and other capital has dried up.

Although in the early stages of industrialisation, China and India are already sources of substantial international capital (McKinsey 2008). They have been active candidates for growing investment in the Australian resource industry because of their capacity to mobilise capital for direct as well as indirect investment in this highly prospective sector of the world economy and because firms that consume raw materials, and policymakers in their home countries, remain anxious to secure resource supplies for the long term, even though demand for some key commodities has eased in the short term.

This is the background to and context in which there has been growing discussion of Australian policies towards Chinese foreign investment in Australia's resource sector.

The argument

The rise of Chinese and Indian demand for resources continues to drive growth in investment in the resources sector in Australia. The scale of the accompanying surge in FDI alone prompts new questions about the role of FDI.

In addition, China and India, in different political contexts, give the State a large role in their economies and a big share of their outward investment is channelled through state-owned enterprises (SOEs), state-owned banks or sovereign wealth funds (SWFs).

Australia and most other industrialised countries have spent the past couple of decades convincing their voters that the private sector, not government, should take the lead in managing most businesses. The global financial crisis has seen a retreat from this philosophy but this has not diminished questioning of the role of the State in foreign investment activities. At the same time, the industrialised countries continue to stress the important benefits that come from foreign investment and run open regimes towards foreign investment—direct and indirect. When confronted by government-controlled foreign investment, it might seem that one of these propositions has to give (Thirlwell 2008).

There are therefore two big questions raised by the prospects of a significant rise in FDI from China into the Australian resources sector. Is the surge of FDI into Australian mining and energy consistent with achieving the traditional gains from foreign investment? And are there particular problems associated with investment from foreign SOEs or state-managed SWFs? These are the two central questions that we shall address in this chapter.

There are corollary questions. FDI from SOEs is conceptually different in character and effect from portfolio (indirect) investment out of SWFs. This distinction is blurry at the edges. A minority stake by a single investor in a project might be accompanied by control through participation in the board of the firm or other arrangements that constrain the management of the project. Policy authorities might also apply different measures in terms of the share of ownership in judging the distinction between direct and portfolio investment.[2] In principle, however, the distinction between passive investment by a portfolio investor and FDI is clear enough. What are the implications of these distinctions? How important is the extent of control of a project by the foreign partner?

Australia's Treasurer, Wayne Swan, has said:

> We usually welcome and encourage some participation by the buyer, because that offers the buyer some security of supply and the seller some stability in the market. But we need to ensure that investment is consistent with Australia's aim of ensuring that decisions continue to be driven by commercial considerations and that Australia remains a reliable supplier in the future to all current and potential trading partners...[I]t follows that as the proposed participation by a consumer of the resource increases to the point of control over pricing and production, and especially where the resource in question is already developed and forms a major part of the total resource, or where the market disciplines applying to public companies are absent, I will look more carefully at whether the proposal is in Australia's national interest. (Swan 2008)

Apart from the extent of control, how important is the home country's policy regime? SOEs operate under different policy regimes in different countries. The regime under which a Swedish SOE operates might be different from that under which Chinese or Indian SOEs operate. Do these differences affect the impact of investment from these different sources? Further, the regime under which SOEs operate changes over time, and it is clearly changing in China. Do these changes need to inform the strategy that host countries might adopt towards FDI from this source?

These are some of the questions that will be discussed in this chapter.

First, there is a brief review of the role of FDI in Australia and the Australian resource sector, including an assessment of the rise of Chinese interests and China's economic relationship with Australia. Then we set out the issues for managing a regime that captures the gains from FDI. We ask whether there are other issues that need to be considered in the case of Chinese FDI. We examine the role of SWFs. We conclude with observations about the implications for Australian policy, as well as how Australian policy strategies might play into policy strategies in China and elsewhere.

The role of FDI in the Australian resources sector and China

FDI plays a particularly important role in the Australian resources sector. Mining accounts for almost one-quarter of all FDI in Australian industry, with the accumulated stock of foreign investment amounting to more than A\$92 billion in 2007 (ABS 2009). In the same year, FDI in manufacturing was estimated to be A\$68 billion (about 18 per cent) and in services about A\$190 billion. FDI has played a key role in the growth of the resources sector, especially in the past half-decade or so, when the annual growth of FDI in the mining sector has averaged more than 10 per cent a year (in 2007, there was an increase of 15 per cent). The confidence in Australia's investment environment has been a crucial element in Australia's ability to attract foreign investment into its resources sector and to take advantage of burgeoning opportunities in the international markets for raw materials—notably in China. Foreign investment plays a key role not only in delivering resource supplies to international markets, but in discovering and proving resource reserves and assets. Without openness to foreign investor participation in the industry, there would be limited willingness to undertake the investment in exploration and development of resources in which FDI has played such an important role. China is already participating actively in the proving of resource deposits (*Australian Financial Review*, 15 August 2008). More than four-fifths of the investment in offshore petroleum and gas exploration and more than one-half of the investment in the exploration and assessment of other minerals that underpin production in these industries today were undertaken by foreign investors (Hartley 1984; ABARE 2007).

FDI has accounted for more than one-third of capital formation in all Australian industry since the turn of the century; in mining and resources, it has accounted for almost half—and in some years a much higher proportion—of total capital formation in the sector. Importantly, foreign investors have played a similarly prominent role in capturing export markets and account for a growing share of minerals exports (ABS 2003.

Foreign and domestic firms are established and highly competitive suppliers of resources to global markets but China has emerged as far and away the fastest growing market for output from the industry—especially for iron ore and natural gas—in the past decade.

China is already Australia's largest overall trading partner and the largest buyer of a range of Australian raw material exports. Japan remains Australia's largest export market, but it can be confidently forecast that China will replace Japan as our largest export market within the next half-decade or less (Drysdale 2008).[3] China's role in the structure of Australia's global merchandise trade is being transformed (Tables 16.1–3).

China is Australia's largest market for iron ore, copper, wool and cotton, and a major and growing market for natural gas. Commodity exports from Australia to China grew at 17 per cent in 2007 and have averaged 19 per cent annual growth in the past decade. Export growth to China has remained important through the global financial crisis. The trade relationship with China is but one element in what has every prospect of becoming Australia's most important overall economic relationship bar none. While global FDI flows fell by 20 per cent in 2008, Chinese outflows doubled—to an estimated US$41 billion (Davies 2009). China's direct investment share is likely to continue to rise. China's direct investment in Australia is said to have risen to US$1.4 billion in the first quarter of 2008. FDI is very important, but it is only one dimension of the growing importance of the Chinese economy to Australia and other countries in the world economy.

Although Australia was the destination for some of China's largest early post-reform foreign direct investments—the Channar iron ore project and Portland aluminium project in the 1980s—China remains a relatively small player in Australian investment.

Table 16.1 Australia's total merchandise trade, by trading partner (per cent)

	1990	1991	1992	1993	1994	1995	1996	1997	1998	1999	2000	2001	2002	2003	2004	2005	2006	2007	2008
Japan	23.2	22.8	21.8	22.0	21.2	19.2	16.6	16.8	16.5	16.1	16.3	16.2	15.4	15.1	15.0	15.5	14.6	14.0	15.7
China	2.6	3.1	3.7	4.2	4.7	4.7	5.2	5.2	5.2	5.7	6.6	7.5	8.6	9.8	11.2	12.7	13.5	14.8	15.2
US	16.8	16.7	15.4	14.6	14.7	14.3	14.8	14.6	16.2	15.7	15.0	13.9	14.0	12.6	11.6	10.4	10.2	9.5	8.7
Sth Korea	4.4	4.5	4.6	5.0	4.9	5.6	6.2	5.8	5.5	5.4	6.1	5.9	6.0	5.4	5.4	5.5	5.7	5.5	5.6
Singapore	3.7	4.1	4.5	3.9	4.1	4.3	3.8	3.8	3.2	4.4	4.2	3.9	3.7	3.3	3.7	4.3	4.5	4.1	5.0
UK	5.1	4.6	4.9	5.1	4.8	4.8	5.0	4.6	5.7	4.9	4.7	4.8	4.6	5.4	4.2	3.8	4.2	4.2	4.3
NZ	4.8	4.7	5.0	5.4	5.9	6.0	6.0	5.9	5.1	5.7	4.9	5.0	5.2	5.5	5.4	4.9	4.2	4.4	3.8
Thailand	1.1	1.2	1.6	1.6	1.7	1.8	1.8	1.8	1.6	1.9	2.1	2.1	2.3	2.5	2.6	3.0	3.1	3.5	3.5
India	0.9	0.9	1.0	1.1	1.0	1.1	1.2	1.4	1.5	1.2	1.1	1.3	1.4	1.8	2.5	2.8	3.0	3.0	3.4
Germany	4.1	3.9	3.8	3.6	3.9	4.2	3.7	3.4	3.9	3.8	3.2	3.4	3.6	3.9	3.7	3.4	3.1	3.1	3.0
ROW	33.3	33.3	33.8	33.5	33.2	34.0	35.8	36.8	35.6	35.2	35.7	36.1	35.2	34.6	34.7	33.7	33.9	33.9	31.9
Total ($b)	84.2	103.3	113.8	125.0	132.7	149.0	155.2	168.1	185.6	188.2	227.1	240.1	247.0	237.8	258.8	294.7	339.7	356.1	448.9

Source: Australian Bureau of Statistics (ABS), Cat. no. 5368.0, Tables 14a and 14b.

Table 16.2 Australia's merchandise exports, by trading partner (per cent)

	1990	1991	1992	1993	1994	1995	1996	1997	1998	1999	2000	2001	2002	2003	2004	2005	2006	2007	2008
Japan	26.6	27.6	25.3	24.9	24.7	23.1	20.2	19.9	19.6	19.2	19.8	19.4	18.6	18.2	18.9	20.5	19.8	19.0	22.6
China	2.6	2.8	3.2	3.7	4.4	4.4	5.0	4.7	4.3	4.7	5.5	6.2	7.0	8.4	9.4	11.6	12.4	14.1	14.8
Sth Korea	6.0	6.3	6.3	7.0	7.3	8.5	9.5	8.0	6.9	7.2	8.2	7.8	8.4	7.5	7.8	7.9	7.5	8.0	8.3
India	1.2	1.2	1.4	1.5	1.4	1.5	1.6	2.0	2.4	1.7	1.7	2.0	2.1	3.1	4.6	5.0	5.4	5.5	6.1
US	11.6	10.0	8.8	8.1	7.2	6.5	6.5	7.5	9.5	9.7	10.0	9.7	9.7	8.8	8.1	6.7	6.2	6.0	5.5
NZ	5.1	4.9	5.3	5.9	6.8	7.4	7.4	7.3	6.4	7.7	6.0	5.9	6.6	7.6	7.5	6.5	5.5	5.6	4.2
UK	3.6	3.2	3.9	4.6	3.7	3.5	3.6	2.9	5.3	4.3	3.4	4.2	4.7	6.9	4.3	3.6	5.0	4.2	4.2
Taiwan	3.6	4.3	4.4	4.4	4.4	4.6	4.5	4.8	4.8	4.8	5.0	4.4	4.0	3.5	3.5	4.0	3.8	3.5	3.8
Singapore	4.6	5.5	6.5	5.2	5.3	5.4	4.1	4.6	3.7	4.7	5.3	4.4	4.2	3.3	2.8	2.8	2.8	2.4	2.8
Thailand	1.2	1.3	1.8	2.0	2.1	2.4	2.2	2.0	1.4	1.7	1.8	1.9	2.1	2.1	2.6	3.0	2.6	2.6	2.4
ROW	33.9	32.8	33.0	32.8	32.9	32.7	35.4	36.5	35.7	34.2	33.5	34.2	32.7	30.8	30.7	28.5	29.0	29.0	25.5
Total ($b)	47.2	53.7	58.3	62.7	64.7	71.6	76.9	84.7	88.9	86.8	110.3	122.5	119.4	107.9	117.7	139.0	163.7	168.3	223.1

Source: Australian Bureau of Statistics (ABS), Cat. no. 5368.0, Tables 14a and 14b.

Table 16.3 Australia's merchandise imports, by trading partner (per cent)

	1990	1991	1992	1993	1994	1995	1996	1997	1998	1999	2000	2001	2002	2003	2004	2005	2006	2007	2008
China	2.7	3.5	4.2	4.7	5.0	5.0	5.3	5.7	6.0	6.5	7.8	8.8	10.1	11.0	12.7	13.7	14.5	15.4	15.6
US	23.5	24.0	22.3	21.2	21.8	21.6	23.0	21.8	22.3	20.8	19.8	18.2	18.1	15.8	14.5	13.7	14.0	12.6	11.8
Japan	18.8	17.6	18.1	19.1	17.8	15.5	13.0	13.7	13.8	13.4	13.1	13.0	12.3	12.5	11.8	11.0	9.8	9.6	9.0
Singapore	2.5	2.7	2.4	2.6	3.0	3.2	3.4	3.0	2.8	4.1	3.2	3.4	3.4	3.4	4.4	5.5	6.1	5.6	7.2
Germany	6.4	6.1	5.8	5.8	6.0	6.7	6.0	5.6	6.0	5.7	5.0	5.7	5.7	6.2	5.8	5.6	5.1	5.2	5.0
Thailand	1.0	1.2	1.3	1.2	1.3	1.3	1.4	1.6	1.7	2.2	2.4	2.3	2.5	2.8	2.7	3.1	3.6	4.2	4.5
UK	7.0	6.2	5.9	5.7	6.0	6.0	6.4	6.4	6.0	5.3	6.0	5.3	4.6	4.2	4.1	4.0	3.6	4.3	4.4
Malaysia	1.4	1.6	1.7	1.7	1.8	2.0	2.2	2.5	2.8	3.2	3.7	3.3	3.1	3.3	3.9	3.9	3.8	3.9	4.0
NZ	4.4	4.6	4.6	4.9	5.0	4.7	4.7	4.4	4.0	4.0	3.8	4.0	3.8	3.9	3.7	3.5	3.1	3.3	3.4
Sth Korea	2.4	2.5	2.7	3.0	2.6	2.9	3.0	3.6	4.3	3.8	4.1	3.9	3.7	3.6	3.5	3.3	3.9	3.2	2.9
ROW	30.0	30.0	30.9	30.3	29.8	31.1	31.7	31.7	30.4	30.8	31.2	32.2	32.7	33.3	32.9	32.6	32.6	32.7	32.3
Total ($b)	37.1	49.6	55.5	62.3	68.0	77.4	78.3	83.3	96.7	101.5	116.9	117.7	127.6	129.9	141.2	155.7	176.0	187.8	225.8

Source: Australian Bureau of Statistics (ABS), Cat. no. 5368.0, Tables 14a and 14b.

The current scale and structure of Chinese investment across the Australian economy are described (Table 16.4).

Chinese FDI approved by the Foreign Investment Review Board (FIRB) amounted to almost A$10 billion in 2005–06 and 2006–07, of which about A$8 billion or 80 per cent was in minerals and resources. The Australian Treasurer reported in his speech of 4 July 2008 that, since November 2007, he had received applications to the value of A$30 billion for investment projects from China (*Australian Financial Review*, 5 July 2008). Should these investments materialise, the increment to Chinese FDI would represent a large jump in China's foreign investment presence in Australia, but it would still leave China a much less important investor than the United States or the United Kingdom, both of which now have less sizeable trade relationships with Australia than does China. The data for the fiscal year to 2008 have not yet been published (as of June 2009). Foreign investment approvals through the FIRB are commonly higher than investments actually realised, as measured by the Australian Bureau of Statistics (ABS). Approved foreign investment inflows into Australia (according to the FIRB) rose, however, by 82 per cent in 2006–07, compared with the previous year, with inflows increasing from A$85.6 billion to A$156.4 billion. The United States was the largest source of investment (A$45 billion or 29 per cent of the total). Next were Singapore (A$18 billion), Mexico (A$16.8 billion) and the Netherlands (A$12.8 billion). From this perspective, a jump of A$30 billion in investment from China would hardly be out of proportion.

As measured by the ABS, Chinese investment inflow into Australia averaged only A$180 million annually in the past decade. By 2008, the accumulated stock of Chinese investment in Australia stood at A$7.9 billion (more than twice the level of two years earlier and on par with that of Taiwan). The ABS reports that of that total, A$3.1 billion is direct investment (the balance being portfolio flows). As of 2008, China's FDI in Australia represented less than 1 per cent of the total stock of FDI in Australia (A$393 billion). Its concentration in the resources sector increases China's share of resource investments in that sector but it still holds a relatively small share in that sector (in 2007, the stock of direct investment in the minerals sector in Australia was about A$90 billion).

Table 16.4 Chinese investment in Australia by industry, as approved by the Foreign Investment Review Board, 1992–2007 (A$ million)

Year	No.	Agriculture, forestry and fisheries	Manufacturing	Mineral exploration and resource processing	Real estate	Services and tourism	Total
1993–94	0	0	0	0	0	0	0
1994–95	927	0	1	42	426	52	522
1995–96	267	0	6	52	137	31	225
1996–97	102	10	3	5	176	17	210
1997–98	0	0	0	0	0	0	0
1998–99	0	0	0	0	0	0	0
1999–2000	259	35	5	450	212	10	720
2000–01	0	0	0	0	0	0	0
2001–02	237	0	47	20	234	10	311
2002–03	0	0	0	0	0	0	0
2003–04	170	0	2	971	121	5	1100
2004–05	206	2	0	39	181	42	264
2005–06	437	0	223	6758	279	0	7259
2006–07	874	15	700	1203	712	11	2640

Source: Department of Treasury various years, Foreign Investment Review Board. Annual Reports, Department of Treasury, Australian Government, Canberra, <http://www.firb.gov.au/content/publications.asp?NavID=5>

Investment in the resource sector by Chinese enterprises has remained active through the global financial crisis (arguably it has become even more so) as bank finance and other investors have retreated from the market. A review of significant activities in the past 12 months shows a range of strategies that might be expected in the resource sector:

- some propose to take ownership of particular projects, such as the agreement by Xinwen Mining to pay A$1.5 billion for Linc Energy's Bowen Basin coal tenements in Queensland in September 2008 (although at the time of writing in 2009, the deal had yet to be completed)
- some establish the right to explore, such as Shenhua Energy's reported payment for a licence to explore coal deposits below the Liverpool Plains in New South Wales in October 2008
- some take a majority share in the company, such as China Nonferrous Metal Mining Group's agreement to take a majority stake in Australian rare-earths miner Lynas Corporation Limited in May 2009
- some take up minority positions, such as Hunan Valin Iron and Steel Group's purchase of 16.5 per cent in Fortescue Metals Group in February 2009, or the proposal by Ansteel to increase its minority shareholding in Gindalbie Metals in May 2009.

These are transparent transactions, unlike many Japanese investments, in which many parameters are hidden in joint venture arrangements.

Three cases of Chinese investment in the Australian resource sector have attracted particular policy attention:

- Chinalco's investment in Rio Tinto
- Sinosteel's takeover of Midwest and its bid for Murchison
- Minmetals purchase of OZ Minerals.

These are discussed in more detail in Box 16.1. The commentary on these projects focused on their effect on competition, their impact on cooperation between Australian companies and their implications for security issues. In all cases, the matters could have been resolved within the existing regulatory structures and in all cases the strategy of Chinese investors appeared consistent with corporate commercial interests.

Box 16.1 Three case studies

In February 2008, BHP Billiton announced a hostile bid to take over Rio Tinto. Chinalco and Alcoa also bought 9 per cent of Rio Tinto at that time. By the end of 2008, BHP had withdrawn its bid and then in February 2009 Chinalco proposed to extend its ownership to 18 per cent in order, it was reported, to provide funds to help refinance Rio Tinto debt accumulated in its purchase of Alcan. The purchase was consistent with Chinalco's announced international strategy to that time, and also provided access to Rio's assets of hydro-powered aluminium smelters, acquired from Alcan.

The Chinalco proposals raised issues about foreign investment by a government-owned firm, about the impact of the proposal on competition and, in the case of the 2009 offer, about the extent of control that the ownership share implied. Commercial criteria decided the matter when, in June 2009, Rio Tinto management withdrew from the arrangement with Chinalco—but not before extensive regulatory review, which has left an increased residual of uncertainty around investment from China.

The February 2008 purchase had triggered the attention of the FIRB under the new guidelines for FDI by SOEs, which we discuss in the body of the chapter. On Chinalco's investment, the Treasurer, Wayne Swan, said the Australian Government needed assurance that investment proposals from SOEs and sovereign funds were commercial and did not intend to advance strategic or even political objectives. In July, Swan added that the government would 'more carefully consider proposals by consumers to control existing producing firms'. The Treasurer pointed out that this would be a concern especially if the resource was big and already developed and if the proposed buyer was moving to 'a point of control over pricing and production' (Maiden 2009). On 24 August 2008, the Treasurer approved investment by Chinalco in up to 11 per cent of the Rio Tinto Group (or 14.99 per cent of Rio Tinto Plc, the arm of the Rio Tinto Group that was listed on the London Stock Exchange). The Treasurer also imposed a number of undertakings on Chinalco, including not to raise its shareholding any further without fresh approval and not seeking to appoint a director as long as its shareholding was less than 15 per cent. The FIRB returned to give attention to Chinalco in 2009 after the new proposal and the board, soon after the bid, announced it would require an extended period to mid-June to review the proposal. Rio management withdrew from the arrangement before this date.

The second set of issues related to the capacity of Chinalco to affect the iron ore price paid by Chinese steel mills. The Australian Competition and Consumer Commission (ACCC) in March 2009 released its opinion that the takeover would not lessen competition in any relevant market (ACCC 2009). The ACCC explained that any attempt to lower the world price through increased production (assuming Chinalco had the ability to drive such investment), so as to benefit consumers such as Chinese steelmakers, would lead to drops in output by other suppliers, which would then cause world prices to rise again, or else Rio would have to bring on project after project to keep the price down. The price drop could not be sustained. The ACCC also noted that this strategy required a 'China Inc.' view of the world.

In addition to the Treasurer's approval, Rio Tinto's shareholders needed to agree to the US$19.5 billion investment, which would double Chinalco's equity stake in Rio Tinto. There were reports of shareholder resistance and, given the improved outlook for resource markets, in June 2009, Rio announced that the proposal would not proceed. Rio had to pay a break fee to Chinalco. At the same time, Rio entered into a joint venture with BHP Billiton to raise funds from merging their West Australian iron ore businesses.

Another case of interest was Sinosteel's takeover of Midwest Corporation in 2008. This was the first hostile takeover by Chinese investors. Previously, Murchison Metals, a neighbour of Midwest, had been bidding for Midwest. If Midwest and Murchison had merged before Sinosteel's acquisition of Midwest, Sinosteel, even though already a shareholder, would have had less control over the projects. Sinosteel then held up the Murchison deal and itself took over Midwest, for which the Treasurer provided approval in December 2007. With full ownership of Midwest, Sinosteel could secure an off-take agreement for its output, which would otherwise have had to be negotiated. Having bought Midwest, it then paid to manage the merger with Murchison, which it now appears to be planning to purchase. The Treasurer has so far approved Sinosteel ownership of Murchison up to 49.9 per cent (Sinosteel had applied for 100 per cent but withdrew that application). Midwest and Murchison mine a pair of deposits and there are advantages in a merger, including the cost savings from exploitation of the neighbouring deposits, stockpile efficiencies, better sequencing of the development, coordinated exploration and the advantages of blending the ores of different qualities plus a greater capacity to raise funds. Also, the WA Government has chosen a Murchison infrastructure proposal for a port and rail link to the mid-west area of Western Australia.

On 16 February 2009, OZ Minerals reported that Chinese trading group Minmetals had made a bid for OZ Minerals, which had been working on options to repay debt. The FIRB process here was more important than in the Midwest case. The OZ Minerals directors had recommended the proposal but, on 27 March 2009, the Australian Treasurer rejected Minmetals' bid based on national security concerns regarding the flagship Prominent Hill mine's location in the defence-sensitive Woomera area—too close to the defence facility's prohibited-area weapons testing range. On 1 April 2009, Minmetals revised its bid. The revised offer excluded the Prominent Hill mine. The Treasurer approved it on 23 April 2009. The miner's bankers had agreed to an extension of the refinancing deadline to 30 June to allow the Minmetals transaction to proceed.

Capturing the gains from FDI

Foreign direct investor participation in the economy generates a range of benefits including higher incomes, productivity and competitiveness through providing new technology, know-how, marketing and access to lower-cost capital as well as opportunity for shifting risks. The principal benefits that are likely to be brought by Chinese foreign investor participation in Australian resource projects at this time are that they might bring additional capital and links to rapidly growing markets. At the same time, there are issues to be managed and resolved in capturing the full benefit from foreign investment.

Here attention is focused on FDI in the resource sector. There is a rich literature on foreign investment in other industries, which deals with a range of general issues (Drysdale 1972; Caves 1978; Dosi et al. 1990; Borensztein et al. 1998; Hanson 2001; Barro and Sala-i-Martin 2004; Dunning and Lundan 2008).

In the minerals sector, because of its capital-intensive nature and its geographical remoteness, benefits tend to be concentrated in returns to government associated with national ownership of the resources and to sectors such as engineering, financial and commercial services and transportation, which are closely linked to mining. These characteristics are said to restrict the benefits from FDI in the resource sector in developing countries because of weaknesses in taxation systems and because of the limited linkages between the resource sector and other sectors in those economies (UNCTAD 2007:140, 168). There are higher levels of local procurement in industrialised, resource-rich host economies that are the home base for the globalising mining-supply businesses that rank among the largest and most profitable companies in the world (UNCTAD 2007:Box IV.3); Australia counts itself in this category.

The pervasive impact of mining sector activity, despite its heavy concentration geographically in Western Australia and Queensland, can be seen in its effect on incomes, employment and the key macroeconomic indicators right across the Australian economy (Department of Treasury 2008:16–20).

The scope of benefits in the resource sector

FDI in the resource sector offers a number of advantages to the host country including the provision of capital, technology, know-how and access to markets. These benefits are substantial given the scale, technological complexity and long project lives that typify resource investments in Australia.

In addition, FDI is often part of an integrated set of mining and industrial activities. UNCTAD (2007:111) identifies an overall trend of increasing integration between mining and smelting, particularly in aluminium but also in iron ore. These linkages provide a basis for the marketing and distribution of the output of mineral projects. Risks are shared along the production chain. This is an additional benefit of FDI in the development of large-scale resource projects.

Vertical integration is not the only way to manage project risks. Other options include the use of long-term contracts between independent firms, complemented by portfolio capital flows. Smith (1980) explains the rationale for the combination of long-term contracts with arrangements for setting prices. They serve as a means of maximising the value of projects and achieving an efficient distribution of risks. The contracts also allow the mining company to raise finance for large projects, which in mining have long lead times and produce outputs with specific characteristics. Buyers then have to commit to investments in complementary processing methods or at least face some costs in adjusting their operations to outputs from different sources. As Smith explains, the result is that buyers and sellers in these markets operate portfolios of bilateral trade or sales and procurement links.

Provision of equity capital to the project or the mining company by the buyers of the output demonstrates another form of commitment by them. Control is not required, but may be sought depending on the nature of the project—although even an investment to a level that is less than required for control may still meet the definition of FDI. If that investment by the buyer also reduces the cost of finance to the mining company (by allowing that company to ease what otherwise would be restrictions on its capacity to raise debt) then it adds to the surplus available for distribution.

These circumstances are those that are likely to dominate Chinese investment interest in the Australian resource sector. Chinese investors overwhelming are likely to want a stake in projects that provide a link to markets in China and offer an additional source of capital, and to want to invest in partnership with Australian or other foreign firms that bring management know-how and technology as well as capital to mining projects.

Managing the issues with resource sector FDI

Significantly, the main host country's benefits from resource project development accrue via income flows, including to governments. There are issues related to the presence of foreign capital in resource sector projects, including with the management of the income flow from them. Resource projects are associated with the presence of variable rents. They involve the development of resources that are not replaceable and the global stock of which has scarcity value because of its size and its uneven distribution geographically. The value of the resource in this circumstance—at least for infra-marginal projects—enjoys a premium or rent over the cost of extraction. UNCTAD (2007:Box VI.3) lays out some options for capturing these rents, including taxes based on revenue, output and profit. There are trade-offs between the costs of collection and administration of these taxes and their effects on economic efficiency.

The payments by minerals companies to governments at all levels in Australia (other than for services) can be broken down (Figure 16.1). These data exclude income taxes paid by non-resident management and employees. The figure reveals that output-based taxes and licensing fees paid to state governments are a relatively small proportion of the total tax take compared with taxes on income. Income taxes have an effect on the incentive to invest compared with taxes on pure profit (Garnaut and Clunies Ross 1975, 1983) while output taxes affect the incentives to exploit a deposit. The composition of the doughnut in Figure 16.1 suggests the tax allocation in the Australian resources sector is skewed towards the collection of revenues from resource firms via income taxation.

Figure 16.1 Taxation payments to governments, 2006–07 ($million)

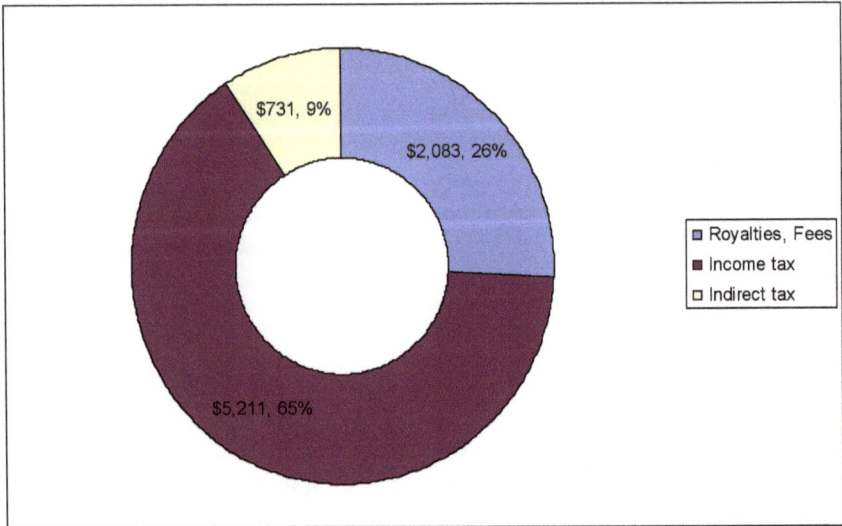

$731, 9%

$2,083, 26%

$5,211, 65%

□ Royalties, Fees
■ Income tax
□ Indirect tax

Source: < http://www.minerals.org.au/information_centre/minerals_industry_survey_report/publications2 >

Inefficient taxation regimes run the risk of collapse as circumstances change. The minerals and energy sector tax regime in Australia is complicated by the Australian federal system and the evolution of the distribution of taxation powers between the Commonwealth and the states, but it is legislatively and politically robust. In federal jurisdictions, such as those that cover the offshore production of oil and gas, a variant of a resource-profits tax regime applies, although the primary form of non-income taxation of onshore projects is through state-levied royalties.

The profitability of long-lived resource projects can change over time, creating incentives to change the fiscal arrangements where political and legislative systems are not robust, especially in periods in which there is a substantial increase in the rent value of resources occasioned by sharp rises in the terms on which they are traded, such as has been the experience in recent years (Duncan 2006). UNCTAD (2007) notes that many studies find that taxation regimes in minerals projects are regressive; it discusses (Box VI.5) options for more progressive regimes of the kind that are in part in place already in Australia.

In an advanced economy, the perception of an unfair and inefficient distribution of rents in projects can emerge, especially in the context of rising prices. This might not be an issue in the management of existing projects but could hinder new projects, which might operate on the same terms as existing projects. Chinese investment in Australian minerals is a consequence of the growth in demand in China. That growth in demand has contributed to rising prices in the same way that, in the 1960s and 1970s, the growth of Japanese demand saw a rise in Australian and global commodity prices. As investment arrives in host countries such as Australia to take advantage of new profit opportunities in resource production and trade, the distribution of rents becomes an issue in policy debate. There could be scope to gain from the implementation of more efficient taxation regimes. Hogan (2007) argues for the translation of arrangements for oil and gas in Australia to onshore minerals, but the established taxation arrangements for onshore minerals are the product of a long and complex history of fiscal relations between the Commonwealth and the states and are unlikely to change soon, even in the context of the current federal taxation and fiscal arrangements reviews. As Hogan (2007:100–1) concludes:

> Significant information on the net cash flow of resource projects is required to administer the petroleum resource rent tax. Extending a profit based royalty such as the petroleum resource rent tax to onshore mineral resources would involve significant transitional costs and increase the information requirements for administering resource taxation arrangements in Australia. There are also likely to be a number of issues that would need to be resolved in replacing the current systems that apply across several jurisdictions with a consistent mineral resource rent tax—for example, the taxation treatment of failed exploration projects would need to be considered (companywide deductibility of exploration expenditures is an important component of the petroleum resource rent tax).

There is another issue to do with taxation that arises in resource projects that are owned and controlled by the buyers of output from the project as part of an internationally integrated operation. This is the familiar issue of the opportunity for transfer pricing when there are not arm's-length transactions between firms. The importance of transfer pricing lies, of course, in its potential to reduce the taxation take of the host country through understatement of resource project profits.

The aluminium industry—in which international vertical integration is pervasive, significantly because of the importance of the specific technical characteristics of inputs across a production chain—has traditionally been the industry in which transfer pricing potentially presents the most important challenge to Australian taxation authorities.

In such cases, the taxation authorities can declare the appropriate price of output in determination of tax obligations, even when there is no readily observable arm's-length price of output. These are circumstances that require active taxation authority attention. Where participation in ownership does not involve control (a minority equity holding or partnership without control), the question does not arise.

A second major set of issues concerns the local and global environmental effects of resource sector projects. This concern applies to some extent to all resource projects. If projects add to environmental degradation, that is a consequence of a failure to bring home to investors the consequences of the project. In other words, it is the result of the failure of the host country to correct the market failure associated with the environmental externality and is not related to the presence of foreign investment as such.

Are there specific environmental issues associated with projects that involve foreign investment? Do investors in resource projects seek a haven from their domestic regulatory environment or do they apply global standards? UNCTAD (2007:147) reports that most large mining companies apply at least their home standards and that in many cases rigorous codes are also applied to subcontractors. Large and established multinationals have a better environmental performance compared with smaller local companies. They 'introduce and diffuse higher standards and more advanced technologies for environmental protection' (UNCTAD 2007:148). UNCTAD (2007:148) does note that some new entrants in resource sectors are based in countries with relatively weak environmental legislation, which involves a risk, but it concludes that environmental performance depends on 'host-country regulations and the capacity to implement them'.

A third set of issues concerns the social impacts of projects. In Australia, most mining investments are in remote locations and the principal social impact is on Indigenous communities. Although it has not been the case in the past, the framework for settlement of mineral leasing rights is now subject to more robust arrangements and public scrutiny. International and domestic mining companies are also at the forefront of the development of Indigenous employment programs. While there are other social and environmental issues in more populous parts of the country that arise in the development of minerals and resource projects (such as has been the case in the Hunter Valley or is currently the case in the Liverpool Plains around BHP Billiton's coal development), they are not distinctively associated with foreign investment projects.

In brief, we have identified a number of issues that are sometimes raised about the impact of FDI in a host economy, including those associated with the management of income flows and with the environmental and social impacts of projects. In all cases, these problems arise not from the presence of foreign investment as such but because of inefficient policy in the host economy. Capital flows run the risk of reducing welfare if there are domestic distortions or weaknesses in the regulatory or policy framework. If these policy distortions or weaknesses are evident and important, the solution is a domestic reform program, rather than restriction of the inflow of foreign capital.

Is Chinese FDI in the resource sector different?

Investment flows in the resource sector can take the form of FDI or portfolio flows, either as an independent investment or as part of a package of risk-management tools. The motivations for FDI have been discussed in some detail above and extensively in the literature (Dunning and Lundan 2008). The gains from investments via FDI provide a return on assets that is specific to the investing firm and for which participation in production (rather than licensing) is an efficient method of earning that return.

Portfolio flows are not necessarily associated with these firm-specific assets, do not involve management of the assets in which equity is acquired and do not involve control over the operations of firms or other entities in which equity is held, except through the effect of entry or exit from ownership of those assets on their price. In principle, therefore, there is every reason why the interest of portfolio investors in the mining sector and other sectors of the Australian economy should be welcomed. It adds to the stock of capital to which the country has access for investment in profitable resource sector and other activities.

There are good reasons for the buyers of natural resources also to be investors in projects, as noted above. There are also reasons why buyers might wish to seek control in projects, which, because of product characteristics, logistics or the lumpiness of the investments involved at both ends, are efficiently part of an integrated international production chain. As we have also noted above, this has been a characteristic of efficient investment in the resource sector for many years, including in cases in which end users of the product are controlling investors in projects that are integrated into international operations. So it is a new development in policy for the Treasurer to make it explicit that projects in which there is participation in ownership of projects 'to the point of control' by resource buyers will be routinely subject to more intense scrutiny (see the earlier quotation). This step increases the restrictiveness of access to the resources sector by foreign participants. The circumstances under which it might be justified need to be examined very carefully since it makes Australia potentially a less attractive location for investment and source of supply for a range of resource products for which this condition has not previously applied.

Another concern that is sometimes expressed is that Chinese investors might use their influence to lower prices of iron ore, so as to benefit Chinese steel-makers. This requires a 'China Inc.' view of the world, as the ACCC (2009) explained in its review of the Chinalco deal discussed above (Box 16.1).

The question of government ownership

In the case of Chinese FDI, there is the additional question of whether government or state ownership should matter in the treatment of applications to invest. Chinese FDI is not the only FDI in which government ownership could be important. Growth in the number of projects in which interest is being expressed by Chinese entities with some measure of government ownership has, however, been a factor in attracting policy attention. This includes SOEs and SWFs.

The Australian Government has responded with an elaboration of policy on screening foreign investments. In February 2008, it announced a set of guidelines that is reproduced in Appendix 16.1. These are the guidelines that are being applied in consideration of the Chinese and other FDI proposals that were discussed earlier and they include reference to whether:

- an investor's operations are independent from the relevant foreign government
- an investor is subject to and adheres to the law and observes common standards of business behaviour

- an investment could hinder competition or lead to undue concentration or control in the industry or sectors concerned
- an investment could impact on Australian Government revenue or other policies
- an investment could impact on Australia's national security
- an investment could impact on the operations and directions of an Australian business, as well as its contribution to the Australian economy and broader community.

The guidelines assert that 'proposed investments by foreign governments and their agencies (for example, [SOEs and SWFs]) are assessed on the same basis as private sector proposals. National interest implications are determined on a case-by-case basis' (Appendix 16.1). The guidelines go on to state, however, that 'the fact that investors are owned or controlled by a foreign government raises additional factors that must also be examined' (Appendix 16.1) in the administration of foreign investment controls. This, it is argued, reflects 'the fact that investors with links to foreign governments may not operate solely in accordance with normal commercial considerations and may instead pursue broader political or strategic objectives that could be contrary to Australia's national interest' (Appendix 16.1).

This argument creates uncertainty about foreign investment policy towards Chinese investment and is inconsistent because it includes a dimension that is 'additional' to the test of 'national interest'. This additional test, we demonstrate below, is unnecessary. The 'national interest' test has, in the past, been an adequate yardstick by which to manage the participation of FDI in the resources and other sectors of the economy. The additional tests on government-owned entities appear to discriminate against Chinese FDI proposals, since so many of them involve government-owned entities. There are other foreign investment policy regimes—for example, in Canada[4]—that incorporate provisions about state-owned firms, but it is not clear whether these provisions make sense for Australia.

Additional scrutiny of government ownership

The nature of the 'additional factors' that could demand a test of suitability beyond the 'national interest' test is difficult to imagine. There are three main possibilities.

1. FDI investments involving state ownership and dominant shareholding and control might be used as a vehicle for shifting profits back to the home country through underpricing exports. This might be a problem only if: a) the government-owned firm is the buyer of the resource or is directly compensated by the home state for losses incurred; and b) the government-owned firm dominates the host-country market, preventing the host-country taxation authorities from declaring the value of output against benchmark competitive prices. In these circumstances, there is a clear 'national interest' case for restricting foreign investment on monopoly grounds. It is not necessary to identify any 'additional factors' flowing from state ownership in order to reach this conclusion.

2. FDI investments involving state ownership and dominant shareholding and control might be used as an instrument for subsidising the development of 'excess capacity' or 'extra-marginal' projects and to ratchet resource prices down. This might be a problem only if the government-owned firm has total market power in the particular resource market concerned. In this circumstance there is a clear case for restricting foreign investment on 'national interest' grounds and, again, identification of 'additional factors' associated with state ownership is not necessary. The recent determination by the ACCC in respect of Chinalco's offer for an increased share in Rio Tinto demonstrates that Australia has the policy regime and institutions necessary to deal rationally and comprehensively with issues of this kind. The governments of resource-deficient countries might provide, and have in the past provided, capital subsidies to resource or energy developments by private investors or state investors for 'resource security' reasons in times of resource scarcity and tight markets. Acquiring a dominant position through a particular government-owned firm is likely to be a very blunt and ineffective instrument for achieving that policy objective. The evidence from the history of Japanese policies that extended subsidies to resource developers is littered with projects that did not survive a long-term market test.

3. FDI investments involving state ownership and dominant shareholding and control might be used to pursue political or strategic goals inconsistent with the efficient development and marketing of national resources. In such cases, again, clearly the 'national interest' dominates all other considerations. In a case in which a strategic resource—say a uranium project that had dominant-supply status—was either a trade or the foreign investment target, political and security issues

need to be dealt with in a state-to-state framework. In less strategic contexts, all firms that invest abroad—private as well as public—are ultimately subject to the laws and policies of the countries in which they are incorporated (at home and in the countries in which their subsidiaries operate) and questions of extra-territoriality do arise in the operation of firms internationally and have to be covered by state-to-state dealings.

In all of these cases, a 'national interest' test is adequate to handle the issue, whether the foreign investment is government owned or privately owned. Note that these issues do not arise at all for any foreign investment in which there is minority participation without control, by either a government-owned or privately owned firm.[5] The former cases are extreme and unusual. The latter cases are, as we have shown, by far the most common in which Chinese state-owned investments are involved in the Australian resource sector.

Some might argue that investment by a government-owned enterprise is likely, of its nature, to be inefficient and resource wasting. Government-owned enterprises have their origins in bureaucratic systems and have governance structures that are not subject finally to the disciplines of the market. Would Singtel, a Singapore Government-owned telecommunications provider and investor in Optus, have qualified for scrutiny merely on that ground? Whatever the firm-specific advantage a government-owned foreign investor in the resource industry brings to a project (commonly it will be a marketing link involving integration of operations along a production chain or access to additional capital), the value it puts on the asset will be tested ultimately in the market. It has been the practice for an assessment of the managerial capacity of a foreign investor not to form part of the review process. That a foreign investor is government owned hardly seems grounds for now departing from that very sensible practice.

In fact, the empirical evidence suggests that state-owned foreign investors have performed well (Young and Lu 1998). Multinational SOEs from Eastern Europe perform similarly to other foreign firms. There is also no evidence of the use of state power or privileged information in their business abroad. The goal of these ventures appears to be simply to operate successfully within the confines of the market. Our case studies also demonstrate the consistency of investment strategy with commercial motivation by Chinese investors.

Market disciplines on Chinese firms

The *a priori* identification of a class of investment proposals as deserving of special scrutiny introduces an element of prejudgment into the foreign investment review process, departing from the well-established and respected case-by-case approach. It is unfortunate that this is occurring at a time when it is strategically important that Australia, and other sophisticated market economies, rather than being cautious about the participation of Chinese state-owned firms, welcome it. State-owned firms in China are increasingly subject to the disciplines of the market at home. They have preferred access to domestic credit through the state-owned banking system but on terms that are, given that distortion, increasingly commercially based.[6] The prevalence of state-owned firms is wider in China than was the prevalence of state ownership, strictly defined, in the resource-consuming and resource-investing industries in Japan 30 or 40 years ago, but their entrenchment in the market is not so different. Chinese companies in which the State has a stake are usually publicly listed at home and increasingly in Hong Kong and abroad. Corporate organisation and corporate governance in China are in a state of transition and are evolving towards a system increasingly governed by market institutions.

As Woetzel (2008) says:

An out-of-date impression of state-owned companies distorts the picture of China's competitive landscape and masks both opportunities and threats facing multinationals. A more current view would, for example, have them consider more favourably the value that certain state-owned companies might bring to a global partnership. A realistic multinational must also recognize that they will become more attractive to top talent and, probably, more innovative. Both developments will ratchet up the level of competition.

Thornton (2008), a director on the board of large Chinese state-owned firms, observes:

[O]fficials at the highest levels [in China] recognize the need to put in place what might be called a modern system of corporate governance. They know that they'll be required to meet certain standards when they list their major companies in public markets in Hong Kong, London, or New York. They're also increasingly convinced that better corporate governance leads to better business results, greater efficiencies, wealth creation—all of those things that are good for companies, people, and the country. They have seen that even non-traded corporations like Saudi Arabia's Aramco have adopted leading corporate-governance practices.

Australia's dynamic economic and political interests

Australia's economic and grand political-strategic interests are in supporting the momentum towards market-based corporate governance in China—and engaging with it. Practical engagement recommends welcoming investments from Chinese firms because, through their fuller participation in the Australian market and other markets abroad, they subject themselves to the disciplines of robust and well-governed market institutions. Unnecessary regulation of capital from this source into the Australian market will not only be detrimental to Australian economic interests by driving it to other markets—possibly less supportive of reform of corporate structures and corporate behaviour—it is likely to encourage a retreat to appeals to the power of the State in ways that are likely to be damaging to our long-term economic and political interests. The application of special conditions for these investments would reinforce the perception of the primacy of regulatory solutions over market solutions and help sustain the dominance of the bureaucracy over the market in China.

Sovereign wealth funds

There is also the question of the potential role of China's SWFs in the Australian market for equity in the resource sector (Farrell et al. 2008; Wood 2007; JP Morgan Research 2008; Monitor Group 2008; Beck and Fidora 2008; Zhang and He 2008). Concerns about SWFs have included the following ideas (Truman 2008): that governments might mismanage the funds, including paying insufficient attention to corrupt practices; governments might manage the funds efficiently but for non-profit purposes (for example, by directing them towards the protection of national champions or promoting particular development strategies at home); SWF decisions might lead to 'financial turmoil' (as it was alleged of hedge funds); and foreign governments might have conflicts of interest with the managers of the assets in which they invest.

Wariness about SWFs' investment intentions appears unjustified. These funds seek diversified investment and higher returns in international equity investment like other portfolio investors, although they also have become more active in the mergers and acquisitions market. They add to the stock of capital for investment in this and other sectors and the capacity of the firms in which they invest to take advantage of the growth of trade and business opportunities. Should a SWF take a controlling stake in a particular enterprise, its investment can and should be subject to the same review and 'national interest' test as that of other investors. There is also a general interest in improving the standards of transparency and accountability of all SWFs, including our own, Futures Fund, which does not rank highly according to these standards (Truman 2008).

The effect of policies directed selectively at Chinese state-owned investment is not confined to these investments; it is much broader. Australian decisions about FDI in which there is Chinese state ownership or about investments from a Chinese SWF cannot be prevented from influencing the views of other investors, including the managers of other SWFs, about the desirability of investing in Australia.

The scale of these funds is now significant and growing. Truman's (2008) data on SWFs around the world cover three such funds in China, which now ranks ninth in terms of offshore assets (with total assets of US$272 billion, of which US$135 billion is invested offshore). The total value of SWFs, according to Truman's data, is more than US$5000 billion, of which nearly US$3500 billion is international assets. Singapore has more than US$330 billion invested offshore.

Truman is concerned that the adoption of thoughtless protectionist policy towards a particular country's SWFs because of wariness about their investment behaviour is likely to be counterproductive. He suggests instead the international adoption of a blueprint of good practices that would refer to decision making based on economic grounds alone, a commitment to good governance, a commitment to fair competition with privately owned investors and respect for host-country rules.

Additional tests on this class of investment from China and decisions in each case are likely to make it more difficult to raise capital from others, such as Japan. Uncertainties about rules on Chinese foreign ownership, such as caps on control, would impede capital flows more generally and raise the possibility that such caps might be applied more widely. At least some of the opportunities created by the growth in demand in China are likely to be lost. The current ambiguities are damaging to Australia's economic and long-term political-strategic interests.

Conclusions

There is no persuasive case for any change in direction over control of foreign direct capital inflows in response to the recent surge of interest of Chinese foreign direct investors in the Australian resources sector. The participation of the Chinese SWFs in equity investments in Australia also does not present any particular problem that cannot be dealt with appropriately within the policy framework that has been in place for some time. Chinese investors are under-invested in Australia, given the importance of China in Australia's trade, including and especially as a market for Australian resources, and given China's increased importance in global capital markets. Unless we deliberately constrain it to our own cost, China's share in Australian trade and in global trade and capital markets is destined to continue to grow and China's share in the direct and indirect ownership of Australian assets could easily grow commensurately.

Anxiety about the growth of foreign investment by China is as unfounded as it was in earlier times over the growth in foreign investment by Japan, which accompanied the emergence of Japan as Australia's major economic partner and a major supplier of capital to world markets.

Australia has a world-class mining sector in which the largest and most competitive mining firms—Australian and, to a very great extent, already foreign-owned—are heavily involved. The mining sector is deeply linked into and integrated with the rest of the Australian economy. The taxation and regulatory framework within which the mining sector is governed is well established and robust. While some have suggested that the Australian taxation regime could be improved to ensure that the Australian public captures a higher share of the rents from high-class mine investments or from unusual periods of high profit in the industry (Hogan 2007), the taxation regime is not a matter of active policy concern or public debate. If the efficiency of the taxation regime is a matter of public concern, we have argued, that is a matter that needs to be addressed through reform of the taxation regime and its impact on foreign and domestic firms—not a matter that is appropriately dealt with through controls or restrictions on FDI inflows. If there are environmental or social issues that require public policy intervention in the sector, they are issues that need to be dealt with through initiatives in environmental and social policy that impact on domestic and foreign-owned operations—not through controls over foreign-owned companies alone.

In brief, none of the usual and general arguments that might be advanced in caution about FDI participation in the sector applies in any substantial degree to the circumstances in Australia.

Increased uncertainty about the treatment of Chinese FDI in the resources sector is, at the margin, likely to damage the potential growth of the sector and Australia's full and effective participation in the benefits from Chinese economic growth through the growth of its market for industrial materials. An important objective is to assuage nascent Chinese corporate and policy strategies aimed at containing the growth of Australian market share. These strategies are familiar instruments in the pursuit of minerals and energy security by resource importers (Lesbirel 2004). There is the added risk that application of 'additional' policy tests with respect to Chinese investment creates uncertainty about and impediments to investment from other sources as well.

It might seem a puzzle as to how Australia got itself into this pickle over Chinese FDI. A few final words on that situation and what might be a sensible way out of it could be helpful.

The rapid rise of China caught many by surprise, although some Australians and Australian institutions have been on the leading edge of thinking about those developments. The intensification of Chinese investment activity in the Australian resource sector has also come swiftly, although it has been gathering strength for some time. These developments alone do not explain the recent elevation of policy interest in Chinese investment in the Australian resource sector or the discomfort of the previous Australian government or the present government in dealing with the issue.[7] A series of events contributed and it illustrates our argument as to the value of a generally applied national interest test to investments of this type. Two events were of particular importance.

The first event was the high-profile takeover bid by BHP Billiton for Rio Tinto (Box 16.1), which opened up the question of Chinese investment in Australia. Whether it occurred to the architects of the BHP Billiton takeover strategy or not, a merger between the two largest international iron ore suppliers in the world was bound to excite interest in China, the largest iron ore market in the world. Subsequently, there was the bid by Chinalco for a higher stake in and a more comprehensive strategic alliance with Rio Tinto. Chinalco, already a significant international investor in mining projects around the world, moved to secure an initial minority stake in Rio Tinto in early 2008.

Here is not the place to speculate about where this corporate activity will end, but brief comment is in order on the implications of the development for framing policy towards FDI that incorporates state ownership. As noted in Box 16.1, the Australian Treasurer, after a recommendation by the FIRB, approved the investment by Chinalco in up to 14.99 per cent interest in the Rio Tinto Group. This share was less than the 'substantial interest' level of 15 per cent that applied under the FIRB policy (<http://www.firb.gov.au/content/_downloads/General_Policy_Summary_April_2008.rtf>),[8] and the Treasurer made the determination under the new guidelines applying to SOEs. Chinalco has moved to take a 'substantial interest' in Rio Tinto, so this new circumstance has to be considered by the FIRB under Australia's foreign investment rules. In the event, Rio Tinto's change of heart meant that no official decision was required.

The second event was Sinosteel's investments in the mid-west region of Western Australia. It had applied to take over Midwest, a WA iron ore company, which was approved in November 2007 just after the Rudd Government assumed office. As explained in Box 16.1, Sinosteel also targeted Midwest's neighbour, Murchison, and it continues to wait for the FIRB ruling on its application. Sinosteel's interest in Murchison will have been increased by the recent WA Government decision to ask a Murchison consortium to build a new port to serve the region. It has been suggested that a wholly Chinese-owned infrastructure network in the WA mid-west might be an obstacle to delivering iron ore to other markets. Again, this issue can be dealt with by the kind of conditions that the WA Government has routinely imposed on other infrastructure developments. The scale and structure of these investments do not suggest any considerations of 'national interest' or effects on competition or strategic importance that might recommend their non-approval.

These and the other projects discussed in Box 16.1 have introduced some political confusion into the discussion of Australia's foreign investment regime in the past year. Some of the confusion seems to relate to uncertainty about how to respond to the growth of Chinese investment interest in the Australian resources and energy sector. The issues of state ownership of investment, competitiveness in markets and political or security matters are not appropriately dealt with through additional restrictions and tests on Chinese or other foreign investment proposals. Uncertainty about these issues already runs the risk of hindering development of the industry's potential and damaging our longer-term political and security interests. Much of the uncertainty, however, has also been introduced by interested commercial and political parties in play around the market (Box 16.1).

The best way to dispel the uncertainty and confusion is through:

- reassertion of the market framework within which all foreign investment proposals are examined in Australia
- initiation of government-to-government arrangements for routine consultation between Australian and Chinese authorities that would serve to facilitate scrutiny of competition, corporate governance and financial transparency issues and have the practical effect of strengthening that framework over time.

The detail of the initiative we suggest here will need to be the subject of discussion and careful study elsewhere.

Acknowledgments

We are indebted to a large number of people for information, advice and assistance in the preparation of this chapter. Shiro Armstrong and Darien Williams provided research assistance at the East Asia Bureau of Economic Research (EABER), as did Claire Hollweg and Uwe Kaufmann at the School of Economics at the University of Adelaide, and they deserve our special thanks. Earlier versions of the chapter have been presented at the Crawford School of Economics and Government, The Australian National University's China Forum, the China Energy Research Institute and Peking University's Center for China Economic Research. We are grateful to colleagues in all those forums and to officials at the Australian Treasury for valuable feedback. We are especially grateful to Ligang Song, Ross Garnaut, Shiro Armstrong and colleagues in the Crawford School's seminar series, who provided comments on various drafts. We are, of course, alone responsible for whatever deficiencies it continues to contain.

References

Albanese, T. 2008, Winning strategies for global champions, Speech to Australia-Israel Chamber of Commerce and Industry, 16 June.

Australian Bureau of Agricultural and Resource Economics (ABARE) 2007, *Australian Commodities*, December, Australian Bureau of Agricultural and Resource Economics, Canberra.

—— 2008, *Australian Commodities*, June Quarter 08.2, Australian Bureau of Agricultural and Resource Economics, Canberra, <http://www.abare.gov.au/publications_html/news/news/news.html#>

Australian Bureau of Statistics (ABS) 2003, *Foreign Ownership of Australian Exporters and Importers, 2002–03*, 5496.0.55.00, Australian Bureau of Statistics, Canberra.

—— 2009, *International Investment Position—Australia: Supplementary statistics, 2008*, 5352.0, Australian Bureau of Statistics, Canberra.

Australian Competition and Consumer Commission (ACCC) 2009, *Chinalco (Aluminium Corporation of China)—Proposed acquisition of interests in Rio Tinto plc and Rio Tinto Lt*, 25 March, Australian Competition and Consumer Commission, Canberra, <http://www.accc.gov.au/content/index.phtml/itemId/501191>

Barro, R. and Sala-i-Martin, X. 2004, *Economic Growth*, The MIT Press, Cambridge, Mass.

Beck, R. and Fidora, M. 2008, *The impact of sovereign wealth funds on global financial markets*, ECB Occasional Paper, no. 91 (2 July 2008), European Central Bank, Frankfurt am Main, Germany, <http://ssrn.com/abstract=1144482>

Borensztein, E., De Gregorio, J. and Lee, J. W. 1998, 'How does foreign direct investment affect economic growth?', *Journal of International Economics*, vol. 45 (1 June), pp. 115–35.

Caves, R. E. 1978, 'Policies towards trade in raw materials', in J. G. Crawford, S. Okita, P. Drysdale and K. Kojima (eds), *Raw Materials in Pacific Economic Integration*, Croom Helm, London, pp. 288–311.

Crawford, J. G., Okita, S., Drysdale, P. and Kojima, K. (eds) 1978, *Raw Materials and Pacific Economic Integration*, Croom Helm, London.

Davies, K. 2009, 'While global FDI falls, China's outward FDI doubles', *Columbia FDI Perspectives*, no. 5, 26 May, <http://www.vcc.columbia.edu/www.vcc.columbia.edu>

Department of Treasury 2008, *Budget Papers*, Department of Treasury, Australian Government, Canberra.

—— 1995–2007, *Foreign Investment Review Board. Annual Reports, 1995–2007*, <http://www.firb.gov.au/content/publications.asp?NavID=5>

Dosi, G., Pavitt, K. and Soete, L. 1990, *The Economics of Technical Change and International Trade*, Harvester-Wheatsheaf, New York.

Drysdale, P. 1970, 'Minerals and metals in Japanese–Australian trade', *The Developing Economies*, vol. 8, no. 42 (June), pp. 198–218.

—— 1988, *The Economics of International Economic Pluralism: Economic policy in East Asia and the Pacific*, Columbia University Press and Allen & Unwin, New York and Sydney.

—— 2008, 'Deepening Asian integration and regional cooperation arrangements', in Asian Development Bank, *Emerging Asian Economies*, Asian Development Bank, Manila.

Drysdale, P. (ed.) 1972, *Direct Foreign Investment in Asia and the Pacific*, The Australian National University Press, Canberra.

Duncan, R. 2006, 'Price or politics? An investigation of the causes of expropriation', *Australian Journal of Agricultural and Resource Economics*, vol. 50, no. 1, pp. 85–101.

Dunning, J. R. and Lundan, S. M. 2008, *Multinational Enterprises and the Global Economy*, Edward Elgar, Cheltenham, United Kingdom.

Farrell, D., Lund, S. and Sadan, K. 2008, *The New Power Brokers: Gaining clout in turbulent markets*, July, McKinsey Global Institute.

Garnaut, R. and Clunies-Ross, A. 1975, 'Uncertainty, risk aversion and the taxing of natural resource projects', *The Economic Journal*, vol. 85, no. 338 (June), pp. 272–87.

—— 1983, *The Taxation of Mineral Rents*, Oxford University Press, Oxford.

Hanratty, P. 1996, *Inward direct foreign investment in Australia: policy controls and economic outcomes*, Research Paper, no. 32 (May), Parliamentary Research Service, Department of the Parliamentary Library, Canberra.

Hanson, G. H. 2001, *Should countries promote foreign direct investment?*, UNCTAD G-24 Discussion Paper Series, no. 9 (February), United Nations Conference on Trade and Development and Harvard Center for International Development, Geneva and Cambridge, Mass.

Hartley, P. R. 1984, 'Foreign ownership and the Australian mining industry', in L. H. Cook and M. G. Porter (eds), *The Minerals Sector and the Australian Economy*, Allen & Unwin, Sydney.

Hogan, L. 2007, *Mineral resource taxation in Australia: an economic assessment of policy options*, ABARE Research Report 07.1, Australian Bureau of Agricultural and Resource Economics, Canberra.

JP Morgan Research 2008, *Sovereign Wealth Funds: A bottom-up primer*, 22 May, JP Morgan Chase Bank, NA, Singapore.

Korporal, G. 2008, 'China warns Labor on investment curbs', *The Australian*, 2 July 2008.

Kloppers, M. 2006, *Resourcing Asian Growth*, BHP Billiton, Melbourne, <http://www.bhp.com.au/bb/home.jsp>

Kearney, A. T. 2007, *Foreign Direct Investment Confidence Index*, Global Business Policy Council, New York.

Lesbirel, H. S. 2004, 'Diversification and energy security risks: the Japanese case', *Japanese Journal of Political Science*, vol. 5, pp. 1–22.

McKern, B. 1976, *Multinational Enterprises and Natural Resources: Foreign investment in the Australian minerals industry*, McGraw-Hill, Sydney.

Maiden, M. 2009, 'Canberra and share rally remake Rio game for Chinalco', *Age*, 5 May 2009.

Monitor Group 2008, *Assessing the Risks: The behaviors of sovereign wealth funds in the global economy*, Monitor Group, New York.

Smith, B. 1980, *Long term contract arrangements and financing arrangements for minerals developments*, Research Paper, no. 72 (September), Australia Japan Research Centre, Canberra.

Stevens, M. 2008, 'China faces mining investment curbs', *The Australian*, 26 June 2008.

Stoeckel, A. 2008, *Sovereign Wealth Funds: Friend or foe*, Centre for International Economics, Canberra.

Streifel, S. 2006, *Impact of China and India on global commodity markets: focus on metals and minerals and petroleum*, Background paper for *Dancing with Giants: China, India, and the global economy*, Institute for Policy Studies and The World Bank, Washington, DC.

Swan, W. 2008, Australia, China and this Asian century, Speech to the Australia-China Business Council, Melbourne, 4 July 2008.

Thirwell, M. 2008, 'Sharing the spoils of China's rise means negotiating some tricky investment twists and turns', *The Australian*, 7 July 2008.

Thornton, J. 2008, 'Governing China's boards: an interview with John Thornton', *The McKinsey Quarterly*, August.

Truman, E. 2008, *A blueprint for sovereign wealth fund best practices*, Peterson Institute Policy Brief, PB08-3 (April), Peterson Institute, Washington, DC.

United Nations Conference on Trade and Development (UNCTAD) 2007, *World Investment Report 2007: Transnational corporations, extractive industries and development*, United Nations Conference on Trade and Development, Geneva and New York, <http://www.unctad.org/Templates/webflyer.asp?docid=9001&intItemID=4361&lang=1&mode=downloads>

Woetzel, J. R. 2008, 'Reassessing China's state-owned enterprises', *The McKinsey Quarterly*, August.

Wood, A. 2007, 'The sovereign wealth fund game needs new rules', *The Australian*, 3 November 2007.

Young, S. and Lu, T. 1998, 'Internationalization of Chinese enterprises: key issues for the future', *Long Range Planning*, vol. 31, issue 6, Strathclyde International Business Unit and Institute of World Economics and Politics, CASS, Glasgow and Beijing.

Zhang, Y. and He, F. 2008, *China's sovereign wealth fund: weakness and challenges*, Research Center for International Finance Working Paper, no. 0823 (December), Institute of World Economics and Politics, Chinese Academy of Social Sciences, Beijing.

Endnotes

1. These indexes measure the formal requirements for investment approval, and these requirements will have an effect in deterring investment, although not necessarily in investment approval outcomes. On this last measure, Australia might rank as a less restrictive regime.

2. The Australian policy authorities in the past would appear to have judged a share in ownership of 15 per cent to constitute a significant direct investment, although a much lower share, of about or less than 10 per cent, has attracted policy interest. Technically, a foreign stake of 10 per cent in an investment qualifies that investment for inclusion in the data for FDI.

3. It is likely that this will occur sooner (in the coming year or two) because of the sharp lift in the relative growth of China compared with other markets in the global economic crisis.

4. See the Canadian guidelines at: <http://www.ic.gc.ca/epic/site/ica-lic.nsf/en/lk00064e. html#state-owned>

5. A structure of minority holdings through joint venture, as discussed earlier in this chapter, or the procurement of a position on a board may permit a measure of control that requires scrutiny in either privately owned or government-owned or related investments.

6. Their access to funds from that source for foreign investment is constrained by commercial discipline, as recent experience with investment in the Indonesian power sector appears to attest.

7. For early press comment on the policy issues and response see Stevens (2008) and Korporal (2008).

8. See the earlier discussion of the plasticity that has appeared in this test in the chapter.

Appendix 16.1 Principles guiding consideration of foreign government related investment in Australia

Australia maintains a welcoming stance towards foreign investment in recognition of the substantial benefits that it provides to our community.

The purpose of Australia's foreign investment screening regime is to ensure that foreign investment into Australia is consistent with our national interest. The Treasurer can reject proposals that are deemed contrary to the national interest or impose conditions on them to address national interest concerns.

Significant foreign investment proposals must be notified to the Australian Government and examined by the Foreign Investment Review Board (FIRB). This includes all proposed investments by foreign governments and their agencies. This requirement is a longstanding feature of Australia's foreign investment policy that has been maintained in place by successive governments.

While the FIRB plays an important advisory role, determining whether a proposal is consistent with the national interest is ultimately a matter for the Treasurer.

To ensure they are consistent with Australia's national interest, the FIRB examines whether proposed foreign investments may have any adverse implications for Australia's national security or economic development and ensures they are consistent with any specific foreign investment legislation in areas such as transport and telecommunications. It also examines whether proposals have implications for other Government policies, competition and the operations of Australian businesses.

If the Treasurer forms a view that a foreign investment would be inconsistent with Australia's national interest, it may be blocked or made subject to conditions to address any problems that have been identified.

Guidelines for foreign government investment proposals

Proposed investments by foreign governments and their agencies (eg., state-owned enterprises [SOEs] and sovereign wealth funds [SWFs]) are assessed on the same basis as private sector proposals. National interest implications are determined on a case-by-case basis.

However, the fact that these investors are owned or controlled by a foreign government raises additional factors that must also be examined.

This reflects the fact that investors with links to foreign governments may not operate solely in accordance with normal commercial considerations and may instead pursue broader political or strategic objectives that could be contrary to Australia's national interest.

The Government is obliged under the *Foreign Acquisitions and Takeovers Act 1975* to determine whether proposed foreign acquisitions are consistent with Australia's national interest. In examining proposed investments by foreign governments and their agencies, the Australian Government will typically have regard to the following six issues.

1. An investor's operations are independent from the relevant foreign government.

In considering issues relating to independence, the Government will focus on the extent to which the prospective foreign investor operates at arm's length from the relevant government.

It also considers whether the prospective investor's governance arrangements could facilitate actual or potential control by a foreign government (including through the investor's funding arrangements).

Where the investor has been partly privatised, the Government would consider the size and composition of any non-government interests, including any restrictions on governance rights.

2. An investor is subject to and adheres to the law and observes common standards of business behaviour.

To this end, the Government considers the extent to which the investor has clear commercial objectives and has been subject to adequate and transparent regulation and supervision in other jurisdictions.

The Government will examine the corporate governance practices of foreign government investors. In the case of an SWF, the Government would also consider the fund's investment policy and how it proposes to exercise voting power in relation to Australian companies.

Proposals by foreign government owned or controlled investors that operate on a transparent and commercial basis are less likely to raise additional national interest concerns than proposals from those that do not.

3. **An investment may hinder competition or lead to undue concentration or control in the industry or sectors concerned.**

These issues are also examined by the Australian Competition and Consumer Commission in accordance with Australia's competition policy regime.

4. **An investment may impact on Australian Government revenue or other policies.**

For example, investments by foreign government entities must be taxed on the same basis as operations by other commercial entities. They must also be consistent with the Government's objectives in relation to matters such as the environment.

5. **An investment may impact on Australia's national security.**

The Government would consider the extent to which investments might affect Australia's ability to protect its strategic and security interests.

6. **An investment may impact on the operations and directions of an Australian business, as well as its contribution to the Australian economy and broader community.**

The Government would consider any plans by an acquiring entity to restructure an Australian business following its acquisition. Key interests would include impacts on imports, exports, local processing of materials, research and development and industrial relations.

The Government would also consider the extent of Australian participation in ownership, control and management of an enterprise that would remain after a foreign investment, including the interests of employees, creditors and other stakeholders.

Source: < http://www.treasurer.gov.au/DisplayDocs.aspx?doc = pressreleases/2008/009.htm &pageID = 003&min = wms&Year = &DocType = >

Greenhouse gas emissions reduction
A theoretical framework and global solution

17

Project Team of the
Development Research Centre,
People's Republic of China

Introduction

The Kyoto Protocol, as 'the first game in town', represents significant progress towards reducing global emissions. Its cap-and-trade mechanism and flexible market-based implementation have been valued highly. Meanwhile, there has also been wide criticism (for instance, Nordhaus 2006; EC 2008) of its flaws: 1) small coverage and a lack of effectiveness; 2) countries, especially developing countries, lack incentive to participate; 3) the additionality problem of the Clean Development Mechanism (CDM). To fight effectively against global warming, a more effective post-Kyoto architecture is needed.

Although a variety of alternative proposals aiming to succeed the Kyoto Protocol have their own advantages (Aldy et al. 2003; Aldy and Stavins 2007; Garnaut 2008; Nordhaus 2006, 2008; Stiglitz 2006; Weitzman 1974; Sagar and Kandlikar 1997), each also has its disadvantages. For instance, some require revolutionary changes to establish a framework completely different from the Kyoto Protocol; some are based on the particular interests of certain countries; and some are seen as not sufficiently fair by developing countries, especially by the major emerging emitters.

Although according to the principle of 'common but differentiated responsibilities', developing countries are not required to reduce emissions in the existing Kyoto Protocol, their further involvement is needed in global emissions reduction. Nonetheless, since the rights and responsibilities of each country regarding climate change have not been precisely measured in the unclear term of 'differentiated responsibilities', industrialised and developing countries, especially the big global emerging emitters, feel there is an unfair burden sharing and are accordingly critical of one another. Hence, the new international agreement must be built on a solid basis of fairness and must clearly define each country's rights and responsibilities; otherwise the post-Kyoto protocol is not likely to be self-enforcing or effective.

The objective of this chapter is to develop a theoretical framework for allocating each country's emission entitlements and, by establishing a national emissions account (NEA) for each country, to provide a full-coverage global solution with adequate respect for the rights of developing countries. In section two, we investigate the economic nature of greenhouse gas (GHG) emissions and show how each country's emission (or emission-reduction) behaviour changes once its emission entitlements are clearly defined. In section three, we develop a theoretical framework for how to allocate GHG emission entitlements for each country and provide a NEA-based global solution to emissions reduction. In section four, we use hypothetical data to demonstrate how to establish NEAs for each country and present some findings from the demonstration. In section five, we further explore the implications of the findings and clarify some major issues on climate change. The last section concludes the chapter.

The economic nature of greenhouse gas emissions

The economic nature of GHG emissions is determined by their natural or technical characteristics. First, due to the mobility of the atmosphere, no matter how much an individual country emits, the harm those emissions do is borne by everyone on Earth. Second, the harm of GHG emissions lasts for hundreds of years due to their long lifetime in the atmosphere. For instance, over the course of a century, although half of the carbon dioxide emitted in any one year will be removed, about 20 per cent of it will remain in the atmosphere for millennia (Solomon et al. 2007:824). Most of the greenhouse gases accumulated in the atmosphere have been emitted by industrialised countries since the Industrial Revolution. Third, the harm of greenhouse gases is non-rival, which means that the harm suffered by a person will not be alleviated because of more people taking the harm.

Given current technologies, most production activities need to—directly or indirectly—emit greenhouse gases, although the outputs of units of emissions in different countries vary. Therefore, GHG emissions on one hand impose harm on humans; on the other, they bring benefits to humans. If, however, global greenhouse gases are accumulated in the atmosphere beyond a certain level, their harm will far exceed their benefits. Most scientists agree that global greenhouse gases must be limited in the range of 450 parts per million (ppm) of carbon dioxide equivalent (CO_2-e), otherwise the consequences will be disastrous (Metz et al. 2007; Stern 2007; Garnaut 2008). How to get all countries to take coordinated action to lower their emissions is, however, a great challenge. The key is to provide incentives for each country to lower its emissions through clearly defining and enforcing each country's emission entitlements.

Greenhouse gas emissions bring harm and benefits. The benefits are owned exclusively by the emitting countries, but the harm is borne by all people of all countries on Earth. Since the emission entitlements of each country are not clearly defined, each country then has an incentive to emit as much as possible to the common atmosphere to maximise their benefits. Excessive emissions lead to global warming, the so-called 'tragedy of the commons' (Hardin 1968). If emission entitlements could be clearly defined and all countries could emit subject only to their quotas, each country's emissions behaviour would change and the limitations on global emissions would not be topped. The countries that needed greater quotas could purchase them from others.

The question of 'by how much should a country reduce its emissions' is the same question as 'how much is a country entitled to emit'? Like emissions, emissions reduction also has benefits and costs. The major 'benefit' of emissions reduction is that it can reduce the expected losses caused by global warming. The cost of a country's emissions reduction is reflected mainly in its decreasing output or increasing input. Due to the mobility of greenhouse gases, a particular country bears the full costs of emissions reduction itself, while all countries share the benefits. Therefore, no country has sufficient incentive to unilaterally reduce its emissions and all want to be free riders. Consequently, it is difficult to achieve a rational result of global cooperation to reduce emissions.

If a country could exclusively claim all the benefits resulting from its emissions reduction then the optimal strategy for each country would shift from not reducing emissions to reducing emissions. Unfortunately, in reality, the extremely high costs and technical limitations prevent a country from claiming the benefits to the other countries resulting from its emissions reduction. If, however, the emission entitlements of all countries could be clearly defined then a country reducing its emissions could 'claim' the benefits through the market; its emission quotas for sale would increase or the amount needing to be purchased would decrease.

Hence, the core of the global emissions reduction problem is really one of how to define or allocate each country's emissions entitlements. The Coase (1960) theorem stresses the importance of clearly defined initial property rights for minimising social costs, but does not provide an answer for how to define the initial GHG emission entitlements. Grossman and Hart (1986) and Hart and Moore (1990) stress that, if there are transaction costs, different ownership structures will lead to different performances and there must be one particular ownership structure that is most efficient. Hence, given a global initial emissions rights allocation, an efficient *ex post* global *real* emissions allocation will be achieved through the market. The emissions reduction will occur in the countries with the lowest opportunity costs.

How do we define the initial emissions entitlement of each country? The atmosphere is a typical public resource and, in most cases, Earth's public resources have been 'allocated' on a first-serve principle or have even been obtained through war. Moreover, redefining the distorted historical emissions makes things more complicated. We need therefore to find a fair, objective and simple principle to define or allocate the initial emission entitlements for each country.

A theoretical framework and global solution

A theoretical framework

We use Figure 17.1 to show the time horizon of emissions. The definition (or allocation) of emission entitlements includes two periods: the historical period, T0–T1, and the future period, T1–T2.

Figure 17.1 The time horizon for international emissions rights allocation

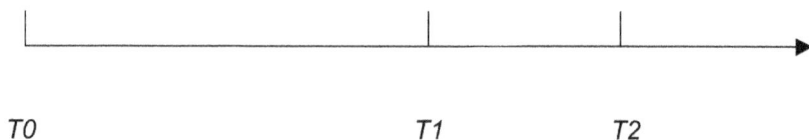

Note: *T0* could represent the point of the Industrial Revolution or another point.[1] *T1* is the current point and *T2* is a point in the future—say, 2050.

The problem of how to define (or allocate) each country's emissions rights can be treated as a problem of preventing a country from imposing extra external harm on the others. No matter how much an individual country emits, the harm from those emissions is borne by everyone on Earth. The GHG emissions of each country cause harm not only to the emitting country, but to all people in all other countries. After the external harms imposed by one another are offset, the over-emitting countries still impose extra harm on others.

The definition of property rights is reciprocal. The emission right can be defined to either the emitter or the victim. Defining each party's property rights is essential for fairness, so the following principle should be adhered to: no country has the right to impose extra external harm on any other country without compensation; or, all countries have the right not to bear extra external harm from any others without compensation. If a country imposes extra external harm on other countries, it should compensate them. Therefore, the emissions level at which no country imposes extra external harm on any other country becomes a benchmark for allocating the initial emission entitlements.

Proposition

A country does not impose extra external harm on any others if and only if each country's per capita emissions are equal. Accordingly, the equivalent per capita emissions are the benchmark for the allocation of initial emission entitlements. If the real emissions of a country are greater than its initial emission entitlements or the global per capita level, it should pay for its extra emissions, and vice versa.

Proof

Since the internal allocation of emission entitlements within a country is not discussed in this chapter, for simplicity, we assume that all people's real emissions within a country are the same and are equal to the per capita real emissions of the country, e_{ij}. The population of a country is N_i, and the world population is $N = \sum N_i$, in which $i = 1, 2...n$ stands for different countries. $j = 1, 2$ stands for two different periods: $T0-T1$ and $T-T2$. The global per capita accumulated emission during period j is $\overline{e_j} = \frac{\sum e_{ij} \cdot N_i}{N}$. Since the harm caused by each person's emissions is borne by all people around the world, the total external damage a person causes to all the other people is the function of $e_{ij}(N-1)$. Everyone on Earth suffering the harm from GHG emissions is the function of $\sum_{i=1}^{n} e_{ij} \cdot N_i = \overline{e_j} \cdot N$.[2] Since the proportion of e_{ij} is due to the emissions by each person, the external harm imposed by the others is the function of $\sum_{j=1}^{n} e_{ij} \cdot N_i - e_{ij}$. Given the assumption that all people's real emissions within a country are equal, the people within a country do not cause extra harm to each other. Therefore, all the extra external harm caused by a person is the extra external harm to the people of all other countries. In the case without a compensation mechanism, the emissions of a person do not cause any extra external harm to any other countries—if and only if:

Equation 17.1

$$e_{ij}(N-1) - (\sum_{i=1}^{n} e_{ij} \cdot N_i - e_{ij}) = 0$$

A country does not impose any extra external damage on any other country, if and only if:

Equation 17.2

$$[e_{ij}(N-1)] \cdot N_i - [(\sum_{i=1}^{n} e_{ij} \cdot N_i - e_{ij})] \cdot N_i = 0$$

Insert $\sum_{i=1}^{n} e_{ij} \cdot N_i = \overline{e_j} \cdot N$ into Equation 17.2 and we have $e_{ij} = \overline{e_j}$. It is the benchmark emission level, satisfying the 'if and only if' condition that 'each country does not impose any extra external harm on any other country'. The benchmark emissions level is the initial emissions entitlement, e_{ij}^r, which will be allocated to each person of each country. Each country's initial emissions entitlement is:

Equation 17.3

$$e_{ij}^{r} = \overline{e}_{j}$$

If the real per capita emissions of a country are greater than its per capita initial emission entitlement—namely, $e_{ij} > e_{ij}^{r}$ —or greater than the global per capita emission entitlement—namely, $e_{ij} > \overline{e}_{j}$ —then it means this country has imposed extra external harm on other countries and should compensate the others for its extra emissions, and vice versa. Using e_{ij}^{t} to indicate the per capita extra emissions of a country, $e_{ij}^{t} = e_{ij} - e_{ij}^{r}$. Assuming p is the price of a unit of emissions entitlement in the international emissions market, or the shadow price when an international emissions trading scheme is not in place, the compensation will be $y = p \cdot e_{ij}^{t}$. QED.

The global distribution of per capita emission entitlements of all countries in different periods is $\left[e_{i}^{r} \right]$. It defines the global allocation of emission entitlements of each country according to the principle that 'no country has the right to impose extra external harm on any other country without providing compensation'. The emissions distribution of each country is therefore based on an objective rather than a subjective standard. After the emission entitlements are clearly defined, the emission entitlements trade will select an optimal global real emissions structure with the least social cost $\left[(e_{i}^{r} + e_{i}^{t}) \right]$. In reality, since it is extremely costly to completely and accurately measure the real amount of emissions, e_{ij}, of each country, there is a trade-off between improving the accuracy of measuring and enforcing each country's emission entitlements and reducing transaction costs. There is therefore always a marginal error between the measured real emissions and the *real* real emissions of each country. Therefore, the situation of $(e_{ij} - e_{ij}^{t}) - e_{ij}^{r} = \varepsilon_{ij} \neq 0$ is always true. The ε_{ij} is refereed as the efficient externalities (Cheung 1970).

Hence, to define or allocate each country's initial emissions rights, the *per capita principle* should be used *consistently* in: 1) all periods—that is, in both T0–T1 and T1–T2; and 2) all countries, including industrialised and developing countries.

National emissions account-based global solution

A country's emissions entitlements are:

Equation 17.4

$$E_{ij}^{r} = e_{ij}^{r} \cdot N_{i} = \overline{e}_{j} \cdot N_{i}$$

If a country's real emissions, E_{ij}, are greater than its emission entitlements, E_{ij}^{r}, it should purchase emissions quotas, E_{ij}^{t}, from other countries.

Equation 17.5

$$E_{ij}^{t} = E_{ij} - \overline{e}_{j} \cdot N_{i}$$

The balance of a country's national emissions account (NEA) is B_{ij}:

Equation 17.6

$$B_{ij} = \overline{e}_{j} \cdot N_{i} + E_{ij}^{t} - E_{ij}$$

According to each country's 1) initial emissions rights (entitlements), E_{ij}^{r}; 2) real emissions, E_{ij}; 3) traded emissions, E_{ij}^{t}, in two periods of T0–T1 and T1–T2, we can then establish an NEA for each country.

Each country's total balance on its NEA by T2 is the addition of 1) its emissions balance during T0–T1, and 2) its new emissions quotas allocated during T1–T2 plus its traded quotas. The balance on each country's NEA then exactly represents their 'differentiated responsibilities' to reduce emissions (or their rights to emit). Once all countries' responsibilities are clearly defined, an effective international and national approach can be developed. The NEA-based global solution includes three steps.

Step 1

Each country's emissions rights during T0–T1 must be defined according to the per capita principle. We can then turn the unclear 'historic responsibilities' of the over-emitting countries into clear NEA deficits, and surpluses for others. Since the traded emission is zero and emission costs are not included in the price of traded goods during T0–T1, embedded emissions, in theory, need to be counted as the real emissions of the importing countries—although it is impractical to measure this.

Step 2

The future global emission amounts during T1–T2 must be scientifically set and then the emissions quotas allocated among all countries according to the per capita principle. Each country's new emissions quotas during T1–T2, plus the NEA balance during T0–T1 are its total emissions caps by T2. Since emissions quotas can be traded and emission costs will eventually be reflected in the price of traded goods, embedded emissions are no longer a particular problem when we measure each county's real emissions.

Step 3

An open and compatible solution must be established for the international collaborative mechanism and the domestic emissions reduction approach to incorporate various existing proposals. The various solutions can then coexist and compete with each other in the NEA framework.

At the international level

Any existing collaborative mechanisms can be used, as long as their effectiveness is eventually reflected in each country's balances of NEA.

International emissions trading scheme (IETS): changes the balance of the NEA of the emission-trading countries.

Joint implementation (JI): changes the balance of each country's NEA.

Clean Development Mechanism (CDM): increases the NEA balance of industrialised countries and decreases the balance of developing countries side-by-side.

International public emissions reduction fund: the widely proposed public fund can also play its role in the NEA framework. The contribution of a country to the fund increases its balance accordingly, while it reduces the balance of the beneficiary countries.

Technology transfer and research and development: their effectiveness needs to be reflected in the NEA.

At the national level

All countries have freedom to choose their domestic approach, as long as they meet their emissions caps by T2. The countries with emission deficits need to clear their deficits by the target year.

1. A country may adopt an emissions trading scheme (ETS), carbon tax, hybrid system, emissions regulation or any other approach at home.

2. Subject to its total quotas by T2, each country may determine the number of its annual emission permits and make a credible emissions reduction (or emissions) road-map during T1–T2.

A demonstration of how to establish a national emissions account

A demonstration

Consider a world consisting of two representative countries: industrial country A and developing country B. Their population, concentrated historical emissions by T1, current annual emissions at T1, global emissions and future global emissions quotas during T1–T2 are in Table 17.1. For simplicity, embedded emissions during T0–T1 are assumed to be zero. A country's NEA is established according to its per capita emissions entitlements, real emissions, traded emissions and population. For simplicity, assume the population remains stable during T1–T2.

Table 17.1 Emissions data for each country (hypothetical)
(person, unit)

	Country A		Country B		World	
	Total	Per capita	Total	Per capita	Total	Per capita
Population at T1	200	-	400	-	600	-
Current annual net emissions (at T1)	400	2	400	1	800	1.33
Concentrated historical emissions during T0–T1	28,000	140	14,000	35	42,000	70
Global emissions quotas during T1–T2	-	-	-	-	30,000	50

- = zero

Step one: calculating each country's NEA balance during T0–T1

The global per capita emission during T0–T1 is 70 units of carbon dioxide. For simplicity, we assume the embedded emission is zero. If country A has over-emitted 14 000 units of carbon dioxide and its emission deficit is −14 000 units of carbon dioxide by T1, the emission surplus of country B is 14 000 units of carbon dioxide (Table 17.2).

Table 17.2 National emissions account during T0–T1

	Country A	Country B	World
Emissions entitlements	70 × 200 = 14,000	70 × 400 = 28,000	42,000
Real emissions	28,000	14,000	42,000
Traded emissions	0	0	0
Balance until T1	14,000−28,000 = −14,000	28,000−14,000 = 14,000	0

Step two: scientifically set the future global emissions target during T1–T2 and calculate each country's NEA balance during T1–T2

The global per capita emissions entitlement during T1–T2 is 50 units of carbon dioxide. The total global accumulated emissions by T2 will reach 72 000 units of carbon dioxide. For simplicity, we do not take into account the removal of greenhouse gases in the short run in this hypothetical example. According to the per capita principle, the allocation of emission entitlements and balances for each country can be calculated (Table 17.3). The total balance for each country is the addition of its balance during T0–T1 and that in T1–T2. The balance exactly represents each country's responsibility for emissions reduction (or entitlements to emit).

Table 17.3 National emissions account during T1–T2

	Country A	Country B	World
Emission entitlements	50 × 200 = 10,000	50 × 400 = 20,000	30,000
Real emissions	Yet to happen	Yet to happen	Yet to happen
Traded emissions	Yet to happen	Yet to happen	Yet to happen
Balance at T1	−14,000 + 10,000 = −4,000	14 000 + 20,000 = 34,000	30,000

The findings from the demonstration

First, it is misleading to simply compare the current annual emissions of different countries at T1. In the example, the current annual emissions of countries A and B at T1 are both 400 units, but their per capita real emissions are very different. The global per capita emission is 1.33 units, while the per capita emission of country B is 1—far lower than the 2 units of country A. Without considering historical emissions, country A over-emits 0.67 of a unit per person per annum, while country B still has 0.33 of a unit to reach the global average per capita level.

Second, it is misleading to simply compare per capita annual emissions of different countries. To show this, we adjust the current annual emissions of country B in Table 17.1 from 400 to 800, then the current per capita annual emissions of the two countries are equal to 2 units. Since the historical emission of country A is higher than that of country B, however, country A has infringed 14 000 units of emission entitlements from country B.

Third, once the emission entitlements of all countries are clearly defined, the real emissions of each country can no longer be used as the measurement for their contributions to global emissions reduction. For instance, in theory, country A can develop all zero-emission service industries and import emissions-embedded goods from country B, while country B, in addition to its own emissions quotas, buys all emissions quotas of country A to develop emissions-intensive industries and exports emissions-embedded manufactured goods to country A. In this case, all global emissions are done by country B, and country A emits zero. This does not mean, however, that country A has made a bigger contribution to global emissions reduction; both countries have made the same contribution. Also, to simply pursue a low-carbon economy is misleading. In this case, country A is a zero-emission economy while country B is an emission-intensive economy, but the welfare of the two countries could be the same.

Fourth, the reason why country A should take more responsibility for climate change is not because it is richer than country B (that is, the so-called different capacities) or because country B has a 'right to development', but because country B bears the harm imposed by the extra emissions of country A, represented by its deficit of −14 000 units. This means that the rationale behind the NEA-based solution is substantially different from those emphasising the capacity difference.[3] Meanwhile, how much responsibility a country should take for climate change is irrelevant to whether or not it is large. A country cannot be required to take more responsibility just because it is big in size. If a large developing country was not a single country but an economic bloc consisting of 30 poor countries, no-one would require the 30 poor countries to reduce their emissions. In reality, however, there is no substantial difference between the two cases.

The advantages of the NEA-based solution

First, this solution is an upgraded version of the Kyoto Protocol: it maintains its advantages but overcomes its flaws.

- It offers full coverage: all countries can be covered. To classify the countries into industrialised and developing countries is then no longer necessary in the proposal. The problem of carbon leakage is also solved once all countries are covered by the new protocol. In practice, it can cover the major emitters first, and then extend further to cover the minor emitters later.

- It offers effectiveness: the global reduction target is built into the proposal, since the global aggregate emission amount in the future is scientifically determined and then allocated among all countries. Also, an accumulated emissions target replaces the percentage target in the Kyoto Protocol.

- The additionality problem of the CDM is overcome. A CDM project will increase the balance of the investing country and accordingly reduce the balance of the host country side-by-side. The NEA approach can therefore not only overcome the additionality problem, it can further extend the CDM to a two-way mechanism—that is, the firms in developing countries can also invest in emissions-reduction projects in industrialised countries.

Second, the vague 'common but differentiated responsibilities' are clearly defined in the proposal. An NEA is an effective tool by which to measure and manage global emissions reductions. Each country's emissions balance exactly represents its responsibility for emissions reduction.

Third, once each country's emissions account is established, emissions reduction becomes a self-interested behaviour: the more a country reduces, the more quotas it can sell or the less quotas it needs to buy. A strong incentive mechanism for global emissions reduction is therefore established.

Fourth, the NEA approach is compatible with various existing international collaborative mechanisms and domestic reduction approaches. The various approaches can compete with each other in the NEA framework.

Fifth, for the countries that are not yet covered by the Kyoto Protocol or that have failed to meet their commitments, their contribution to and responsibilities for emissions reduction are clearly measured and recorded by their NEAs.

Discussions

Contraction and convergence

Since the principle of 'contraction and convergence' was first proposed by the Global Commons Institute in 2000, it has been widely embraced by some industrialised countries. Under contraction and convergence, each country will start out with emission entitlements equal to its current real emissions levels, and then, over time, converge to equal its per capita entitlements, while the overall global budget contracts to accommodate the emissions reduction objective. The problem of convergence is that now that it recognises the per capita principle as a fair principle in the allocation of emission entitlements, the principle should be applied from T0, rather than as late as the 'converged point' in the future (T2). 'Real emissions' is a different concept to 'emissions entitlement'. A country's high/low per capita real emissions cannot justify its high/low emission entitlements. In the process of convergence, the rights and interests of country B are really infringed by country A. In the NEA-based solution, the concept of convergence can still be incorporated, but it now merely means 'convergence of real emissions' rather than 'convergence of emission entitlements'. Each country's gaps between its emission entitlements and real emissions need to be balanced by the traded emissions quotas.

Common but differentiated responsibilities

The principle of 'common but differentiated responsibilities' is a critical one for protecting the rights of developing countries with regard to climate change, but is still not sufficient. Under the existing framework of the Kyoto Protocol, developing countries are not required to reduce their emissions. This makes it look like only the industrialised countries are making a contribution to global emissions reductions, while the developing countries are not. Nonetheless, according to their NEA balances, country A, with 14 000 deficits, should reduce much more, and country B, with 34 000 surplus units, is entitled to claim more compensation from country A. Because the differentiated responsibilities are not clearly defined, however, both the greater responsibilities of country A and the rights of country B cannot be seen clearly in the existing Kyoto framework.

Global public fund on climate change

A focus of international climate negotiations is how industrialised countries can transfer technologies and funds to developing countries for mitigation and adaptation. The proposal for a global public fund for emissions reduction has been widely discussed (Bhagwati 2006; Garnaut 2008:Ch.10). The rationale for why industrialised countries should provide technologies and funds to developing countries is mainly because of the former's historical emissions. Under the unclear differentiated responsibilities, the establishment of such a global fund could be deemed as the resolution of the historical problem—and all countries will be at the same level on emissions reductions. Nonetheless, this rough calculation is avoided in the NEA-based solution. For instance, a country's emissions deficit might be reduced by only 30 per cent after a country has made a big contribution to the global public fund.

The issue of embedded emissions

The issue of embedded emissions has also been widely discussed. In the NEA-based global solution, embedded emissions in different situations have different welfare effects. First, during the historical period of T0–T1, since emission entitlements were not clearly defined and emission costs were not reflected in the price of traded goods, the embedded emissions, in theory, should be treated as the real emissions of the importing country—though it is almost infeasible to be measured in practice. Second, since each country's emission entitlements during T1–T2 are clearly allocated and the emission costs will be reflected in the price of traded goods, it is not meaningful to take into account embedded emissions in the production-approach measurement. Third, if, however, some countries are not covered by the international emissions reduction protocol, the countries not covered will impact on the export industries of the countries producing emissions-embedded goods. Carbon leakage to the countries not covered is inevitable. The solution to this problem is not to relax the emissions reduction targets of the home countries, but to ensure all countries are covered by the international agreement.

Is global warming a market failure?

Global warming is widely seen as a market failure (for example, Stern 2007). This is somewhat misleading. The condition for a market to function is well-defined property rights. Without emissions rights being clearly defined, we cannot expect the market to work on global warming. Defining emissions rights is, however, the job of government. Greenhouse gases are a global public good/hazard. That means we need a global 'government' to provide the public service of defining and enforcing each country's emission entitlements. In an era of globalisation, we need to establish effective global governance, rather than relying on government intervention to solve climate change.

What does the per capita principle mean to large developing countries?

Many people might think that the populous developing countries, such as China, will benefit greatly from the per capita principle; in reality, they will not. The per capita principle merely allocates a low carbon growth model to China, since, according to the principle, China's accumulated per capita emissions can reach only the world average level in the future—much lower than the current high level of real emissions in the industrialised countries. It is impossible for China to adopt a business-as-usual growth model in the future as the industrialised countries did previously. China will be under huge pressure to lower its emissions according to the per capita principle.

Conclusion

Based on the principle that no country has the right to impose extra external harm on any other country without compensation, this chapter has developed a theoretical framework for how to allocate GHG emission entitlements for each country. The historical and future initial emission entitlements should be allocated according to the per capita principle. A country's national emissions account (NEA) can be established according to its emission entitlements, real emissions and traded emissions. The balance of the NEA of each country exactly represents its responsibility for emissions reduction. The optimal global allocation of real emissions can be achieved through the transaction of initial emission entitlements. The embedded emissions during T0–T1 should be taken into account when measuring the real emissions of each country, while it is not necessary to take into account those during T1–T2. The NEA-based global solution aims to cover all countries. In order to improve its effectiveness, however, it might first cover the major emitters and then extend to other countries once they are ready.

The proposed NEA approach is still an in-principle framework and many details are yet to be sorted out. For instance, how and from what point should the historical emissions of each country be measured? How can the future global emissions targets be set scientifically? What sorts of international and national institutional infrastructure are required for the NEA approach? For how long should the emissions deficits of the industrialised countries be eliminated? How can relevant systems of international trading, supervision and implementation be designed? Although the choice of which kind of post-Kyoto protocol to adopt is more a political decision than a purely academic issue, the most essential requirement in order for the protocol to be widely accepted is that it should be built on justification, rather than being decided by arm-twisting. The NEA approach is such a solution, with no bias to any particular countries or interests.

At present, most of the literature on climate change presumes that emissions reduction will conflict with economic development in the short term. With rapid technological innovations in renewable energy, however, there appears to be great potential for a low-carbon economic development model to replace the traditional high emissions growth model. The technological innovation must be driven mainly by market incentives, rather than by government intervention (Romer 1990). The NEA approach provides such an incentive. If the emission entitlements of all countries can be clearly defined and strictly enforced then the market can function well and emissions reduction will become a self-interested behaviour. In the long run, GHG emissions reduction will bring prosperity and sustainability to human society.

Acknowledgments

This chapter is an outcome of the Development Research Centre project Fighting Against Global Climate Change, headed by Yutai Zhang. Project team leader: Shijin Liu. Draft author: Yongsheng Zhang (<zys@drc.gov.cn>). Revised and finalised by: Shijin Liu. Discussants: Junkuo Zhang, Hongchun Zhou, Peilin Liu, Zhenyu Wu and Anbo Xiang. The authors thank the valuable comments, suggestions and criticisms from Shiro Armstrong, Peter Drysdale, Steven Howes, Frank Jotzo, Warwick McKibbin, Yew-Kwang Ng, Ligang Song and Shuntian Yao. The authors are solely responsible for the errors.

References

Aldy, J. E., Barrett, S. and Stavins, R. N. (eds) 2007, *13+1: a comparision of global climate change policy architectures*, Discussion Paper, dp-03-26, Resources for the Future, Washington, DC.

Aldy, J. E. and Stavins, R. N. (eds) 2007, *Architectures for Agreement: Addressing global climate change in the post-Kyoto world*, Cambridge University Press, New York.

Bhagwati, J. 2006, 'A global warming fund could succeed where Kyoto failed', *Financial Times*, 16 August 2006.

Cheung, S. 1970, 'The structure of a contract and the theory of a non-exclusive resource', *Journal of Law and Economics*, vol. 13, pp. 49–70.

Coase, R. 1960, 'The problem of social cost', *Journal of Law and Economics*, vol. 3, pp. 1–44.

European Commission (EC) 2008, *Questions and answers on the commission's proposal to revise the EU emissions trading system*, MEMO/08/35, 23 January, European Commission, Brussels.

Frankel, J. 2007, 'Formulas for quantitative emissions targets', in J. E. Aldy and R. N. Stavins (eds), *Architectures for Agreement: Addressing global climate change in the post-Kyoto world*, Cambridge University Press, New York.

Garnaut, R. 2008, *The Garnaut Climate Change Review*, Cambridge University Press, Melbourne.

Grossman, S. and Hart, O. 1986, 'The costs and benefits of ownership: a theory of vertical and lateral integration', *Journal of Political Economy*, vol. 94, pp. 691–719.

Hart, O. and Moore, B. 1990, 'Property rights and the nature of the firm', *Journal of Political Economy*, vol. 98, pp. 1119–58.

Hardin, G. 1968, 'The tragedy of the commons', *Science*, vol. 162, pp. 1243–8.

Solomon, S., Qin, D., Manning, M., Chen, Z., Marquis, M., Avery, K. B., Tignor, M. and Miller, H. L. (eds) 2007, *Climate Change 2007: The physical science basis. Contribution of Working Group I to the fourth assessment report of the IPCC*, Intergovernmental Panel on Climate Change, Cambridge University Press, Cambridge and New York.

Metz, B., Davidson, O. R., Bosch, P. R., Dave, R. and Meyer, L. A. (eds) 2007, *Climate Change 2007: Mitigation of climate change. Contribution of Working Group III to the fourth assessment report of the IPCC*, Intergovernmental Panel on Climate Change, Cambridge University Press, Cambridge.

Nordhause, W. 2006, 'After Kyoto: alternative mechanism to control global warming', *American Economic Review*, May.

—— 2008, *The Challenge of Global Warming: Economic models and environmental policy*, Yale University Press, New Haven, Conn.

Pew Center on Climate Change 2005, *International Climate Efforts Beyond 2012: Report of climate dialogue at Pocantico*, Pew Center on Climate Change, Arlington, Va.

Romer, P. 1990, 'Endogenous technological change', *Journal of Political Economy*, vol. 98, S71–102.

Sagar, A. and Kandlikar M. 1997, 'Knowledge, rhetoric and power: international politics of climate change', *Economic and Political Weekly*, vol. 32, no. 49 (6–12 December), pp. 3139–48.

Stern, N. 2007, *The Economics of Climate Change: The Stern review*, Cambridge University Press, Cambridge.

Stiglitz, J. 2006, 'A new agenda for global warming', *Economist's Voice*, The Berkeley Electronic Press, University of California, Berkeley.

United Nations Framework Convention on Climate Change (UNFCCC) 2007, *Report of the Conference of the Parties on its Thirteenth Session, held in Bali from 3 to 15 December 2007. Addendum, Part Two: Action taken by the conference of the parties at its thirteenth session*, FCCC/CP/2007/6/Add.1, United Nations Framework Convention on Climate Change, Bonn, Germany.

Weitzman, M. L. 1974, 'Prices vs. quantities', *Review of Economic Studies*, vol. 41, no. 4, pp. 477–91.

Endnotes

1. A major disagreement between industrialised and developing countries centres on which year to start T0 from. This question is open in the proposal, as long as 1) the starting year can be justified, and 2) someone can be held responsible for all the existing emissions in the atmosphere.

2. In reality, the harm different people in different regions suffered cannot be 100 per cent equal, but for simplicity, the assumption of equal harm is acceptable.

3. The NEA-based solution is different from those associating each country's responsibility with its income level (for instance, Pew Center on Climate Change 2005; Frankel 2007; UNFCCC 2007).

Can China rescue the global climate change negotiations?

18

Stephen Howes

China has to make a substantial commitment, though I cannot say what exactly the nature of that commitment ought to be.

— Todd Stern, US special envoy for climate change[1]

Introduction

China's importance in global efforts to reduce greenhouse gas emissions is widely acknowledged. Greater efforts by China to reduce emissions will have large direct and indirect environmental benefits—direct because China is the world's largest emitter and indirect because China is a superpower. Greater efforts by China would induce greater effort by many other countries, developing and industrialised.

China already has policies in place to reduce emissions, including by improving energy efficiency and promoting renewable energy and afforestation (Sheehan and Sun 2008; Garnaut et al. 2008a; Information Office of the State Council 2008). Emissions have, however, grown rapidly in China in recent years: carbon dioxide emissions from fossil fuels—the main source of greenhouse gases—grew on average at 10.5 per cent per annum between 2000 and 2007 (Netherlands Environmental Assessment Agency 2008). Growth in emissions has slowed with the onset of the global recession, and perhaps even gone negative, but it is expected to pick up again with economic recovery. Continued growth of emissions in China at or close to 10 per cent per annum would offset any reduction in emissions in industrialised countries and would discourage global action. What, however, does the world expect of China? What might China agree to do? And what impact could China have on global climate change negotiations, which have been making little progress?

As the opening quote suggests, these are not easy questions. They are also risky questions to answer, since they are live, and the real answers—as against good guesses—might become apparent any day. There are, however, also no more important questions confronting the current round of global climate change negotiations. On these grounds of importance, rather than ease or prudence, I attempt in this chapter to provide an answer to these questions. I claim no special insider's knowledge on climate change policy in China, but rather draw on recently published material.

To provide the necessary context, I begin by summarising the history and status of international climate change negotiations. I then set out a range of non-official views that has emerged from China in recent months, consider their possible implications for official policy and conclude with an attempt to answer the questions set out above.

Continuity and change in international climate change negotiations

If serious international climate change mitigation does get under way in the coming years, the past decade (roughly 1998–2008) will be viewed as the lost decade for climate change. And, if serious international mitigation does not emerge, the mishaps of the past decade will be among the main reasons why.

After the Kyoto Protocol was concluded in December 1997, the US Administration, responding to the US Senate's Bryd-Hegel Resolution of July 1997,[2] stated that it would not push for ratification of the treaty without developing countries doing more. As Todd Stern (1999), then President Bill Clinton's climate change coordinator, indicated in June: 'we are not…intending to submit the treaty for Senate ratification until we have a greater…meaningful level of participation from developing countries, which we don't yet have.'

The diplomatic 'full-court press' launched by then Secretary of State, Madeleine Albright (1998), in support of this objective achieved very little. In hindsight, it was mission impossible, since the United States was essentially trying to reopen an international agreement the ink on which was barely dry. Two developing countries, Argentina and Kazakhstan, expressed interest in voluntarily adopting emissions targets (Victor 2001). Overall, however, developing countries responded with hostile solidarity. China led the opposition. Liu Jiang, head of China's delegation to the Sixth Conference of the Parties under the UN Framework Convention on Climate Change (UNFCCC) in 2000 argued that:

To confuse the different responsibilities between developed and developing countries, to impose new obligations on the latter and even take this as a condition for the Protocol's ratification, will lead to nothing but fierce political confrontations. This, undoubtedly, is a catastrophe for the international community in their efforts to combat climate change. (Liu 2000)

In the end, no developing countries adopted emissions targets. In 2001, under President George W. Bush, the United States announced that it would not be ratifying the Kyoto Protocol.

Fast forward to today and the US focus once again is on developing countries. Todd Stern, now the climate change envoy for President Barack Obama, summed up the current US position earlier this year:

I think the most fundamental issues in this negotiation in general have to do with how we think about, capture and express the actions and the level of undertakings to be taken by major developing countries as well as the developed countries. (Stern 2009)

China's response, a decade later, was also little changed. Developing countries were not the problem. Rather, 'the key to a deal in Copenhagen lies in the "political will" of the developed countries', according to Su Wei, China's chief climate change negotiator (Wu and Huan 2009).

To understand this decade-long stand-off, one has to return to the 1992 Framework Convention on Climate Change (UNFCCC). The UNFCCC, which has been ratified by 192 parties, including the United States, committed industrialised countries to move first, to take, as the preamble put it, 'immediate action…as a first step towards comprehensive response strategies at the global, national, and, where agreed, regional levels'. The Kyoto Protocol to the convention, with its commitment by industrialised countries to reduce emissions by 2008–12 by 5 per cent relative to 1990 levels, was intended to be this first step—but it was never taken. The failure of the United States to ratify the treaty dealt a fatal blow to the protocol's credibility and discouraged effort by those industrialised countries that did go ahead. Few have succeeded in achieving a sustained decline in emissions.

This 'first-step' strategy—let us call it Plan A—has now been discarded. From an environmental perspective, it is too dangerous for developing countries to continue to sit outside the international climate change mitigation regime. Whereas in 1990, developing-country carbon dioxide emissions from the combustion of fossil fuels were about one-quarter of total global emissions, by 2005, they were 40 per cent (IEA 2007a). In any case, the US response to Kyoto has made any first-step strategy politically untenable. Industrialised countries are therefore trying to move towards a Plan B, which involves all major emitters. Under Plan B, industrialised countries are still meant to do more (hence preserving the UNFCCC principle of common but differentiated responsibility), but no longer go first.

The slow progress being made in negotiations bears testimony to the difficulty of this task. Since industrialised countries didn't deliver on Plan A and since Plan B involves asking more of developing countries, it is not surprising that the transition is proving difficult and acrimonious. To use a colloquial expression, industrialised countries don't have a leg to stand on. Moreover, no country is prepared to reopen the UNFCCC itself, yet it is this treaty that commits industrialised countries not only to move first but, moreover, to compensate developing countries for the 'agreed full incremental costs' they will bear for any actions they should choose to take to mitigate climate change (Article 4.3). These provisions provide ample grounds for any developing country to object to any push to a Plan B that requires them to do more.

The distance the world has to cover to reach an agreement at Copenhagen or beyond can be seen from the disagreements in relation to the three main negotiating planks of the 'Bali Road Map', agreed in Bali, Indonesia, in December 2007. The various complexities and strands of the Bali Road Map can be boiled down to three main points (Howes 2009; de Boer 2009):[3]

- industrialised countries should commit to economy-wide emissions reduction targets
- developing countries should take 'nationally appropriate mitigation action'
- industrialised countries should provide financing and other support to developing countries for mitigation and adaptation.

While these three propositions command widespread agreement, the debate about each is intense. Concerning the first, all major industrialised countries have now indicated what their emissions reduction targets for 2020 will likely be. Initial analysis suggests that the likely aggregate industrialised-country reduction will be in the range of 10–20 per cent by 2020 from 1990 levels (Howes 2009). Developing countries, however, are demanding that industrialised countries cut emissions by at least 25–40 per cent, in line with numbers drawn from the *Fourth Assessment Report* of the Intergovernmental Panel on Climate Change (IPCC) and first floated at the Bali conference. Often, the demands are placed at the top end of that range. In its May 2009 submission to the UNFCCC, China called on '[a]ll developed country Parties to the Convention [to] commit to reduce their GHG emissions by at least 40% below 1990 levels by 2020' (Government of the People's Republic of China 2009:63).[4]

There is a similarly sharp divergence of views in relation to the third issue. Developing countries argue that international funding should be provided largely through the public sector and needs to be large (in the range of hundreds of billions of dollars annually). China's May 2009 submission recently called on '[d]eveloped country Parties [to] make assessed contributions by a percentage of annual GDP, e.g. 0.5–1%, in addition to the existing ODA' (Government of the People's Republic of China 2009:68).[5] This would have to be public funding: 'Private sector approach[es] and market-based mechanism[s] can only play a complementary role in addressing climate change' (Government of the People's Republic of China 2009:68). Large funding claims by developing countries tend to be dismissed by industrialised countries as 'ambit claims' (Spiegel Online 2009). They are reluctant to fund mitigation in middle-income developing countries, including China,[6] and argue that funding to developing countries to support their mitigation should be delivered largely by the private sector. The United States' May 2009 submission to the UNFCCC suggests that '[t]he private sector is expected to be a much larger source of funding than the public sector' (Government of the United States of America 2009:8).

The second issue, relating to mitigation actions to be taken by developing countries, is the most complex. The debate is currently about how these actions should be recorded and has not yet reached the more important issue of what they should add up to in terms of emissions reductions. There is agreement that developing countries will not be asked to sign on to binding targets (as industrialised countries will continue to be), but not much beyond that. In general, although there is a range of views among industrialised and developing countries, industrialised countries want developing countries to commit to plans of action, with quantification of the implied emissions reduction and strong international recognition. Developing countries on the other hand stress the voluntary and discretionary nature of the decision to mitigate, and the link to external financing.

The debate in relation to this second plank of the negotiations can be seen by positions put forward by the United States and South Africa. The United States, for example, has called for the new climate change agreement to include for industrialised countries, 'quantitative emissions reductions/ removals' by 2020 and, for developing countries, 'nationally appropriate mitigation actions [up to 2020]…that are quantified (e.g., reduction from business-as-usual)' (Government of the United States of America 2009:4). South Africa, in contrast, recommends that any new agreement contains provision for only a 'register of nationally appropriate mitigation actions by developing countries'. The register would

> initially contain a list of *indicative* mitigation actions proposed and support needed to implement and will include information related to the assumptions and methodology underpinning the proposed action, the emissions that would be avoided, relative to baseline, and the required support for the indicative mitigation actions. (Government of South Africa 2009:97)

The register would be updated annually. The South African position thus accords developing-country actions a lower legal standing than industrialised-country commitments (only the latter would actually appear in the treaty) and links them more tightly to support from industrialised countries.

While the range of views in relation to it is large, it is this second plank of negotiations that represents the biggest hope of a way forward for the current round of climate change negotiations, since it suggests a convergence of views in an area in which disagreements a decade ago fatally undermined the Kyoto Protocol. In particular, it appears that the United States is not pursuing in this round binding emissions targets for developing countries. Industrialised countries are now broadly united in what they are seeking from developing countries—that is, commitments to policies and measures rather than to quantitative targets. The United States has been explicit about this in recent months, including through its recent submission to the UNFCCC and through public statements. For example on 12 June 2009, Jonathon Pershing, the US chief negotiator, was quoted as saying: 'We're saying that the actions of developing countries should be binding, not the outcomes of those actions' (Adam and Goldenberg 2009). In the same month, during his visit to China, Stern was reported as saying, 'We don't expect China to take a national cap at this stage' (You et al. 2009b).

This approach also suggests that developing countries are now prepared to do more. Developing countries in general might still be termed 'reluctant nations' when it comes to mitigation (Victor 2008), but they are certainly less reluctant than they used to be. Their position is expressed well in the G5 (Brazil, China, India, Mexico and South Africa) 2008 statement:

> We, on our part, are committed to undertaking nationally appropriate mitigation and adaptation actions which also support sustainable development. We would increase the depth and range of these actions supported and enabled by financing, technology and capacity-building with a view to achieving a deviation from business-as-usual. (G5 2008)

Whereas the developing-country position embedded in the UNFCCC might be summarised as, 'We'll only mitigate if we want to, and if there is external financing', this new position could be summarised as 'We'll mitigate climate change on our own to some extent, and we will do more if there is external financing'.

This change in positions is for a number of reasons. On the part of the United States, it perhaps represents the lessons of experience. Getting developing countries to sign on to quantitative targets was tried in the late 1990s, and failed. On the part of the developing countries, there is no doubt that the risks of climate change are better appreciated today than they were 10 years ago. Recent projections for the melting of the Hindu-Kush-Himalayan-Tibetan glacial system (the Earth's 'third pole') suggest that 75 per cent of it will have melted within 50 years, with potentially catastrophic impacts on lives and livelihoods across Asia (UNEP 2008).[7] Having the United States back in the negotiating room at least makes a negotiated agreement possible. It also raises prospects of trade retaliation if an agreement isn't forthcoming, and puts the onus on leading developing countries—none more so than China—to be good global citizens.

China itself has said little in relation to this issue of developing-country mitigation action, though its position overall appears to be similar to that of South Africa (NDRC 2009). What domestic action, if any, China might commit to is the subject of the remainder of this chapter.

Views from China

A number of Chinese papers have recently appeared in two distinct areas: global agreements and national targets. What follows below is not intended by any means to be an exhaustive survey, but rather an important sample of relevant arguments and positions.

Papers by the Project Team of the Development Research Centre (2009, Chapter 17, this volume), Pan et al. (2008a) and Cao (2008) have all taken up the issue of the desirable shape of a global agreement. All three argue for a global cap-and-trade regime in which China participates fully. Given China's traditional opposition to such a position, this itself makes the papers interesting. The status of the authors also demands that this body of work be taken seriously. The Development Research Centre (DRC) is the think tank of the National Development Research Council (NDRC), which has carriage of climate change policy in China. Professor Pan Jiahua is a distinguished scholar and adviser to the government on climate policy.

While the three proposals differ in various ways, they all argue that one factor that should be taken into account when the global emissions budget is divided between countries is *cumulative* per capita emissions. Garnaut (2008) shows that most of the industrialised-country targets for 2050 are broadly consistent with a gradual convergence by that date to equal *current* per capita emissions production. An approach that allocated emissions on per capita past rather than future emissions would, however, require much steeper cuts by industrialised countries. For example, by my calculations, the Pan et al. (2008a) paper has the implication that industrialised countries need to commit to emissions reductions of 65 per cent by 2020.[8]

The second set of papers suggests domestic emissions and energy policy targets for China for the next decade. The *Sustainable Development Strategy Report* produced by the Chinese Academy of Sciences (CAS) in March 2009 proposes that

> by 2020, China's low carbon economic development target be set at 40%–60% reduction of energy consumption per unit of GDP over the 2005 level, and CO_2 emissions per unit of GDP be decreasing by about 50%. With support of reasonable and fair technology transfer and financing mechanism[s]…China's carbon emissions could be expected to peak between 2030 and 2040, and then stabilize and start to decline afterwards. (CAS 2009)

A recent paper by Jiang Kejun and his co-authors of the Energy Research Institute (also part of the NDRC) projects a policy scenario in which energy intensity (the ratio of energy consumed to gross domestic product [GDP]) falls by 50 per cent between 2005 and 2020 (Jiang et al. 2009).

Finally, an article by Hu Angang (2009), of Tsinghua University and an adviser to the government, argues that China should peak its carbon dioxide emissions by 2020, return them by 2030 to 1990 levels and by 2050 reduce emissions to half of their 1990 levels.

What sort of impact might these academic analyses and arguments have on official Chinese policy? Given the consensus outlined in the previous section that developing countries will not be called on to take on binding targets at Copenhagen, the global agreement papers are likely to have more of an influence in the longer term. The curious compromise world of 'targets and timetables' for industrialised countries and 'policies and measures' for developing countries, which the international climate change regime appears to be heading for, is best understood as a transitional one. Ultimately, a more harmonised regime will need to prevail, if only for purposes of comparability.[9] Perhaps more and more countries will take on economy-wide targets. If so, the arguments of the first set of papers indicate some of the difficulties the world might face making the transition. Industrialised countries, having already announced medium (2020) and long-term (2050) targets, have a first-mover advantage. Developing countries, however, when they come to accept quantitative targets, are unlikely to be prepared to derive their targets from the residual of an agreed global target and a set of pre-announced industrialised-country targets. They might also want a renegotiation of industrialised-country targets, along the lines of the arguments advanced by these three papers.[10]

The other set of papers seems more relevant for the short term and for the current negotiating framework. As foreshadowed in Garnaut (2008), could China use domestic policies as the basis for an international commitment to mitigate climate change?

China is now preparing its next five-year plan, which will run from 2011 to 2015. China already has a number of emissions and energy-related targets. There have recently been various suggestions from the media that China is gearing up to adopt new targets for the next five-year plan or possibly out to 2020. Media reports suggest that the existing goal for energy-efficiency improvement (a 20 per cent reduction in the energy intensity ratio over the period of the Eleventh Five-Year Plan from 2005 to 2010) could be extended out to 2015 or 2020 (Chen and Miles 2009). Indeed, China already has an implicit goal: the 2005 China National Energy Strategy and Policy 2020 (DRC 2005) sets a goal of quadrupling GDP by 2020 while only doubling energy use, implying a halving of energy intensity. Chinese officials have also recently indicated that the 2020 target for renewable energy could be increased from 15 per cent (NDRC 2007) to 20 per cent (AFP 2009). It has also been reported that a goal to reduce the carbon intensity of output might be adopted (Li 2009). Zhang Xiaoqiang, Vice-Chairman of the NDRC, was quoted in London as saying that 'Beijing was open to the idea of limits on the carbon intensity of its economy… We have taken note of some expert suggestions on carbon intensity with a view to have some quantified targets in this regard. We are carrying out a serious study of those suggestions' (Borger and Watts 2009).

Hu's (2009) recommendations appear to be unrealistic and, by recommending that by 2030 emissions be returned to their 1990 level, ask too much of China. To see this, note that in Garnaut (2008), even under a stringent 450 parts per million (ppm) global stabilisation agreement, China's emissions entitlements in 2030 are still about double their 2000 levels. Let us assume, however, that, in line with CAS (2009) and consistent with Jiang et al. (2009), China adopts an explicit policy of halving its carbon intensity by 2020 over 2005 through some combination of improvements in energy efficiency and increases in the share of renewable energy. This would require an annual average reduction in carbon intensity of about 4.5 per cent between 2005 and 2020.

How ambitious this is depends on what is understood as the current trajectory of emissions. Views differ greatly on this. A halving of carbon intensity by 2020 would require a deviation—of 10 per cent below the Energy Information Administration (EIA 2009) reference case; 28 per cent below the reference case of the International Energy Agency (IEA 2007b); 30 per cent below the McKinsey Global Institute's (2007) projections; 37 per cent below the projections of Garnaut et al. (2008b); and 45 per cent below those of Sheehan and Sun (2008).[11]

Projecting China's trajectory of emissions is difficult for two reasons. First, the policy regime in China with regards to energy is complex and in flux, and it is difficult to estimate the effect of existing measures. As Sheehan and Sun (2008:404) comment, 'the government has relied mainly on "command and control" measures, rather than price or tax measures'.

Second, there is a structural break in about 2000 in the long-term trend of energy intensity (Figure 18.1). It is difficult to know whether the flattening out of emissions intensity since 2000 is a temporary aberration or a new long-term trend. Garnaut et al. (2008b) argue that the historical experience of other developing countries, including rapidly growing Asian countries, suggests that, without policy action, little further decline in emissions intensity would be expected. This in turn would support the case that a target of halving emissions intensity by 2020 is indeed a very ambitious policy, representing a one-third or more deviation from outcomes in which energy efficiency and clean energy are not explicitly targeted.

Figure 18.1 China's energy intensity, 1980–2008

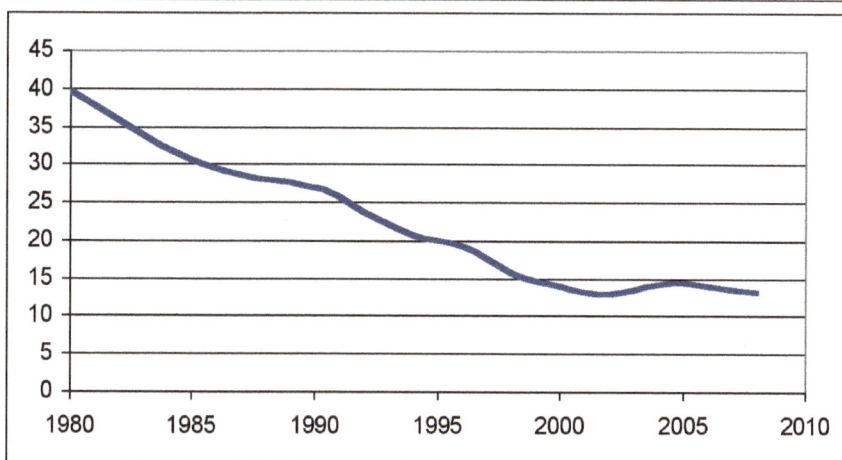

Note: The ratio is energy (in million tons of standard coal equivalent) over GDP (CNY billion at 2000 prices).

Sources: National Bureau of Statistics (NBS) 2008, *China Statistical Yearbook 2008*, China Statistics Press, Beijing, <http://www.stats.gov.cn/tjsj/ndsj/2008/indexeh.htm>; National Bureau of Statistics (NBS) 2009, *Statistical communiqué of the People's Republic of China on the 2008 national economic and social development*, National Bureau of Statistics, Beijing, <http://www.stats.gov.cn/english/newsandcomingevents/t20090226_402540784.htm>

Of course, it is important to stress that such a policy commitment implies that China's emissions will increase. How much depends on growth. With 8 per cent annual average growth to 2020, carbon dioxide emissions would grow by 70 per cent above 2005 levels even with a halving of emissions intensity in this period.

It is, however, equally important to realise that it is inevitable that China's emissions will continue to rise for some time. A one-third deviation from business-as-usual by 2020 is more than what is judged by most to be an equitable or reasonable contribution by China to a stabilisation agreement. For example, the *Garnaut Review* (Garnaut 2008) gave China headroom so that its emissions entitlement at 2020 under an ambitious (450ppm overshooting) global stabilisation scenario was only 10 per cent below business-as-usual. The influential analysis of den Elzen and Höhne (2008) suggests that developing-country emissions need to be only 15–30 per cent below business-as-usual in 2020 for the same scenario.

A policy commitment from China would need to be not only ambitious but credible. There is only space here for a preliminary analysis. So far, China has had limited success in achieving its 4 per cent annual reduction goal for energy intensity—the goal it would need to continue with for another decade to achieve a halving of its carbon intensity. By my calculations, based on the latest available statistics, China had achieved by the end of 2008 about only an 8 per cent reduction in energy intensity since the goal was launched in 2005 (Figure 18.2).[12] That leaves it less than halfway to its 20 per cent target by 2010, with only two years to go. Moreover, most of the reduction was achieved in 2008 and as a result of the global recession (which has hit energy-intensive exports particularly hard) not of Chinese policy.

Figure 18.2 Growth in energy intensity: recent performance and targets

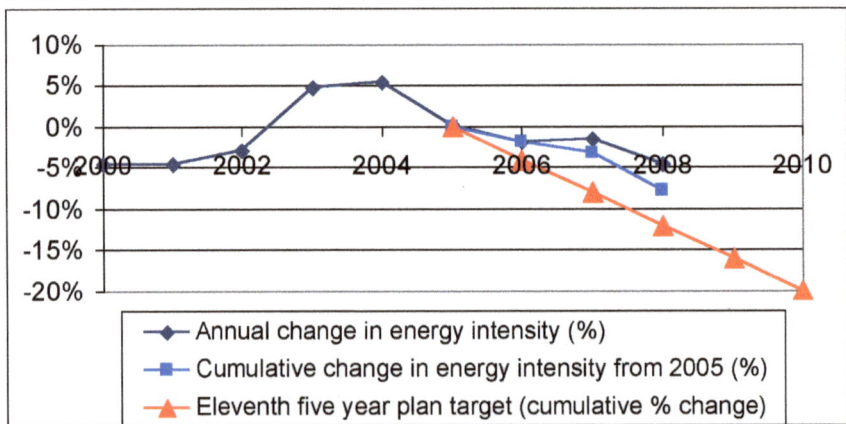

Sources: National Bureau of Statistics (NBS) 2008, *China Statistical Yearbook 2008*, China Statistics Press, Beijing, <http://www.stats.gov.cn/tjsj/ndsj/2008/indexeh.htm>; National Bureau of Statistics (NBS) 2009, *Statistical communiqué of the People's Republic of China on the 2008 national economic and social development*, National Bureau of Statistics, Beijing, <http://www.stats.gov.cn/english/newsandcomingevents/t20090226_402540784.htm>; see also Note 12 and the note to Figure 18.1.

Meanwhile, China's energy mix shows stability, with increases since 2000 in the shares of coal and gas, a reduction in reliance on oil and no change in the share of nuclear and renewable energy (Figure 18.3). If we assume GDP grows at 8 per cent a year from now until 2020, and the energy intensity target is met, renewable energy will have to grow by about 9 per cent annually out to 2020 to meet the 15 per cent target, and by about 11 per cent annually to meet a 20 per cent target. If the share of coal, oil and gas remains constant, increasing the share of renewables to, say, 20 per cent will reduce the carbon intensity of energy by about 15 per cent. If the share of coal relative to oil and gas continues to increase, this will somewhat offset the impact of a rising renewable energy share.

Figure 18.3 China's energy mix, 1990–2007 (per cent)

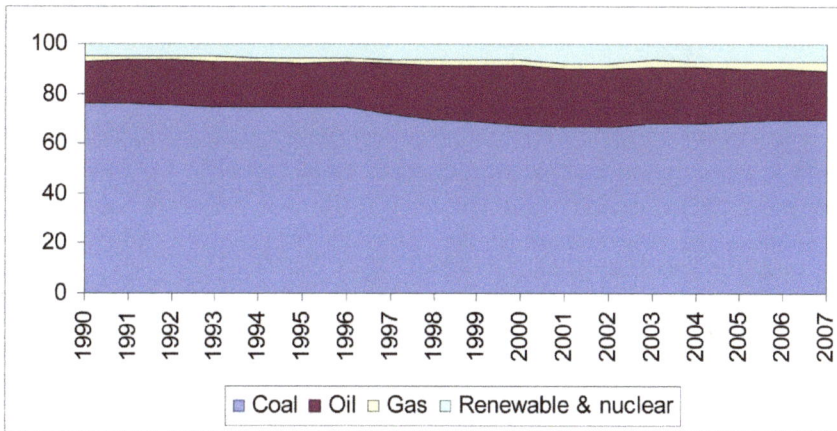

Source: National Bureau of Statistics (NBS) 2008, *China Statistical Yearbook 2008*, China Statistics Press, Beijing, <http://www.stats.gov.cn/tjsj/ndsj/2008/indexeh.htm>

Projections to 2020 (apart from the papers already cited, which obviously argue that a halving of emissions intensity is feasible) give a range of outcomes for what is possible under a reform scenario. A 50 per cent reduction in emissions intensity by 2020 lies about 20 per cent below the policy scenarios of the 2007 IEA projections and Sheehan and Sun (2008).[13] The McKinsey Global Institute's projections are typically more optimistic than others about how quickly energy efficiency can be improved. A 50 per cent reduction target is, however, about 10 per cent below what the McKinsey Global Institute (2007) estimates can be achieved using existing technologies in profitable energy-efficiency improvements, though note that the McKinsey projections are in terms of energy efficiency alone, and the targeted increases in renewable energy would further reduce China's carbon intensity, as discussed above.

In summary, a target for 2020 that aimed broadly at halving China's carbon intensity from its 2005 level would certainly be seen as ambitious. Indeed, the United States has already effectively said as much, with its chief negotiator commenting, in the context of a possible goal for China for the next five years, '[i]f they come up with improvements in energy efficiency, then 20 percent would be an excellent number, a very strong number' (Spiegel Online 2009).[14] Indeed, the target is so ambitious that some might view it as not credible, especially given China's limited success in recent years in reducing energy intensity. Nevertheless, other countries will want to encourage China to adopt an ambitious target rather than cautioning it against making an offer it might not achieve.[15] The direction of policy in China is clear, and the expectation is that an ambitious target would itself provide the impetus for more sweeping reforms in China, including possibly the introduction of widespread carbon pricing.

For China to provide a stimulus to international negotiations, it will need to not only announce a target along these lines but be prepared to make an international commitment to it. If China is not prepared to make a quantitative commitment along the lines expected of industrialised countries, it will need to commit to, say, the halving of emissions intensity as a quantitative, non-binding indicator of what its policies are expected to deliver. Once an international commitment was made, some sort of international monitoring would be expected. If China is not planning to seek international funding for this commitment, then its recent statements suggest that it won't accept international monitoring (NDRC 2009).[16] By the same token, it seems unlikely that, if agreement was in sight, a compromise would not be possible on this issue.

Conclusion

Amid the generally gloomy prospects for climate change negotiations and slow progress in relation to the same, this chapter has drawn attention to the possibility that China will commit to something like a halving of its carbon intensity between 2005 and 2020.

This is far from a sure thing. We still can't say exactly what China will commit to, but we are also not completely in the dark. It is highly likely that China will continue with its energy-efficiency improvement program and it seems quite possible that it will combine this and its renewable energy program into a carbon-intensity (emissions-to-GDP) reduction target for 2015 or 2020. A target to halve emissions intensity by 2020 would clearly meet, if not exceed, the expectations of the industrialised countries. It would be seen as an ambitious, stretch target—possible but not easy to achieve. If put forward as an international commitment—as a quantified, non-binding indicator of expected policy impact—it would more than satisfy the expectations of industrialised countries.[17]

There are various reasons why China might adopt such a target but not be prepared to offer it as an international obligation. Agreement on the form in which such commitments should be made might not be possible. As mentioned, even though there would be no penalties for non-compliance, China might not be prepared to submit to international monitoring and reporting. There is also the large divide between what China is asking from the industrialised countries and what they are offering. The second section of this chapter indicated the huge gaps here in relation to emissions reduction targets and public funding.

Even if the distance between the negotiating parties is too great to be covered in the next few years, and no international agreement is possible, the recent policy developments in China are encouraging. Motivated by concerns about energy security and local air pollution as well as climate change, China appears likely to proceed with the sort of energy-efficiency and clean-energy policies analysed in this chapter regardless of whether an international treaty is in place or not. If the United States passes cap-and-trade legislation, the need for an international agreement to drive national action will be further reduced. The combined example of the world's two superpowers will be much more influential than the penalty provisions of any multilateral treaty. This provides a useful contingency in the event that no treaty can be negotiated or if, once again, the US Senate refuses to ratify any successor treaty. More generally, given the obstacles that will have to be overcome before a successful agreement can be reached, the more countries are committed to national action irrespective of their international obligations, the better will be the outlook for successful international climate change mitigation.

That said, there can be no doubt that the forging of an international agreement would give an important stimulus to domestic action around the world, and in particular would allow industrialised and developing countries to proceed with an understanding that each was doing its agreed 'fair share'. An international offer from China to halve its carbon intensity by 2020, in return for the West doing more in terms of emissions reduction and public funding—while itself a long shot—seems to be the best basis we have for a global deal. While a number of papers have recently called for US–China collaboration on climate change, conceived primarily in technological terms (Chandler 2008; Chu and Thornton 2009; Lieberthal and Sandalow 2009), collaboration on striking a global deal on these terms would be far more influential in unlocking the impasse that has long held back global climate change negotiations.

References

Note: All web references are current as of 16 June 2009.

Adam, D. and Goldenberg, S. 2009, 'US says it will not demand binding carbon cuts from China', *The Guardian*, 12 June 2009, <http://www.guardian.co.uk/environment/2009/jun/12/climate-change-copenhagen>

Agence France-Presse (AFP) 2009, 'China eyes 20 pct renewable energy by 2020: report', *Agence France-Presse*, <http://www.google.com/hostednews/afp/article/ALeqM5iHms-GqSyTR6Yu7xFhZY8nf7Iz1Q>

Albright, M. K. 1998, Earth Day 1998: global problems and global solutions, Press release, US Department of State, Washington, DC, <http://secretary.state.gov/www/statements/1998/980421.html>

Borger, J. and Watts, J. 2009, 'China launches green power revolution to catch up on West', *The Guardian*, 9 June 2009, <http://www.guardian.co.uk/world/2009/jun/09/china-green-energy-solar-wind>

Bradley, R. and Pershing, J. 2009, 'Introduction to sustainable development policies and measures', in K. Baumert and R. Bradley (eds), *Growing in the Greenhouse*, World Resources Institute, Washington, DC.

Cao, J. 2008, *Reconciling human development and climate protection: perspectives from developing countries on post-2012 international climate change policy*, Discussion Paper 2008-25, Harvard Project on International Climate Agreements, Cambridge, Mass.

Chandler, W. 2008, *Breaking the suicide pact: US–China cooperation on climate change*, Carnegie Endowment Policy Brief, Carnegie Endowment, Washington, DC.

Chen, E. and Miles, T. 2009, 'China may extend energy-saving goal to 2020: paper', *Reuters*, 15 May 2009, <http://www.reuters.com/article/rbssEnergyNews/idUSPEK2745720090515>

Chinese Academy of Sciences (CAS) 2009, *Sustainable Development Strategy Report*, Chinese Academy of Sciences, Beijing, <http://www.theclimategroup.org/assets/resources/CAS_2009_Sustainable_Development_Strategy_Report_-_Exec_Summary.pdf>

Chu, S. and Thornton, J. 2009, *A Roadmap for US–China Cooperation on Energy and Climate Change*, Pew Center and Asia Society's Center on US–China relations, Arlington, Va., and Washington, DC.

de Boer, Y. 2009, 2009: the year of climate change, Press release, United Nations Framework Convention on Climate Change, Bonn, Germany, <http://unfccc2.meta-fusion.com/kongresse/090601_SB30_Bonn/downl/090608_UNFCCC_Executive_Secretary.pdf>

den Elzen, M. and Höhne, N. 2008, 'Reductions of greenhouse gas emissions in Annex I and non-Annex I countries for meeting concentration stabilization targets: an editorial comment', *Climatic Change*, vol. 91, pp. 249–74.

Development Research Center of the State Council (DRC) 2005, *China National Energy Strategy and Policy 2020*, Development Research Center of the State Council, Beijing, <http://www.efchina.org/FReports.do?act=detail&id=155>

Energy Information Administration (EIA) 2009, *International Energy Outlook 2009*, Energy Information Administration, US Department of Energy, Washington, DC, <www.eia.doe.gov/oiaf/ieo/index.html>

G5 2008, G5 statement issued by Brazil, China, India, Mexico and South Africa, 2008 Hokkaido Toyako Summit, Japan, 7–9 July 2008, <http://www.twnside.org.sg/title2/climate/info.service/climate.change.20080702.htm>

Garnaut, R. 2008, *The Garnaut Climate Change Review*, Cambridge University Press, Cambridge.

Garnaut, R., Jotzo, F. and Howes, S. 2008a, 'China's rapid emissions growth and global climate change policy', in L. Song and W. T. Woo (eds), *China's Dilemma: Economic growth, the environment and climate change*, ANU E Press and Asia Pacific Press, Canberra.

Garnaut, R., Jotzo, F. Howes, S. and Sheehan, P. 2008b, 'Emissions in the Platinum Age: the implications of rapid development for climate change mitigation', *Oxford Review of Economic Policy*, vol. 24, no. 2, pp. 1–25.

Government of the People's Republic of China 2009, 'Submission to the UNFCCC ad hoc Working Group on Long-term Cooperative Action under the Convention', *Ideas and Proposals on the Elements Contained in Paragraph 1 of the Bali Action Plan Submissions from Parties. Part I*, FCCC/AWGLCA/2009/MISC.4 (Part I) (19 May), United Nations Framework Convention on Climate Change, Bonn, Germany.

Government of South Africa 2009, 'Submission to the UNFCCC ad hoc Working Group on Long-term Cooperative Action under the Convention', *Ideas and Proposals on the Elements Contained in Paragraph 1 of the Bali Action Plan Submissions from Parties. Part II*, FCCC/AWGLCA/2009/MISC.4 (Part II) (19 May), United Nations Framework Convention on Climate Change, Bonn, Germany.

Government of the United States of America 2009, *US Submission on Copenhagen Agreed Outcome*, Government of the United States of America, Washington, DC, <http://www.state.gov/documents/organization/124313.pdf>

Howes, S. 2009, 'Finding a way forward: three critical issues for a post-Kyoto global agreement on climate change', *Indian Growth and Development Review*, vol. 2, no. 1, pp. 75–98.

Hu, A. 2009, 'A new approach at Copenhagen', *China Dialogue*, 6 April 2009, <http://www.chinadialogue.net/article/show/single/en/2892>

International Energy Agency (IEA) 2007a, *CO_2 Emissions from Fuel Combustion: 1971–2005*, International Energy Agency, Paris.

—— 2007b, *World Energy Outlook 2007: China and India insights*, International Energy Agency, Paris.

Information Office of the State Council 2008, *China's Policies and Actions for Addressing Climate Change*, Information Office of the State Council, Beijing, <http://www.ccchina.gov.cn/WebSite/CCChina/UpFile/File419.pdf>

Jiang, K., Hu, X., Zhuang, X., Liu, H. and Liu, Q. 2009, Fuel substitution and diversification in China, Paper presented at ERI-ANU China Energy Conference, Canberra, 14 April 2009.

Li, J. 2009, 'Environmentally-sound tech needed', *China Daily*, 4 May 2009, <http://www.chinadaily.com.cn/bizchina/2009-05/04/content_7740693.htm>

Lieberthal, K. and Sandalow, D. 2009, *Overcoming obstacles to US–China cooperation on climate change*, John L. Thornton China Center Monograph Series, John L. Thornton China Center at The Brookings Institution, Washington, DC.

Liu, J. 2000, Statement by H. E. Mr Liu Jiang, Head of the Chinese Delegation, Minister and Vice-Chairman of State Development Planning Commission of China, Sixth Conference of the Parties to the UNFCCC, <http://www.ccchina.gov.cn/en/NewsInfo.asp?NewsId=5369>

McKinsey Global Institute 2007, *Leapfrogging to Higher Energy Productivity in China*, McKinsey Global Institute, Washington, DC.

National Bureau of Statistics (NBS) 2008, *China Statistical Yearbook 2008*, China Statistics Press, Beijing, <http://www.stats.gov.cn/tjsj/ndsj/2008/indexeh.htm>

—— 2009, *Statistical communiqué of the People's Republic of China on the 2008 national economic and social development*, National Bureau of Statistics, Beijing, <http://www.stats.gov.cn/english/newsandcomingevents/t20090226_402540784.htm>

National Development and Reform Commission (NDRC) 2007, *Medium and Long-Term Development Plan for Renewable Energy in China*, [Abbreviated version, English draft], National Development and Reform Commission, Beijing, <http://www.martinot.info/China_RE_Plan_to_2020_Sep-2007.pdf>

—— 2009, 'Implementation of the Bali Roadmap: China's position on the Copenhagen Climate Change Conference', *China Climate Change Info-Net*, <http://www.ccchina.gov.cn/en/NewsInfo.asp?NewsId=17528>

Netherlands Environmental Assessment Agency 2008, *Global CO$_2$ Emissions: Increase continued in 2007*, Netherlands Environmental Assessment Agency, Bilthoven, The Netherlands, <http://www.pbl.nl/en/publications/2008/GlobalCO2emissionsthrough2007.html>

Pan, J., Chen, Y., Wang, W. and Li, C. 2008a, *Carbon budget proposal: global emissions under carbon budget constraint on an individual basis for an equitable and sustainable post-2012 international climate regime*, Working Paper, December, Research Centre for Sustainable Development, Chinese Academy of Social Sciences, Beijing.

Pan, J., Phillips, J. and Chen, Y. 2008b, 'China's balance of emissions embodied in trade: approaches to measurement and allocating international responsibility', *Oxford Review of Economic Policy*, vol. 24, no. 2, pp. 354–76.

Sheehan, P. and Sun, F. 2008, 'Emissions and economic development: must China choose', in L. Song and W. T. Woo (eds), *China's Dilemma: Economic growth, the environment and climate change*, ANU E Press and Asia Pacific Press, Canberra.

Spiegel Online 2009, 'US wants a "legally binding climate agreement"', Interview with Jonathan Pershing conducted by Christian Schwägerl, *Spiegel Online*, <http://www.spiegel.de/international/world/0,1518,630073,00.html>

Stern, T. 1999, Press briefing by Todd Stern, US President's Coordinator for Climate Change, <http://www.presidency.ucsb.edu/ws/index.php?pid=47854>

—— 2009, Press briefing of the US Delegation to the UNFCCC Climate Change Talks, Bonn, Germany, US Department of State, <http://germany.usembassy.gov/events/2009/mar-29-stern/>

United Nations Environment Program (UNEP) 2008, *Atmospheric Brown Clouds: Regional assessment report with focus on Asia*, United Nations Environment Program, Nairobi, Kenya.

Victor, D. 2001, *The Collapse of the Kyoto Protocol and the Struggle to Slow Global Warming*, Princeton University Press, Princeton, NJ.

—— 2008, *Climate accession deals: new strategies for taming growth of greenhouse gases in developing countries*, Discussion Paper, no. 2008-18, Harvard Project on International Climate Agreements, Cambridge, Mass.

Wu, L. and Huan, G. 2009, 'Top Chinese negotiator urges developed countries to commit more in fighting climate change', *Xinhua*, 1 April 2009, <http://news.xinhuanet.com/english/2009-04/01/content_11109345.htm>

You, N., Li, J. and Fu, J. 2009, 'US will not seek cap on emissions', *China Daily*, 11 June 2009, <http://www.chinadaily.com.cn/bizchina/2009-06/11/content_8272942.htm>

Acknowledgments

I would like to thank Frank Jotzo and Ross Garnaut for their comments, as well as participants at two ANU seminars at which earlier versions of this chapter were presented, and Harry Guinness for his research assistance. All remaining errors are my own.

Endnotes

1. 'Climate envoy's cooperation call', *China Daily*, 23 February 2009, <http://www.china.org. cn/environment/news/2009-02/23/content_17318608.htm>

2. The Byrd-Hegel Resolution, which was passed 95–0, expressed the sense of the US Senate that the United States should not be a signatory to any protocol that would '(A) mandate new commitments to limit or reduce greenhouse gas emissions for the Annex I Parties, unless the protocol or other agreement also mandates new specific scheduled commitments to limit or reduce greenhouse gas emissions for Developing Country Parties within the same compliance period, or (B) would result in serious harm to the economy of the United States'.

3. The argument here is not that these three points provide the basis for the most efficient or effective global agreement, but rather they constitute the most likely basis for a global agreement. de Boer (2009) lists four points. The fourth relates to the governance of funding provided under the third point.

4. A related disagreement is about whether these targets should be met only by domestic emission reductions, as developing countries tend to argue, or by continued use of the Kyoto Protocol flexibility mechanisms, such as international trading and international offsets (the Clean Development Mechanism), as industrialised countries tend to argue.

5. ODA is official development assistance, or aid.

6. 'The convention talks about obligations that might total $100 billion for activities like mitigation. But if you take a look at that, it includes all the mitigation requirements in China, South Korea and Singapore. These are not countries that need financial assistance from the rest of the world to mitigate. After you take those out, you have a much smaller number' (Spiegel Online 2009).

7. Although note that the latest scientific analysis suggests that blame for this should be shared equally between global warming due to greenhouse gases and regional warming of the lower atmosphere as well as soot deposition on snow and ice due to Asia's 'atmospheric brown cloud'.

8. Pan et al. (2008a) assume 40 per cent domestic cuts by 2020 over 2005 for Annex 1 countries and show Annex 1 countries still need to purchase 40 per cent of permits. This corresponds with a commitment to a 64 per cent cut by 2020 over 2005 (40 per cent domestic and 0.4*40 per cent by permits). Similar calculations by India have led them recently to suggest 80 per cent cuts by industrialised countries by 2020 ('Japan, Russia urged to issue 2020 greenhouse goals', *Reuters*, 2009, <htp://www.alertnet.org/thenews/newsdesk/L8653677.htm>).

9. Many economists make a case on efficiency grounds for a 'top-down' harmonised regime, with all countries subject to either emissions targets or similar policies, such as carbon taxes. Others argue for a more 'bottom-up' approach to promote participation and compliance. As discussed in Howes (2009), the approach now being developed—'top down'

for industrialised countries with emissions targets and 'bottom up' for developing countries with country-specific policies—has no real foundation in the literature (though it is perhaps best captured by the idea of 'sustainable development policies and measures'; Bradley and Pershing 2005). Indeed, it has little by way of theoretical rationale, but appears rather to be emerging as a compromise between industrialised and developing blocs.

10. The other issue that China might raise should it opt to participate in an emissions target regime is whether targets should be set on the basis of production (as under Kyoto) or on the basis of consumption, which would favour China given its role as the world's manufacturer. See Pan et al. (2008b) for further discussion.

11. In some cases, no explicit projection for 2020 is given. In these cases, interpolation between, for example, 2015 and 2030 projections was used. The McKinsey Global Institute's base is 2003. The McKinsey figures are for energy intensity; the others are for carbon intensity.

12. A cumulative 7.7 per cent reduction is less than what is reported by China—for example, 10.1 per cent ('China's economy transforming in green revolution', *Xinhua*, 2009, <http://www.ccchina.gov.cn/en/NewsInfo.asp?NewsId=17836>). My figure is obtained by combining data from the *China Statistical Yearbook 2008* (NBS 2008) with more recent data from the 2009 *Statistical communiqué* (NBS 2009). The more recent data pertain to output (from 2006 onwards) and to energy consumption (for 2008 only).

13. The IEA's 'alternative policy scenario' is based on environmental policies for China under consideration at the time the scenario was constructed (2007). Sheehan and Sun's most ambitious policy case is used for this comparison, in which the role of energy-intensive industries is reduced, relative energy prices increase and energy intensities improve in industry and transport. As earlier, interpolation is used to construct 2020 values when they are not available. The McKinsey base is 2003.

14. This chapter focuses on a possible commitment to halve the carbon intensity of output by 2020 over 2005 levels. If the carbon intensity of energy is constant, halving of carbon intensity requires a halving of energy intensity. Achieving this for the period 2005–20 would be consistent with reducing energy intensity by 20 per cent over each of the five-year periods, 2005–10, 2011–15 and 2015–20.

15. This is especially true given the generally poor track record of industrialised countries in meeting their own Kyoto targets.

16. 'Only those actions enabled by measurable, reportable and verifiable support are subject to the "measureable, reportable and verifiable" requirement' (NDRC 2009).

17. The United States' May 2009 submission to Copenhagen indicates that it also would want major developing countries to commit to a peaking year for emissions and to indicate in which year they would take on binding emissions targets. Whether China would make commitments along these lines remains to be seen. Compromises will, however, also likely be forthcoming in the face of an ambitious offer from China.

Moving towards low-carbon economic growth 19

Jinjun Xue

Deng Xiaoping famously proclaimed that 'it doesn't matter if a cat is black or white, so long as it catches mice'. This rejection of ideological purity and embrace of pragmatism became the basis of China's new development model. The new approach led to 30 years of rapid economic growth, directing China toward a new place in the global economy. This development has, however, not been without cost. The environmental impact of China's rapid industrialisation has been particularly severe. Deng may not have been concerned with the colour of the cat, but we might now be concerned if the mouse is blackened by pollution. This chapter analyses the potential for environmental issues to act as a constraint on economic growth. A growth model that displays characteristics of an environmental Kuznets curve (EKC) is developed to assess the most recent data.

The EKC derives from long-run empirical observations across countries. It is observed that environmental degradation associated with economic growth increases most rapidly at low levels of per capita income. As income grows, the additional degradation due to each successive economic gain slows until it eventually peaks. As per capita income continues to grow, degradation eventually diminishes.

An implication of the EKC is that environmental degradation could act as a constraint on future economic growth. This chapter develops a theoretical model for incorporating environmental constraints on economic growth, but allowing for the possibility of innovation in environmental technologies as well as government policies that fortify the environment. A modified EKC is then estimated for China.

The chapter is composed of four parts. Section one discusses the EKC and illustrates how environmental pollution can act as a potential constraint on economic growth in some circumstances. Section two provides a growth model that assumes that technological innovation with regard to environmental measures can render environmental constraints on economic growth redundant and, in turn, promote sustainable development. Section three tests the hypothesis by drawing on data from China and presents a new EKC developed from time series. Section four discusses the main findings and offers some tentative conclusions.

The EKC model with environmental constraints on growth

The Kuznets curve originated as a theory illustrating the relationship between economic growth and income inequality—that is, the income Kuznets curve (IKC) (Kuznets 1955). In recent years, it has been developed into a model showing a process of high economic growth accompanied by high environmental pollution. In this chapter, we will discuss a growth model, incorporating environmental constraints, and highlight how pollution influences the path of economic growth.

The structure and implications of the EKC

Paralleling the IKC model, the EKC model describes the dynamic relationship between gross domestic product (GDP) growth and pollutant emissions as an inverted U curve. Pollution per capita will increase rapidly as the economy accelerates in the take-off stage, reaches a peak (turning point) in the high growth stage and then decreases in the stable growth stage. Through this process, the EKC assumes that the pollution problem will be solved gradually and the economy will arrive at a stable growth stage eventually (Figure 19.1).

The EKC is a market fundamentalist-based model and it suggests that pollution will be reduced automatically by the market mechanism as an economy matures. Consequently, there is no need for government intervention in the economy (for example, via a strong environmental policy regime).

Most analysis and country-based case studies, however, show that the progression from a high-pollution regime to a low-pollution regime can be more protracted if there is no strong government policy intervention, if distortions exist that sponsor inefficient practices or if technological progress/transfer linked to improvement in the environment is not pursued aggressively. Furthermore, damage to the wider environment while the EKC is on its upswing could be so pervasive that it impinges on current and future economic growth.

Figure 19.1 Traditional EKC

P (Emission of CO_2, SO_2, etc.)

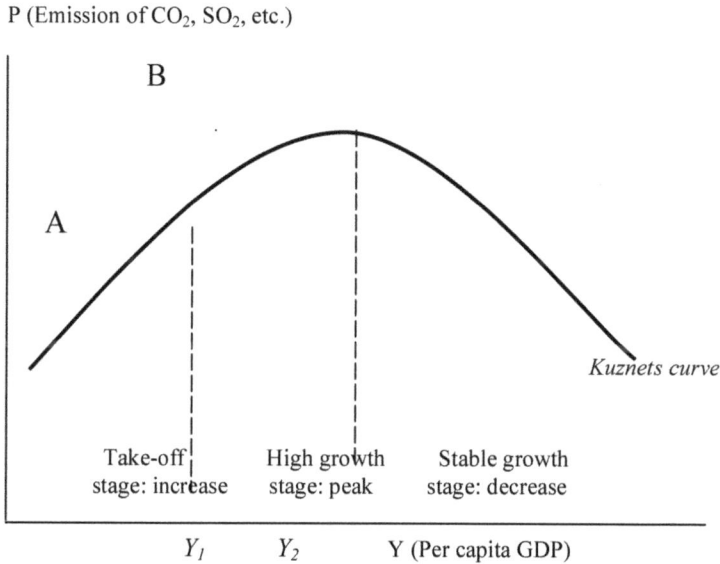

Source: Based on the Kuznets hypothesis in Kuznets, S. 1955, 'Economic growth and income inequality', *American Economic Review*, vol. 45, no. 1, pp. 1–28.

In studying the case of China, it has been argued that the extensive damage to the environment is primarily a consequence of its high growth and mass consumption of energy and the distorted policy of economic development (*Nature*, no. 5, 2005); therefore we cannot wait for an early arrival of the gradual sustainable development predicted by the EKC. In other words, we have to seek a new approach based on the revised EKC that can help China out of its current state of high growth-accelerating pollution and find a way to shorten the process of transition from a high-pollution to a low-pollution stage of development.

An environmentally constrained EKC without technological progress

Considering the unique case of China, and the search for a new EKC, it is useful to set a formal framework of economic growth as a benchmark. A short discussion of the theory of economic growth is therefore in order.

A growth model without technological progress

In the growth theory literature, the Cobb-Douglas production function illustrates that capital investment and the labour force are the only factors determining the quantity of production. Following the inferences of this function, we assume that the economy is driven by capital, but that technological progress is absent. In light of this, the Cobb-Douglas production function can be expressed as Equation 19.1.

Equation 19.1

$$Y^N = F(K,L) \text{ or } Y^N = K^\alpha L^\beta$$

in which L = capital investment, L = labour force and $\alpha = (1-\beta)$.

Because saving is equal to investment in the Keynesian equilibrium of national income, s can be interpreted as investment and i includes physical investment and human capital. Here, we define human capital as labour force, therefore we can develop the equation into a Harrod-style growth model (Harrod 1948) as Equation 19.2.

Equation 19.2

$$G = s/k$$

or

$$\frac{dY}{Y} = \frac{dK}{K}\omega_K + \frac{dL}{L}\omega_L$$

in which A = growth rate, A = saving rate, A = coefficient of capital, which can be defined as the ratio of input–output, ω_E = the elasticity of capital and ω_E = the elasticity of labour.

A growth model with technological progress

The Harrod-style growth model stresses the absolute role of savings or investment in the process of economic growth but ignores the role of technological progress. To modify the model, we change the economy into a modern economy by introducing the factor of technological progress, A, into the production function. The above production function can therefore be rewritten as Equation 19.3.

Equation 19.3

$$Y^A = F(K, L, E)$$

or

$$Y^N = AF(K, L)$$

Based on the new production function, we can transfer the Harrod-style model into the Solow model in which technological progress (designated as dA/A) is included (Equation 19.4).

Equation 19.4

$$\frac{dY}{Y} = \frac{dK}{K}\omega_K + \frac{dL}{L}\omega_L + \frac{dA}{A}$$

in which ω_E is economic growth. Explicitly, the Solow model demonstrates that technological progress is the decisive factor in modern economic growth (Solow 1956). Because technological progress is an external factor, however, the Solow model is treated as an endogenous growth model and, implicitly, the economy will grow with constant returns to factors of production.

A growth model with an environmental constraint but without technological progress

Now we can develop an EKC model in which the environmental factor, E, is considered. As a consequence, we get the following production function (Equation 19.5).

Equation 19.5

$$Y^A = F(K, L, E)$$

in which ω_E is economic growth available and E equates to the environmental factor, which can be defined as the cost of environmental pollution, and is negatively related to economic growth.

By introducing E into the growth model, we can develop a new growth model incorporating the environmental factor (Equation 19.6).

Equation 19.6

$$\frac{dY}{Y} = \frac{dK}{K}\omega_K + \frac{dL}{L}\omega_L - \frac{dE}{E}\omega_E$$

Here, dA/A is the cost of environmental pollution measured by the ratio of investment in environmental control in GDP and ω_E is the elasticity of resource consumption.

The environmentally constrained EKC model

To explain the relationship between economic growth and environmental change, we introduced the environmental factor into the EKC model and constructed an environmentally constrained EKC model. This aims to show that when the economy grows at an accelerating speed, as a side product of mass consumption of energy (for example, coal and crude oil), environmental pollution (for example, emissions of sulphur dioxide, carbon dioxide, and so on) will become more and more problematic. Furthermore, the pollutants will cause damage not only to nature, people and society, but to economic growth because they will induce huge cost and place a heavy burden on the economy. As a result, the economy will have to invest in environmental measures in order to improve economic performance and the quality of people's lives. In other words, the cost of environmental pollution and investment in pollution-control measures will have a significant impact on GDP growth and induce a constraint on future economic growth. This is what we defined as the cost of high growth or 'the black mice effect', using Deng Xiaoping's description about mice.

To illustrate the cost of high growth, consider in Figure 19.2 an EKC with a binding environmental constraint. It demonstrates that at the high-growth stage, in the absence of technological change, increasing pollution will induce a strong environmental constraint on the growth path of per capita GDP. As a result of environmental degradation, the growth path of per capita GDP might not go up but will instead bend in the direction of a low-speed, unstable-growth position. Accordingly, the distorted growth path will delay arrival at the turning point (peak) and not enable the economy to reach the third stage—that is, stable growth with low pollution, as shown by the EKC—and it will remain in a stage of low growth and high pollution.[1] As a consequence, many mice become black mice.

Figure 19.2 The EKC with environmental constraint

E (Emission of SO_2, CO_2, etc.)

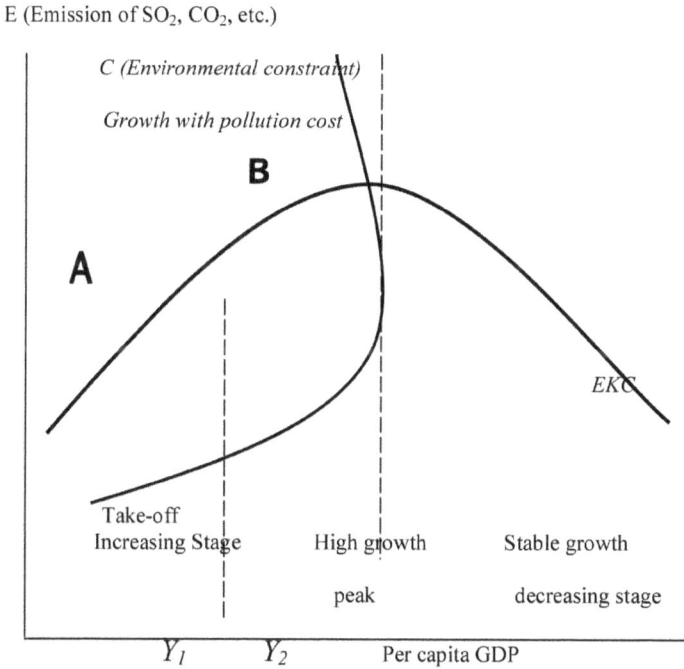

A new EKC with environmentally related technological progress

In this section, we will develop a new EKC model that incorporates technological progress driving positive environmental outcomes into the basic neoclassical growth theories discussed above.

Economic growth with pollution-suppressing technology

Here we introduce pollution-suppressing technology into the EKC system to derive sustainable economic and environmental development.

To evaluate the applicability of our hypothesis, we will perform a simulation assuming a set of growth rates. We presume that the EKC includes a pollution-suppressing technology, which can guarantee sustainable development. Therefore, production functions of gross output can be written as Equations 19.6 and 19.7.

Equation 19.6

$$Y^N = AK^\alpha L^\beta , \; \alpha + \beta = 1$$

Equation 19.7

$$R = BK^\gamma L^\delta , \; (\gamma + \delta) > 1$$

Here, we assume $\gamma + \delta$ exceeds unity. This means that the pollution-suppressing technology possesses the nature of increasing returns to scale.

With these conditions, we can get a new growth model for sustainable development (Equation 19.8).

Equation 19.8

$$\frac{dY}{Y} = \frac{dK}{K}\omega_K + \frac{dL}{L}\omega_L + \frac{dA}{A} + \frac{dT_E}{T_E}\omega_{TE}$$

in which dA/A = technological progress for production, dT_E/T_E = environmentally related technological progress and ω_E = elasticity of environmentally related technological progress.

There are two kinds of technologies being used in this mode. One focuses on production (for example, energy-saving technology, sulphur-deodorant technology, and so on) and the other on environmental controls (for example, energy-saving technology, sulphur-deodorant technology, and so on). Figure 19.3 is a demonstration of the new EKC based on this model.

The new EKC shows that by introducing environmental-control technology, the growth path of per capita GDP can move forward gradually while pollution emissions increase slowly at first, tending to decrease and finally arrive at the third stage in which ideal sustainable development can be obtained and environmental pollution can be contained in a reasonable manner. The model implies, however, that per capita GDP should grow at a reasonable speed with effective pollution control but not at high speed and beyond the environmental burden.

Figure 19.3 A new EKC with a growth model for sustainable development

E (Emission of SO_2, CO_2, etc.) per capita

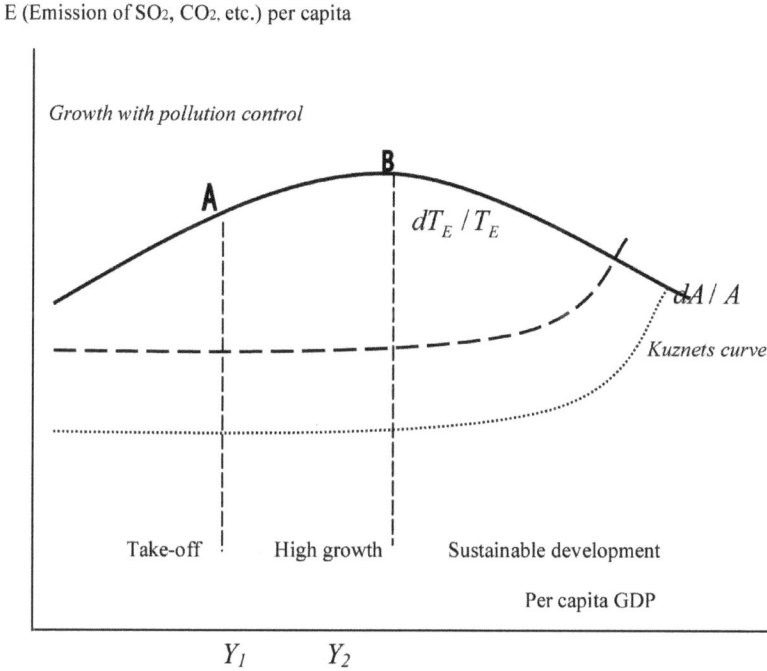

Growth with pollution control

B

A

dT_E / T_E

dA / A

Kuznets curve

Take-off　High growth　Sustainable development

Per capita GDP

Y_1　　　Y_2

Source: Author's own schema.

The flying-geese model and catch-up effect

According to historical data, most industrialised countries spent between 50 and 200 years overcoming the trade-off between economic growth and environmental pollution. For example, it took the United Kingdom 185 years to reach its peak of carbon dioxide emissions, while it took the United States 135 years. It took even the East Asian miracle economy of Japan more than 100 years from the Meiji era to reach its peak year in 2005 (CAS 2009:45), as well as suffering from a painful experience of 'the four big pollution diseases' (Xue et al. 2002). Meanwhile, some empirical studies show that most countries pass the turning point of their EKC at income levels of US$10 000–23 000 (at 1990 prices). There are, however, some exceptions; South Korea is one example. It took only 40 years from 1946–97 for South Korea to reach the peak point of its carbon dioxide emissions—at $4114 per capita GDP. This phenomenon can be explained by the flying-geese paradigm—an Asian version of the theory of catch-up.

The flying-geese paradigm was developed by Japanese scholars as a way to view the technological development of South-East Asia, with Japan as a leading power. In the theory, Kaname Akamatsu (1962) postulated that Asian nations would catch up with the West as part of a regional hierarchy in which the production of commoditised goods would continuously move from industrialised countries to developing ones. The underdeveloped nations in the region could be considered as being 'aligned successively behind the advanced industrial nations in the order of their different stages of growth in a wild-geese-flying pattern'. Using the theory, we can distinguish that one important factor that has induced the shortcut in the Kuznets curve of South Korea might be foreign direct investment (FDI) and its export-oriented economy.

Here, the effects of foreign capital introduction can be summarised in the following way. The introduction of foreign capital induces technological transfer to developing countries. The multinational cooperation brings with it new products in which new technologies, including environmentally related technology, are embodied. Through the production of the new products, developing countries can catch up with industrial-country technology, especially environmentally related technology, in a relatively short time.

It also introduces international standards of environmental control and greatly improves the environmental management of invested countries by stimulating the production of environmentally friendly products.

It brings environmental management and know-how to the developing countries and improves management by introducing new production methods (Toyota Production System, TPS, is one example).

It brings domestic enterprises into environmental investment and environmentally friendly product development by driving competition between foreign and domestic enterprises.

It improves people's attitudes towards the environment and brings about changes in human behaviour, which in turn induces improvements in production activity.

The above functions can than generate a catch-up effect and improve productivity and environmental quality in a short rather than a long period.

The tunnel effect of the EKC

Recently, the idea of a low-carbon economy has become a popular idea for dealing with global warming issues. One of the methodologies used is the so-called 'tunnel effect' (Figure 19.4), which is a combination of the flying-geese model and the EKC.

Figure 19.4 The tunnel effect model

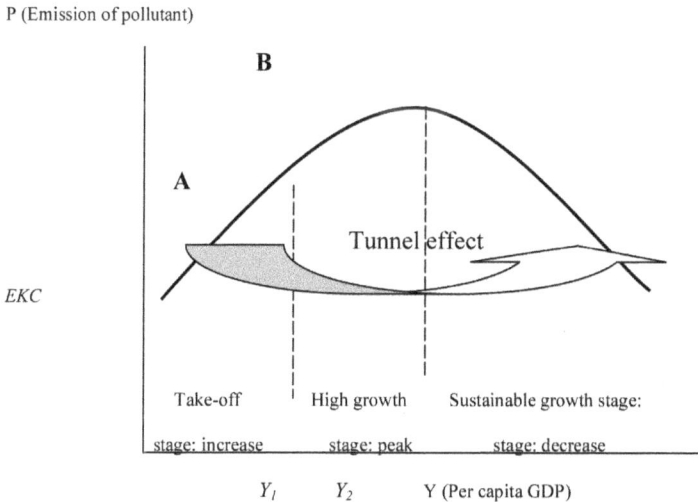

P (Emission of pollutant)

B

A

Tunnel effect

EKC

Take-off stage: increase

High growth stage: peak

Sustainable growth stage: stage: decrease

Y_1 Y_2 Y (Per capita GDP)

Source: Author's own schema.

Figure 19.4 shows that one economy can take a shortcut from the first stage to the third stage through the tunnel. The tunnel effect can be described as a result of the catch-up effect and the effects of technological transfer through the FDI activities summarised above. The following conditions, however, will determine whether the tunnel effect can be realised.

1. The amount and speed of technological transfer from industrialised to developing countries.

2. The absorption capability of the accepting country, including human resources, management, institutional change, technology application and so on.

3. Technological innovation to utilise the efficiency of technological application in the developing country.

4. Policy orientation (one example is the low-carbon economy development path followed by some countries).

441

The Chinese EKC

In this section, we test the new EKC hypothesis using historical Chinese data.

The high-growth–high-cost pattern

China has been experiencing high growth with a correspondingly high cost of environmental degradation. Some estimates put the figure for the cost of environmental degradation as high as 15 per cent of GDP.[2] We review the evidence on environmental pollution in China in its high-growth period.

Table 19.1 is an international comparison of economic growth. It shows that China has high growth rates comparable with Japan and other Asian late-comer industrialisers, but China's high-growth period has been more protracted than the others. What we can draw from this is that the phase of accelerating environmental pollution per capita in China could be more serious and the painful period might last longer than in other economies. In other words, it could take much longer for China to ensure that the EKC moves from the increasing to the decreasing phase of the curve.

Table 19.1 An international comparison of high-growth periods

Countries and regions	Period	Years	Annual growth rate
Japan	1958–73	15	9.7
	1973–88	15	3.6
	1988–93	5	3.0
South Korea	1962–77	15	9.6
	1977–87	10	8.0
	1987–95	8	8.1
Taiwan	1962–77	15	10.1
	1977–87	10	8.7
	1987–95	8	6.6
China	1978–96	18	10.6
	1981–90	10	9.4
	1991–2000	10	10.1
	2001–05	5	9.5
	1978–2008	30	8.9

Sources: Economic Planning Agency of Japan 1996, *Asian Economy 1996*, Economic Planning Agency of Japan, Tokyo, Japan; National Bureau of Statistics (NBS) 2008, *China Statistical Yearbook 2008*, China Statistics Press, Beijing.

Figure 19.5 shows that as per capita GDP grows, energy consumption grows at a much higher rate. Meanwhile, Figure 19.6 shows that pollutants such as sulphur dioxide, waste water, solid waste and exhaust-gas emissions are increasing at a high rate. Smog dust is alone in displaying a increasing trend.

Figure 19.5 GDP growth and energy consumption in China, 1983–2005

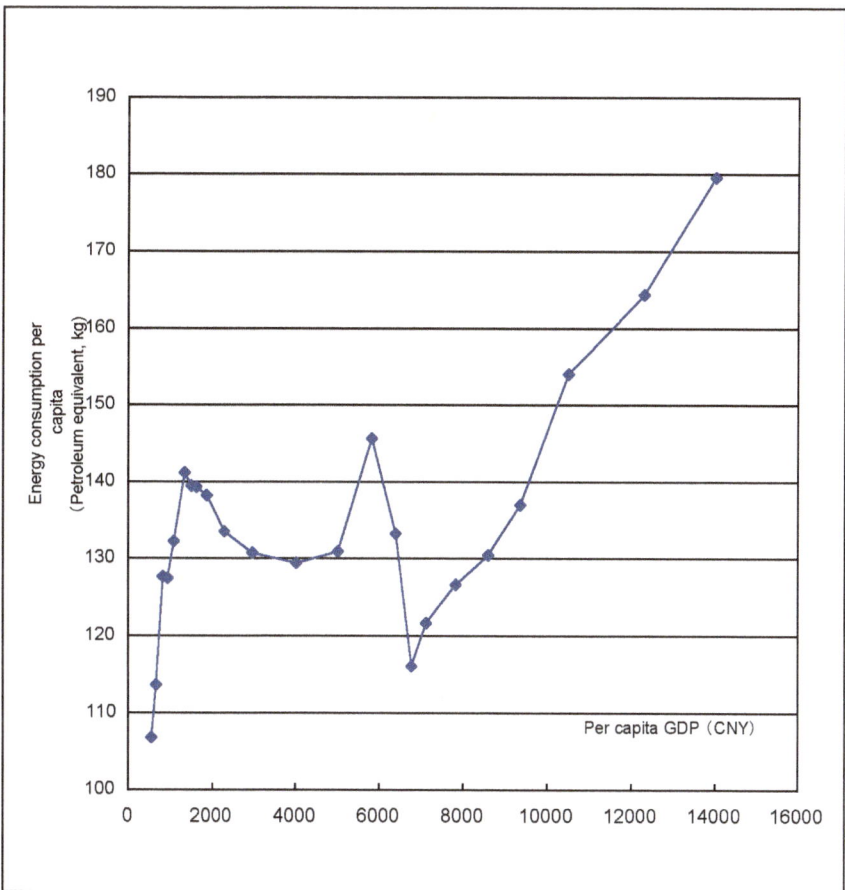

Source: National Bureau of Statistics (NBS) 2006, *China Statistical Yearbook 2006*, CD-ROM version, China Statistics Press, Beijing.

Figure 19.6 Pollutant emissions in China (log tonnes)

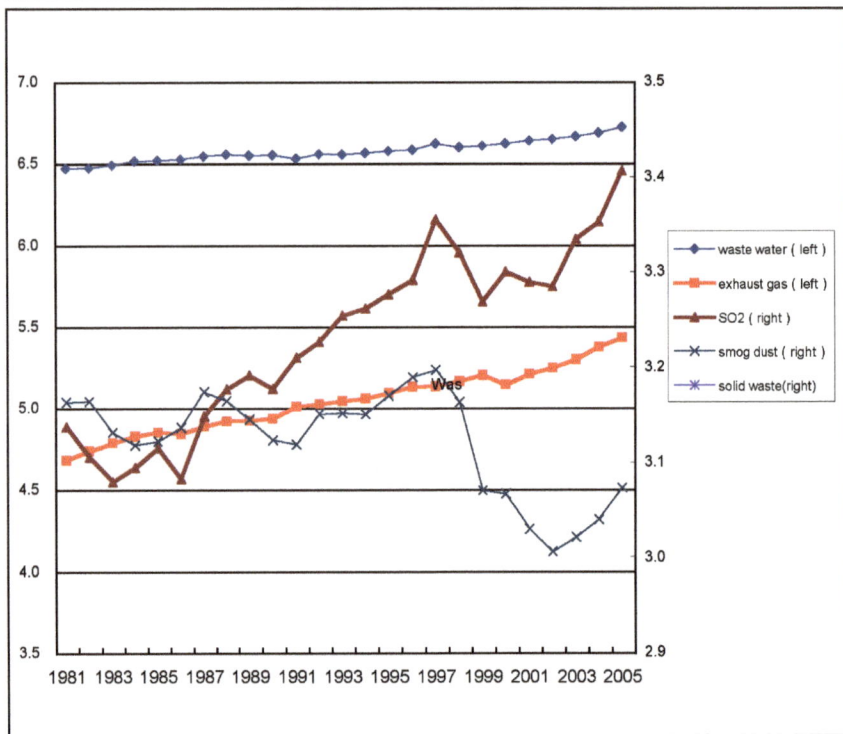

Source: National Bureau of Statistics (NBS) various years, *China Statistical Yearbook*, China Statistics Press, Beijing; State Environmental Protection Administration (SEPA) various years, *China Environmental Statistics Yearbook*, China Environmental Yearbook Press, Beijing.

The China EKC

Using the data sets of per capita GDP and per capita carbon dioxide emissions and sulphur dioxide emissions, we shaped China's Kuznets curve using carbon dioxide emissions data from the World Bank's *World Development Indicators* (2008) and sulphur dioxide data from the *China Statistics Yearbook* (NBS 2008). We found that carbon dioxide and sulphur dioxide emissions have very high correlations with GDP growth (Figures 19.7 and 19.8). More importantly, we found that both the EKCs of China appear to still be very much in the second stage and have not arrived at the turning point. This means that environmental pollution in China will continue to worsen for some time if the Chinese Government introduces no further restrictions to control pollution.

Figure 19.7 China's EKC (carbon dioxide emissions and GDP per capita, 1980–2006)

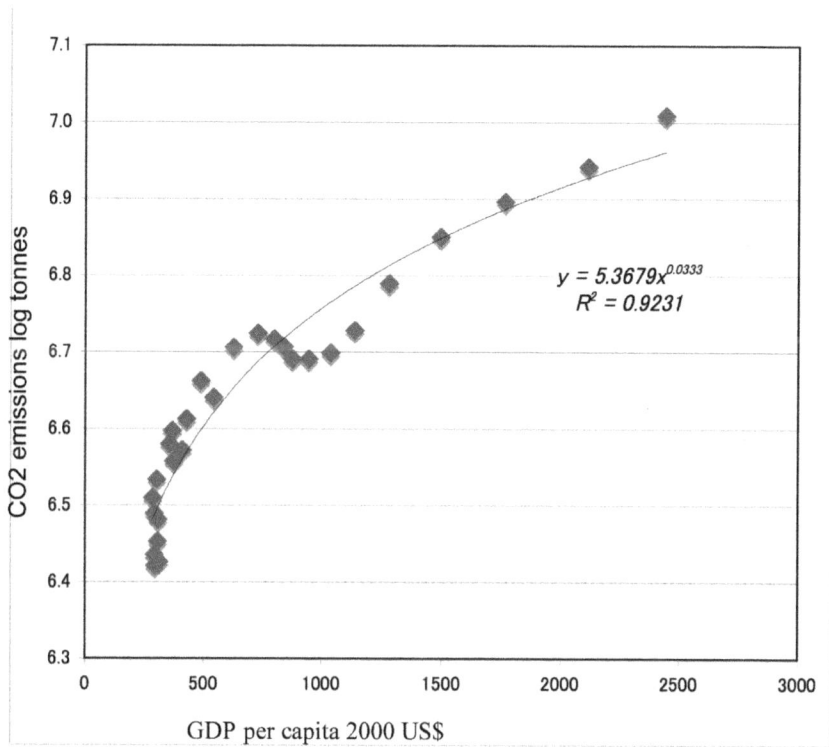

$$y = 5.3679x^{0.0333}$$
$$R^2 = 0.9231$$

X-axis: GDP per capita 2000 US$

Y-axis: CO2 emissions log tonnes

Source: Author's own estimation.

Can China catch up?

As discussed earlier, it is possible for a developing country to catch up with industrialised countries in terms of environmental improvement. The question here is whether China can catch up.

To answer this question, we analyse the trends of unit consumption of energy and unit carbon dioxide emissions through international comparison.

Figure 19.9 shows that China is at a high level of energy consumption measured by tonnes of petroleum equivalent per CNY1 million. Figure 19.10 shows the same outcome, but with a decreasing trend in per capita carbon dioxide emissions. This shows there is a possibility for China to take a shortcut in reducing pollution and increasing the pace of improvement of environmental quality.

445

Figure 19.8 Sulphur dioxide emissions and GDP per capita, 1981–2006 (log tonnes)

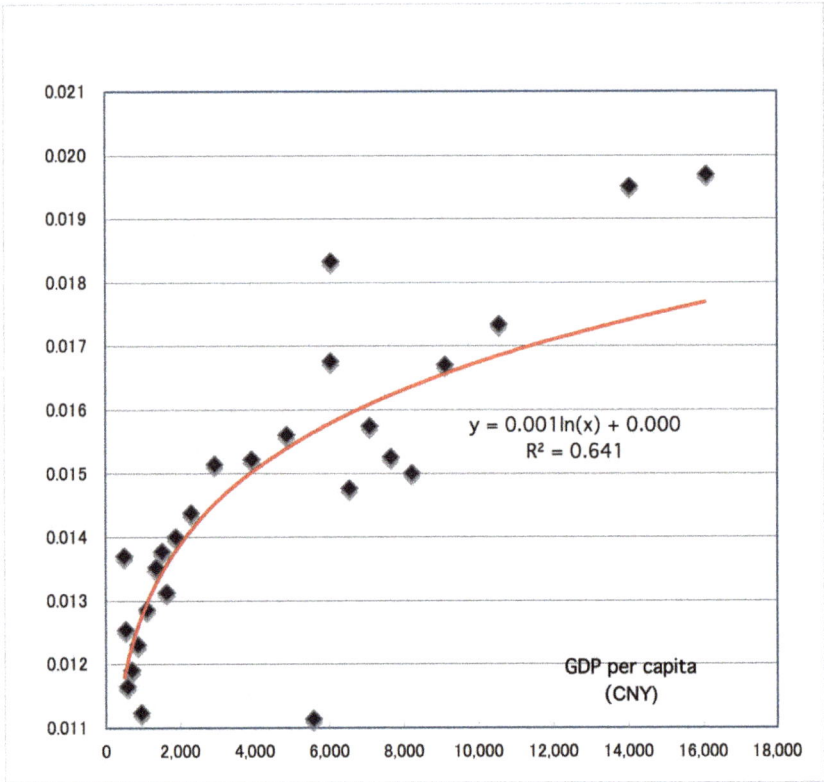

Source: Author's own estimation.

In searching for the reasons for the decline of per capita carbon dioxide emissions, environmental technological progress and investment in pollution control are possibilities. Ninomiya (2005) estimated that environmental technological progress contributed one-third of sulphur dioxide emissions reduction during 1980–2005.

We believe, however, that the Chinese EKC has less to do with the free market economic mechanism than with strong government policy on environmental protection. In other words, the apparent path of the EKC—increasing to a peak before decreasing—shows that government policy is active and fruitful in the area of environmental improvement. For example, we saw the restriction or banning of highly polluting cars and taxis during the period.[3]

Figure 19.9 Energy consumption per tonne per CNY1 million GDP (tonnes petroleum equivalent)

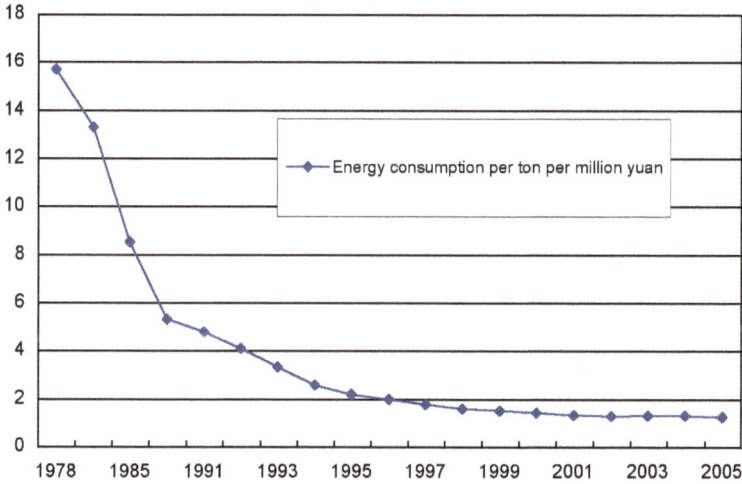

Source: National Bureau of Statistics (NBS) 2006, *China Statistical Yearbook 2006*, CD-ROM version, China Statistics Press, Beijing.

Figure 19.10 Carbon dioxide emissions per 100 GDP production, 1990–2006

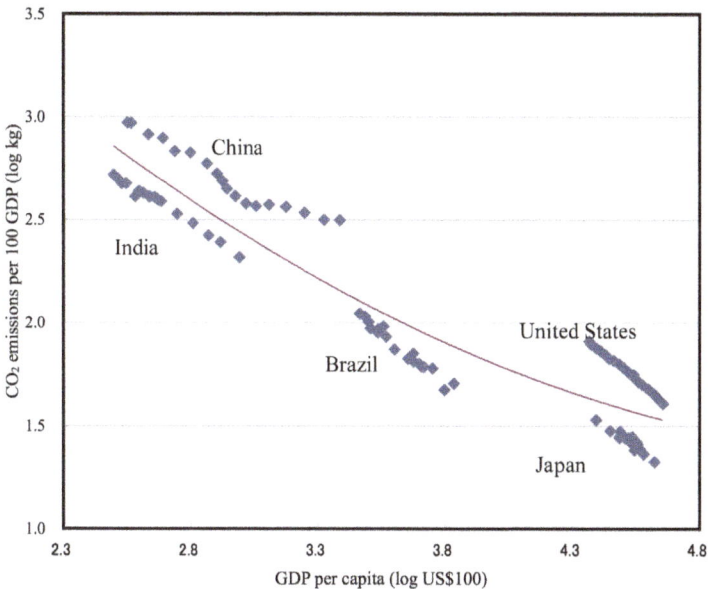

Source: Calculated using the data from World Bank 2008, *World Development Indicators 2008*, CD-ROM version, The World Bank, Washington, DC.

As we know, the Chinese Government has been promulgating a substantial number of regulations on pollution control and has invested large amounts of money in environmental improvement schemes (Figure 19.11). Just as there are wide regional differences in economic growth and income distribution, the same can be said of investment in environmental controls. As with regional income disparity in China, there are large differences in environmental investment (Figure 19.12). Data show that the provinces in eastern China—such as Guangdong, Jiangsu, Zhejiang and Shandong—have invested the most in pollution control, while the figures for the provinces in central and western China, such as Guizhou and Gansu, are much lower.[4]

Figure 19.11 Pollution control investment and its share in GDP

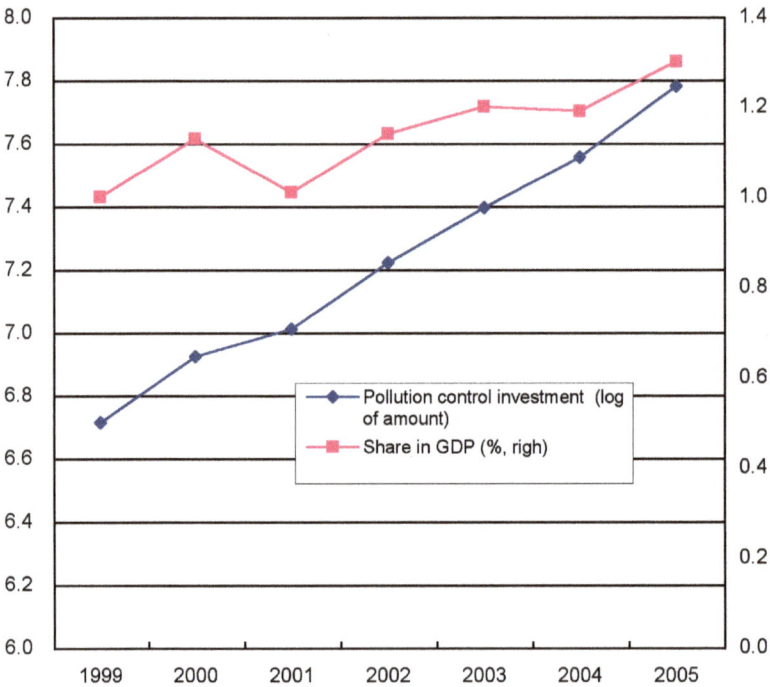

Source: National Bureau of Statistics (NBS) 2006, *China Statistical Yearbook 2006*, CD-ROM version, China Statistics Press, Beijing.

Figure 19.12 Pollution control investment by region, 2005

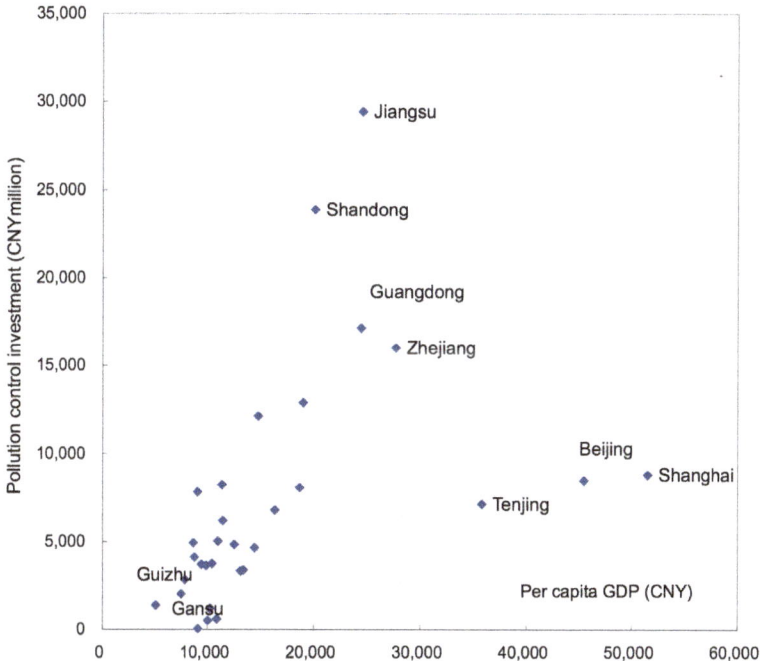

Source: National Bureau of Statistics (NBS) 2006, *China Statistical Yearbook 2006*, CD-ROM version, China Statistics Press, Beijing.

As we assumed in the conditions of the new EKC, *E* is a negative value and is therefore being counted as a cost in relation to GDP. Similarly, the environmental control investment or environmental improvement investment presents a huge cost to the Chinese economy.

There are many reasons for environmental pollution in China—for example: the priority afforded to heavy industry as part of the State's development strategy, the shortage of investment in environmental controls, differentiation among the regions and the so-called 'pollute first, control second' thinking, which also existed in the 1960s in Japan.[5] Here, we focus on a single reason. The factor we want to stress is the heavy reliance on coal and the subsequent sulphur emissions in energy consumption. Figures 19.13 and 19.14 demonstrate that China's reliance on the consumption of coal and its structure of energy consumption have not really changed since 1978.

Figure 19.13 Structure of energy consumption, 1978

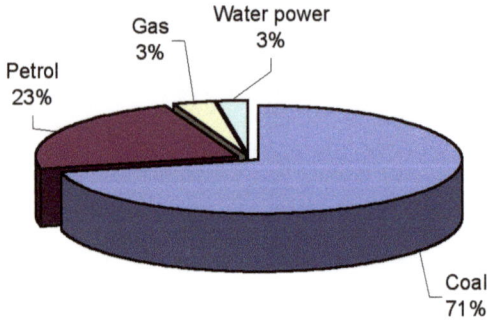

Gas 3%

Water power 3%

Petrol 23%

Coal 71%

Source: National Bureau of Statistics (NBS) 2006, *China Statistical Yearbook 2006*, CD-ROM version, China Statistics Press, Beijing.

Figure 19.14 Structure of energy consumption, 2005

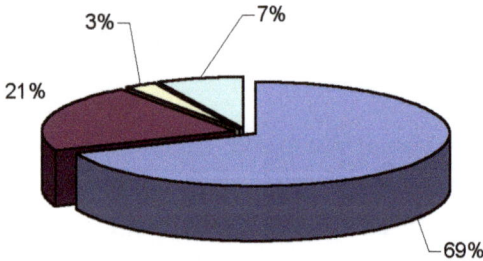

3%

7%

21%

69%

Source: National Bureau of Statistics (NBS) 2006, *China Statistical Yearbook 2006*, CD-ROM version, China Statistics Press, Beijing.

Conclusion

This chapter discussed the Chinese EKC and showed that during the high growth stage, environmental destruction could constrain future economic growth. This is what has been called 'the cost of high growth'. Our environmentally constrained growth model demonstrated that increasing pollution could induce a strong environmental constraint on economic growth and force the growth path to fall into a trap of low growth–high pollution. It was argued that the benevolent path of the theoretical EKC would not appear without the introduction of appropriate pollution-suppressing technologies.

Our adapted growth theory assumes, however, that the technological innovation of environmental measures can solve the environmental constraints placed on economic growth and, in turn, can promote sustainable development. The new EKC derived from this analysis shows that pollution-suppressing technology can push an economy onto the traditional EKC path. In other words, it promotes the growth path to arrive at the third stage—namely, the stage of sustainable development. The theory also illustrates that pollution can be reduced through technological progress/transfer. Endowing this factor with increasing returns to scale in an adapted neoclassical framework allows the system to generate a sustainable model of growth in output per capita. The importance of this theory is that it gives countries with environmental issues a chance to solve their problems and catch up with industrialised countries through a shortcut in economic development.

The Chinese case illustrates that environmental pollution has been worsening seriously since the beginning of its period of high growth. China is a production factory for the world but also a pollutant factory for the world. The per capita and unit data of carbon dioxide emissions indicate, however, that it is possible to reduce pollution and improve the environment through the environmental policy and environmentally related technological progress. Recent developments indicate that policy changes need to be made to expedite the market-based turning point for environmentally friendly growth.

Consequently, it will be a long march for China to arrive at the third stage of its EKC and realise sustainable development. It is time for China to transform its development pattern from 'black growth' to 'green growth' and change the coloured mice to white or return the mice to their natural colours.

China created an economic miracle in the past 30 years and we expect that China can create another miracle in its environmental protection in the next 30 years.

References

Akamatsu, K. 1962, 'A historical pattern of economic growth in developing countries', *Journal of Developing Economies*, vol. 1, no. 1 (March–August), pp. 3–25.

Chinese Academy of Science (CAS) 2009, *China Sustainable Development Strategy Report 2009*, Science Press, Beijing.

Economic Planning Agency of Japan 1996, *Asian Economy 1996*, Economic Planning Agency of Japan, Tokyo, Japan.

Harrod, R. 1948, *Towards a Dynamic Economics: Some recent developments of economic theory and their application to policy*, Macmillan, London.

Kuznets, S. 1955, 'Economic growth and income inequality', *American Economic Review*, vol. 45, no. 1, pp. 1–28.

Liu, J. and Diamond, J. 2005, 'China's environment in a globalizing world', *Nature*, vol. 435 (30 June).

National Bureau of Statistics (NBS) 2006, *China Statistical Yearbook 2006*, CD-ROM version, China Statistics Press, Beijing.

—— 2008, *China Statistical Yearbook 2008*, China Statistics Press, Beijing.

—— various years, *China Statistical Yearbook*, China Statistics Press, Beijing.

Ninomiya, Y. 2005, 'An empirical analysis of economic growth and SO_2 emission in China—examination of the environment Kuznets curve', *Journal of International Cooperation Studies*, vol. 21, no. 1.

Rawski, T. 2002, 'Measuring China's recent GDP growth: where do we stand?', *China Economic Quarterly*, vol. 2, no. 1 (October).

Solow, R. 1956, 'A contribution to the theory of economic growth', *Quarterly Journal of Economics*, vol. 70.

State Environmental Protection Administration (SEPA) 2006, *China Green National Accounting—Study Report 2004*, [Public version], National Bureau of Statistics, Beijing.

—— various years, *China Environmental Statistics Yearbook*, China Environmental Yearbook Press, Beijing.

World Bank 2008, *World Development Indicators*, The World Bank, Washington, DC.

Xue, J. and Arayama, Y. 2004, 'Western development and environment problem in China', in C. Yulian and L. Hai Ying (eds), *Western Development Project in China: The actual problems and the policy*, Finance and Economics Press, Beijing.

Xue, J., Arayama, Y. and Peng, J. (eds) 2002, *Economic Growth and Environment Issues in China*, Northwest University of Finance and Economics, Dalian.

—— 2003, *Economic Development and Environment Control in China: Theory and the actual*, Northeast University of Finance and Economics, Dalian.

Endnotes

1. Here, we define 'growth' as the growth rate of per capita GDP.

2. According to Liu and Diamond (2005), the cost of environmental damage to the economy is 8–15 per cent of China's GDP. Meanwhile, an official research report estimated a cost of CNY51 billion from environmental damage in 2004—3.05 per cent of total GDP. The share will reach 6.8 per cent, however, if environmental damage is not controlled with current technology (SEPA 2005).

3. There could be other reasons for this result. One might be the data problem as summarised by the 'Rawski puzzle', which states that the official statistical data, especially GDP growth, are not coordinated to the growth of energy production and consumption (Rawski 2002). The data published in the *Statistical Yearbooks* are therefore suspicious because we know that data collection related to pollution is very difficult and the statistical system for such data is not yet mature in China.

4. For the issue of regional difference in environmental controls, see Xue and Arayama (2004) and Xue et al. (2003).

5. For the experiences of high growth and high pollution in Japan and China, see Xue et al. (2003).

Index

www.ingramcontent.com/pod-product-compliance
Lightning Source LLC
Chambersburg PA
CBHW051442270326
41932CB00035B/3381